Praise for *Cartography and*

MW00512472

"The Luyia defy assumptions about African ethnicity. With neither myth of common descent nor shared vernacular speech, this modern community is yet no colonial invention. These least 'tribal' of Kenya's peoples mapped their own territory of civic pluralism. In this new departure in ethnic studies, Julie MacArthur persuasively subverts our conventional wisdom."
    —John Lonsdale, Emeritus Professor of Modern African History, University of Cambridge

"*Cartography and the Political Imagination* breaks new ground in Kenyan historiography with its focus on western Kenya. This detailed and sophisticated study argues that Luyia ethnic architects used cartography to create a demographically inclusive, politically pluralistic, and progressive cosmopolitan community. It is refreshing to read a book on Kenya that does not focus on Mau Mau or the Kikuyu. MacArthur's exemplary study of a regional history will be indispensable to scholars of ethnogenesis and cartography in Africa and elsewhere."
    —Kenda Mutongi, Williams College

"The Luyia have long represented a potential test case for the limits to the invention of ethnicity. MacArthur's rich study does not disappoint. It reveals how a series of external influences—land pressures, gender panic, and the drawing of administrative boundaries—led the Luyia to define themselves through appeals to locality rather than shared ancestries. Its most fascinating contribution lies in its treatment of Luyia practices of counter-mapping."
    —Paul Nugent, Centre of African Studies, University of Edinburgh

"MacArthur's exploration of the historiography of ethnicity in Kenya combines theoretical sophistication with innovative and deftly interdisciplinary methodological work, along with a knack for personalized storytelling. In *Cartography and the Political Imagination*, MacArthur has knit together a diverse and complex array of actors, plot lines, and forms of evidence (archival, cartographic, oral), resulting in a fascinating and important piece of historical scholarship."
    —Heidi Gengenbach, University of Massachusetts, Boston

Cartography and the Political Imagination

To Michael
From
Nancy
Editor extraordinaire!

NEW AFRICAN HISTORIES

SERIES EDITORS: JEAN ALLMAN, ALLEN ISAACMAN, AND DEREK R. PETERSON

*Books in this series are published with support from the
Ohio University Center for International Studies.*

David William Cohen and E. S. Atieno Odhiambo, *The Risks of Knowledge: Investigations into the Death of the Hon. Minister John Robert Ouko in Kenya, 1990*

Belinda Bozzoli, *Theatres of Struggle and the End of Apartheid*

Gary Kynoch, *We Are Fighting the World: A History of the Marashea Gangs in South Africa, 1947–1999*

Stephanie Newell, *The Forger's Tale: The Search for Odeziaku*

Jacob A. Tropp, *Natures of Colonial Change: Environmental Relations in the Making of the Transkei*

Jan Bender Shetler, *Imagining Serengeti: A History of Landscape Memory in Tanzania from Earliest Times to the Present*

Cheikh Anta Babou, *Fighting the Greater Jihad: Amadu Bamba and the Founding of the Muridiyya in Senegal, 1853–1913*

Marc Epprecht, *Heterosexual Africa? The History of an Idea from the Age of Exploration to the Age of AIDS*

Marissa J. Moorman, *Intonations: A Social History of Music and Nation in Luanda, Angola, from 1945 to Recent Times*

Karen E. Flint, *Healing Traditions: African Medicine, Cultural Exchange, and Competition in South Africa, 1820–1948*

Derek R. Peterson and Giacomo Macola, editors, *Recasting the Past: History Writing and Political Work in Modern Africa*

Moses E. Ochonu, *Colonial Meltdown: Northern Nigeria in the Great Depression*

Emily S. Burrill, Richard L. Roberts, and Elizabeth Thornberry, editors, *Domestic Violence and the Law in Colonial and Postcolonial Africa*

Daniel R. Magaziner, *The Law and the Prophets: Black Consciousness in South Africa, 1968–1977*

Emily Lynn Osborn, *Our New Husbands Are Here: Households, Gender, and Politics in a West African State from the Slave Trade to Colonial Rule*

Robert Trent Vinson, *The Americans Are Coming! Dreams of African American Liberation in Segregationist South Africa*

James R. Brennan, *Taifa: Making Nation and Race in Urban Tanzania*

Benjamin N. Lawrance and Richard L. Roberts, editors, *Trafficking in Slavery's Wake: Law and the Experience of Women and Children*

David M. Gordon, *Invisible Agents: Spirits in a Central African History*

Allen F. Isaacman and Barbara S. Isaacman, *Dams, Displacement, and the Delusion of Development: Cahora Bassa and Its Legacies in Mozambique, 1965–2007*

Stephanie Newell, *The Power to Name: A History of Anonymity in Colonial West Africa*

Gibril R. Cole, *The Krio of West Africa: Islam, Culture, Creolization, and Colonialism in the Nineteenth Century*

Matthew M. Heaton, *Black Skin, White Coats: Nigerian Psychiatrists, Decolonization, and the Globalization of Psychiatry*

Meredith Terretta, *Nation of Outlaws, State of Violence: Nationalism, Grassfields Tradition, and State Building in Cameroon*

Paolo Israel, *In Step with the Times: Mapiko Masquerades of Mozambique*

Michelle R. Moyd, *Violent Intermediaries: African Soldiers, Conquest, and Everyday Colonialism in German East Africa*

Abosede A. George, *Making Modern Girls: A History of Girlhood, Labor, and Social Development in Colonial Lagos*

Alicia C. Decker, *In Idi Amin's Shadow: Women, Gender, and Militarism in Uganda*

Rachel Jean-Baptiste, *Conjugal Rights: Marriage, Sexuality, and Urban Life in Colonial Libreville, Gabon*

Shobana Shankar, *Who Shall Enter Paradise? Christian Origins in Muslim Northern Nigeria, ca. 1890–1975*

Emily S. Burrill, *States of Marriage: Gender, Justice, and Rights in Colonial Mali*

Todd Cleveland, *Diamonds in the Rough: Corporate Paternalism and African Professionalism on the Mines of Colonial Angola, 1917–1975*

Carina E. Ray, *Crossing the Color Line: Race, Sex, and the Contested Politics of Colonialism in Ghana*

Sarah Van Beurden, *Authentically African: Arts and the Transnational Politics of Congolese Culture*

Giacomo Macola, *The Gun in Central Africa: A History of Technology and Politics*

Lynn Schler, *Nation on Board: Becoming Nigerian at Sea*

Julie MacArthur, *Cartography and the Political Imagination: Mapping Community in Colonial Kenya*

Cartography and the Political Imagination

Mapping Community in Colonial Kenya

༈

Julie MacArthur

OHIO UNIVERSITY PRESS ༈ ATHENS, OHIO

Ohio University Press, Athens, Ohio 45701
ohioswallow.com
© 2016 by Ohio University Press
All rights reserved

Cover art: (*background*) C. W. Hobley, map of Kavirondo, 1898. Hobley,
"Kavirondo"; (*upper right corner*) sketch map of Jeremiah Nabifwo's property.
19 January 1959, KPA, WD/4/5; (*lower left corner*) sketch map of M. Mbango s/o
Linyonyi's property. 16 June 1956, KNA, PC/NZA/3/15/68.

Printed in the United States of America
Ohio University Press books are printed on acid-free paper ⊗ ™

26 25 24 23 22 21 20 19 18 17 16   5 4 3 2 1

Library of Congress Cataloging-in-Publication Data
Names: MacArthur, Julie, 1982– author.
Title: Cartography and the political imagination : mapping community in
  colonial Kenya / Julie MacArthur.
Other titles: New African histories series.
Description: Athens, Ohio : Ohio University Press, 2016. | Series: New
  African histories | Includes bibliographical references and index.
Identifiers: LCCN 2016005708| ISBN 9780821422090 (hc : alk. paper) | ISBN
  9780821422106 (pb : alk. paper) | ISBN 9780821445563 (pdf)
Subjects: LCSH: Luyia (African people)—Kenya—History. |
  Ethnicity—Political aspects—Kenya. | Cartography—Political
  aspects—Kenya. | Cartography—Social aspects—Kenya. | Kenya—Ethnic
  relations—History.
Classification: LCC DT433.545.L88 M33 2016 | DDC 305.896395—dc23
LC record available at http://lccn.loc.gov/2016005708

Contents

Illustrations

Acknowledgments

This book is the product of the support and guidance of many individuals and institutions. I have amassed a number of intellectual and personal debts during the course of this project, which spanned the better part of a decade.

First and foremost, immense thanks go to my former supervisor and generous adviser thereafter Derek Peterson for his constant support and insightful guidance. Over the past ten years, Derek's commitment and intellectual rigor has provided inspiration, challenge, and, at times, some needed tough love. This project is also particularly indebted to the pioneering work and tireless encouragement of John Lonsdale. When I first e-mailed John as an undergraduate student in Toronto, eager but unsure of my next step, I could not have imagined that he would not only respond and introduce me to the topic that would come to form this book but also become a central mentor and champion for this research. John's own work began in western Kenya, and his enthusiasm, generosity, and staggering memory opened the door both intellectually and personally.

I was privileged to count Megan Vaughan and John Iliffe among my mentors at Cambridge; both provided immeasurable advice and direction throughout this project. The African History Group and World History Seminar at the University of Cambridge provided critical spaces to present chapters and ideas as they developed. Special thanks also to Sean Hawkins, Paul Nugent, Bruce Berman, David Anderson, Lynn Thomas, Ruth Watson, Chris Youe, Terence Ranger, Peter Wafula Wekesa, Bethwell Ogot, Pamela Khanakwa, and Justin Willis for their invaluable counsel and feedback over the years. The final chapter of this volume benefited greatly from a fellowship with the National History Center's International Seminar on Decolonization in 2009. I am grateful to the organizers and intellectual mentors, Wm. Roger Louis, Philippa Levine, Marilyn Young, Dane Kennedy, and Jason Parker, and to my fellow seminarians for the rich discussions that forced me to think in more conceptual and cross-regional ways. The University of British Columbia and the University of Toronto have also provided intellectual homes over the years of revision; colleagues too numerous to name at both institutions have prompted me to think about this project in new and exciting ways.

In eastern Africa, I am extremely grateful to Peterson Kithuka and Richard Ambani at the Kenya National Archives for helping track down missing files and providing crucial insights into the mazes of files held in the archives. In particular, Richard generously offered his encyclopedic knowledge of the archives and his own personal connection to the histories of western Kenya to the service of this research. Special thanks also go to chief archivist Eliakim A. Azangu for providing permissions for the reproduction of images from the Kenya National Archives. Claire Médard introduced me to the intimidating world of fieldwork and provided me with my first home in western Kenya. Very special thanks to my research assistant, Henry Kissinger Adera, for his invaluable work and company. I am also indebted to the many men and women in western Kenya who gave up their time to recount their own personal histories and in particular the men of the Luyia Council of Elders and their families. I am especially grateful to J. D. Otiende, an impressive historian in his own right, for his candor, his hospitality, and his incisive historical memory. In Uganda, this research was supported by the Makerere Institute for Social Research and their former director, Nakanyike Musisi, whom I am now privileged to count among my colleagues at the University of Toronto. The institute also provided a great home during the first stage of revisions for the book while I held a Visiting Research and Teaching Fellowship under the directorship of Mahmood Mamdani. I owe a great debt to my colleagues and graduate students there for their deep intellectual commitment and the spirited exchanges we enjoyed.

The research for the original doctoral project was funded by the Gates Foundation (2006–9) and the Cambridge Overseas Research Scholarship (2006–9). At the University of Cambridge, Trinity Hall, the Faculty of History, and the Centre of African Studies generously provided funds for field research through the Smuts Memorial Fund, the Prince Consort Fund, the Members' History Fund, the Holland Rose Fund, and the UAC Nigeria Travel Fund. The Social Sciences and Humanities Research Council of Canada postdoctoral fellowship (2010–12) also provided critical funds that helped transform this project from a doctoral thesis into an academic monograph. I sincerely thank these institutions for their generosity and commitment to research.

I am grateful to Ohio University Press, Gill Berchowitz, and the editors of the New African Histories series for their patience, their insightful counsel, and their belief in my vision for this project. In particular, I am grateful to Allen Isaacman for his intellectual and personal engagement, and his commitment to young scholars. I would also like to thank the two anonymous reviewers for their careful readings and constructive criticism.

Undertaking this project would not have been possible without the encouragement and moral support of friends and family. To fellow scholars Emma Hunter, Matt Carotenuto, Myles Osborne, Stacey Hynd, Lindiwe Dovey, and Alex Corriveau-Bourque, thanks for the friendships, arguments, and support in the field. Friends too numerous to name across eastern Africa also opened doors, shed light on complex local politics, and offered welcome diversions over the years. To fellow historians Julia Laite and Jen Grant, thanks for the many years of debate, wine, and cupcakes, and for reminding me of the light at the end of the tunnel. Special thanks to Alban Rrustemi and Gregory Hughes for their immense personal and "technical" support over the years. To my TIFF family, thanks for "transforming the way" I see the world and for the annual "breaks." And finally, my sincerest thanks to my sisters for their constant encouragement; my nieces for their boundless curiosity and uplifting spirits; my father, whose passion for history and debate inspired my own; and my mother, the intrepid and tireless editor, for her incisive insights, sense of humor through painstaking edits, and unwavering support.

Abbreviations

ACK	Anglican Church of Kenya
ADC	African District Council
APA	Abaluyia Peoples Association
AWA	Abaluyia Welfare Association
AWF	African Workers' Federation
BFBS	British and Foreign Bible Society
BPU	Buluhya Political Union
CMS	Church Missionary Society
FAM	Friends African Mission
FUM	Friends United Mission
IAI	International African Institute
IBEAC	Imperial British East Africa Company
KADU	Kenya African Democratic Union
KANU	Kenya African National Union
KAU	Kenya African Union
KCA	Kikuyu Central Association
KLC	Kenya Land Commission
KNA	Kenya National Archives
KPA	Kakamega Provincial Archives
KTWA	Kavirondo Taxpayers' Welfare Association
LNC	Local Native Council
NARA	US National Archives and Records Administration
NCA	Nyanza Central Association
NKCA	North Kavirondo Central Association
NKTWA	North Kavirondo Taxpayers' Welfare Association
NLTC	Native Land Tenure Committee
OAU	Organization of African Unity
TNA:PRO	The National Archives: Public Records Office
UNA	Uganda National Archives

Mapping Political Communities in Africa

ON 25 August 2009, Perus Angaya Abura sat drinking her morning tea in her home, in the Amalemba Estates outside Kakamega, in Kenya's Western Province, anticipating a knock at her door from a "census enumerator." The 2009 Kenya census sparked controversy when government officials opted to resurrect a section on ethnic background on their questionnaires. Responding to concerns over ethnic violence, official manipulation, and minority rights, Kenyan officials expanded the list of forty-two "tribes" recognized in the last census a decade before to 114. The new list contained several tribes Perus had identified with at various points in her long life.[1] For the first time, "Kenyan" appeared as an option on a national census. "Luyia," the ethnic group ascribed to Perus since the first colonial census, in 1948, when she was but a teenager, also appeared.[2] Under "Luyia," a collapsible list of several different names unfolded for the first time: "Kisa," the administrative name given to the clans within Perus's home location during the colonial demarcation of 1909; and "Isukha," her husband's community and thus the community of her children, now appeared as official ethnic identities. Here laid out before Perus were some of the multiple identities she had come to wear: in Perus's words "Kenyan, Luyia, Kisa, Isukha, how can I choose? I am all of these."

Official inquiries into ethnic identity in Kenya threatened to pour salt on the fresh wounds of violence and political instability that engulfed the country after the 2007 national elections. The tightly fought campaign between incumbent Mwai Kibaki's Party of National Unity (PNU) and the opposition Orange Democratic Movement (ODM), led by Raila Odinga, quickly gave way to allegations of electoral fraud and massive demonstrations. The violence that ensued was graphically depicted by both Western media and many in the Kenyan government as "tribal" or "ethnic" in nature: the evils of political tribalism—the pitting of tribal communities against each other in an all-out competition for political power and resources—again rearing its ugly head in postcolonial Africa.

The opposition party ODM was born out of popular protests against Kibaki's proposed constitutional reforms in 2005 that did little to limit executive power or reform "Kenya's 'top heavy' political system."[3] Headed by a "pentagon" of five leaders with prominent Luo politician Raila Odinga at the helm, ODM hitched its campaign onto deeply historical arguments, telling histories of lost sovereignty, prophesizing interethnic cooperation, and envisioning a devolved, federated state.[4] Their strategy was a regional one: each of the five leaders in the pentagon represented a different regional polity, and their platform promised a more equitable "sharing of the cake" across the country. Debates during the campaign highlighted the multiple social inequalities, historical grievances, and regional disparities in development that cut across simplified "tribal" allegiances.[5] The two months of postelection violence left over one thousand people dead and seven hundred thousand internally displaced and ended with a compromised coalition government, with Kibaki continuing as president and Odinga instated in the newly created position of prime minister. Ethnic arguments certainly played a role in voting patterns and in the subsequent violence, but to label the two-month conflict that inaugurated 2008 as merely the cyclical bloodletting of "age-old tribal hatreds" was to misread not only the deep social anxieties and urgent political questions at stake in these elections but also the complex histories of the making and unmaking of political communities in eastern Africa.

Ahead of the 2009 census, newspapers, blogs, and other popular forums filled with debates over the nature of identity in Africa. In an article for the *Standard*, Otuma Ongalo pondered his census choices:

> I'm a son of a Luo man from Nyanza and Mnyala woman from Kakamega who migrated from Ugunja and established a home among the predominantly Bukusu in Bungoma in early 1960s. . . . Part of my family born before mid 1960s speaks fluent Luo, Kinyala and Kibukusu. . . . I'm married to an Isukha woman but our children cannot speak Kisukha, Kinyala, Luo or Kibukusu. So, when enumerators turn up in our homestead they will find a nation, not a tribe.[6]

Mama Ida, wife of Prime Minister Raila Odinga, drew laughs when she responded to the census question with, "I'm half-Luo, half-Luhya—you know, 50–50!"[7] With no provision for such mixed families, Ida Odinga was enumerated as a Luo, the community of her husband.[8] One columnist jokingly pictured these plural families as products of a distinct moral economy: "exchanging goats for the tribe."[9] In western Kenya, as across the country, long histories of migration, intermarriage, and interethnic exchange complicated bureaucratic efforts to align people into neatly ordered columns of sanctified and unchanging tribal groupings. As Ongola's response eloquently captured, the grammar of identity had a history and a geography that made sense of the plurality and multiplicity of identities in postcolonial Africa.

In response to petitions from "minority communities" in this minority nation, respondents for the 2009 census would be "at liberty to break away from the broader Luhya, Kalenjin, Mijikenda, Swahili or Kenyan Somali and identify with one or the other of the numerous sub-groupings under them."[10] The groups targeted in this process of disaggregation at first glance appeared quite diverse, and yet they shared a common history of ethnic imagination at odds with contemporary understandings of ethnogenesis. All extend across national and colonial borders; all have recent histories of confederal alliances among diverse communities; and all have been at the forefront of federalist debates and secessionist campaigns in postcolonial Kenya.[11] Of the Mijikenda, a confederation of nine communities along Kenya's coast, Justin Willis has argued that their modern articulation of ethnicity was "a history, and an identity, of recent origin; a truth whose ambiguity is constantly reflected in historical presentation."[12] It was this ambiguity, this plurality and dissent within territorially unbound ethnic bodies, that government officials in Kenya painted as potentially subversive and destructive to national stability.

The census enumerator never arrived at Perus's door. Despite a projected success of 97 percent of households across the country, delays, errors, and confusion marred the census in the Western Province, returning only 79 percent of its recorded household data.[13] Perus's dilemma, though, revealed a deeper history of the multiplicity and ambiguities of belonging in postcolonial Africa.

In all these recent political developments in Kenya—the 2005 constitutional referendum, the 2007 elections, the 2009 census, and again in the 2013 elections—one question plagued officials and repeatedly grabbed headlines: how will the Luyia answer?[14] With the second-highest voting numbers in the country, the Luyia represent a powerful regional power broker and crucial factor in any electoral contest. However, the political plurality of Luyia constituents consistently defied the tenets of political tribalism, never historically voting as a bloc. Despite representing the most hotly contested, diversely populated, and historically oppositional province during the 2007 Kenya elections, the province did not witness the levels of violence and retribution that spread around its borders. Even with one of their "own," in the form of Musalia Mudavadi, vying for the presidential seat in 2013, Luyia voters continued their tradition of defiantly plural politics, splitting the vote yet again between multiple candidates and parties.[15]

The political landscape of western Kenya is "slippery" terrain: "just as the Luhya's favourite food, 'mrere' is slippery, so too is anyone that banks on the Luhya to vote in bulk for them."[16] Many have asked whether they were indeed a proper "tribe": in the words of one Kenyan columnist, the Luyia were "created by the colonial administration some time in the 1940s. They did not exist before then and have no history as a 'tribe.'"[17] And this questioning of Luyia "credentials" as a tribe extends far beyond Kenya's popular and political discourses: mentors, advisers, and colleagues at academic conferences and in casual conversations have similarly asked me, "but are the Luyia *really* a tribe?"[18]

These questions formed the original stimulus for this book, asking how and to what ends the Luyia community developed this seemingly plural and unpredictable ethnic identity. Indeed, the "Luyia" did not exist as a discrete ethnic appellation before the 1930s; precolonially, and well into the colonial era, they were instead multiple discrete and distinct political communities that defied ethnic categorization and crossed environmental, linguistic, and colonial boundaries. Nevertheless, in 1948, after four decades of British rule in Kenya, a previously unknown ethnic name suddenly appeared atop the first official census. From nonexistence, the "Luyia" appeared with 653,774 enumerated and named constituents. By the 2009 census, Luyia numbers had risen to 5.3 million, the second-largest ethnic affiliation in the country. Despite their recent and self-conscious history of ethnogenesis, Luyia elders interviewed throughout my research described their community within the idiom of "tribe": to be Luyia was to be "of the same blood," to "gather together," to "speak the same language."[19]

This story, then, begins in this slippery terrain, in the undulating landscape of what would become western Kenya. From the shores of Lake Victoria to the foothills of Mount Elgon, the immense ecological and topographical variety of this compact region invited a complex mix of African settlers from divergent migratory routes and linguistic backgrounds. While European geographers and administrators mapped a singular, neat territory to order this complex landscape, its diverse inhabitants proved resistant to would-be state builders. With the discovery of gold in their lands in the 1930s, a territorial crisis prompted local political thinkers to imagine, for the first time, an enlarged ethnic polity in western Kenya.

The threats to land and local moral economies brought by colonial rule prompted many communities across eastern Africa to imagine new ethnic polities. However, for the communities of western Kenya, no single vernacular language ever united their disparate speakers; no common narratives or mythic founding father bound their members within historical lineages; and no set of cultural practices defined their community membership. Lacking these traditional, or at least recognizable, reservoirs of ethnic politics, Luyia political thinkers instead mapped new limits of authority, moral accountability, and political community along territorial lines: they worked to territorialize custom and institutionalize plurality; they mobilized a civic language of territorial nationalism to rationalize their differences; they imagined a territory of cosmopolitan people bound not by common lineage or past myths but by a common geographic imagination. While narratives of ethnogenesis among the Luyia claim no common founding father or point of origin, they insist on a geographic identity. This geographic space, defined by the regional networks and exchanges made necessary by environmental interdependence and the multiplicity of communities, provided the most constant source of inspiration and mobilization for the creative re-imaginings of the Luyia community.

While framed, and continually frustrated, in the colonial terms of the ethnos, the creation of a plural and civic-minded Luyia identity proved impressively durable, and flexible enough to allow Luyia partisans to defend against encroaching European settlers and African neighbors, to productively navigate the politics of loyalism and dissent during the Mau Mau rebellion, and to foster a vibrant and fiercely plural political culture. Understanding this dynamic, confounding, and diverse political project requires a reassessment of current theories of ethnogenesis, prompts an investigation into the geographic imaginations of African communities, and provides a challenge to contemporary readings of community and conflict in Africa.

LINES OF ARGUMENT:
IMAGINED POLITICAL COMMUNITIES

This book advances three lines of argument based on three intertwined concepts that while abstract and multiple in their meanings have material and situated implications and reflect the high stakes and changing political economies of African political imagination. The first follows the argument of "imagined communities," to use Benedict Anderson's now famous phrasing, of understanding national and ethnic identities as thoroughly historical and intrinsically creative processes.[20] Such imagined communities formed on the basis of multiple impetuses: national, religious, linguistic, ideological, and genealogical. Yet while ethnos provided the language for much of this imagination in colonial Africa, what was imaginable had historically contingent limits. To address the constraints and possibilities of these imaginings, the second line of argument seeks to unpack the emergence of a particular form of ethnic patriotism that demonstrates the complex interplay of nativism and cosmopolitan pluralism within African political thought. Finally, I argue that these seemingly contradictory claims were made possible by the mobilization of geographic imaginations capable of articulating and at times enforcing the boundaries of inclusion and exclusion. At its analytical core, this study argues for a social history of cartographic political imaginations.

In colonial Africa, the European belief that all Africans belonged to timeless, bounded, primordial "tribes" meant ethnicity was the only framework recognized by imperial surveyors, missionaries, and colonial officials, and in turn became the dominant language of African culture and politics. But this does not mean that African imaginations of tribe, and later nation, were merely "derivative discourses" trapped in European constructs and ideologies.[21] While most contemporary historians shy away from the term, due to its imperial roots and primordial implications, *tribe* has rarely represented a problem for self-description within African patriotic discourses. Indeed the idiom of "tribe" has proven incredibly resilient despite the vilification of its twin head, "tribalism." While I hesitate to endorse a wholesale rehabilitation of the term, the language of *tribe* continues to hold great relevance and currency in the everyday political imaginings of self and society in Africa.

Until the late 1970s, these two analytical thrusts—one viewing tribes as primordial communities bound by blood kinship relations and the other viewing tribes as instrumental political identities, circumstantial and open to manipulation—governed both colonial and academic understandings of ethnic identity.[22] Both these theories understood ethnic identity as a fact and their tenets continue to dictate popular representations of Africa, as witnessed in the aftermath of the 2007 Kenya elections. However, both failed to account for the continuing salience and changing meanings of ethnicity in contemporary African societies.

In the 1980s a new cohort of African scholars questioned the "fact" of ethnic identity and championed a new theoretical model that still dominates today. In Leroy Vail's seminal edited volume *The Creation of Tribalism*, contributing scholars theorized the "invention of tradition" through the codification of customary law, the standardization of African languages, and the effects of migrancy on the construction of new lines of community under colonial rule. As John Iliffe argued, "Europeans believed Africans belonged to tribes; Africans built tribes to belong to."[23] For these constructivists, ethnicity was not a fixed condition but rather a modern expression of historical processes, socially constructed by colonial officials, European missionaries, and African political thinkers.

Postcolonial studies have largely endorsed these instrumentalist and constructivist approaches, picturing ethnicity as an industry, as a crisis of citizenship, and as a "shadow theatre" of historical production.[24] A new thrust seems to be reinvigorating primordialist arguments and debates around whether colonial regimes did, in fact, invent ethnic and racial hierarchies or rather simply added a new language for racial or ethnic thinking.[25] In global and transnational studies of ethnogenesis, there exists a growing trend toward examining the "entanglements" of ethnicity, the interrelationships of ethnicity, race, nationalism, class, gender, and sexuality.[26] In colonial contexts, these studies examine ethnogenesis both as a strategy of subaltern resistance and as a means of exercising and consolidating dominance.[27] Despite Richard Werbner and Terence Ranger's warning that the "story of ethnic difference in Africa threatens to overwhelm the larger debate about postcolonial identity politics," recent studies continue to emphasize instrumental political manipulation, lineage-based myth making, and the colonial legacies of the dichotomy between customary and civic models of belonging.[28]

Fixated as the constructivists have been on the colonial moment, what they still fail to account for are the very real attachments to and emotive potential of ethnic identification witnessed in modern Africa. As John Lonsdale has argued, "Ethnicity can scarcely be invented, or warmly shared, in a historical void."[29] The limits of "invention" soon became apparent even to its founding thinkers.[30]

More recent scholarship on ethnicity in Africa has heeded Lonsdale's call to interrogate the moral debates and imaginative processes marshaled by African communities in the making of ethnic identities. In his groundbreaking work on Kikuyu society and the moral economy of the Mau Mau rebellion, Lonsdale redirected scholarly attention toward the internal moral debates of ethnic polities.[31] He argued that "moral ethnicity" was primarily a culture of personal and civic accountability: "To debate civic virtue was to define ethnic identity."[32] Ethnicity thus represented a moral and political arena in which African communities debated and continually reimagined notions of belonging and citizenship, social obligation and civic responsibility, and moral authority and political leadership. In doing so, Lonsdale opened up the timeline of ethnic invention and created a language that allowed scholars to interrogate ethnicity as a creative moral project: in the words of Thomas Spear, to shift scholarly focus to "the dynamics of traditions, customs and ethnicities; on the contradictions of colonial rule; on shifting resource endowments and access; on how African and European intellectuals reinterpreted traditions in the colonial and postcolonial context; and on why others believed them."[33]

While the "invention of tradition" school of thought and the more thorough accounting of "moral ethnicities" continue to offer important frameworks, both suffer from two interrelated shortcomings. First, scholarship in this vein too often takes the "inventors" of political communities at their word, elevating their versions of constructed community at the expense of the multiple, dissenting, and competing forms of community developed within and outside the linguistic and territorial confines of the "tribe."[34] Just as "invention" was not limited to the colonial period, neither was it the sole domain of the African cultural brokers who wrote patriotic histories. Tim Parsons has recently shown the "diverse ways of being" for the Kikuyu in colonial Kenya by refocusing attention away from the "inventors," who constructed the illusion of consensus toward the ordinary "people who crossed ethnic boundaries."[35] As Rogers Brubaker and Frederick Cooper argued in their oft-quoted but often misunderstood essay, an emphasis on identity, in its equally problematic "hard" and "soft" conceptions, can often mask the more complex, multiple, and mobile processes of identification.[36]

Second, the focus on the singularizing political imaginations of these "inventors" has obscured or at least sidelined other forms of imagination, and in particular geographic imaginations, that helped make these political imaginations viable or attractive in the first place. While such "inventions" were subject to constant revision by multiple actors, they were not open to just any interpretation. The material and symbolic base available for such imaginations conditioned and constrained the projects of ethnic "inventors." As will be seen throughout this study, regional processes of exchange and interdependence created what Paul Richards has called a "common grammar" of social experience, despite differences in language, culture, or political organization.[37] Across Africa, these "common grammars" emerged from common geographic visions and provided a mechanism for rationalizing plurality and managing dissent within ongoing projects of ethnogenesis.

ETHNIC PATRIOTISM:
BETWEEN NATIVISM AND COSMOPOLITANISM

"Ethnic patriotism" provided a particular currency in the moral economy of colonial eastern Africa: "ethnic" because of the particular colonial investment in the language of tribe and "patriotic" because of the in-turn investment by African political thinkers in the construction of a patria, a fatherland with countrymen to feel kinship among and a territory to defend.[38] In the comparative politics of patriotism in eastern Africa, ethnicity offered a historically contingent and politically viable form of community building.[39]

Despite presenting one of the clearest cases of ethnic "invention," where the terms of a Luyia ethnic identity literally did not exist before the 1930s, the history of ethnic imagining among the Luyia has received surprisingly little scholarly attention, especially in comparison to the pioneering and voluminous scholarship on ethnicity coming out of Kenya.[40] Newly "Luyia" historians began writing partisan histories as early as the 1940s, in line with patriotic history-writing projects taking place across Africa in the late colonial era.[41] After the impressive body of work by Gideon Were, however, the historical and cultural production emerging from western Kenya tended to take as its subject the so-called subtribal ethnonationalisms.[42] While scholars in various fields have traveled to western Kenya for their case studies of socioeconomic, educational, and religious change, the majority of these texts focus on specific communities that fall under the Luyia banner, neglecting the complex tensions and negotiations of difference among the constituent groups who came to form and at times refuse this corporate body.[43]

The most common explanation for the Luyia identity has fallen along constructivist lines, picturing the "Luyia" as a creation, either of colonial officials or of local political thinkers, "former students of Makerere College on analogy of BaGanda."[44] Yet the framework of the "invention of tradition" fails to account for how these actors fashioned an ethnic project without a common stock of historical myths and without a founding father from whom to imagine a patria. Unlike the more maximal cultural projects of the Luo Union, the Kikuyu Central Association, and the Haya Union farther afield, or even the more federalist projects of the Mijikenda and the Kalenjin, the "invention" of Luyia ethnic architects was not of a unified traditional past but rather of a corporate present and an interdependent future. While ethnogenesis among the Luyia seems to provide a challenge to scholars of "invention," which perhaps explains their omission from this historiography, the large body of scholarly work on ethnicity signals the particular value and competitive nature of ethnic patriotism in colonial Kenya.

Luyia ethnic patriots emerged out of a particular set of discourses and social experiences within the colonial world. Take for example the life and political work of Ephraim A. Andere. Born in 1920 in Namasoli, North Kavirondo, Andere had a typical, if fairly elite, education at the Alliance High School before distinguishing himself as a writer and political thinker at Makerere College in Uganda.[45] Upon his return to the district, in 1940, he gained a reputation as a respected schoolmaster at the prestigious Nyang'ori Primary School and later at Maseno School. But Andere's real achievements were in the realm of ethnic patriotism. As general secretary of the Abaluyia Welfare Association, Andere worked toward the federation of smaller locational and clan associations under a Luyia umbrella. In 1948 he spearheaded the campaign that would put the Luyia name atop the first national census in Kenya. Throughout the 1940s he worked tirelessly with the Luyia Language Committee, whose goal it was to create one Luyia language out of the multiple and stubbornly diverse dialects in the region. Throughout Kenya, language committees proved a common tool for ethnic patriots and a training ground for burgeoning political leaders. In 1947 all three nominations for the Legislative Council from western Kenya—Philip Ingutia, Paul Mboya, and B. A. Ohanga—played significant roles in their respective Luyia and Luo language committees.[46] The Kalenjin Language Committee similarly included future politicians Daniel arap Moi and Taita arap Towett.[47] While a Luyia language failed to materialize, for Andere this linguistic endeavor went hand in hand with his political and demographic work.

Andere's name would be become most closely associated with the formulation of Luyia customary law in the 1950s. The project was ambitious and fraught. The overwhelming variety of customary practices among the constituent communities of the Luyia stumped early administrators, clogged local courts, and led to endless parochial conflicts among neighbors. For Andere, consolidating customary law seemed a natural extension of his earlier patriotic work. As secretary of the Luyia Customary Law Panel, from 1951 to 1954, Andere deliberately worked to bring in a diversity of panelists to avoid the appearance of favoritism or domination by particular communities that had doomed the Luyia language project.[48] He further petitioned for representatives to come not from elders and chiefly authorities but from young politicians, teachers, and ethnic patriots like himself. Together, these young technocrats set out to define a common set of principles usable in various fields of local governance, political organization, language, and moral discipline. In multiple customary law publications, Andere ordered and tabulated the plurality of Luyia customary practices into a seemingly singular, coherent document.[49] These publications are, however, quite amusing to read, riddled as they are with complicated tables, competing terminologies, sections on "local variations," and recurrent qualifications. In Andere's masterful hands, plural and dissenting cultural practice became the defining rather than defeating feature of Luyia "customs," allowing for a variety of readings and open to constant revision. The creation of Luyia customary law was a technocratic feat and a victory for Andere.

Ethnic patriots did not work in isolation; they were members of complex social networks that clustered around religious denominations, schooling, government positions, and experiences of urbanism and international schooling. Andere served as longtime committee member on *Muluhya*, a magazine published by Luyia students at Makerere, alongside fellow ethnic patriots W. B. Akatsa and J. D. Otiende, among others. It would be fellow nominee Otiende who would recommend Andere for nomination to the Legislative Council in 1948.[50] Ahead of the first national election, in 1957, the local council chose Andere to tour the district and collect testimony with the Coutts Commission alongside important politicians W. W. W. Awori and Pascal Nabwana.[51] On panels, committees, and district councils, Andere worked alongside nearly every current and future political figure from western Kenya and made the work of ethnic patriotism into a profession.

Ethnic patriotism did not altogether offer a social identity as such. Rather, ethnic patriotism offered a self-conscious form of work, an occupation taken up in the context of a specific colonial context. While Luyia ethnic patriots shared similar biographies, and clusters did emerge, they also diverged and came from a variety of denominational and local filiations. Some, like Paul Agoi, moved in and out of these registers. After over a decade working in the native administration as a headman, councilman, and member on several boards, into the 1930s Agoi recognized the shifting tides and the growth of ethnic patriotism as a viable form of work. He became the president of the North Kavirondo Taxpayers' Welfare Association, where he protested local land policies and called on the people of North Kavirondo to name themselves. Before the Kenya Land Commission in 1932, Agoi revealed the growing sense of territorial nationalism within this project when he pronounced that the "proper boundary of the Black man is Mombasa."[52] In 1940, Agoi capitalized the colonial administration's attempt to coopt young ethnic patriots and became chief of the Maragoli. While progressive and well remembered for his visit to Kenyan troops serving in the Middle East in 1943, as chief, Agoi embarked on a different kind of politicking.[53] He began turning inward and fashioning himself along the lines of an invented royal tradition using symbolic elements from the Logoli past. He wore a special robe of leopard skins and took the title of Owuluyali (His Highness). In response to the institution of the Locational Council, whose nominations rested outside his control, Agoi formed his own advisory council, the Bulindi bwo Woluyali.[54] Soon fellow ethnic patriots Lumadede Kisala and Solomon Adagala became suspicious of Agoi's dynastic ambitions. They charged Agoi with undemocratic behavior and forced his early retirement in 1950.

Agoi's miscalculations reflected a fairly unique quality and tension within the Luyia version of ethnic patriotism; Luyia leaders who made such parochial calls to past reservoirs of power soon found themselves out of step. While inventions of tradition and "tribal fantasies" were crucial components of the work of ethnic patriots across eastern Africa, Luyia ethnic patriots were also, from a very early stage, cosmopolitan patriots.[55] The tension between nativism, characterized by autochthonous claims to pure ancestry and rooted geographies, and cosmopolitanism, defined by cultural mixing and mobility, has marked modern African politics of identity. Some have argued that both were colonial imports.[56] Yet, both have much longer histories and wide currency in African thought. If we take Kwame Anthony Appiah's central principles of cosmopolitanism—pluralism, revisionism or "fallibilism," and an obligation to strangers—then the Luyia have always been cosmopolitans.[57] Across Kenya, eastern Africa, and out into an international diaspora, to be Luyia is to say *mulembe*.[58] As explored in chapter 1, for centuries this term greeted visitors and strangers alike by asking where they had been, where they were going, and entreating them to come and go in peace.[59] The formal call and response reflected the mutual obligation contained within such greetings.[60] What Appiah hints at, but never fully develops, is this long history of cosmopolitanism—of plurality, of mobility, of multilingualism, and of multiple identities—among African communities. This left Appiah open to criticisms that his "cosmopolitanism" was Eurocentric and available only to the privileged few.[61] And yet it was in the confrontation between these local, historically rich cosmopolitanisms and colonial "modernity" that many of these communities became nativist, rather than the other way around; and the two were not mutually exclusive.

Nativist discourses of immutable, bounded tribes provided a certain capital within the colonial economy. Older cosmopolitanisms survived, however, and were mobilized within anticolonial politics and ethnic patriotisms alike, aiming not so much at eliminating differences as at recognizing and navigating through them.[62] Cosmopolitanism, in Appiah's view, was precisely about this kind of conversation without the necessity of consensus: "Even people who share a moral vocabulary have plenty to fight about"—a sentiment echoed in many Luyia proverbs.[63] So while Andere and others took up the ethnic work of linguistic consolidation and the codification of customary law, their culturalist projects revealed not the suppression of difference but rather their insistent pluralism. The direction of this work—the ability of ethnic patriots to navigate the tensions between nativism and cosmopolitanism and to subsume their constituents under patriotic discourses—was never entirely new, nor did it remain in their hands alone.

These ethnic patriots shared another common feature: they were all men. As Lonsdale has noted, "Patriotic history tends to be masculine history."[64] While "patriotic" men formed the intellectual core of much of this work, they often called upon women to carry the weight of their inventive projects, to comport themselves as the bearers of children, of morality, and of their community's cultural values. African women, by their biology and social energies, reproduced the moral communities these men sought to fashion. As scholars of the "invention of tradition" took the "inventors" of ethnic communities at their word, African women often disappeared in their studies of ethnic identity: as Leroy Vail put it, "Ethnicity's appeal was strongest for men, then, and the Tswana proverb to the effect that 'women have no tribe' had a real—if unintended—element of truth in it."[65] Though some impressive studies have looked at African women's agency in subverting male authority, in carving out new spaces of work and morality, and in crafting nationalist agendas, these studies often placed women as a category apart from the study of ethnic imaginings.[66] Writing on this problem among Marakwet women in colonial Kenya, Henrietta Moore argued that "in such a situation, women are invisible, sunk, contained within the 'naturalised' domain of the dominant ideology."[67] The reactive fallback notion of "the invisible woman" within ethnic studies has allowed for uncritical approaches to this subject.[68] African women often disappeared in histories of ethnic imagining precisely because "patriotic" men sought to subsume them.

Ethnic identity for Luyia women was not so much "invisible" or even "subsumed" as it was transformable. While culturalist projects like the Luo Union and the Haya Union sought to rein in the moral conduct and reproductive capabilities of their women, Luyia entrepreneurs shied from these cultural politics and instead integrated "Luyia" women strategically into their demographic projects through a progressive discourse of universal suffrage and ethnic diversity. In theory, intermarriage among Luyia groups required women to follow their husband's customs and raise their children within the patrilineal culture. As Charles Ambler noted for the nineteenth century, patrilineal absorption allowed women to move between groups with ease, without requiring the special initiations often demanded of foreign men.[69] However, with a private wink and a nod, wives and mothers transmitted many aspects of their former cultural identities to their children in language and custom.[70] That women could carry ideas, customs, languages, and networks throughout the territorial space of the Luyia underpinned the processes of interpenetration and intermarriage that defined the very plural nature of the late colonial Luyia discourse. Perus's dilemma before the census enumerator dramatized the tensions that existed for women in the production of ethnic communities.

For such women, cosmopolitan ethnic patriotism was then, in many ways, second nature. While Luyia political thinkers remained more concerned with electoral projects and census numbers than with any culturalist agenda, they still engaged in a gendered discourse of morality, movement, and home. The tension between a gendered nativist politics and a progressive cosmopolitanism proved a critical, if challenging, feature of Luyia ethnic patriotism. This cosmopolitan ethnic patriotism also proved potentially dangerous: patriotic competitors would decry such cosmopolitanisms as rootless, ungrounded, so much so that being "cosmopolitan" became an insult often hurled in their direction.[71] As will be seen throughout this story, the limited and often failed cultural projects of Luyia entrepreneurs in language, gender discipline, customary law, and history writing prompted a more minimalist approach to the formulation of political community and revealed the attenuated character of this ethnic project.

Despite the recent historiographical emphasis on fluctuation, negotiation, and cultural production in the imagining of ethnicity, these models continue to rely on a teleological insistence on ethnic invention, enforced consensus, and exclusion. Gabrielle Lynch's recent work on the Kalenjin, whose composite communities, like those of the Luyia, came to be recognized by this appellation only in the 1940s, has argued that this ethnic alliance succeeded through the consolidation of lineage-based myths of origin and an "emotive (and inherently exclusive) narrative of territorial association."[72] What is still missing is a way to understand the plurality and dissent not only at the borders but also within these patriotic discourses and the multiple and overlapping localities in which they evolved.[73] While the Luyia were not unique in this process, they were perhaps uniquely self-conscious. The imagining of a Luyia community reflects less an exception to the rules of ethnic invention and more the creative energies mobilized to rationalize plurality and dissent. Luyia ethnic architects grounded their patriotism within a distinct geographic vision. Lacking the consensus and consolidation of a more thoroughgoing culturalist agenda, they were left with a mapped outline from which to build a new form of demographically inclusive, politically plural community. For Luyia cosmopolitans, territorial nationalism provided a language, a form of argumentation capable of tapping into the geographic imaginations, multiple sites of identification, and histories of regional interdependence and interaction among their plural and irrepressibly diverse constituents.

GEOGRAPHIC IMAGINATIONS: MAPPING POWER, COUNTERMAPPING DISSENT

In an interview with the editors of the French Marxist geography journal *Hérodote* in 1976, Michel Foucault begins by defending his lack of interest in geography as a subject.[74] When confronted with the profusion of spatial and geographic metaphors in his work—position, displacement, terrain, archipelago, landscape—Foucault defends these terms as reflecting more historical and political power structures rather than geographic ideas in and of themselves. By the end of this exchange, however, the editors prompt Foucault into an about-face: "I must admit . . . Geography acted as the support, the condition of possibility for the passage between a series of factors I tried to relate. . . . Geography must indeed necessarily lie at the heart of my concerns."

Geography and the encounters between communities and the landscapes they inhabit have long produced sites of imagination and contestation through which African communities expressed their histories, their moral economies, and the limits of their political communities. And yet, as Foucault realized, despite a profusion of geographic metaphors, very little scholarly attention has interrogated the geographic imaginations behind these metaphors that made possible the variety and durability not only of knowledge production and power structures but also of subaltern political imaginations.[75]

The spatial turn in African history over the past few years has prompted a move away from restrictive, relatively recent, and colonially contingent national and ethnic units of analysis toward a focus on "regions": geographic spaces defined by the extent of "networks of interaction, whether political, economic, social, or cultural."[76] This regional approach not only breaks away from colonial timelines and boundaries but also exposes the diverse and dissenting interactions and exchanges within these spaces. This is not to suggest, as some have, a simple replacing of an "ethnic" grammar with a "geographic" one; rather, this approach responds to Achille Mbembe's call for an investigation into the *"imaginaires* and autochthonous practices of space."[77] These "imaginaires" revealed themselves in many forms: in the histories told; in the geographic work of language, customary practice, and demographic control; and in the spatial delimitation of land, movement, power, and belonging.

Social formations among the constituent communities of the Luyia reflected an "imbrication of multiple spaces" of belonging, exchange, and authority before colonial conquest.[78] While this geographic imagination continued to inform the organization of political relations and strategies of resistance into the colonial period, the territorial outline drawn by imperial surveyors offered a new coherence, a framework from which new political thinkers could claim the right to speak for an enlarged ethnic constituency. Contrary to instrumentalist understandings of colonial boundaries constructing ready-made ethnic territories from which African politicians mobilized their constituents, colonial maps did not invent new identities wholesale but rather introduced new tools in the visual illustration of history and community.[79] Mapmaking provided a way of "writing the world," a way of making legible spatial relationships and territorial claims.[80] And while geography constituted social practice, cartography, as introduced in the colonial era, became political action.

A recent historiographical trend has focused on the importance of mapping and strategies of territoriality to the imperial project. For Lord Curzon, boundaries represented "the razor's edge on which hang suspended the modern issues of war or peace, of life or death to nations."[81] Geography made possible the possession of distant territories, bringing "light" to dark, unknown places and peoples: "To govern territories, one must know them . . . unless a region is first conceived of and named, it cannot become the specific subject of a map."[82] Historians have made great use of geographer Robert Sack's theory of territoriality to reconstruct the links between territory and power, geography and governance, and mapmaking and identity. In Sack's terms, "'territoriality . . . forms the backcloth to human spatial relations and conceptions of space. . . . Territoriality is the primary spatial form power takes."[83] Territoriality was then a strategy of social interaction, of rule, and of state building.[84]

Taking inspiration from Benedict Anderson's seminal text *Imagined Communities*, two pioneering studies in this young field, Thongchai Winichakul's *Siam Mapped* and Christopher Gray's *Colonial Rule and Crisis in Equatorial Africa*, both emphasized the instrumental role of imperial mapmaking in the formation of new ethnic and national communities.[85] Both studies began by sketching the cognitive mapping of space that existed before the intervention of colonial geography.[86] Winichakul explored the sacred topographies of Buddhist thought alongside the ancient maps of Southeast Asia to demonstrate the "coexistence of different concepts of space."[87] Gray, on the other hand, built on Jan Vansina's theory of "cognitive *landscapes*" that spatialize ideology on an intimate scale.[88] For Gray, the cognitive mapping of kinship and clan hierarchies among the stateless communities of South Gabon allowed for the development of a socially defined form of territoriality.[89] For both Winichakul and Gray, the introduction of colonial mapmaking constrained local practices of space, imposed imperial understandings of geography, and encoded boundaries as the delimiters of new ethnic and national bodies.

Historians of colonial territoriality have investigated the use of mapping in the spatial organization of gender relations, the micropractices of power and governmentality, and the relations and identities formed on frontiers and across borderlands.[90] Postcolonial studies have further looked at colonial boundaries variously as artificial barriers, as delimiters of citizenship, and as conduits of exchange and interaction.[91] But the underlying argument remains virtually the same: the introduction of modern mapping technologies marked a radical break that displaced older forms of geographic knowledge and prompted new formulations of community and identity. By focusing too narrowly on imperial and "official" maps, these studies risk eliding the "cartographic anxiety" that such processes produced and occluding the ways Africans, or indeed subalterns across the colonized world, informed, contested, and appropriated these colonial impositions.[92]

The introduction of cartography reflected broader histories of scientific exchange and literacy in the colonial world. Imperial state builders, according to James Scott, required spatial ordering to make their power legible, but these "state fixations" were often frustrated—unmapped lands were not blank spaces waiting to be filled, and local populations did not "stand idly by when surveyors came into view."[93] Cartography represented a contested enterprise in which local communities, as much as European experts and scientists, worked to produce knowledge and constitute communities. In counterpoint to the work of Tim Mitchell and Scott, mapping was not the sole property of high-modernist imperial planners.[94] Mapping, as a tool of power, imagination, and dissent, was much more broadly distributed and proved to be a useful political strategy for subaltern activists and ethnic patriots alike. Whether by the state or in the hands of local amateur surveyors, mapping obliged both cartographers and readers to understand themselves in relation to the map.

The colonial obsession with territorial ordering and cataloguing incentivized the development of cartographic literacy and produced distinct modes of competition in local moral economies. Mapping, as with all colonial strategies of rule, was a negotiated, historically contingent process. Africans, serving as guides, porters, and assistants in the work of mapping of western Kenya, quickly leaned lessons in reconnaissance, surveying, triangulation, and a whole host of cartographic techniques and languages. Missionary and later government schools held formal classes in geography. In the 1940s, District Social Welfare Officer Ryland reported that geography was among the most popular subjects at his Development Centre.[95] Though the exact lessons and mapmaking exercises used by missionary and government teachers remain difficult to ascertain, mapping proved an indispensable tool in the emerging colonial economy.

In classrooms, in courtrooms, and before colonial land commissions, Africans practiced their cartographic skills and produced maps to defend their landholdings and household economies. The most explicit training ground for local mapmaking skills came from colonial courts. In her study of mapping in Mozambique, Heidi Gengenbach noted that "of all types of colonisers' maps, cadastral maps impinged most directly and disruptively on the lives of Africans."[96] Land cases called upon claimants to draw instrumental pictorial representations of their farms and surrounding environments. Native tribunals in western Kenya were constantly congested with land cases that often dated back over generations and included multiple overlapping claims.

Court cases were replete with competing maps that used increasingly sophisticated methods of representation. Symbols and legends guided the court's readings of these maps. When "trespassers" entered the farmland of recently deceased Jeremiah Nabifwo, his sons created a detailed map of their father's landholdings to present to the court.[97] A "key" guided the court through mazes of dotted lines, shaded spaces, and interlocking properties (fig. i.1). Nabifwo's sons worked to prove the

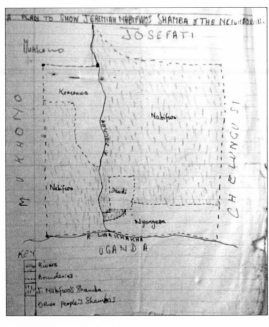

FIGURE I.1. Sketch map of Jeremiah Nabifwo's property. 19 January 1959, KPA, WD/4/5.

violation of their father's lands by visualizing the rivers, borders, and tenant farms that defined the limits and terms of access to his property.

In other cases, claimants sketched detailed histories into the landscape. In the case of M. Mbango s/o Linyonyi, a map offered multiple decades of information, tracing lines of ownership, use, court appeals, and competing claims (fig. I.2). In such maps, individual claims overlapped, intersected, and at times competed with larger claims to clan lands. These cases became increasingly complex by the late colonial period as plaintiffs moved in and out of the district, complicating land claims that often privileged use and mapped accuracy over genealogy and custom.[98] These land maps revealed the increasing sophistication, complexity, and careful attention to pictorial detail of cartographic representation in western Kenya.

This mapmaking was never, however, a simple translation of the world of experience into the world on paper, as argued by Sean Hawkins. Hawkins drew too sharp a distinction between literal maps and cognitive mappings, seeing cartographic practices as a "text" that imposed new forms of historical consciousness.[99] The transnational literature on territoriality is often inclined to contrast a notion of precolonial spatial fluidity and multiplicity with colonial mapped fixity, indeed mirroring the literature on ethnic identity.

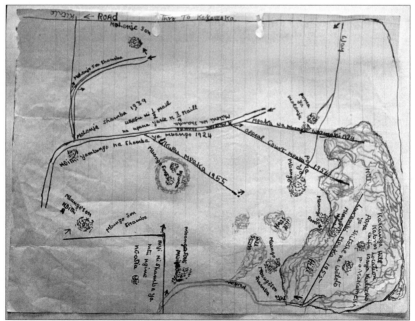

FIGURE I.2. Sketch map of M. Mbango s/o Linyonyi's property. 16 June 1956, KNA, PC/NZA/3/15/68.

As cartographic literacy gained prominence, new mapping techniques grafted onto older environmental and social negotiations on the ground. Claimants in western Kenya continually demanded that maps of landholdings be substantiated through reference to older measures of land tenure and asked for the intervention of elders "who know very much about our grand-grand fathers boundaries."[100] Courts often required "proofs" of boundaries in the physical landscape and expert testimony alongside pictorial representations. Maps produced for the courts were taken out to the disputed areas, where lines on the page were matched to physical realities. In the case of Musa Mamai versus Jonathan Wepukhulu over land in Kolani, Chief Barasa called for observers from the surrounding population to witness the new boundary demarcation. At the site of the conflict, Mamai and Wepukhulu both agreed for the "boundary to run as drawn on the . . . map."[101] In other cases, maps were "drawn" on the floor of the court itself.[102] Maps produced for these colonial land courts never provided the final word on landownership; rather, local communities debated, negotiated, and redrew these maps. While colonial mapping affixed land to the page as never before, these practices grafted on top of older environmental and social negotiations on the ground and encouraged the production of new cartographic metaphors and symbols.

The cases of Jeremiah Nabifwo, M. Mbango, Musa Mamai v. Jonathan Wepukhulu, and others illuminated a much larger trend. Mastering mapping skills was proving increasingly indispensible to local competitions over scarce resources. Chiefs and district officials often remarked on the quality of maps in their judgments. Further, these maps became part of a permanent record, an archival patrimony that was frequently called up in later land disputes. While geographic literacy served "symbolic, cognitive and pedagogic" roles, mapmaking itself became an instrumental resource for the reproduction of class, wealth, and power in the moral economy of western Kenya.[103]

But the importance and uses of mapping went far beyond this instrumental function. Mapping also proved a critical tool for ethnic patriots, particularly for those ethnic patriots whose constituents were also cosmopolitan and plural. Maps could provide the engines to transform their "social energy into social work."[104] Local cartographic practices, both on an intimate and on a patriotic scale, allowed for the development of what contemporary geographers term countermapping. Also called ethnocartography, countermapping refers to community-based mapping projects, particularly in postcolonial and indigenous land cases, used to "resist the power of the state."[105] As contemporary legal systems, both local and international, consider carefully drawn maps obligatory and often paramount evidence in questions of land rights, countermapping provided the means to make the land claims of indigenous peoples "legible" and legally viable.[106] In recent years, technological advances such as geographic information systems and the Global Positioning System have democratized the tools of mapping and aided these countermapping campaigns. While these new technologies have added to the "excitement" around such projects, countermapping also relies heavily on a much wider range of lower-tech and lower-cost techniques, such as sketch mapping and scale model constructions.[107] Countermapping offered the power, or at least potential, to transform individual land into property and communal land into territory. In this way, countermapping served both a counterhegemonic purpose—mapping against the state— and a generative purpose, capable of mapping new states of political imaginations.

The social work of countermapping has a much longer history than assumed in the literature on indigenous rights and community based activism. If defined as an essentially counterhegemonic practice, then countermapping preceded cartography, as local communities used spatial strategies to resist state-builders of all kinds. In a recent study, James Scott has demonstrated how "hill peoples" in central Asia used spatial strategies to escape state builders, taking refuge in remote hills that served as spaces not only of resistance but also of "cultural refusal."[108] "Statelessness," in this conception, should not be understood as disorganization or as a lack of social structures but as a strategy and an art form. Spatial analysis has opened new avenues for the study of social formations characterized by heterarchy, systems of organization exemplified by overlaps, multiplicity, and divergent yet coexistent patterns of relations, power, and authority.[109] Whether in parallel or in contest with hierarchal systems, heterarchy provided a strategy of "(horizontal) social complexification," and a means of evading or checking centralizing political forces.[110] While the kindom of Buganda used spatial organization to order power and discipline their subjects, this same spatial ordering also allowed members of the court to allocate measures of accountability: through the complex spatial organization of different forms of religious and political leadership, citizens of Buganda "made their rulers accountable not by centralizing power but by keeping things complicated."[111] Alternative sites of authority also provided overlapping mappings of power and strategies of resistance, as in healing sites and the territorial spirits of the Great Lakes region.[112] Absent the cartographic tools of mapping, states and local actors alike used spatial strategies to organize and contest power, to assert and avoid obligations, and to define and redefine community.

The arrival of imperial cartography elevated the power of the map in Africa and offered new opportunities for countermapping resistance. Sumathi Ramaswamy has drawn attention to the geographic work of those she termed "barefoot cartographers": amateur mapmakers who adopted the tools and symbols of "command" cartography to produce and reinscribe the mapped "logo" of the nation.[113] While such terminology risks reifying an orientalist dialectic between the naked, unscientific nature of local geographic imaginations and the booted, scientific work of imperial cartographers, it does importantly dislodge the practices of mapping from its official uses and point to the popular and patriotic production of mapmaking cultures. The drawing of maps and the clerical work involved in defining and defending territory provided partisans across Africa with another avenue for self-representation, for recasting their histories, and for forwarding their political agendas. For Luyia ethnic patriots, mapping enabled them to order and naturalize the space of belonging, to marshal their plural and often dissenting constituents, and to minimally outline their political and cultural project along territorial lines. There was thus "no catastrophic erasure by the natives of 'precolonial' or 'indigenous' conceptions of land with the arrival of new modalities of visualizing territory ushered in by the colonial state through the mediation of the modern science of cartography."[114] Rather, mapping provided a concrete tool mobilized by local patriots in the articulation of new identities in a wider and increasingly crowded political arena.

In a recent study on the "spatial factor" in African history, Allen Howard and Richard Shain have suggested that "perhaps the 'ethnic' approach to African history has most determinedly blocked the application of spatial analysis."[115] The present study works to redress this gap, creating a dialogue between the voluminous historiography on ethnic identity and the growing literature on territoriality and geographic imaginations. Instead of understanding territory as solely part of high-modernist colonial projects or as simply a strategic resource of "political tribalism," this study suggests a methodological shift toward exploring the multiple ways local communities and ethnic patriots adopted and reworked mapping strategies to their own ends. Linking the study of moral ethnicity with territorial politics, this study further investigates the ongoing debates over the meaning of the Luyia political community, debates often expressed as arguments over maps and borders. Boundaries, be they cognitive or geographic, both marked and managed the extent of political communities. Colonial mapping strategies produced new geographic imaginaries and a form of "map-mindedness" appropriated by African communities in their reformulations of identity, community, and territory.[116]

A NOTE ON SOURCES

In a recent nonfiction piece on Kenyan visual artist Wangechi Mutu, compatriot Binyavanga Wainaina began with a historical declaration: "We are made by our archives."[117] In the context of a study of encounters— between people and landscape, between the colonial map and local geographic imaginations, between systems of knowledge and grammars of community—this statement rings especially true. The research for this project necessitated an engagement with multiple historical modes and my own encountering with a wide variety of sources—archival, vernacular, oral, and pictorial—across multiple times and spaces.

Researching a borderland that exists at the crossroads of several competing histories required archival work across three continents, from the borderlands of Uganda and Kenya through to Birmingham and Cambridge, England, and even across the Atlantic to Richmond, Indiana.[118] Such archives included national, provincial, missionary, and personal holdings. Sources from the Uganda National Archives, in Entebbe, presented a relatively untapped and rich, if elusive, avenue for exploring regional and cross-boundary histories. Missionary records from across three continents, too often used only in missionary or religious histories, provided rich evidence of linguistic projects, political work, and the interaction of new religious ideas with the patriotic imagining of new communities. Newspapers, both vernacular and national, offered important insights into local and national transformations in political thinking and language. The present study also pays particular heed to the documentation of oral testimonies in court cases, in colonial commissions, and in local history-writing projects. While set within the performative theaters of colonial production, this kind of testimonial documentation allows the "voices" of African petitioners to be read in and through colonial documents.[119]

More exceptionally, this project makes extensive use of archival maps. Geographic literacy produced its own "tin-trunk" literature, to use Karin Barber's terminology, found in the personal, hidden documentation produced by elites and nonelites alike that helped advance African political argumentation.[120] Maps drawn for local land courts, in partisan histories, in political tracts, and for colonial boundary commissions produced a vast archive of cartographic representations. These sources do, however, present challenges. As they are often viewed as addenda or supplements, they are particularly susceptible to disappearance and destruction. On a recent visit to the Kenya National Archives, I found that one of the largest files of maps submitted to the Kenya Regional Boundaries Commission, which provided much of the evidence for chapter 9 of this volume, has now disappeared in the process of recataloguing. Maps mentioned in reports, petitions, land cases, and other correspondences were often impossible to trace. The material nature of maps, which require frequent handling and copying, also make these sources susceptible to deterioration. Many of the maps I consulted were falling apart, literally offering only fragments of the past. Still, the variety of maps drawn by official hands as well as those drawn by local landowners and ethnic patriots provide a particularly rich source base. As with literacy itself, these maps revealed the "hidden powers" of territory inscribed on paper.[121] Long passed over or ignored entirely, the symbols and cartographic metaphors operating inside and outside the map itself provide a means of accessing and interrogating evolving arguments over geographic imaginaries.

In the tradition of social history, an extensive oral history project conducted over the course of 2007 and 2008 also sought to capture the testimony of elders from what is, in many ways, the last colonial generation. Since the pioneering work of Jan Vansina, oral history has privileged "tradition" and the ability of the historian to separate verifiable truths from the performative aspects of oral accounts.[122] However, over the past twenty years or so, a major theoretical and methodological shift has moved toward the use of oral histories as important sources unto themselves, with all of their subjectivity, theatricality, and ambiguity.[123]

Life histories have become a particularly popular means of accessing the social world and alternative histories. In my own work, early group interviews collecting oral traditions quickly gave way to more personal, life history–style interviews. My first forays into group interviews were often interrupted and at times hijacked by local political officials or self-appointed village experts. While these interventions produced valuable and insightful contestations, they took control of the interview process and setting away not only from me as an interviewer but moreover from the chosen interviewees, whose histories did not always match the priorities and privileged narratives of "official" figures. The life history format, though still embedded in wider familial and communal networks that meant interviews were rarely a one-on-one event, allowed for a greater degree of intimacy, privacy, and rigor.

The primary nucleus of informants came from the Luyia Council of Elders, a formal organization composed of twenty men, each representing a recognized constituent community within the Luyia fold. While representing themselves as the producers and guardians of this ethnic project, these men rarely subsumed their divergent narratives or personal histories under a codified historical narrative. Rather, the variety of politics espoused by these elders revealed the diversity of political thought and the competing forms of community still debated within their council meetings. In interviews with these sanctioned male elders, wives, sons, daughters, neighbors, and onlookers often interjected, providing a wider range of engagements and new sources of historical perspectives. Other informants came from a broad cross-section of backgrounds, from former rebel fighters to local men and women who had never traveled outside western Kenya, and from the first female councillor to a former vice president.

The sheer number of different dialects and languages in the region was overwhelming. Every interviewee spoke multiple languages with great fluency. To clear this linguistic hurdle, I opted to allow informants to choose the language of the interview, and if necessary interpreters would be chosen in consultation with the informant. Many chose to speak in English, allowing them, as one elder put it, to control the "terms of their translation," though debates on appropriate terms and translations were common. And yet, as explored in chapter 4, the choice of language may also reflect deeper concerns of the interviewees around political and intellectual positioning.

I was often amusingly reminded of my own position as a single, white, female, and specifically Canadian, researcher. When meeting with former rebels of the Dini ya Msambwa movement in Kimilili, I was asked why "white Canadian women always want to know about Dini ya Msambwa"—referring of course to the pioneering work of Audrey Wipper on the movement in the 1970s.[124] Msambwa followers had crafted very formal, if not always strict, gender discipline practices. My position as both an honored guest and as a woman caused some dissension among the group as to where I should sit: in outdoor meetings and formal gatherings, men and honored guests would be given the often-limited chairs while women customarily sat on the ground. A compromise of sorts was reached when a "chair" of animal skins was constructed on the ground for me to sit on—the "invention of tradition" in action. I was acutely aware in this context that the women in the group would not be able to add their voices freely, adding strategic silences, though not absences, that were only partially overcome with further, more intimate and informal interviews.

In another case, a prominent Bukusu businessman accompanied me to an interview with a well-respected elder on Bukusu customs, Mzee Mombasa as he was known to friends.[125] Mzee Mombasa made repeated pronouncements that outsiders, and more specifically women, could not bear witness or be privy to the sacred inner workings of Bukusu customs. And yet the interview proceeded as usual, with my Bukusu interlocutor repeating my questions verbatim and Mzee Mombasa responding in my presence, though officially acknowledging only my male companion.

Perhaps the most impinging but also revealing context for this project was the political. The majority of the interviews took place during the 2007 electoral campaigns in Kenya and their direct aftermath in 2008. This heightened political context inevitably shaped the oral histories collected. Informants continually related and compared their life histories to the contemporary social and political issues being debated in the campaigns.[126] At times, the elections would directly intervene into the interview process: several interviews with important former trade unionist and independence leader Arthur Aggrey Ochwada had to be suspended and postponed when a fleet of black SUVs appeared on the horizon, indicating that Ochwada's close friend and political confidante, current vice president Moody Awori, had traveled home to seek his counsel.[127] Among the Dini ya Msambwa former rebels and family members of former leader Elijah Masinde, election time always proved frenetic as local politicians vied to sit on Masinde's stool in the Msambwa shrine—a sign of prophetic approval.[128] The atmosphere at these interviews was palpably charged, as former rebels and extended family members sought to position themselves as the guardians of this history and its political import for contemporary electoral contests. In this setting, the past refused to stay past: the pasts expressed were restless, mobile, and irrepressibly present.

These life histories are not left to tell an unmediated narrative. Rather, I treat these testimonies as social texts that, when read with and against documentary archives, provide important contexts, heated points of debate, multiple and often fragmented meanings, and critical historical interventions. Further, they helped me map a kind of intellectual and social network throughout western Kenya and beyond. Like the past itself, these interviews rarely stayed put: stories, and even actual interviews, crossed borders and traveled to urban centers. Daily I would travel by local bus, bicycle, and foot up to six or seven hours with my research aide, Henry Kissinger Adera (yes, his father was a great admirer of Kissinger). Henry provided a crucial service, not only as my point of access to many of the interviewees but also as an interlocutor and impressively diplomatic negotiator. As a Luo, and son of an important elder on the Luo Council of Elders, Henry stood somewhat outside of the political histories and tensions of the Western Province. Many interviewees encouraged him to join politics, saying he could win even in the Western Province. His introductions and interventions proved indispensable, as did his company as a fellow traveler through unpredictable terrains. This study owes much not only to these formal interviews but also to the debates about politics and competing versions of history discussed with Henry and with a wide array of fellow passengers on long *matatu* bus rides across the country and on the backs of *boda boda* bicycles throughout western Kenya.

CHAPTER BREAKDOWN: A ROAD MAP

The imbrication of so many manifestations of geographic imaginations of community required this study to traverse a wide intellectual terrain. While following a chronological and thematic logic, each chapter builds on different kinds of geographic work, investigating the multiple meanings and uses of mapping: as activity, as metaphor, as colonial science, and as patriotic idea. Each chapter tracks episodes of geographic encounter that when read together comprise the intellectual architecture of the construction of and contestations over the making of the Luyia identity in colonial Kenya.

In Chapter 1 the diverse communities of western Kenya find their varied geographic imaginations confronted and eventually transformed by the power of the map. The ecologically rich and topographically diverse terrain of western Kenya taught its African settlers lessons in agronomy, social organization, and political authority. Using linguistic analysis, oral sources, and recorded narratives of migration and settlement, this chapter first reconstructs the evolving forms of identification and geographic practices that existed up to the late nineteenth century. These precolonial geographies of interpenetration, of itinerant territorialities, and of regional exchange were neither lost nor completely displaced by the arrival of colonial cartography; rather, local inhabitants reworked their spatial conceptions and geographic practices to countermap the tools of surveyors and contest imperial geographies. Some, like the Wanga, invested early in imperial cartography, providing men, supplies, and local, though self-promoting, knowledge to the British as they "beat the bounds" of these new boundaries. Others negotiated and subverted the work of imperial cartographers, pushing through colonial boundaries, sabotaging the symbols of surveyors, and drawing their own maps alongside older practices of space. In this encounter between different geographic imaginations, mapping became both the tool of territorial acquisition and the means of its subversion.

Chapter 2 traces the transformation of mapping from a novel tool in local competitions over resources, power, and patronage into a tool of patriotic imagination. In the early decades of colonial rule, internal struggles over chiefly authority and local definitions of lineage and land rights fractured along clan and administrative lines. Local political actors reformulated kinship and invented ancestors to defend their diverse practices of land tenure and political authority from colonial hierarchies and bureaucratization. Boundaries became flashpoints in these contestations, and cartography became an instrument of political action.

Into this picture of competitive mapping, the discovery of gold in North Kavirondo threatened African land rights on an ever-larger scale. Conflicts over land and mineral rights encouraged local political thinkers to begin thinking of an enlarged ethnic polity in western Kenya as a means of defense against colonial interventions into their lands and competition with their African neighbors. Before the Kenya Land Commission of 1932, representatives from North Kavirondo consolidated their diverse practices of land tenure, suppressed recent internal fragmentations over political authority and kinship measures, and transformed local practices of mapping into a means of imagination. Before they had a name, these representatives declared themselves the spokesmen of a "tribe," and the map provided the concrete evidence of their political existence.

While chapter 2 reveals the impetus for this patriotic investment in the map, in chapter 3 this investment pays dividends, informing innovations in the patriotic work of ethnogenesis and history writing. Having declared themselves a tribe, ethnic patriots in western Kenya went in search of name. In choosing Luyia—a term that translated for many as the fireplace where the elders of clans would gather—these young political thinkers turned away from the genealogical arguments created by naming communities after mythic founding fathers and instead chose a corporate name that privileged a horizontal drawing together of discrete, autonomous clans into one discursive and political space. This innovation would prove a larger trend: later ethnic projects, like the confederate Mijikenda or the Kalenjin who literally called to each other by naming themselves "I say to you," employed ethnic names that similarly spoke to a new political ethos of kinship and community.[129] The interwar period proved a high tide for this kind of ethnic patriotism. Throughout the 1930s, Luyia patriots worked fill this mapped space with historical and "emotional" resonance through the creative work of writing histories, electing leaders, and defending the political, moral, and territorial borders of this novel community.[130]

Chapters 4 and 5 then follow the emergence of a new, more self-consciously fashioned generation of Luyia ethnic patriots in the 1940s who embarked on patriotic work in multiple fields—linguistic, demographic, and customary—to rationalize the diversity among their disputatious constituents and defend their work against the deconstructive politics of the locality. In Chapter 4 recent graduates from Uganda's Makerere College championed the work of the Luyia Language Committee to standardize one written Luyia language out of the multiple and distinct dialects of the region. The work of language consolidation created an environment of competitive linguistic work, often faltering precisely on the translation of terms that related to land, power, and belonging. This linguistic work threatened to undermine oral traditions of accommodation and flexibility and promoted defensive vernacular cultures. While no printed vernacular-Luyia linguistic culture ever materialized, "speaking Luyia" remained central to "being Luyia."

In Chapter 5 the moral anxieties of the early 1940s, manifested in crises over land, mobility, and gender discipline, prompted a turn to the locality that threatened to disaggregate the fragile work of Luyia ethnic patriots. As sons and daughters left western Kenya in ever-larger numbers, smaller-scale ethnic associations formed to defend diverse moral economies and to enforce a gendered discourse of male fraternity and female deviancy through the creation of urban football teams and "anti-prostitution" campaigns. By the late 1940s this turn to the locality and concern over movement and morality took its most dramatic form in a crisis over female circumcision. Controversy sparked when young women of the Tachoni were found to be engaging in secret circumcision ceremonies or leaving the district to be circumcised. These conflicts were about more than customary and gendered control: they were about the demographic health of the community and about the very frontiers of respectability.

The crisis over female circumcision brought home the limits of plurality and threatened the progressive and mannered values purported by Luyia cultural brokers. In response, the new generation Luyia politicians embarked on electoral and demographic projects that sought to make national politics consequential for local political thought. The duality and incompatibility of ethnicity and nationalism have dominated the study of African history in the twentieth century. Although local narratives of nationalism have challenged the national metanarratives reified in the postcolonial era, it is of equal importance to break down the national center—ethnic periphery model.[131] Nationalism did not, as some have argued, necessarily represent a "mortal challenge" to the work of ethnic patriots.[132] The circular movement of leadership and ideas created feedback and strategic borrowing between national and ethnic imaginings. Luyia leaders were, in some ways, ideal protonationalists—coming from a young ethnic project that privileged the language of territorial nationalism and cosmopolitan patriotism over calls to genealogical depth or ethnic conformism.

With the cultural projects of the 1940s faltering, territorial nationalism provided Luyia entrepreneurs a language, a form of argumentation capable of tapping into the geographic imagination of their plural constituents. Through census campaigns, electoral projects, and cultural reforms, Luyia leaders in the late 1940s transformed the Luyia ethnic project from the messy, fractured politics of the locality into a vehicle of national politicking. They managed a careful balance between a cosmopolitan, territorial nationalism and a rooted ethnic discipline, mapping an ethnic homeland in western Kenya through the enforcement of customary control and the formulation of gendered and territorial belonging.

In chapters 6 and 7, the late colonial politics of loyalism and dissent prompted a remodeling of the Luyia idea and entrenched the map and the politics of territoriality as tools of dissent and imagination. While much of the research on national politics in Kenya has followed a teleological path tracing whether the Kenya African Union (KAU), the first national political party, eventually led to the militant Mau Mau rebellion, accessing the "deep politics" of late colonial Kenya requires a decentering of this national history and an examination of the negotiated spaces not between binary poles but rather among the plural expressions and uses of territorial nationalism.[133] The national crisis posed by the Mau Mau rebellion polarized the political landscape of Kenya, between ethnic and national, educated elite and worker, and loyalist and radical. Too often administrators, political commentators, and historians have labeled those beyond the borders of central Kenya as unproblematically "loyal," outside the conflicts and moral debates of the Mau Mau rebellion. In western Kenya, however, the politics of loyalism and dissent not only already existed but also prompted Luyia cultural brokers to forward an idea of plural political community capable of providing flexibility and opportunities to exercise agency in the late colonial era.

The religious and anticolonial Dini ya Msambwa movement challenged both colonial and ethnic patriotic geographies. Through their religious pilgrimages, cultural reforms, and anticolonial activism, these frontier rebels threatened to unground the progressive discourse and civic reputation cultivated by Luyia patriots. By the late 1940s both colonial officials and Luyia thinkers had come to organize law and culture territorially, fixing diverse communities to "tribal" geographies and disciplining those who moved beyond these territorial confines. Unwittingly, the Dini ya Msambwa movement acted as antecedent for later debates around closed ethnic geographies and colonial counterinsurgency tactics later perfected during the Mau Mau rebellion.

In the 1950s, as the Mau Mau rebellion prompted a new kind of ethnic politicking, Luyia political thinkers fashioned a more flexible form of territorial consciousness. Chapter 6 traces the social history of this new Luyia idea that would allow Luyia cosmopolitans, farmers, and workers to move more freely through Kenya's polarized political landscape. The chapter does not aim simply to insert another region, another ethnic group, back into the history of Mau Mau and 1950s Kenya.[134] Neither does it assume that simple comparison or jockeying for position between Mau Mau and western Kenya's own rebellion, in the form of Dini ya Msambwa, is enough. Rather, it argues that the myopic study of Mau Mau and anticolonial dissent more broadly solely from the perspective of central Kenya has left a great deal of the story out, not only of Mau Mau itself but also of the larger context of social change in eastern Africa at the time. In the 1950s, Luyia political thinkers marshaled a theory of ethnic pluralism and mapped a moral geography of belonging to navigate the Emergency era politics of loyalism and dissent.

As decolonization neared, the Kenya Regional Boundaries Commission of 1962 witnessed the ascendency of the map in debates over the terms of sovereignty and alternative models of political community. While many recent studies of African history have made an admirable and long overdue move away from the colonial/postcolonial periodization, the end point of this study, in chapter 7, comes in the 1960s precisely because of the self-conscious remapping of community that occurred during decolonization and that was subsequently suppressed, though not erased, in postcolonial discourses. During the Kenya Regional Boundaries Commission, mapping became the primary tool of dissent, as it was those African communities most invested in the reengineering of colonial boundaries ahead of independence that would engage in this competitive mapmaking. In countless memorandums and political tracts, Luyia organizations demanded their own territory by redrawing colonial boundaries, shoring up demographic numbers, and telling cartographic histories of lost sovereignty. Chapter 7, more than any chapter preceding it, turns to a more thorough examination of the literal, pictorial maps drawn by ethnic patriots to visualize their histories of community, sovereignty, and belonging and to contest spatial, territorial, and political relations on the eve of independence. Within these debates, the geographic imaginations explored through this study proved to be the most constant and most affecting doctrines of the Luyia ethnic identity. While often frustrated, such alternative political imaginations found in the map a way of visualizing their claims. For both nationalists who sought to maintain colonial boundaries and dissenters seeking alternative political futures, the map became the fetish of postcolonial belonging.

~

In tracing the contested genealogy of cartographic political imagination in western Kenya one constant emerged: where land divided, territory united. Where the mapping of land enabled competitive claims to resources and locality, the mapping of territory enabled the imagining of a patriotic idea. Internal dynamism characterized the Luyia ethnic project and fostered an almost defiant history of cosmopolitan patriotism, federal belonging, and rooted pluralism. And yet, this is not to say the Luyia were entirely unique. As dramatized in Perus's dilemma before the 2009 Kenya census, the question for many Kenyans, and indeed Africans more broadly, was not so much one of identity but of the multiple and overlapping sites of identification; not so much of ethnicity but of the creative and unfinished process of ethnogenesis.[135] And while ethnogenesis provided the language, geographic work often provided the practice.

1 ⤳ The Geographies of Western Kenya

> Slippery ground does not recognize kings.
> —Abaluyia proverb[1]

FROM THE shores of Lake Victoria to the foothills of Mount Elgon, the landscape of what would become western Kenya undulates with immense ecological and topographical variety, from gentle hills and flat-bottomed valleys to deeply gorged rivers fringed with lush tropical rainforests. For centuries, African settlers moving through this area greeted each other with the term "Mulembe." In its many variations, "Mulembe" asked visitors where they had been, where they were going, and entreated them to come and go in peace.[2] A Luganda-English dictionary defined the term as "may he bring you in peace to your community."[3] Community members struck the *murembe* tree, with its brilliant red flowers, to undo taboos or to consecrate peace between warring communities.[4] Despite its wide use across eastern Africa, Luyia elders in western Kenya claimed the term as central to their formulations of community, migration, and home: anywhere they traveled, "to be Muluyia was to say 'Mulembe.'"[5]

The environmental diversity northeast of Lake Victoria invited a host of African settlers to cultivate the land and graze their cattle. Diverse migratory routes and relatively recent patterns of settlement created a linguistically and culturally mixed region: in the words of the doyen of Kenyan history, Bethwell Ogot, "lying in an ancient migration corridor, the traditional history of the district is one of the most confused and complex in the whole of East Africa."[6] This traditional history was a continual source of contention and argumentation, complicated by regional networks of trade and cultural exchange across complementary ecological zones. Migrating communities practiced a particular form of itinerant territoriality, a portable ideology of territorial control and belonging that linked networks of clans to particular tracts of land. African communities settled into niche environments and developed a diverse range of small-scale and defensive clan structures characterized by multiple and over-lapping systems of authority. The precolonial space of the lake region represented a dynamic area of expanding frontiers, heterarchical social formations, and ethnic interdependence.[7]

Colonial conquest enclosed these frontiers and mapped new lines of exchange, community, and power. First circumnavigated by Henry Morton Stanley in 1875, the lake region was known to early traders, explorers, and colonial administrators as the Nyanza basin and its people as Kavirondo.[8] Colonial conquest brought all the imperial instruments of state fixity—map, census, and tax—to bear on these diverse and decentralized African communities. Colonial geographers enlisted local inhabitants as amateur surveyors, guides, and porters to track rivers and navigate forests, to set out survey beacons, and to "beat the bounds" of their newly demarcated boundaries. The new maps introduced by imperial cartographers at the turn of the century imposed a top-down geographic vision that over-wrote local conceptions of space and fixed named African communities to particular mapped territories. However, Africans around and across these newly mapped boundaries turned their spatial strategies to resistance, sabotaging the work of colonial surveyors, adopting new cartographic practices and symbols, and purposefully mistranslating their own geographic conceptions to countermap colonial geographies. The construction of colonial boundaries fostered new geographic imaginations of labor, obligation, and resistance and precipitated the remapping of authority, moral community, and competing territorialities in the making of western Kenya.

ENVIRONMENT AND SOCIETY: MAPPING PRECOLONIAL COMMUNITIES

As John Iliffe argued in his seminal text *Africans*, the history of the African continent and its peoples must be understood against the backdrop of a diverse and difficult environment.[9] In his study of the Taita in Kenya, Bill Bravman put the point succinctly: "Geography is not exactly destiny . . . but it has powerfully influenced the history of the people who live there."[10] In the Great Lakes region, the ability to control and profit from this rough and potentially rich environment provided the primary source of tension for precolonial societies.[11] This geographic space, however, was more than just a backdrop against which diverse African political systems, social relations, and material cultures evolved: this space, both physical and cognitive, was dynamic and ever changing, inspiring and constraining the geographic imaginations of these communities over time.

Northeast of one of eastern Africa's Great Lakes, named Lake Victoria in the nineteenth century by British explorer John Hanning Speke, lies a land of immense ecological and topographical variety. Created by a faulting in the geological crust, two main reliefs dominate the topography: the fertile lake plateau composed of a broad belt of granite soils studded by massive granite boulders and the drier highlands that flank the region to the north and east, where cool, moist air nurtures healthy volcanic soils. Altitudes range from 3,770 feet (1,150 meters) along the shores of the lake to over 7,050 feet (2,150 meters) on the slopes of Mount Elgon.

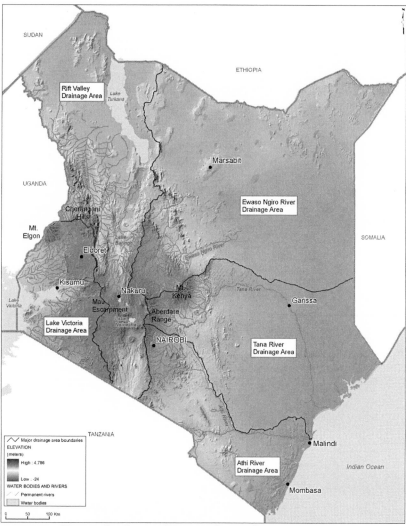

FIGURE 1.1. Topographical map of Kenya and magnification of western Kenya. World Resources Institute, *Natural Benefits in Kenya.*

This geomorphology has been described as "pockets": although predominantly grassland savanna, bordered by equatorial forest to the north and tropical rainforest to the east, a series of interlocking ridges, hills, and valleys alternate to create an undulant plain. Two distinct seasons keep the region fairly regularly well watered: the dry season, from mid-December to mid-February, and the rainy season, from March to December, with annual rainfall between 61.7 and 76.3 inches.[12] A tilt in the African Plateau allows water to flow through numerous rivers and streams from northeast to southwest and drain into the lake. This varied relief created a great diversity of agro-ecological zones with niche economic and settlement potentials.[13]

This distinct and varied terrain formed a migratory corridor in eastern Africa that invited a long history of human settlement.[14] In the "classical age" of African settlement in the Great Lakes region, from 1000 BCE to 400 CE, new developments in ironwork and crop production encouraged more intensive agricultural practices and the development of more settled and complex social and political systems. Early evidence of scattered settlements of southern Cushites, Bantu, and southern Nilotic groups existed in the southern regions around the lake, joined by an influx of Kalenjin- and Maa-speaking settlers further north at the turn of the millennium. Scholars have dated the current settlements to the

FIGURE 1.2. Southern view from Mount Elgon. Photo by author, March 2007.

A. *Nandi Range and Nyando Valley*

B. *Descent from Equator Hill, South Maragoli*

FIGURE 1.3. Photos of North Kavirondo. Wagner, *Bantu of North Kavirondo*, vol. 1, plate 1.

fourteenth and fifteenth centuries.[15] Though still a point of heated debate, most historians concur that Bantu settlements existed before the arrival of the Nilotic Luo from the Sudanese north in the late fifteenth century.[16] Luo migrations dislocated these Bantu settlements, creating two distinct northern and southern blocks of Bantu communities around Lake Victoria: the Bantu communities of the north and the Gusii, or Kisii, of the south.

Those Bantu populations pushed north by the arrival of Luo settlers settled into the ecologically diverse and productive region northeast of the lake extending up to Mount Elgon. The sixteenth century marked an explosion of new settlements and population growth that put pressures on cultivation, cattle, and land. The arrival of the Nilotic Teso in the mid-seventeenth century marked another important shift, as Teso-Bukusu/Bagisu wars over the next few centuries created a wedge between these two communities around Mount Elgon.[17] Bantu and Luo settlers continued to arrive well into the eighteenth century, penetrating the outline of this region from multiple routes and settling into productive agricultural and fishing niches around the lake.

This linear narrative of migration and settlement in the region, however, belies the urgent and contentious argumentation at stake in the telling of these histories. Narratives of how and when particular groups arrived in the region have been recast to fit partisan projects of ethnic imagining throughout the colonial and postcolonial era. Bethwell Ogot's pioneering text *History of the Southern Luo*, for example, was the product of ongoing partisan history projects among Luo intellectuals.[18] Ogot's dual volume *Luo Historical Texts* created an "archival patrimony" that obscured the intellectual work of other Luo historians.[19] While early partisan historians such as Shadrack Malo and Samuel Ayany "consciously and unconsciously suppressed the signs and substance of discoordination and contention" to achieve a harmonized Luo past, Ogot went a step further, offering "the careful and patient reader a view of a people, a nation, Canaan, constructed out of critical tensions and conflicts over land, political domination, and domestic insecurity."[20] Luo historians drew their constituents in line through direct descent from their fifteenth-century founding ancestor, Ramogi. Across the various projects of ethnic imagining in Kenya, patriotic historians wrote of unified and purposeful migrations to subsume divergent claims, to draw their partisans in patrilineal descent to a mythic founding father, and to promote the past as a model for contemporary threats to their moral communities.[21]

Further north, Gideon Were produced a similar archival reference entitled *Western Kenya Historical Texts*, cataloguing the oral clan histories of Bantu and Kalenjin settlers.[22] In his history of these migrations, Were drew a sharp distinction between the largely settled and agriculturalist Bantu communities and their pastoralist neighbors, who, in the nineteenth century, were "still busy expanding northwards into their present territories."[23] In this way, Were glossed over the multiple and complex migrational routes of Bantu agriculturalists to lay claim to a longer history of settlement. However, unlike Ogot, Were was harder pressed to create an overarching historical narrative out of the stubbornly diverse clan histories of these Bantu settlers, with no "Ramogi" common ancestor or common linguistic grounding. While Ogot could provide a unifying thrust to Luo migrations, Were was continually obliged to acknowledge the diverse origins of his subjects. At stake in these partisan histories were urgent concerns over land rights, community membership, and the future moral discipline of the history teller's audience. Indeed, many of these early patriotic histories have been, unintended or not, transformed into evidence in contemporary land disputes and familial conflicts over custom.[24]

In the texts of Were and others, the diversity of the communities in this lake region refused to be aligned. The multitude of migratory routes visualized in their maps reflected the diverse linguistic and historical backgrounds of these new settlers (figs. 1.4, 1.5). Clan histories of these migrations varied over time and space and reflected the variety of social organizations and political objectives of their tellers. Under pressure from overcrowding, disease, warfare, and would-be state builders, migrations often followed localized and uncoordinated clan lines that gave birth to new community formations. Many Bantu clans told of their historic origin in Egypt ("Misri" among Bantu speakers), then traveling down through Bunyoro and Buganda, providing a mythic point of origin and hinting at a stated or royal past.[25] Others emphasized their diverse migratory origins traveling through carefully recalled landmarks and difficult terrains to defend their cultural distinctiveness and political sovereignty. These "narrative maps" sketched a history of complex spatial relations, movements, and important sites such as forts and shrines along a migratory journey that strategically culminated in the construction of a regional homeland in their current settlements.[26]

The histories of these migrations and settlements, whether Bantu, Kalenjin, Luo, or Maasai, must be understood not as the forward march of coherent ethnic groups but rather as complex histories of social interaction

FIGURE 1.4. Migrational map by Günter Wagner. *Bantu of North Kavirondo*, 1:23.

and multiple movements over centuries. These small-scale migrations led to fluid regional patterns of interaction and integration across ethnolinguistic divides: as Were argued, "The Abaluyia owe their origin to the interaction of many diverse cultural and linguistic groups stretching back to over one thousand years."[27] Individual clans in the southern areas of Buhayo, Kisa, Marama, and Tiriki self-consciously trace their lineages to mixed Bantu, Kalenjin, Luo, and Maasai origins.[28] The clans of the Tachoni claimed their roots among both the early Uasin Gishu settlers and the later arrivals of Bantu clans passing around Mount Elgon.[29] In the space northeast of Lake Victoria, clans of various linguistic backgrounds formed strategic alliances through intermarriage and absorption, making every clan multiethnic from their very arrival. As Luyia historian John Osogo put it, "The history of our people has been at the local level, the story of the interaction of the clans."[30] The residue of this regional culture of exchange persisted in the systems of trade that developed, in shared linguistic features, and in the assimilation of cultural practices.

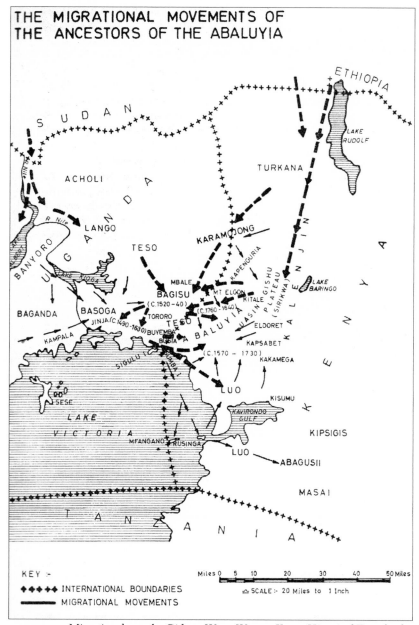

THE MIGRATIONAL MOVEMENTS OF
THE ANCESTORS OF THE ABALUYIA

ETHIOPIA

SUDAN

LAKE
RUDOLF

ACHOLI

TURKANA

R Nile
LANGO

BANYORO

TESO

KARAMOJONG

U G A N D A

K E N Y A

KAPENGURIA

MBALE

BAGISU
(C.1520-40)

MT ELGON

UASIN GISHU
(SIRIKWA)
PLATEAU

KITALE

LAKE
BARINGO

K
A
L
E
N
J
I
N

LAKE KIOGA

BAGANDA

BASOGA

TESO

TORORO

JINJA (C.1490-1630)

BUYEMBA

BUSIA

A   B   A   L   U   Y   I   A
(C.1570 - 1730)

ELDORET

KAPSABET

KAKAMEGA

KAMPALA

SIGULU

LUO

SESE

KISUMU

LAKE

KAVIRONDO
GULF

VICTORIA

KIPSIGIS

MFANGANO

RUSINGA

LUO

ABAGUSII

MASAI

T   A   N   Z   A   N   I   A

KEY :-
♦♦♦♦♦♦ INTERNATIONAL BOUNDARIES
▬▬▬ MIGRATIONAL MOVEMENTS

Miles 0   5   10   20   30   40   50 Miles
△ SCALE :- 20 Miles to 1 Inch

FIGURE 1.5. Migrational map by Gideon Were. *Western Kenya Historical Texts,* back cover.

The uneven and varied environment encouraged niche settlements and the development of specialized agronomic practices according to environmental capabilities and regional patterns of exchange. In the south, rich soils and compact valleys proved ideal for the intensive cultivation of major crops such as sorghum, sweet potatoes, beans, and bananas. In the more expansive plains of the north, a mix of cultivation and cattle ranching provided a middle ground of trade and political interaction between agriculturalists and pastoralists. A small body of research on precolonial trade networks in western Kenya suggests the influence of inter-ethnic interaction on the making of precolonial communities.[31] Markets developed early in the eighteenth century to facilitate trade across economic specializations. In the 1930s German anthropologist Günter Wagner recorded a lengthy history of precolonial markets from a Logoli elder: "The people of many different tribes assembled there . . . and in those years everybody who wished to obtain anything he liked could go to that market."[32] Northern Bantu settlers frequented these markets in search of fish and livestock, while the Luo came for the grains brought by Bantu agriculturalists, mostly millet and sorghum. From their new agricultural neighbors, Kalenjin-speaking pastoralists adopted a number of terms involved in cultivation and food production, including words for "beans," "flour," and "to weed."[33] Northern Bantu populations similarly borrowed cattle-keeping terms and practices from their Kalenjin and Nilotic neighbors. As Jean Hay found, even between the divergent Bantu and Dholuo language groups, the terms for "homestead, wooden hoe, sorghum, maize, beans, and a number of other crops are essentially the same . . . suggesting extensive cultural contacts and influence in economic matters."[34] Economic interdependence and trade fostered cultures of exchange and integration across ethnolinguistic divides.

These complementary environments also fostered the development of specialized skills. The availability of great deposits of iron ore in the Samia hills prompted its settlers to specialize as blacksmiths, peddling their skills across the region. The Banyore, located in the well-watered hills of Bunyore, were recognized as rainmakers and consulted as experts throughout the region. The sharing of professionals and specialists across clans traced a regional network that further encouraged cultural exchange. In border regions, many informants pointed to the adoption of place names and linguistic features from their Kalenjin neighbors. The Tiriki adopted Kalenjin age-set names, arguably one of the defining features of male-community membership.[35] The Tiriki, frequently at war with their Logoli neighbors in the nineteenth century, often allied with Nandi clans.[36] The adoption of Kalenjin age-set names may have allowed young men to identify allies in warfare despite linguistic and cultural divisions. The relative practice of circumcision, both male and female, among these groups also attested to complex historical exchanges. The practice of circumcision varied greatly despite contemporary popular beliefs that all Bantu communities in this region practiced male circumcision, in contrast to their uncircumcised Luo neighbors, but not female circumcision, in contrast to their Kalenjin and Maasai neighbors. Early European explorers noted the falsity of such common beliefs, recording a variety of practices ranging from elaborate male circumcision ceremonies to the absence of any form of circumcision.[37] These exchanges of experts and customary practices blurred the environmental and social lines seemingly dividing these groups. Ideas of community and production were not confined in this era by notions of enclosed ethnic communities but rather grew out of geographic interdependence, pragmatic comparative work, and strategic cultural borrowing.

OF CLANS AND TRIBES:
TERRITORY, AUTHORITY, AND BELONGING

It was this "slippery ground," this environment of rich diversity, interdependence, and fluidity that, in the words of one proverb, did not "recognize kings."[38] Alongside lessons in agronomy and social interdependence, this environment taught its first settlers to develop independent small-scale polities characterized by heterarchy, unique languages of political and social organization, and distinct cultural practices in land and authority.

Precolonial studies of eastern African societies often emphasized the flexibility of local identities as necessary for "establishing relative positions on the cognitive map of expanding frontier societies."[39] Early oral historians pinpointed the clan as the most stable and fruitful source of historical information and genealogical periodization: unlike the "invented" tribes of 1970s historians, clans were "out there," in the words of Jan Vansina.[40] Recent scholarship has criticized these evolutionary and lineage-based models and has begun to interrogate the moral and intellectual organization of precolonial African communities. In their classic study on the Luo identity in Siaya, David Cohen and E. S. Atieno Odhiambo argued that "friendship fortifies kinship," a challenge to mainstream anthropology that treats kinship as "an enclosed autonomous locus of structure."[41] In her study of the Bagisu, close relatives of the Bukusu on the Ugandan side of Mount Elgon, Suzette Heald demonstrated that segmentary lineage systems and descent-based kinship ideologies were not inherently at odds with the practices of territoriality or creative reformulations of kinship.[42] Less the basic and innate structure of community envisioned by colonial administrators and European anthropologists, clans were the historical products of imaginative social work and provided a locus of belonging amid multiple shared sites of identification and interaction.

Among those who settled northeast of Lake Victoria, the clan was often the largest and most constant source of identification and support. The clan acted as a unit of agency, a tool in the management of social relations that offered cognitive structure to mappings of community and territory.[43] Clans were often a heterogeneous mixture of families and small groupings linked together by common ancestry, common migration, or common settlement. However, the terms of membership and size of the clan were as flexible as the new environments in which they settled required. Exogamy, the practice of marrying outside the clan, and patrilineal descent underlined the gendered nature of community membership. Wagner found that "each tribal community (particularly its male half) derives its 'group consciousness' first and foremost from the belief that all or the large majority of its constituent clans have descended in an agnatic line from a mythical tribal ancestor."[44] However, as earlier alluded, the primacy of descent and ancestral myths proved more illusory than this unqualified assertion.

As with partisan histories of migrations, the nomenclature of "clan" and "tribe" represented terms of imagined political communities continually contested and reworked within larger cultural projects. Some larger "tribal" associations of clans, such as the Wanga, the Logoli, and the Bukusu, did emerge in the eighteenth and nineteenth centuries; but these communities were the products of the same imaginative work as clan communities on a larger scale. For the purposes of this study, these "tribal" names suggest not articulated structures of political authority but rather larger communities of clans that were recast in the colonial era to defend precolonial autonomy.

Beyond changing ethnonyms and constraining lineage-based models of kinship, the basis of clan formations in western Kenya relied on the ability of the group to effectively settle and civilize new ecological niches. Neil Kodesh has argued that the variety of terminology for clan structures in the Great Lakes region, including *ubwoko* in Kinyarwanda, *kika* in Luganda, and *ruganda* in Lunyoro, suggests that "the ideology and practices of clanship developed along different lines in various settings within the region."[45] Among the Bantu communities of this compact area, terms for clan organization varied from *oluhia* and *olugongo* to *ibula* and *ehiri*.[46] These terms reflected not only varying forms of political organization but also the varied environments that constrained as well as sheltered.

Environmental conditions taught these inhabitants lessons in how to structure political and social relations. Ecological niches prompted the development of specialized economic production and skills that fostered distinct communal identities. Some, like the larger groups of the Tiriki and the Bukusu, became frontier communities as they settled on steep hills and beside rich forests that offered opportunities for expansion.[47] The expanding Bukusu promoted strong military leadership (in the figure of the *Omugasa*), built fortified, walled villages into the landscape, and transformed territorial *msambwa* ancestral spirits into "ancestral ghosts," akin to those in Buganda, so that they could inhabit the caves and springs of their new territories.[48] Throughout eastern Africa, msambwa sites on the edges of settlements provided important sacred spaces linking the "health of the land" to the health of residents and their descendants.[49] Living on the imagined edge of this landscape, these frontiersmen would pose distinct problems for both colonial officials and ethnic architects seeking to territorialize ethnic identity.

Others, such as the southern clans of the Bahayo, Banyore, Batsotso, and Idakho settled into pockets isolated by hills and ridges and well suited for intensive agriculture. Among these more dispersed settlements, patriarchal clan heads and councils of elders provided only symbolic leadership linked to their ability to amass material and human wealth and maintain peaceful relations.[50] Among the large but scattered clans of the Logoli, the *weng'oma*, or "one of the drum," would beat a drum across the hills to gather clan heads together in times of war.[51] Early anthropologists such as Wagner viewed these systems of political authority as "inarticulate," not "linked up with clearly defined rights and privileges, such as usually associated with institutionalized chieftainship."[52] Even in warfare, as Sir Harry Johnston noted, precolonial raiding patterns were individualistic and "almost entirely defensive."[53] However, despite these varied structures, political authority was neither "inarticulate" nor merely "defensive": political power among the communities of western Kenya was heterarchical, organized along horizontal lines that allowed for flexible patterns of interdependence, defense, environmental management, and multiple sites of authority.[54]

One glaring exception existed alongside this depiction of decentralized political life. The Wanga crafted the most hierarchical political culture in the region, having a royal family and a king, the *nabongo*, who ruled over Wanga clans. Much has been written on the Wanga royal family and the power struggles between different clans over leadership.[55] The Wanga kingdom functioned somewhere between the large and powerful lake kingdoms further west and the more horizontally organized communities of the east.[56] Simon Kenyanchui better described the Wanga political structure as "a confederation of co-equal clandoms."[57] Later political accounts would map the extent of the Wanga kingdom from Lake Victoria to Lake Naivasha, but little evidence supports this expansive claim and the numerous clans described above jealously guarded their autonomy against claims of rule or tribute by Wanga kings.[58] In the nineteenth century, Wanga monarchs used Maasai mercenaries to extend their range of tribute and territorial rule, prompting these independent communities to seek refuge in their protective environments and buttress their own political structures against these monarchical state builders.

The first Europeans to arrive in the region were greeted by the recently ascended Nabongo Mumia, who quickly offered the new arrivals hospitality and aid. For many colonial administrators and later historians, the Wanga kingdom provided a recognizable political structure ideally suited to their ends and interests. Colonial administrators saw in the Wanga kingdom a hierarchical system of authority that could be usefully extended over the decentralized communities of the area. Later local politicians saw in the Wanga's monarchical history a useful narrative of precolonial political sovereignty and organization. By the end of his study, Were became preoccupied with the hypothetical future of the Wanga kingdom had the British not interrupted its consolidation and expansion.[59] The centralization of the Wanga kingdom, however, has not only been overstated by colonial officials and partisan historians but has also overshadowed the complex political interplay and almost defiant tradition of decentralization among the majority of western Kenya's inhabitants.

Relations among these diverse but interdependent communities were not "of coercion and control but of separate but linked, overlapping yet competing spheres of authority."[60] Heterarchy allowed for multiple religious, political, and economic sites of power and identification to exist in parallel. Each clan maintained autonomous control of their own political affairs and yet depended on wider networks for economic, spiritual, and social exchange. Within and outside the reach of the Wanga kingdom, heterarchy also provided a measure of accountability, as it did within the kingdom of Buganda, further west.[61] Among the Wanga, clans organized themselves in circular spatial patterns around the royal family, at once buttressing and constraining the power of the king. Succession was not determined necessarily by descent but rather by a council of clan elders who considered multiple factors.[62] Strategic intermarriages and political negotiations with the various clans of the Wanga ruling elite allowed non-Wanga clans to maintain a great deal of autonomy and protection.[63]

Outside the reach of Wanga tribute, clans used horizontal and complex systems of social organization, strategic alliances, and spatial encampment. The term *oluhia*, from which later cultural entrepreneurs would find a name for their imagined community in the 1930s, reflected this heterarchy and the primacy of place in the social formations of the region. Sometimes translated as clan or clansmen, *oluhia* in many of the languages in the region referred to the "fire-place on a meadow," where the heads of associations of clans would meet.[64] The oluhia served as a sort of assembly site for initiation rituals, for political negotiations, and for the burial of clan heads: it was a "microcosm . . . the place of practical everyday life."[65] This term embodied the horizontal coming together of representatives from different clans in one symbolic and physical space, reflecting the close relationship between place, belonging, and communal identity among these diverse communities.

Despite these multiple sites of identification, land and the practices of territoriality played crucial roles in the spatial organization of belonging. For Osogo, limited tribal structures represented loose linguistic and cultural affinities, while clans performed their most important function as "owners and bequeathers of property," or, more accurately, land use.[66] Land tenure practices varied greatly across the region, producing "different systems from a common background."[67] A common term for the clan and clan territory, *olugongo*, literally translated in many linguistic traditions to "a ridge."[68] Within each olugongo, the clan leadership determined how to allot land to each family and how to absorb and manage the land claims of "strangers." Although clan heads were responsible for negotiating internal boundary demarcations, the limits of their olugongo were "known by their natural boundaries."[69] Uncultivated virgin bush land, *oluangeraka*, or "what is beyond" among the Logoli, allowed clan lands to expand and contract in response to seasonal environmental changes, demographic pressures, and interclan disputes.[70] This practice facilitated crop rotation and the strategic fallowing of lands to avoid the overuse of any one area of cultivation. The *edzinzalo*, a common term for uninhabited mile-wide buffer zones, similarly provided an important precolonial territorial strategy for managing conflict over land and resources. During war times, these buffer zones provided fields of contest and a space for the meeting of warring factions; however, "in times of peace, grazing [was] communal."[71] Wagner noted that these buffer zones acted as political frontiers, as clans did not enforce the "subjugation of neighbouring" groups but rather enacted a strategy of "political integration through territorial continuity of clan."[72] The terms and practices of land tenure in the nineteenth century reflected the processes of segmentation—of fission and fusion—that characterized social formations on still-expanding frontiers.[73]

Niche settlement patterns translated directly into distinct practices of territoriality. Among the Banyore, the hills they inhabited became central to their "situational identity."[74] The Bunyore hills, from whose geographic characteristics clans found their names, represented not only the place where their forefathers first settled but also a protective barrier that defined friends from foes. In the other direction, place-names taken from clan names or important individuals also told stories of migrations and interethnic exchange.[75] Terms for lineage often overlapped with a sense of geographic enclosure. The terms *enyumba, eshiribwa, and indzu* all could be translated as both lineage and the physical enclosure of the clan or gateway of a homestead.[76] In Marama, minor clans who had only recently joined the larger network were referred to as *emikuru*, veranda poles that propped up the household structure of the larger clans.[77] As Christopher Gray has argued, the mistranslation of these terms into simply "land," "clan," or positions of authority by later colonial administrators would elide "the whole complex series of obligations and duties owed to lineage heads by their dependents, and as such . . . the relations of production for these societies."[78] This linguistic variety revealed the intimate connection between community formations and the territory they inhabited.

Despite the multiplicity of precolonial social relations, the practice of territoriality was central to the functioning of these communities. This was not the "aterritorial kinship ideology" Gray found practiced in Gabon.[79] Aterritorial practices did provide social entities with the flexibility to account for complex trade and exchange patterns as well as pressures on the land, whether from the environment or warfare. However, African communities in this region practiced a form territoriality that developed out of their complex migrations and niche environmental settlements. As introduced at the outset of this chapter, the greeting term *mulembe* carried within it this itinerant territoriality that linked who one was with where one came from and where one was going. Addressing the territoriality of these clans, Wagner lamented that "the extent of the geographical 'horizon' of the various sub-tribes in pre-European days I found very difficult to discover. The traditions of some tribes refer to places which are hundreds of miles away from their present homes."[80] Wagner's frustration rested in the mobile form of territoriality practiced by these settlers, carried within kinship ideologies and modes of political authority. Clan representatives often recounted their histories as a people on the move: they "moved in clans" and carried into their new settlements a sense of territorial community membership.[81] Despite long migrations and new environmental settlements, clans often repeated former spatial configurations in their new settlements, reestablishing the spatial ordering of families and figures of authority.

By the nineteenth century many of the communities northeast of Lake Victoria lived as agriculturalists in defined territorial settlements, despite constant pressures from expanding agriculturalist neighbors and continuing cultural and economic trade with surrounding pastoralists. However, the nineteenth century brought with it a time of political and environmental upheaval in eastern Africa, what Gideon Were termed the "age of confrontation."[82] Population growth and continued migrations in the first half of the century caused almost constant warring. Although on the periphery of long-distance trading emanating from the coast, by the late nineteenth century Swahili traders were regular visitors to the area and stories of the infamous slave trader Sudi of Pangani circulated widely, though actual slave trading in the region seems to have been limited.[83] From 1890 the Nyanza basin suffered a series of droughts and diseases that decimated much of eastern Africa.[84] The devastating rinderpest outbreak that caused widespread stock loss, as well as a smallpox epidemic in the 1890s, compounded by the arrival of colonial conquest, undermined traditional practices of land and bush management that had kept disease at bay.[85] These factors forced communities to push into the bush in search of new lands, thus unleashing the threat of trypanosomiasis, or sleeping sickness, spread by tsetse flies across the region.[86] By the end of the century the political and territorial sovereignty of the communities northeast of Lake Victoria was under threat—from expanding neighbors, from disease and drought, and from the arrival of imperial surveyors.

BEATING THE BOUNDS: THE MAKING AND UNMAKING OF IMPERIAL GEOGRAPHIES

From the earliest explorations of Henry Morton Stanley, Joseph Thomson, and Frederick Jackson, explorers, administrators, and missionaries wrote widely of the rich diversity and warm hospitality they encountered northeast of Lake Victoria.[87] These first European visitors universally commented on the plentiful food production, the variety of languages, the diversity of cultures, and the "confusion" of political structures among the African inhabitants they called Kavirondo. Early explorers described the Kavirondo as "industrious" and the "most moral of all tribes."[88]

Morality and gender relations seemed to preoccupy these early European visitors to the lake region. They marveled at the Kavirondo men and women working in the fields together in complete nudity. Comparing the naked Kavirondo women to the covered "ladies of Lamu," Sir Charles Eliot mused, "In Africa, female respectability is in inverse ratio to the quantity of clothes worn, and the beauties of Kavirondo, who imitate the costume of Eve, are said to be as virtuous as she was when there was no man but Adam in the world."[89] As attested to in postcards and photographic collections, the "naked Kavirondo" became an alluring tourist attraction in these early years of imperial travel in eastern Africa (fig. 1.6).[90] Images of naked women standing in fields, pulling a hippo across the shore or sunbathing on rocks became collectibles for travelers from coastal traders to Theodore Roosevelt.[91] Early explorations and imperial travels pictured "Kavirondo" as an untouched landscape, remote and unknown, filled with culturally exotic and morally "naked" people.

The term Kavirondo first appeared to administrators as a distant mapped space on E. G. Ravenstein's maps near the end of the 1870s.[92] In 1884, Joseph Thomson noted with surprise that "Kavirondo does not at all occupy the place which has been assigned to it on the map."[93] Bewildered by the sheer "number of *very distinct tribes*," the term Kavirondo was applied to both the Nilotic and Bantu communities of the lake region, though it progressively came to more specifically denote "all those natives speaking Bantu dialects west of Busoga and north of Kavirondo Bay."[94]

Bringing this confusion under colonial control required the remapping of local geographies. In 1890 the Imperial British East Africa Company (IBEAC, or IBEA) signed treaties with "Sultan Mumiya" of "Upper

FIGURE 1.6. Mombasa postcard, postmarked 1899.

Kavirondo," with the nabongo, or king, of the Wanga, and with the Bukusu clan head "Majanja, Sultan of the Kitosh."[95] In signing these treaties, these two leaders ostensibly "ceded to the said Company all his sovereign rights and rights of government over all his Territories, Countries, Peoples and Subjects." Ravenstein's map for the IBEAC visualized the area of Kavirondo as an important thoroughfare in the economic trading path between the coast and the large kingdoms of the Uganda Protectorate, centering on the town of Mumias. Nabongo Mumia provided the British with a base for trade running between the coast and Uganda and ample supplies of food and manpower for their journeys (fig. 1.7). The space northeast of Lake Victoria, however, remained barely surveyed. Early maps traced complex webs of escarpments and rivers amid whole sections of undifferentiated landmass. Treaties and other informal arrangements led to the incorporation of the region as the Eastern Province of the Buganda Protectorate in 1894.[96] Misreading the political landscape of this region, colonial officials pictured its communities as "unsettled," with no recognizable systems of political structure aside from the Wanga

FIGURE 1.7. IBEAC map of East Africa, 1891–92, by E. G. Ravenstein. Lugard, "Travels from the East Coast."

kingdom. In 1895 it became C. W. Hobley's task to "gradually establish an administration over the various sections of the turbulent collection of tribes, collectively known to the coast people as the Kavirondo."[97]

For Hobley, this reconnaissance work was one of both topographical surveyance and ethnographical investigation (fig. 1.8). The ethnonyms identified by Hobley curved and contorted amid a mess of complex topographical features, aiming to organize space in ethnic terms. The crowded "Isukha" branched out from and over rivers and forests; the "Marama" curved and fitted into a pocket of empty space; the "Ketosh," the name known to Hobley for the Bukusu clans, stretched and expanded across vast territories in the north. In this early map, the territory of these ethnonyms

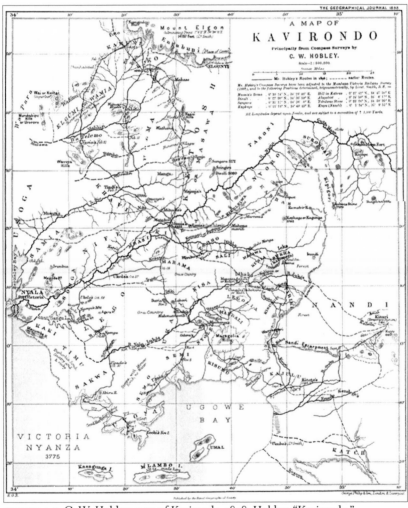

FIGURE 1.8. C. W. Hobley, map of Kavirondo, 1898. Hobley, "Kavirondo."

remained amorphous and undefined either by geographic markers or internal boundaries. In his 1896 report on Kavirondo District, Hobley noted, "The fact of the county being split up into so many sub-tribes without any really powerful Chiefs has induced a more complicated situation than would otherwise be the case."[98] As Sean Hawkins has argued, the failure to read topographical features that functioned as "mnemonic devices" in local cognitive mappings led the British to believe these communities had no "inscribed past" and no geographic system of social organization.[99]

More than mere lines on a page, colonial mapping practices worked to transform previously relational geographies of exchange and community into top-down, scientific, and measurable demarcations. Local geographical concepts proved difficult to translate, as they were relational and relative rather than constant abstract points of reference.[100] The fixed compass points of north, south, east, and west had no corresponding terms in any of the local languages. The term *masaba* for most communities translated as north but referred specifically to Mount Masaba, known by colonial officials as Mount Elgon, the northern frontier of this region.[101] In the Trans Nzoia, an area parallel to the mountain, *masaba* translated as west. Group names like Isukha and Idakho translated as forward and backward or lower and thus similarly reflected situated, geographic relationships and histories of migration and settlement.[102] The Luo referred to the Banyore as "those people from the other side of the hill."[103] Spatial relations thus shifted depending on the positioning of the subject. Colonial conquest not only imposed new and ever more fixed territorial boundaries but also brought with it a new vision of geographic relations.

Conquest and pacification expeditions from 1894 to 1908, numbering fifty separate military operations as catalogued in John Lonsdale's authoritative account, helped fill in Hobley's map and establish internal boundaries around his curving ethnonyms.[104] The hierarchical Wanga kingdom provided the British with a ready army of Wanga and Maasai troops mobilized not only against their Bantu neighbors but also in battles against the Sudanese mutiny of 1897 and Luo and Nandi uprisings.[105] Other communities in the region reacted to colonial incursions with varying degrees of interest, trade, alliance, and resistance. Many viewed the British as pawns of Wanga territorial ambitions.[106] The construction of colonial sovereignty required a great deal of violence and the use of what Christopher Vaughan has called a "hybrid regulatory order," an ambiguous and not always controlled devolution of power and the means of violence to local chiefs, particularly in border regions.[107] The most protracted resistance came from the Bukusu, whose battles at Lumboka and Chetambe's Fort received vivid portrayals in both Hobley's writings and local oral narratives.[108] Lonsdale pointed to the relative geographic isolation of the Bukusu population, in the northernmost extent of the region around Mount Elgon, as key to their protracted resistance to outsiders.[109] As in precolonial conflicts, the slopes and caves around Mount Elgon provided safe haven for those escaping the grasp of would-be state builders.[110] After winning the final major battle against the Bukusu, in 1895, "Hobley had no more to fear from the Luyia. He had been greatly aided in their pacification by their historic disunity."[111] This "historic disunity," however, can in actuality be understood as a strategy, an alternative way of thinking and practicing geographic and social relations, and a means of resistance that while failing to prevent colonial conquest persisted in dogging colonial rule.

Christian missionaries arrived by similar paths as explorers and colonial surveyors from earlier positions in Uganda and on the coast at the end of the nineteenth century. Tales of Bishop James Hannington's visit, in 1885, and Mumia's warning to him not to travel to Buganda, where he died soon after, have taken on legendary status. The North Kavirondo District was unique in the region for the sheer number of missionary groups that gained footholds, numbering as many as ten by the 1920s. The American Quakers with Friends African Mission (FAM) were the first to establish themselves, in 1902. In quick succession the Catholic Mill Hill Missionaries, the Church of God (originally known as the South African Compounds and Interior Mission), and the Anglican Church Missionary Society (CMS) all founded missions in these early years. Colonial officials hoped mission influence would help bring the "most independent and unruly" Bantu communities under colonial control.[112] Missionaries made deals with local elders and competed for land claims to secure territorial "spheres of influence" as first laid out in the 1885 Treaty of Berlin.[113] These negotiations for evangelizing rights in particular areas added yet another layer of mapping onto the multiple colonial processes of territorial demarcation. However, unlike the territories of colonial administration, religious spaces were not always contiguous. Mission grounds and Christian villages crossed, jumped, and intersected different community spaces, creating hybrid sites of cultural contact and imposition, refuge, and exchange. This more dispersed spatial organization would have distinct consequences for later political and social movements.

Colonial conquest brought with it a flurry of mapping projects, from the railway that arrived at Kisumu in 1901 to the carving out of roads, trading posts, and administrative sites. The administrative mapping of the Uganda Protectorate created internal boundaries and delimited top-down spaces of administration and authority that could now be imposed and altered by British bureaucrats, even at great distances (fig. 1.9). In 1902 a

FIGURE 1.9. Map of the Uganda Protectorate, 1902. Johnston, "Uganda Protectorate, Ruwenzori."

decision from the Foreign Office in London to dramatically redraw the eastern boundary of the Uganda Protectorate prompted a more concerted mapping of colonial boundaries in eastern Africa. With the boundaries of the Uganda Protectorate already mapped, British officials in London could, by the stroke of a pen, transfer a large portion of the Central Province and all of the Eastern Province of the Uganda Protectorate to the East Africa Protectorate, renamed the Kenya Colony in 1920.

The motivations behind this transfer remain difficult to assess.[114] The arrival of the railway at Kisumu, in 1901, provided at least one factor in the reorientation of the province, aiming to maintain the whole railway from the coast under one authority (fig. 1.10). As the arrival of the railway and road surveys demonstrated, Kavirondo was increasingly being positioned on the map not as a midpoint on the way to Uganda but as a terminus of trade and administration emanating from the coast. Further, the concurrent arrival of white settlers in the highlands prompted calls for land and labor within the boundaries of the East

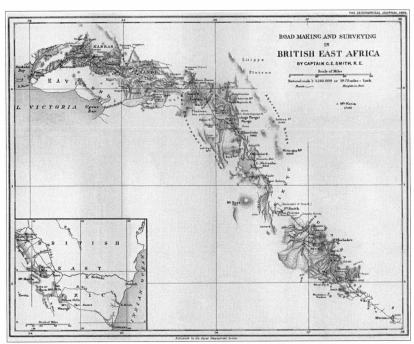

FIGURE 1.10. Map of road making and surveying in British East Africa. G. Smith, "Road-Making."

Africa Protectorate. Nyanza Province, formed out of this enlarged western frontier, effectively placed one of the most agriculturally productive and densely populated areas in the region at the disposal of this rapidly developing settler colony.

Negotiations over the drawing of this new boundary revealed the competing knowledge systems involved in the colonial mapping projects. While some argued for the use of the "scientific" determinants of topographical features as "natural" boundaries, others argued ethnographic considerations should be paramount.[115] The director of surveys, Raymond Alan, later laid out the "scientific" argument against Sir Frederick Jackson's preference for foothills that often corresponded to the environmental ridges of clan boundaries: "As a surveyor, I prefer watersheds as the latter are definite and ascertainable and the former [foothills] cannot be determined by anyone and are, therefore, purely artificial."[116] Conflicts over the meaning and placement of boundaries often pitted imperial geographers against the "men on the ground" responsible for local governance.

At the turn of the century, Sir Harry Johnston, special commissioner of the Uganda Protectorate, and many other men on the ground favored the gradual amalgamation of the two protectorates and thus petitioned for a boundary that would entail the least disturbance possible to ethnolinguistic groupings. A flurry of correspondence in 1901 argued for the "well-known boundaries" that had been secured through *barazas*, meetings with African elders and clan leaders.[117] For reasons obscured in the historical record, in 1902 the Foreign Office backed the "natural frontier" proposed by Sir Clement Hill in London, despite protests from the men on the ground that this new frontier "did not readily coincide with tribal boundaries."[118] Although the scientific arguments for "natural" boundaries prevailed, even these features remained disputed. In his later economic study of the region, Hugh Fearn argued that there was greater territorial logic in using the Nandi escarpment as the new boundary, placing the Bantu tribes in Uganda and the Luo in Kenya.[119] Imperial debates over the logic of boundaries highlighted the conflicts and contradictions of colonial rule in eastern Africa.

It again fell to C. W. Hobley to demarcate the new boundary of the North Kavirondo District. In theory, this new district would contain all the Bantu tribes northeast of Lake Victoria, bordered by Uganda to the west, the Luo to the south, and the Kalenjin and Maasai in the Rift Valley to the east and north. In reality, the "Hobley line" ran through Lake Victoria, along the Sio River in the south, and jaggedly over Mount Elgon in the north, effectively dislocating the Samia community around the Sio River and severing the closely related Bagisu and Bukusu around Mount Elgon.[120] Indeed the Hobley line cut through and across many of the curving ethnonyms he himself originally mapped in 1898 (fig. 1.11). This reorientation transformed the Nyanza region into a borderland, a space thoroughly caught between two colonies that were rapidly differentiating in terms of local governance, European settlement, and African rights. Interterritorial disputes over the exact limits of this border persisted throughout the colonial period and well into the postcolonial era.[121] This process of remapping would have profound effects on the alignment and geographic imaginations of political communities in both territories.

Despite the 1902 boundary agreement, as late as 1927 the boundaries of North Kavirondo remained in flux.[122] The creation of these boundaries first occurred on paper, redrawn over the detailed maps of the Uganda Protectorate, with written descriptions of boundaries circulated in British proclamations. Surveyors and administrators then set out on boundary tours, enlisting African laborers to carry heavy stones for cairns, erect large stone pillars, set beacons, and dig trenches across the new interterritorial boundary with Uganda and against the expanding

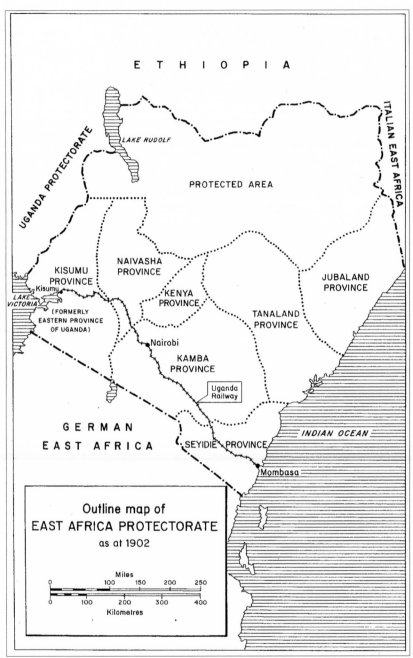

FIGURE 1.11. Map of the East Africa Protectorate, 1902. Beachey, *History of East Africa*, xii.

white highlands.[123] Colonial administrators would then take elders, head-men, and local villagers out to "beat the bounds" of the new boundaries, using drums and ornamental ceremonial flair.[124] In this way, the impe-rial instruments of territoriality imposed a top-down cartographic spatial ordering while enlisting local communities to invest in the construction of these boundaries.

Officials used survey maps, the construction of roads, and the col-lection of taxes to construct and consolidate meaningful boundaries. As the colonial administration envisioned Nyanza Province as a poten-tially rich source of labor and cash crop production, the enforcement of boundaries became a tool in the territorial control of work and local production. With the arrival of the railway, the colonial administration introduced cotton and maize as new export commodities. While cotton production foundered due to local resentment and low prices, maize proved a profitable and exportable cash crop, quickly overtaking tra-ditional crops such as millet, sorghum, and cassava as the staple food of African diets, particularly for laborers.[125] North Kavirondo was fast becoming the "granary of East Africa" and the largest pool of potential laborers in the young colony.[126]

Colonial officials also used borders and taxes to direct the flow of labor. Roads in North Kavirondo emanated out east and north from the administrative base in Mumias to direct the flow of labor and commerce away from Uganda and toward work on the railways, new European settlers' farms in the highlands, and government public works projects within the limits of the new colony. Colonial commissioners worked to "impress all people with the necessity for their young, unemployed men going out to work."[127] Much to the frustration of colonial officials, Afri-can laborers from North Kavirondo negotiated seasonal contracts to fit agricultural cycles and displayed a preference "to work month by month and their dislike of definitely binding themselves by a written contract."[128]

Many defied colonial demands on their labor and resources by migrating across the still poorly defined Ugandan border. Farmers on the Ugandan side of the border similarly evaded forced cotton cultiva-tion and military conscription by crossing into western Kenya.[129] These movements were not without risk and insecurity. Kenyan and Ugandan officials responded with joint taxation collections and punitive actions against clans on either side of the border.[130] In 1917, as Kenyan officials raised hut taxes to fund World War I efforts and pressured chiefs to supply constant labor for the Carrier Corps, fifty Wamia families were forced to return to North Kavirondo from Uganda, where they had fled.[131] The ad-ministration also put strict restrictions on the movement of cattle, seeing any form of pastoralism as "opposed to social or political advancement" and using boundaries to control the spread of sleeping sickness and rinderpest.[132] Administrators introduced "census books" for the registration of residents within a given boundary to help control movement and enforce the payment of taxes.[133] While chiefs went around their territories counting huts, they also subverted these processes by offering refuge to competing communities. In the case of Chief Sudi, his entire census had to be thrown out as he was found to have collected taxes and census data on villages on Mumia's side of the border.[134] Border patrols and the introduction of identity permits in the form of the *kipande* reinforced territorial boundaries as a central feature of colonial governance.

After quashing the final throes of outright resistance, in 1908, British officials set about demarcating internal boundaries and an effective local administration. That same year, Geoffrey Archer, acting district commissioner of North Kavirondo, began his demarcation tour.[135] Archer found the undulating landscape of North Kavirondo, with its "many fixed points and much open rolling grasslands," a "good training ground" for practicing his surveying skills.[136] Archer enlisted local inhabitants as porters, guides, and aides and taught them lessons in cartography as he triangulated locations and called out instructions on the placement of markers. Archer gained a strong reputation for managing clan disputes across the interterritorial boundary and securing local support for "unsatisfactory" boundaries, earning him the difficult job of delimiting the Northern Frontier District and later the governorship of British Somaliland at the young age of thirty-two.[137] Although officials professed a desire to make administrative boundaries coincide with the "tribal" areas mapped by Hobley, Archer struggled to collect accurate clan numbers and to consolidate boundaries along the lines of "native laws and customs."[138] Archer complained that the "Kavirondo are the most pronounced land grabbers."[139] Like Francis Fuller among the Asante in the Gold Coast, Archer believed that boundaries fixed to a topographical map would make sense of the confusion of local customs;[140] and yet, as Sara Berry argued, "However precisely they were drawn on paper, boundaries could be remarkably elusive in practice."[141]

The Wanga royal family and their emissaries invested early in the ideology of boundaries and acted as surveyors in the creation of the basic units of authority and territorial control within the district. Nabongo Mumia and his half brother Murunga were the only Africans officially consulted on Archer's demarcation tour.[142] Archer sent out Wanga chiefs as territorial agents to construct "locations," the smallest administrative unit in the district. In this initial demarcation, only eight locations were drawn around the multiple communities of the region. Throughout the demarcation tour, the Wanga proved not only their usefulness but also their ability to benefit from the colonial processes of mapping. As later reported by Provincial Commissioner C. M. Dobbs, Archer gave "Mumia the biggest sub-district as . . . he alone had 'capable men who are fit to be appointed as headmen over the various sub-divisions of this area.'"[143]

Between 1904 and 1909 the British elevated their Wanga allies to the position of chiefs over the diverse range of clans never previously subject to Wanga power. On 15 November 1909, the colonial government confirmed their alliance with the Wanga by appointing Mumia "paramount chief" over the entire district. This official title would come to haunt the British administration as later African politicians attempted to claim the legitimacy and authority of a paramount chief. Colonial officials reinforced the new "native authority" of Wanga chiefs with the power to arrest, issue orders on the movement of people, compel labor, preside over local disputes, and collect taxes.[144] In the Wanga the British found the local source of "indirect rule" they needed to enforce colonial boundaries.

However, written into the very processes of boundary demarcation and colonial authority were the tools of its subversion for local actors. Countermapping strategies reflected both local geographic practices and the adoption of colonial technologies of mapping. The most commonly used tactic, as had been the case for centuries, was evasion. Local inhabitants, particularly along the interterritorial border, strategically moved throughout geographic networks that extended around and beyond these new borders to evade tax collection, to defy new authorities, and to confuse colonial officials. These cross-border movements took on cyclical patterns and created new networks later used in illicit trade and movements of rebellion. Others, particularly in the north and east, found refuge in the hills and mountains that provided geographic protection from the reaches of the state. While these movements built on and created networks of clan associations, they also produced new sites of conflict, as different communities responded to colonial impositions and incentives in diverse ways.[145] Border clashes in the early years of colonial rule continually disrupted the work of colonial surveyors and often arose strategically to pressure colonial officials, who often only addressed the complete demarcation of locational boundaries as a result of these local "boundary riots."[146] The construction of colonial boundaries was a messy affair, continually interrupted and confused by the activism of local communities.

Local activists also used previous geographic knowledge and their early lessons in cartography to subvert the work of colonial surveyors, through subterfuge, trickery, and outright manipulation. Africans destroyed cairns, moved beacons, and uprooted pillars to move the colonial boundaries set by surveyors. Often the same men who carried and placed the boundary beacons for the British during the day were suspected of, or boasted of, removing them by night.[147] In one example, Wanga chief Murunga was said to have warned the Bukusu that the British wanted to cut them off from land in the northern area of Kamakoiya. Murunga advised the local population to take the beacon and move it, using the British officers' lack of mastery over pronunciation of river names to trick them into accepting the new boundary.[148] The arrival of new European settlers in the Trans Nzoia lands north of the Kamakoiya River after 1912, however, would again push this boundary back and constrict the northern expanses of the district.[149] The environment, too, revolted against the symbols of boundary demarcation as grasses and shrubs overgrew beacons and hid boundaries from view.[150] These countermapping strategies became so pervasive that in 1911, British officials proclaimed harsh penalties for the "destroying or moving or diminishing the utility of *any Land Marks fixed by public authority.*"[151] Colonial officials suggested the use of increasingly permanent markers such as "iron posts sunk in cement" and cairns alongside survey pegs within African farmlands that more starkly mapped the landscape.[152] However, the symbols of surveyors continued to prove susceptible to the countermappings of African activists.

Colonial surveyors thus encountered what Raymond Craib has termed the "fugitive landscapes": territories characterized by multiple and overlapping geographic systems that were not landscapes at all but "places created and recreated through the prisms of memory, practical wisdom, use and collective decision making rather than the lens of instrumentation."[153] This confrontation between competing geographic imaginations of place and space would not result in a total victory for imperial cartography. Hungry for novel technologies and adept at adapting them to their own purposes, Africans found in mapping just such an instrumental tool to make claims to new landscapes of power and resources. By World War I, the number of locations had expanded to eighteen, mostly as a result of protests and the disaggregation of recognized ethnic communities, though more than half the lands and diverse communities of North Kavirondo remained under Wanga rule. These boundaries did not succeed in imposing a "master narrative" of authority and exclusionary rights.[154] The lines drawn by Hobley and Archer, while fugitive and continually contested, did, however, provide a new cartographic grammar for future debates over governance and the territorial horizons of ethnic communities.

⟜

IN THE making and unmaking of competing territorialities in western Kenya, early settlers built autonomous clan structures within niche environments and mapped larger networks of interaction, exchanging goods, services, people, and ideas across this uneven terrain. While the fixed and rigid maps of colonial geographers imposed new fields of conflict and debate onto the diverse communities of North Kavirondo, they also introduced new ways of "writing the world," new tools for competing over local resources, and new strategies for resisting imperial impositions. Local activists combined these early lessons in cartography with local geographic knowledge and spatial strategies to countermap the hegemonic project of imperial geography. In an ironic twist, it was perhaps Hobley's first map—with its curving, overlapping, and expanding ethnonyms—that most directly reflected the heterarchy and shifting geographic relations of communities in western Kenya. As colonial officials worked to consolidate their rule, the need for more clearly demarcated lands and more hierarchical forms of political authority prompted local political activists to rework and reimagine their traditions of geographic and political community. The grounds of authority and community in western Kenya, it seemed, would remain "slippery," and defiant to the recognition of "kings."

2 ⌒ Land, Gold, and Commissioning the "Tribe"

.

IN HIS ethnographic study of the "Bantu of Kavirondo," conducted in the 1930s, Günter Wagner illustrated how the naming of a child often derived from a recent "conspicuous event," such as an epidemic, drought, or famine.[1] It was just such a conspicuous event that gave birth to a new community in western Kenya: the Kakamega gold rush. Prospectors first panned gold in the streams of Kakamega in March 1931. Within a few months, more than two hundred Europeans flooded the most densely populated and closely cultivated southeastern locations of North Kavirondo in search of gold.[2] With the discovery of gold, British parliamentarians took exception to the most fundamental doctrines of the Native Lands Trust Ordinance, passed only a few months earlier. The ordinance had fixed and legally enshrined land in the Native Reserves "for the use and benefit of the native tribes of the Colony forever." Before breaking for Christmas in 1931, Parliament rushed through an amendment allowing for indefinite land appropriation by the state in the reserves. The amending of the Native Lands Trust Ordinance raised serious questions among British officials, African subjects, and international commentators regarding colonial trusteeship, African rights, and landownership within the colony.

The Kakamega gold rush intervened into the history of North Kavirondo at a time of intense local debates over land tenure, political authority, and kinship. By the 1920s early sporadic acts of resistance against British-imposed chiefs and newly cut boundaries transformed into an all-out political campaign. While local activists redrew the limits of authority and community through campaigns of civil disobedience and cross-border activism, locational leaders forwarded themselves as the rightful defenders of customary practice and the political sovereignty of their constituents. The discovery of gold, however, threatened these diverse local moral economies and prompted African thinkers to reimagine the meaning of territory and belonging. As farmers countermapped the incursions of miners into their lands, political leaders from the district stood before the Kenya Land Commission of 1932 and appropriated the colonial map to lay claim to an enlarged political community. In front of this commission, representatives from North Kavirondo subordinated divergent historical accounts, suppressed internal competition over land, and invested in a patriotic mapping of territorial identity to gain leverage over white miners, British bureaucrats, and encroaching European farmers.

A moment of territorial crisis, the Kakamega gold rush marked a dramatic transition in the formulation of local political thought in North Kavirondo. While the deconstructive cartographic work and defense of local moral economies in the 1920s reflected the plural and dissenting traditions of political community in western Kenya, the gold rush provided a common threat that gave energy to new geographic imaginings and prompted ethnic entrepreneurs across western Kenya to adopt the colonial map and declare themselves "a tribe."

THE ANTI-WANGA CAMPAIGN AND THE LIMITS OF "DECENTRALIZED DESPOTISM"

The gold rush surfaced at a high point of political debate and communal reorganization in North Kavirondo. The creation of administrative locations imposed new geographies of power and community (see chapter 1). In the early years of colonial rule, political life organized around these locational lines as local communities sought to define new terms of kinship and map new political communities.

For much of the interwar period, campaigns against colonially imposed, predominantly Wanga chiefs preoccupied locational politics. The practice of "decentralized despotism" in North Kavirondo relied heavily on the extension of Wanga chiefs over vast territories of non-Wanga subjects.[3] The Wanga royal family had worked with British surveyors to divide the territory of western Kenya and claim a monarchical authority that extended far beyond any traditional systems of rule. Wanga power in the colonial era rested on the transformation of inflated monarchical traditions into administrative authority. With little local legitimacy, the rule of these Wanga chiefs was often heavy-handed and taxing. This "despotism," however, had its limits. Political authority was a continually contested aspect of colonial life. As John Lonsdale argued, the imposition of this administrative system "had not so much created previously non-existent political units, as translated the actual or pretended genealogical relationships between clans into that very power nexus from which secession and migration had been the traditional refuge."[4] While local communities continued to mobilize precolonial strategies of resistance, the new geography of power imposed by colonial rule also created new contexts for dissent and imagination.

As early as 1909 local communities voiced their opposition to the "foreign rule" of Wanga chiefs in terms of political sovereignty: "They pointed out that every tribe had its own Chief and that they wanted theirs; in other words it was Utsotso for Watsotso. This was not a petition but a declaration of rights."[5] Previously autonomous and porous clans forged alliances within their locations to contest Wanga power on the grounds of historical autonomy and cultural difference. Into the 1920s the sporadic protests against Wanga chiefs transformed into a widespread anti-Wanga movement. Although these campaigns centered on Wanga chiefs, they were symptomatic of a much larger movement against any chiefs or authorities deemed foreign by local constituents.

Anti-Wanga activists and dissenters against newly appointed chiefs used multiple strategies to defend claims to autonomy and authority. Political protest ranged from uncoordinated, largely reactive confrontations to large-scale mobilizations of civil disobedience. Bukusu farmers defied labor summons from the infamous Wanga chief Murunga, refused to pay taxes, and illegally crossed into the Trans Nzoia and Uganda, territorial strategies they had used against imperial surveyors in previous decades.[6] In Idakho protesters against the rule of the Isukha chief Milimu mounted a campaign of "boycott and civil disobedience."[7] Idakho farmers divided by the interlocational boundary tracing the Yala River led infiltration campaigns, flooding Chief Milimu's northern stronghold. Farmers across the district engaged in cross-boundary cultivation and hut burnings to renegotiate colonial boundaries. While these campaigns fitted within longer local histories of competition over scarce resources and patronage, they represented much more than parochial conflicts over power and particular tracts of land: they were a form of argument, countermapping colonial attempts to define the limits of political communities.

Anti-Wanga campaigns prompted local political thinkers to reframe divergent accounts of the past and mobilize kinship networks along the borders of the location. Petitioners wrote genealogies and migratory histories that contested colonial boundaries. The borders of the Marama location fused together forty-two clans of diverse origins under a name of foreign origin and the rule of Wanga chief Mulama, brother to Mumia.[8] Mulama's public pronouncement that certain clans in North Marama were truly of Wanga origin prompted the diverse, autonomous clan heads of the location to invent a mythical common ancestor, Mulafu, in defense of a broadened kinship network.[9] In Isukha, despite ample evidence indicating their communal name translated as "forward" or "in front," locational leaders, too, claimed the name came from a founding ancestor to defend their historical right to a chieftaincy against Idakho protestors.[10] Local communities circulated myths of common ancestors to foster new kinship ideologies, to renegotiate locational authority, and to get their names on the map.

While some reimagined traditional reservoirs of protest, others used new social forces brought with colonialism to contest colonial structures of rule. Conversion to a rival mission provided one means for local activists to distinguish themselves and argue for a social identity separate from that of the ruling chief. This competitive conversion added a religious topography to these movements, as rival missions provided support, both physical and moral, to their converts against chiefs. In Idakho, Protestants held their own barazas in open confrontation with the Catholic chief Milimu's official local meetings. FAM converts among the Logoli and the Bukusu spoke loudly against the moral abuses of "foreign" chiefs, mobilizing traditional elders to present an alternative model of political and moral authority.[11]

Contests also emerged within the same missions, as a new generation of young mission-educated workers and politicians challenged chiefly authority. In 1928, CMS converts working as railway employees in Nairobi brought charges of polygamy against Chief Mulama.[12] The Church found Mulama guilty and promptly ordered his excommunication. Conflict in Marama between different clans and mission adherents came to a head over CMS festivities held on ancestral lands and led to a pitched two-day battle and the deaths of two participants.[13] In the 1920s, Mulama worked to buttress his chiefly power with political work, serving on the recently minted Local Native Council (LNC) and chairing the North Kavirondo Taxpayers' Welfare Association (NKTWA), the first political organization based exclusively in North Kavirondo.[14] By the late 1920s, however, the leadership of the NKTWA had shifted away from chiefly personalities toward a "younger generation of semi-educated young men" who wore badges in the fashion of self-help proclaiming "forward with the work of our hands."[15] And while the administration blamed these "upstart" Christian converts for the political instability in the district, on the ground campaigns against unpopular chiefs were much more diffuse and broadly mobilized.

Though the colonial administration resisted bowing to these local movements for self-representation, by the late 1920s the limits of "decentralized despotism" became impossible to ignore. The Wanga had outlived their political usefulness. In 1926, Samia activists successfully deposed their Wanga chief, Kadima, on charges of corruption. In 1930, Wanga chief Were of the Waholo location was among the first "to bow gracefully to the storm and to retire."[16] Facing mounting conflict in Marama, the administration finally suspended Mulama from his post in 1935. Elders in North Marama promptly evicted Mulama from his land, sparking an unending battle over his property rights in the location. The retirement of Chief Murunga from the Bukusu locations in 1936 bookended the dramatic demise of Wanga domination in the region.

Geographies of power and communal obligation were at the heart of many of these campaigns, and colonial administrators responded by parceling out land given to the Wanga in early imperial surveys. By 1931 the number of locations in North Kavirondo had increased from eight to twenty-five (fig. 2.1). In the interwar period, these newly won borders took on new significance. Low, popular political campaigns against foreign chiefs traced the borders of the location and prompted local political actors to infuse these territorial limits with new ideas of kinship. As Bill Bravman noted, in the Taita hills political communities under colonial rule refashioned "social identity to shape thought and action in contexts where lineage and neighbourhood-based ideologies were losing salience, or never had much purchase."[17] Activists clogged local land courts and produced competing maps that revealed the scarce resources at stake in these more overtly political campaigns. The anti-Wanga campaigns revealed the limits of "decentralized despotism" in the face of plural political traditions and the imaginative geographic work of local activists in countermapping new terms of kinship, new lines of community, and new strategies of dissent.

PERFORMING TRADITION: THE CODIFICATION OF NATIVE LAND TENURE

In 1930 the colonial administration responded to these mobilizations of competing and inventive traditions by launching the North Kavirondo Native Land Tenure Committee (NLTC) to establish a legal framework for land and customary law.[18] Over seventeen nonconsecutive days between July and October 1930, the committee heard testimony on questions of land acquisition, landownership, boundary demarcation,

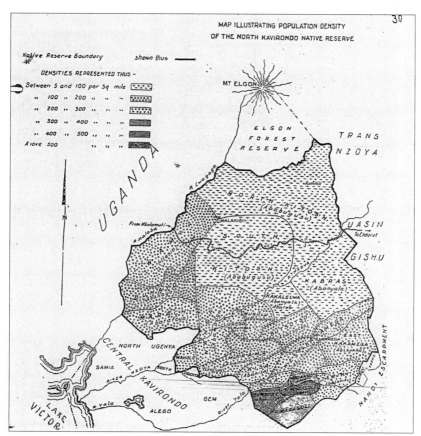

FIGURE 2.1. Map of population densities in North Kavirondo. "Report of Committee on Native Land Tenure in the North Kavirondo Reserve," October 1930, CMS, G3X A5/25.

stranger or tenant rights, the selling of land, grazing rights, and the position of women. Those called to testify as experts on local customs represented the locational administrative elite, chiefs, and headmen, many of whom were concurrently fending off campaigns against their authority. The administration hoped this committee would put to rest many of the anti-Wanga campaigns and border conflicts plaguing the district. However, locational leaders turned the work of the committee into a platform for performing diverse traditions of land tenure and political authority. Locational representatives arranged evidence of migrations, cultural practices, and land laws to promote divergent accounts of history and tradition against homogenizing colonial policies, "foreign" forms of political authority, and competing neighbors.

Colonial commissions such as the NLTC called on African "speakers" and "witnesses" to take part in a particular form of performative political theater. As Lonsdale argued in the case of the Kikuyu, representatives within these dramas told stories of their past as much to create "a knowledgeable audience" as to convince colonial officials.[19] In the face of colonial expropriation, Kikuyu narratives of tradition, migration, and great leaders served as proof of their civility and their coherence as a political community. In western Kenya, Osaak Olumwullah similarly argued that the Banyore before the committee maintained the "façades of community and consensus . . . erected at front-stage level but at the same time dismantled through commentaries made backstage."[20] Yet despite the attempts of locational leaders to construct this façade of political coherence, in the theater of the NLTC the audience talked back.

The North Kavirondo NLTC was a public spectacle, with daily audiences numbering in the hundreds. Throughout the proceedings, testimony had to be suspended to allow for lengthy debates over lineages, migratory routes, and land rights. Authorial notes by an unknown hand qualified the transcript with audience interjections, asides, and corrections. In one such case, this authorial hand recorded the "admission" that several groups representing themselves as landowners in North Kitosh were actually recent settlers from Uganda. These moments of interruption revealed the discursive nature of political thought in North Kavirondo. Just as Lonsdale argued for the inherent skepticism of the Kikuyu people in the face of prophets, the proceedings of the NLTC revealed the skepticism of North Kavirondo's inhabitants toward those who claimed centralized authority.[21] Audience members refused to be silent witnesses to this drama, actively interjecting their voices into the cultural production of authority and tradition.

For the diverse representatives before the NLTC, the "common stock of stories" available to Kikuyu spokesmen did not exist. None claimed a common founding father, common migratory path, or common set of prophetic figures from which all communities in the district sprang. Their stories, instead, fractured purposefully to defend the autonomy and autochthony of their particular communities. Fault lines appeared in their diverse accounts of clan histories, migration, and land tenure practices.

Locational representatives produced histories that drew together the congeries of clans within their specific territories. Representatives told clan histories through codified lists of clan names, clan heads, and clan settlements. When Chief Sudi rose to provide an authoritative account of Bukusu clans, "considerable confusion and dissension" erupted among audience members. The committee adjourned the meeting so that a "correct list" of clans could be compiled. Bukusu headman Dominiko Sianju returned with an impressive table in hand, an extensive list of the names of clans and their current heads from across the Bukusu locations. Representatives actively reformulated ancestry and kinship networks through the secretarial conceit of the list to defend novel political communities built in and around colonial boundaries. In the Kisa location, multiple narratives of founding fathers and important lineages coexisted. Lala, representative for Kisa, had to be replaced when audience members charged him with erasing one of the founding father's sons from his official list. For Lala, erasing this "son" put his own clan in more direct line of descent from the founding father. Representatives argued that this tabulated "common ancestry" provided evidence of the community's "natural boundary."[22] However, what is clear from the ethnographic work of Wagner, representations before the NLTC, and the historical texts of patriotic historians J. D. Otiende, Gideon Were, and John Osogo, is that accounts of founding fathers and lists of clan names were in constant flux, responding to contemporary conditions and the complicated arithmetic of kinship. For local representatives, the process of tabulating kinship through list making provided a central grounds for the political work of aligning constituents and enclosing dissent.

In reality, these clan histories were quite shallow. Although the committee concluded that "almost every tribe has a history of migration," most representatives avoided or denied these histories entirely.[23] Conducting his research at the same time, Wagner also noted the "meagreness of traditions" of migration.[24] Many representatives claimed to have "no tradition of migration." Often representatives traced their clan histories only to the moment of arrival in their present settlements. While contemporaneous anthropological sources cast these communities as "people on the move," representatives pictured their constituents as thoroughly settled, undisputed owners of their lands as witnessed at the arrival of colonial rule.[25] Embodied in the figure of C. W. Hobley, whose primary task was to bring spatial order to this disarray of decentralized agriculturalists, colonial conquest and imperial mapping emerged as the most prominent "common stock" of stories told to defend a history of political autonomy from Hobley's Wanga allies. Representatives told uncluttered histories, geographically pitching the birth of their people as a discrete corporate body within the grounds of their current administrative units, sewing different threads of clan movements together within the location. These shallow traditions of migration suppressed diverse linguistic origins and naturalized western Kenya as a rightful, autochthonous homeland. Locational representatives and audience members produced and reproduced histories of migration and settlement before this committee to build recognizable, bounded "tribes" for the benefit of colonial commissioners.[26]

These local histories also served to reinforce divergent claims to landownership. Two schools of thought emerged in the testimony for the defense of land acquisition: the right of force and the right of first cultivation. While Chief Mulama argued in his opening address that "the first man to come into this country acquired his rights by strength," most claimed land rights through the civilizing of previously unoccupied and untilled land. All locational representatives firmly stated that there was no tradition of selling or buying land. Differences in land practices reflected the environmental diversity and political decentralization of the local land economy (see chapter 1). Before this commission, this diversity was turned to political strategy. Most representatives placed landownership firmly under the control of clan heads. Only Wanga representatives spoke of a differentiated system whereby the nabongo owned the "soil" of the corporate territory, the clan controlled its own boundaries, and individual heads of families owned their homesteads. Many representatives, whose constituents were in the throes of anti-Wanga campaigns, defended their historic autonomy through repeated references to never having paid tribute to any "king" or foreign patron. Very few clans claimed to practice any formalized system of boundary demarcation beyond the use of physical landmarks, such as stones, trees, and furrows. Locational representatives promoted divergent traditions of land tenure to secure their own position as the rightful guardians and arbitrators of their community's customs.

Testimony before the committee provided a window into the fragmented, argumentative, and discursive nature of political thought in North Kavirondo. Apparent from this testimony was a strong skepticism toward centralized authority. Even among the highly centralized Wanga, audience interruptions forced Chief Mulama to adjust his list of Wanga clans at several points. While the anti-Wanga campaigns prompted political thinkers to voice dissenting versions of history to offer proof of their right to particular tracts of land and of their traditions of political autonomy, their evidence before the NLTC reflected more the heterarchy and overlapping nature of traditional practices and long-running arguments over authority in western Kenya. Representatives continually disagreed on the land rights of women, customs involving inheritance and the distribution of land among clan members. While these practices often overlapped or intersected across different locations, representatives remained intent on accentuating the cultural and often linguistic nuances of their particular cultural traditions.

Despite this plural and dissenting picture of land tenure in North Kavirondo, the NLTC recommended the codification of native land tenure practices into a stratified legal land register to include "the name of the tribe, the name of the clan, the name of the clan head, descriptions of external boundaries, the name of contiguous clans, and the number of families with holdings."[27] The codification of previously negotiated processes involving strangers or tenant rights effectively placed land tenure outside the immediate control of the clan. With no title deed, dependents and smaller clans were reliant on benevolent landlords for use of their land. In response, smaller clans in North Kavirondo began demanding an "oath" from the government to secure their land. Land conflicts between locations subsequently called up evidence given before the committee as proof. The testimony given before such commissions were thus self-consciously understood not solely as opportunities to debate competing versions of land traditions but moreover as strategic tools in the documentation of evidence for future conflicts over land rights.

The LNC warned the district commissioner that the failure to implement the findings of such enquiries would mean that "further enquiries would only be met by lying answers."[28] The years 1930 and 1931 were a time of heightened politicking over land and authority. The depression of 1929 further exacerbated land conflict in North Kavirondo, collapsing local export prices and throwing both labor and cash cropping into crisis. A severe locust infestation ravaged North Kavirondo in 1931, causing food shortages and crop destruction: many locations lost up to 60 percent of their maize and *wimbi* (brown millet) crops.[29] And it was at this point that the discovery of gold would interject dramatically thrust these local contests onto the national stage.

THE KAKAMEGA GOLD RUSH

The discovery of gold forever altered the landscape of land and political thought in western Kenya. With gold in their eyes, "colonial officialdom" swiftly reduced the Native Lands Trust Ordinance, guaranteeing the inalienable land rights of Africans in the reserves "for-ever," to a "scrap of paper" (fig. 2.2).[30] This dramatic reversal of colonial trusteeship prompted local political thinkers in western Kenya to refocus their defense of diverse cultural practices and defend territory beyond the limits of the location.

Mr. L. A. Johnson, a farmer in Kenya and frustrated gold seeker from ventures in Tanganyika and the Klondike of Canada in the 1890s, first panned gold in the streams of Kakamega in March 1931.[31] Prospectors soon discovered alluvial gold in the rivers of the Isukha, Idakho, Bunyore, and Tiriki locations. The gold rush in Kakamega was part of a larger regional story of gold mining in the lake areas of eastern Africa in the 1930s, particularly in the Lupa region of Tanganyika and throughout Nyanza Province.[32] The gold rush came at a time when the depression and the sudden drop in prices for agricultural exports exposed the weakness of the settler economy. Gold-mining ventures represented a new frontier and a new avenue for economic survival, if not gain, for European settlers. In 1930, Europeans in Nyanza Province numbered 1,106. By 1932 this number had more than doubled, reaching 2,282 floating and largely unchecked European miners flooding the most densely populated southeastern locations of the North Kavirondo, counting four hundred Africans per square mile (see fig. 2.1). Expectations were high, with many speculating the region's gold deposits to be a "bigger thing than Johannesburg."[33]

By the end of 1931 the administration had issued four hundred permits to European prospectors, originally sold for one pound each. Mining claims grew from 309 in 1930 to 1,074 in 1931 and continued to skyrocket until reaching a peak of 23,158 registered claims in 1934.[34] After 1934 gold mining shifted from predominantly independent alluvial mining to reef mining, undertaken by large companies such as Rosterman Gold Mines Ltd., Tanganyika Concessions Ltd., the Eldoret Mining Syndicate, and the Kentan Gold Areas Ltd. At its peak, mining employed 14,943 Africans, with the peak of locally sourced employment around seven thousand.[35] Numbers employed in the mining sector steadily declined after 1935. By 1936 the European population decreased by more than five hundred as the small miners and alluvial workers departed, these sources of gold having been depleted in just under five years. The large companies also began a steady decline in the subsequent years as no ore body of sufficient quantity was ever discovered. As an economic and industrial project, the gold rush was all but finished by the mid-1940s.

The gold rush sparked a major war of words across the colony, in the British press, and in both houses of Parliament. The loudest outrage focused on the amending of the Native Lands Trust Ordinance of 1930.[36] This document, translated and circulated among African communities throughout the colony, was not just colonial legalese from a distant metropole but rather represented a central doctrine guaranteeing African land rights in the reserves: the "native Magna Carta."[37] The amendment, rushed through Parliament in 1931, allowed for the reversal of the ordinance's key principles. Most important, the colonial state could now compensate for land alienation in cash, obviating the pledge to provide equivalent replacement land for the reserve. Lord Passfield, former secretary of state for the colonies and instrumental figure in imposing the

Native Lands Trust Ordinance on a resistant pro-settler Kenyan government, charged the British government with a "breach of faith": monetary compensation for land loss could never be equivalent or just as "the areas set aside for the Reserves were not set aside for individuals nor for families nor even for the present generation, but for the tribes. If you gave every individual proper full compensation you would still have broken faith with the tribe."[38] The issue of compensation brought into sharp focus the conflict between notions of individual and group forms of ownership. The integrity of "tribal lands" was the very foundation of the colonial concept of Native Reserves. The amendment of the Native Lands Trust Ordinance gave miners free rein in the reserves, stripping the local population of the land rights and safeguards bestowed on them by the ordinance.

A large body of scholarship on the history of mining in Africa has explored the arrival of mining companies and subsequent shifts in modes of production and labor practices.[39] As argued in the well-documented cases of southern Africa, labor migrancy and compound life led to new forms of male identity and shifts in familial structures through links back to the countryside. However, these studies say little about the effects of mining projects in densely populated areas and their effects on changing land strategies, and on African social life and political thought.

Until recently, the Kakamega gold rush figured only tangentially in studies of the industrial or high political developments surrounding this short-lived El Dorado.[40] While Priscilla Shilaro's recent study represents the first comprehensive account of British policymaking and industrial developments, it unfortunately misses an opportunity for a rich local history.[41] Projecting back an ethnic unity in North Kavirondo allowed these authors to make definitive statements on the "Luyia indigenous economy" before this political community had even been named and to neglect the more nuanced and long-lasting social and intellectual effects of the gold rush.[42] The most dramatic impacts of the gold rush came not from its industrial implications but rather manifested in its interjection into the longer history of political thought and territorial imaginings of community in western Kenya.

Initial responses to the gold rush exposed the weakness of district-wide African organizations. The colonial government bypassed the LNC and the local land board where mining was concerned, in open defiance of the Native Lands Trust Ordinance: in the words of Chief Native Commissioner Armigel V. de Wade, it would be "a farce" to consult these advisory bodies; since "it is pretty sure that they are going to disagree if they are consulted, why consult them?"[43] The first petition against

SENSATIONAL FIND OF OLD IRON AT KENYA.   *(Copyright in all countries.)*

FIGURE 2.2. Gold rush cartoon. *Evening Standard*, 9 February 1933.

gold mining penned by the Kavirondo Taxpayers' Welfare Association (KTWA) was easily dismissed by the Colonial Office, who pointed out that the signatories were not from the affected area, being a Luo-dominated organization, and were therefore unqualified to speak for others in the province.[44] Later politicians from adjoining locations in North Kavirondo would receive the same dismissive treatment. For the colonial government, the question of gold extraction was one of individual land rights and compensation. Districtwide organization as yet had little currency with the government or among local communities.

The gold rush led to a new wave of mapping in the district, both more intimate and more intrusive. The first "evil" of the gold rush according to the district commissioner was that of "blind pegging."[45] The process of pegging included the staking out of pieces of land with wooden pegs to enclose the space where prospectors would examine reefs for their gold-bearing potential. Pegged-off areas, usually measuring around six hundred by three hundred feet, dotted the landscape as miners furiously competed to stake their claims. Miners also used pegs and beacons to surround trenches and prospecting pits that further ripped into the land. In the words of the Kakamega district officer, "Daily, hills and ridges are being so covered, and all this is right among the natives' *bomas* and *shambas*."[46]

As already illustrated, pegging was a common technology of acquisition and alienation in colonial mapping and often implied more than the mere plotting of territory. Colonial surveyors, railways, and mission stations all used pegs to delineate excisable spaces.[47] In 1924, FAM missionaries complained to the commissioner of lands of the countermapping strategies used by local inhabitants to contest the appropriation of their lands: the pegs FAM used to demarcate their missions stations were "easily . . . lifted out of the ground and carried off by natives."[48] In 1927, the chief native commissioner ordered that the survey pegs used to carve out the limits of the Native Reserves should be reinforced with stone cairns erected in contiguity with each peg on the reserve side of the boundary. Not only would cairns provide a more "conspicuous" and permanent boundary, they would also "lessen the risk of displacement of the peg."[49] These tools of land surveyors were often the target of sabotage and spatial reorganization (see chapter 1). Pegs, in their impermanent and movable form, were particularly susceptible to territorial strategies of resistance.

On the eve of the gold rush, the district had already witnessed a shift from indirect colonial influence to a more interventionist agricultural policy.[50] State compulsion had dramatically increased the land under cultivation through clearing bush lands and included extensive trenching to prevent soil erosion. For many African farmers, mining trenches symbolized the physical cutting off of landholdings and thus further provoked fears of land alienation. Prospectors dug trenches up to forty feet deep along prospective reefs, with only "a few shillings" paid in compensation to the local populations affected.[51] Lord Lugard described the region as "over-run by Europeans digging enormous pits and trenches all over the place, among the villages and in the cultivation, and pegging out the whole countryside as an earnest of future operations."[52] The haphazard, extensive, and "blind" manner in which individual European miners pegged off claims and dug trenches became the main focus of early resistance.

COUNTERMAPPING THE MINERS: UPROOTING PEGS AND DEBATING MORALITY

In its earliest forms, resistance to mining reflected the threat posed not only to individual land rights but also to moral communities. Concerns over pegging and the moral corruption of local communities manifested in countermapping resistance strategies and gendered discourses of corruption and civility.

Early responses to miners were spontaneous, confrontational, and based on household defense. Blind pegging incited the suspicions of local communities as the uninhibited marking of their land bore striking resemblance to British mapping operations that had effectively redistributed land in the past. Resistance to pegging and the digging of trenches emerged in stages. First, farmers refused miners access to their land and resisted pegging operations. In one instance early in 1932, a young girl attacked a European miner with a pole after he struck her father for refusing to allow the miner into his property.[53] Interference with pegging operations often resulted in the administration withholding the meager compensation offered for the disturbed land.[54] The second stage of resistance involved the strategic planting of crops to restrict pegging or at least demand compensation for any lost crops. These cultivation strategies echoed earlier strategic cropping practices during border disputes and anti-Wanga campaigns. And last, the outright removal of pegs provided the most persistent, and most prosecuted, form of resistance. In August 1932 the first of such clashes made it to the court system, with many Isukha, Idakho, and Logoli imprisoned for short sentences for the removal of pegs.[55] Throughout the 1930s, intelligence reports were replete with cases of pegs being pulled up in the mining areas.[56]

Uprooting pegs, whether of surveyors or miners, was not an entirely novel countermapping strategy. In studying precolonial land tenure practices, Wagner pointed out that, among the Logoli, a man announced his intention to cultivate a particular plot by setting ablaze a number of trees surrounding the area and staking off the area with poles or sticks.[57] These poles then served as symbols of landownership and "if someone else thought he had a prior claim he would remove the markings."[58] The competing land claims would then be taken to the clan elders, the older claim gaining recognition if it could be proven through witnesses. For the Logoli, uprooting the pegs of miners was a political action taken to declare prior claims to the land.

The solution offered by the colonial administration was to support the militarization of pegging. They provided miners with askaris, local soldiers, to "explain compensation." The chief native commissioner translated and circulated a pamphlet on mining in the reserves specifically targeting the question of pegs: "Why do people put pegs in?"[59] Miners replaced wooden pegs with more permanent stone markers, just as surveyors had reinforced boundary pegs with cairns. In 1933 miners discussed organizing themselves more formally "for self defense," and proposed the formation of a local unit of the Kenya Defence Force.[60] As gold deposits quickly depleted, the effects of prospecting and pegging proved to be more invasive and detrimental than the actual mining of gold.

The rapid arrival of white prospectors also raised moral concerns about the effects of industrialization on the local population. Kenda Mutongi has written evocatively on the dramatic "social impact" of the gold rush in Maragoli, placing its effects within a longer narrative of religious conversion, conflict between converts and "nonconverts," and the influence of "secular civilization."[61] The Isukha and the Idakho in the most immediate mining areas staunchly refused contract labor in the mines, furiously battling to protect their land. Some credited Catholic influence in Idakho and Isukha with sheltering local populations from the lures of mining and political activism alike.[62] Their Logoli neighbors, on the other hand, went to the mines by the thousands. Mining offered Logoli men, 50 percent of whom spent most of their time engaged in labor contracts outside the district, with relatively highly paid labor positions closer to home. Logoli mineworkers exercised multiple means of negotiation, from labor freeze-outs to seasonal contracts built around harvest times. The Kenya Mining Association responded to this chronic labor instability by petitioning to import laborers from elsewhere. FAM missionaries and their Logoli converts, who dominated the mining areas, began strategically positioning church services in the mining compounds, preaching in Kiswahili to reach the "workmen of many different tribes."[63]

Labor opportunities threatened the control of fathers and of missionaries over young men who sought monetary gains in the mines. Nonconverts flaunted their new consumer goods—Vaseline and enamel cups—bought with the gains earned working in the mines while FAM converts mocked nonconverts for their inappropriate and unmannered "use of the goods of civilization."[64] Local market vendors increased the price of their wares for these new consumers, both European and African.[65] FAM missionaries lamented, "The average African cannot see the evil that is being brought into their midst by this so called civilization, but many of our church people do see it and grieve over the changed conditions."[66] FAM witnessed a dramatic decline in its membership during these years, as breakaways and "backsliders" left the church. The inability of the missions to adequately address these moral concerns would, later in the decade, open space for new African organizations to claim the mantle of moral custodianship in the district.

Many expressed concerns over the moral implications of mining and increased white settlement in the district in gendered terms. Elders complained at a 1933 baraza that women should not be allowed to work or reside in the mining camps for fear of moral corruption.[67] The KTWA voiced early concerns, in resolutions later published in the British press, over the corruption not only "of personal morality but also valuable native custom."[68] Ezekiel Apindi petitioned the House of Commons that the influx of Europeans would cause the breakdown of "our tribal life. . . .

The old good customs and tradition inherited form our fore-fathers will perish. . . . We dread it most because in Africa bad Europeans does commits [sic] illicit acts of taking some of our girls and spoiling their good character thereby becoming bad women."[69] Two years later, a Jeanes School teacher from East Kakamega complained that settlers were trying to buy local women.[70]

A common pairing, the arrival of mining projects increased such charges of prostitution in the southern locations of North Kavirondo. Local leaders depicted prostitutes as foreign, morally dangerous, and criminally inclined, imported along with migrant laborers, particularly from among the Nandi.[71] Since the early years of colonial rule, female pastoralists, and Nandi women in particular, were singled out as the first "prostitutes," their mobility and position near towns giving them access to wider markets and new forms of employment. As early as 1909, travelers "noted that Nandi 'women were notorious from Mombasa to Kisumu,' and that many were prostitutes in Nairobi."[72] Nandi women in North Kavirondo were regularly accused of spreading "disease and corrupting the local youth of both Sexes" in the district.[73] By 1933 members of the LNC debated means for expelling the "alien women" accused of prostitution from the district.[74] These kinds of rumors and accusations reflected multiple threads in local political thought: the work of comparative patriotisms, the demographic work of moral communities, and the increasingly gendered and ethnic language of social control.

The colonial government, too, worried about the type of European influence that the miners brought. As early as January 1932, the district commissioner of Kakamega issued a warning to all European prospectors:

> Rumours have reached me that certain advances have been made to Local Girls. I would warn any one who thinks he has come to such a friendly agreement that the native of these parts is an expert at Blackmail. . . . I need hardly say in what an awkward position a European would be placed if such a charge were brought against him, and how difficult it would be, form the very nature of the case to defend himself successfully. Further, in all probability, the case would have to go to the Supreme Court for Trial.[75]

A flurry of correspondence between the Colonial Office and administrators in Kenya worried over the uncontrolled and sudden influx of "undesirable" Europeans, floating throughout the district with no formal settlement.[76] Colonial officials attempted to legalize the expulsion of "undesirable" Europeans from the goldfields and on at least one occasion ordered the removal of a compensation assessor from the province due to his cohabitation with "prostitutes."[77] Chief Mulama expressed a fear of "half castes" as part of a moralizing discourse and general panic over sexual discipline and demographic control emerging in this period.[78] These moral anxieties, argued in gendered, racial, and religious terms, emerged as the discovery of gold threatened the stability of the household both physically on the ground and morally on familial controls over the behavior of young men and women.

Resistance to pegging and concerns over moral corruption mapped new geographies of conflict and community in western Kenya. European miners appeared to be shrinking the space of African land rights through progressively intrusive measures and threatening not only Africans' livelihoods but also their control over their households. Although these early forms of personalized resistance continued throughout the decade, the arrival of the Kenya Land Commission (KLC) under the direction of Sir Morris Carter in 1932 provided a forum for the expression of a new type of resistance, this time organized around the boundaries of the reserve. As in earlier conflicts over authority, localized political resistance provided the fuel for political leaders to demand a remapping of political community.

KENYA LAND COMMISSION: MAPPING THE TRIBE

At a meeting of the North Kavirondo LNC a year before the arrival of the KLC, Chief Murunga of the Bukusu locations demanded from the acting chief native commissioner a "map" to be "framed and put up" on the wall that would say, in the words of fellow councillor John Omandu, "The land is ours," the "property of the natives for ever."[79] In 1931 emerging political actors Paul Agoi and Lumadede Kisala argued that the Native Land Trust Ordinance had given them "complete possession of the land within the gazetted boundaries."[80] Subsequent meetings all echoed this call for a map, to be framed and hung on the walls of the council to prove their ownership of the land. In May 1933, a year after the KLC visited North Kavirondo, colonial officials handed Chief Murunga a tin case packed with a series of maps and typed descriptions of the boundaries to keep on behalf of the LNC.[81]

This obsession with getting a "map" marked a shift in the geographic imaginings of community and power. The amending of the Native Lands Trust Ordinance effectively destroyed the sanctity of native land tenure in the entire reserve and rolled back the imagined frontiers of African lands in western Kenya. For members of the LNC, the "map" would make legible their claims to land, to sovereignty, and to a legitimate political community. With the arrival of the KLC, in September 1932, local politicians opted to stop fighting the colonial map and instead embrace it, transforming the map from tool of colonial control into a tool with which to defend their political communities. Through the map, the communities of western Kenya would become a "tribe."

The KLC was given the specific mandate of reviewing "the working of the Native Lands Trust Ordinance, 1930."[82] The gold rush was the most immediate "administrative difficulty" the KLC had to contend with in the assessment of the ordinance. The commission was also charged with defining the boundaries of the White Highlands. These two concerns, of incoming miners and of encroaching white settlers, provided political leaders in North Kavirondo with a common set of grievances. When read alongside the testimony of the NLTC of 1930, the evidence given by North Kavirondo representatives revealed the profound effects of the gold rush on local political thought and the mapping of political communities.

The inhabitants of North Kavirondo gave surprisingly little evidence before this itinerant theater, especially as compared to the lengthy testimonies given before the NLTC and the voluminous testimonies given by other communities throughout Kenya. However, voices from North Kavirondo were not silent; rather, North Kavirondo representatives before the KLC altered and consolidated their diverse agendas. Although a scattering of individuals and missions presented memorandums, the most striking and succinct evidence was given by a selection of LNC members at Mumias on 12 September 1932.[83] With very little dissension, the LNC selected many of the same speakers who had given testimony to the NLTC "to speak on behalf of the tribe": Chief Mulama, Chief Sore, Canon Jeremiah Awori, Dominiko Muzulu, Paul Agoi, and Lumadede Kisala.[84] After their verbose and detailed defenses of autonomous, plural, and decentralized political communities before the NLTC, these six men now stood in front of the KLC and declared themselves representatives of "the tribe." This tribe, as yet unnamed, found its genesis in the defense of a mapped territory before the KLC.

In front of the KLC, North Kavirondo representatives seemed unconcerned with detailing land tenure practices and defending individual land rights. Indeed, all North Kavirondo representatives argued against private or individual land registration. While Fiona Mackenzie has found that Kikuyu representatives defended their claims through "genealogical depth" and detailed accounts of the "transgenerational transmission of lands," North Kavirondo representatives made no attempt to call up lineages or clan traditions to justify landownership, as they had before the NLTC.[85] Indeed, it was only North Kavirondo district commissioner C. B.

Thompson who provided detailed lineages and migrational histories before the commission. Instead, the disparate Bukusu, Wanga, Logoli, and other representatives made repeated references to "our country," "our people," and "our land," naturalizing the territorial space of the entire district as "ours" and thereby suppressing internal divisions, competition over resources, and plural political practices.

The gold rush had revealed the necessity of imagining themselves as representatives of a territorial whole, of defending the "Native Reserve" against the arbitrary amendments of British bureaucrats and invasions of white miners. The boundaries of the Native Reserves delimited more than just territory: they served as colonial markers of ethnic homogeneity, spaces that determined land rights, political authority, and customary practices. The discovery of gold in North Kavirondo reversed African land rights in the Native Reserves, undermined colonial calls to benevolent trusteeship, and prompted political actors to enlarge the territorial limits of their imagined political communities.

The limits of the Native Reserve provided a new "we," a "tribe" for which North Kavirondo representatives could speak. Chief Sore of East Kakamega called on the colonial government to "cut the dog" and pronounce the boundaries of their "whole" territory. This precolonial oath, called *okulya imbwa* among the Logoli, included a ceremony in which warring communities speared a live dog to seal a peace: the "enmity between them was supposed to pass out and die away in the same way as the cries emitted by the dog."[86] In front of the KLC, Sore reconfigured the kinship strategies of oathing to secure the land of the entire reserve. Chief Mulama similarly demanded a "guarantee of our frontier," not through individual titles but rather through a title deed "for the whole of our land." North Kavirondo representatives petitioned the colonial government for a deed to their territory much as members of the Progressive Kikuyu Party asked for "title deeds for the whole country of the Gikuyu and for a 'line' to be drawn around the whole Gikuyu country."[87] Without any warring parties, North Kavirondo representatives were actually more successful than Kikuyu petitioners in consolidating their claims to territorial remapping. North Kavirondo representatives kept the proceedings free from individual or locational land disputes, or even conflicts with their Luo and Kalenjin neighbors, instead narrowly focusing on drawing boundaries between their constituents and European miners and settlers.

To map the frontier of this new political community, representatives consolidated their land claims around the extreme limits of the district: land alienation in the mining areas of the south and the "lost" expansion land in the north. The pegs and beacons first of surveyors and then of miners prompted local populations to understand these symbols as markers of landownership, as the necessary step "before a map could be mapped." When Chief Murunga demanded a "title deed of the reserve," in May 1932, Reverend Jeremiah Awori explained that it was the result of the "fear of losing their lands" prompted by the beacons that now appeared within, and not just around, the reserve.[88] Before the KLC, Lumadede Kisala reiterated this fear of continued land loss in the south: "We are afraid, when we see the pegs set out by the miners, that our land will be taken."[89] The encroachment of European settler farms in the south, around Kaimosi, provided further proof of the compression of the Native Reserve.

In the north, the central issue was lost lands in the Kipkarren and Kamakoiya areas of the Trans Nzoia. The Kamakoiya River, "well-marked and well-known to everyone," served as a convenient "natural" boundary for colonial mappings of the North Kavirondo Reserve.[90] Many representatives told of the compression of the northern frontier after the arrival of white settlers following World War I, which rendered many of the local inhabitants squatters on their own land.[91] Chief Mulama reported that "before the Kipkarren farms were given out there was a man called Kakai who was a headman there. He is there still, as a squatter." Mulama called for a new frontier with "the Europeans": in the northern expanses "we never made any agreement to set a boundary with the Europeans." Chief Mulupi echoed these calls that the Kipkarren farms had never been formally demarcated: Mulupi had "no recollection of a surveyor coming . . . nor do I remember the Elders of Kabras being called to discuss the boundary." North Kavirondo representatives constricted their land claims to cognitively map this new political community along the borders of the reserve, to defend against the encroachment of miners and white settlers, and to roll back the frontier of this mapped territory.

The "map" thus provided consolidators with legible proof of their political work: it justified their project to colonial commissioners while simultaneously encouraging constituents in North Kavirondo to expand their geographic imagination and to take ownership of a patriotic territory, framed and hung on the wall for all to see. This centralized discourse offered cultural brokers in North Kavirondo leverage over the European farmers and miners impinging on their land by consolidating a territorial "us" against foreign expropriators. North Kavirondo representatives echoed the strategy of the Nyeri Kikuyu representatives, whose petitions to the KLC "carefully delineated the boundaries of Gikuyu territory, rolling back white farmers' plantations in an onslaught of boundary-drawing."[92]

By not playing into parochial debates over clan lineages, North Kavirondo representatives pushed back against the encroachment of the White Highlands and mapped North Kavirondo as the rightful ethnic homeland of a tribe as yet unnamed but territorially distinct.

Moreover, representatives from North Kavirondo simultaneously participated in another form of mapping in front of the KLC: the mapping of a nation. As the KLC was tasked with defining the boundaries of the White Highlands, it prompted petitioners to defend their territories in racialized and ethnicized terms, reducing the nation to spheres of separate, territorially distinct communities. While the gold rush led local actors in North Kavirondo to imagine a larger polity on the district level, it also galvanized the first imaginings of a national identity delimited by colonial geographies. Common land grievances and colonywide protests against the amending of the Native Lands Trust Ordinance allowed for ethnic groups across the colony to imagine themselves as a collective of colonized people in one territory that extended from "the Coast to the Great Lake."[93] Paul Agoi eloquently testified that the "proper boundary of the Black man is Mombasa (i.e. the sea)."[94] This east-to-west spatial orientation mapped the geographic imagination of an emerging Kenyan nation through reference to its national contours in iconic natural landmarks: the coast and Lake Victoria. The rejection of a White Highlands carved out of this territorial expression tied disparate communities across the colony together. As the colonial government mapped increasingly racialized spaces of community in Kenya, local partisans began to argue for territorial nationalism alongside ethnic claims.

The unified front provided by North Kavirondo representatives strategically suppressed the internal debates of locational politics. Indeed, the KLC meeting at Mumias was delayed due to local unrest over questions of land tenure. The district commissioner reported that "small clans, fearing that the enquiry might establish them as tenants and not landlords, raised an outcry, and feverish counting of their numbers, designed to show their magnitude and importance, began in more than one location."[95] This type of population counting and census padding became a common strategy in the face of colonial policies of state simplification and resource competition. North Kavirondo representatives glossed over the question of landlord and tenant rights and strategically fought against individual titles, instead petitioning for "title deeds only . . . to guarantee the natives their tenure of the land. Internally only the boundaries between Chiefs required arrangement and demarcation."[96] Before the KLC, locational representatives presented a centralized political vision within the district to defend their own internally divergent interests.

The North Kavirondo administration pictured the KLC testimony as surprising and baseless, as "native claims to land were made which I never heard of before and . . . having no real grievances about land, they felt called to invent some."[97] In a certain sense, the administration was correct: the claims of the North Kavirondo representatives were indeed novel. However, the administration misinterpreted the process of "invention" that was in fact underway. Where the administration saw the invention of false land claims, North Kavirondo representatives invented claims to a larger ethnic territory based on the district boundaries colonial administrators had worked so diligently to define. In their representations to the KLC, these chiefs and headmen turned the colonial belief in larger tribal cohesion to their own advantage, forwarding themselves as the rightful spokesmen of a unified "tribe" and a patriotic territory.

&

THE GOLD rush sparked a territorial crisis for both British officials and local political actors at a crucial juncture in the history of political thought in western Kenya. The discovery of gold led to a transformation in the mapping—physical, legal, and moral—of political communities in North Kavirondo. The pegs of miners intruded into the households of farmers already busily mapping their landholdings in locational conflicts over resources, borders, and authority. But the discovery of gold also proved a "problem for *all*."[98] Just as campaigns against colonially imposed chiefs obliged clan heads to consolidate kinship networks and land tenure practices along locational lines, so too did the arrival of miners and the encroachment of white settlers prompt African thinkers to suppress their divergent locational interests and to map a new ethnic territory along the frontiers of the district.

In 1934, District Commissioner E. L. B. Anderson noted the inevitable influence of the gold rush on local political thought: it was "inevitable that in the course of time, individual resentment having subsided, politically minded individuals should organize opposition on general grounds."[99] In adopting the map as symbol of the "tribe," political thinkers in North Kavirondo made a patriotic investment in the territorial idea. These "general grounds" provided the basis for the formation of the North Kavirondo Central Association (NKCA), who began the political work of imagining an ethnic identity out of the multiple communities of North Kavirondo. The gold rush proved to be the "conspicuous event," to use Wagner's term, that gave birth to a new political community in western Kenya. Mapped both physically and cognitively as one territorially discrete people, this new political community went in search of a name, a past, and a moral community.

3 ⤚ Ethnic Patriotism in the Interwar Years

THE INTERWAR period in eastern Africa witnessed a dramatic surge in ethnic patriotisms.[1] The patriotic work of African entrepreneurs was comparative and political, but moreover it was competitive and geographic.[2] African patriots were busy in these years writing histories, cultivating local loyalties, and mapping homelands in a race that was by then not only ethnic but also, in nascent form, nationalist.

Across Kenya, African communities used shared names to call each other to account and draw each other in line. Through shared names, the Gusii and the Kikuyu invoked a common founding father, Mogusii and Agikuyu respectively, and thus a common past. For ethnic entrepreneurs in western Kenya, choosing a patriotic name was a deliberate and self-conscious process. Their name, Luyia, chosen by a select few who had succeeded where others had failed, reflected the detachment of naming from this genealogical emphasis and instead privileged a new geographic sensibility, a horizontal drawing together of discrete, autonomous clans into one discursive and political space. Later ethnic projects would follow suit, often employing names that worked to create a new political ethos of community out of kinship metaphors, as with the confederate naming of the Mijikenda, literally translated as "nine towns" or "nine homesteads," or the Kalenjin, whose name translated as "I say to you."[3] Through their naming, ethnic entrepreneurs in western Kenya called their constituents to gather around the oluhia, the communal fire, to discuss past victories, to debate contemporary concerns, and to imagine future communions.

After the Kenya Land Commission, a new sense of urgency and self-conscious competitiveness accompanied an increase in political activism. During the Kakamega gold rush, political thinkers in North Kavirondo had redrawn the territorial limits of political community to protect their land from the onslaughts of gold miners, British bureaucrats, and white settlers. In its wake, a group of young mission converts and teachers formed the North Kavirondo Central Association (NKCA) as an intellectual front for the patriotic work of building a new regional polity. Building on the geographic work of the KLC representatives, the NKCA reconfigured individual land claims in North Kavirondo into a defense of a patriotic territory and forwarded itself as the custodian of a moral community. The NKCA set about defining "our land," "our women," and "our rights" through petitions, court cases, and public displays. As the effects of the gold rush subsided, the NKCA attempted to peg its plural constituents to a territory through the creative work of naming and writing patriotic histories. As the colonial state extended its reach into the very soil of African lands, the NKCA engaged in comparative national work and integrated common experiences of compelled agricultural work and land dispossession to extend its reach throughout the district. Spurred by the enlarged political vision fostered by the gold rush, the early ethnic patriots of the NKCA worked to fill in this mapped geographic outline with a name, a history, and a political and moral ethos for a new ethnic community in colonial Kenya.

FROM WELFARE TO PATRIOTIC POLITICS

Though the gold rush exposed the impotence of districtwide bodies such as the LNC and the NKTWA, it also prompted the development of a new political ethos among political thinkers who called upon their disparate communities to envision themselves as members of a corporate body. After the bold testimony of more senior political figures before the KLC, young entrepreneurs in North Kavirondo took up the political work of territorial integration and ethnic imagining.

Rumblings of a new political organization began directly following the KLC near the end of 1932.[4] At first isolated, the new political voices of teachers, young administrators, and Christian converts converged in the southeastern locations around the mining areas.[5] In 1930, District Commissioner E. L. B. Anderson blamed internal conflicts and missionary shortages for creating a space "for politics to usurp the place of religion and for these 'schools' to become in some cases centers of sedition."[6] FAM's inability to provide moral and material defense against the gold rush prompted wide-scale desertion and a ready ground for political converts. These frustrated and educated young men formed the NKCA out of the political space created by the gold rush and the failure of local district bodies, be they missionary, administrative, or political. The NKCA's first president, Andrea Jumba, worked as a FAM schoolteacher and clerk to the chief in Tiriki, though his roots were in Idakho. Other prominent members, such as John Adala, Lumadede Kisala, and Moses Muhanga, shared similar biographies. These men represented the first in the district to take up the work of ethnic patriotism full-time, none holding any full-time employment during this period despite their education. By 1935 the NKCA listed four hundred members, mostly from the southern locations of Tiriki, Maragoli, Bunyore, Idakho, and Isukha, from which its leadership hailed.

Colonial administrators and missionaries feared the gold rush had opened a dangerous political space now filled not only by young "upstarts" but also by the increasing presence of "politically active" Kikuyu farmers from the Central Province. In June 1933 intelligence reports suspected numerous Logoli and Tiriki laborers of paying subscriptions of two shillings to a group of Kikuyu mineworkers in the hopes of getting "a document from King George!"[7] FAM missionaries worried about the "Africa for the African" movement brought "by the Kikuyu people who came up to work with the miners."[8] In the words of leading FAM missionary Jefferson W. Ford, Kikuyu influence had "invaded the Province . . . a number of our Elders and leaders had been caught by the subtleties of the movement, not knowing the hidden character of it."[9] While these charges reflected little more than speculation and paranoia on the part of missionaries and the administration, they did reveal the shifting tenor of local political thought.

Colonial administrators linked this Kikuyu influence to the political activities of the Kikuyu Central Association (KCA), who had only recently clashed with missionaries and the colonial government over female circumcision in the Central Province.[10] As argued in the previous chapter, the gold rush prompted African thinkers across the colony to remap ethnic and national identities. Indeed, the gold rush marked the first time that future nationalist leader Jomo Kenyatta would write about the struggles of an ethnic group in Kenya outside his own Kikuyu.[11] Administrators belittled the founders of the NKCA as "undoubtedly offspring of KCA."[12] In 1934 the warden of mines argued that the publication of the amendment to the Native Lands Trust Ordinance "appears to have effected a working agreement between the NKCA and the KCA."[13] And while these statements, too, reflected colonial exaggeration more than any concrete alliance, the KCA provided at the least a model, revealing the increasingly comparative nature of African patriotic work. Erasto Ligalaba, the NKCA's first secretary, worked with KCA members in Nairobi from whom he garnered organizational tips and strategies, as well as a template for the association's name.[14] Archival and oral sources revealed frequent dual membership and strong ties between the NKCA and the KCA.[15] If not full cooperation or coordination, the KCA at a minimum offered an exemplar for comparison, an early instance of the kind of patriotic work required in the new colonial political economy.

While colonial officials and missionaries worried over Kikuyu influence in the reserve, a new political ethos was beginning to take form on the roads between the reserve and urban centers. The leadership of the NKCA, epitomized in Ligalaba, heralded a "new phenomenon in Nyanzan politics," a new generation of urbanized, educated, traveled men.[16] Ligalaba had only recently returned to the district from Nairobi, where he had worked on the government Kiswahili newspaper *Habari* and the Indian newspaper *Democrat*. As John Spencer has found, "twenty-six out of thirty-three informants in North Kavirondo who identified themselves as former NKCA members" lived outside the district during much of their membership.[17] In 1933 the "Nairobi Committee" of the NKCA, comprising Andrea Jumba, John Adala, and Lumadede Kisala, collected 900 shillings from constituents in North Kavirondo and delivered the funds to Nairobi to help Kenyatta in England.[18] The main architects of this new political culture shared common experiences of teaching, missionary work, and migrant labor outside their home locations and revealed a new orientation and comparative thrust to the political and geographic imaginings of the interwar period.

THE NKCA: TERRITORIAL PATRIOTS AND MORAL CUSTODIANS

From this tentative debut, the NKCA embarked on a project of territorial defense and ethnic consolidation not unlike that of the KCA in the 1920s, forwarding itself as the moral custodians of a new polity.[19] The initial strategies of the NKCA worked to transform the sporadic and localized protest of African farmers against miners into a defense of a patriotic territory. Presenting themselves as territorial surveyors, NKCA members began coordinating protests against the use of pegs, concrete beacons, and open trenches.[20] The timing of the NKCA's emergence, at the end of 1932, was no coincidence: the testimony of North Kavirondo representatives before the KLC earlier in the year had provided a "tribe" and a patriotic territory for which this new association could claim the role of spokesmen.

Just as locational activists invoked the evidence given to the NLTC as legitimizing proof of clan land claims, the NKCA invoked the evidence recorded by the KLC as substantiating proof of their ethnic constituency in North Kavirondo. In one of their earliest petitions, Jumba and Adala presented the "Kavirondo Objections" to the conclusions of the KLC report.[21] In this petition the NKCA flaunted its mastery of colonial documentation by buttressing their arguments with specific page references from the published testimony. The petition included an enumerated list of land claims throughout the district, transforming disparate property battles fought in local courts into a defense of patriotic territory. The NKCA surveyed settlements and farms from south to north and demanded all land in the Native Reserve be native owned: no European farms should fall within the "sphere of the Native Reserve." NKCA petitioners provided their own comparative analysis of the evidence and outcomes of the NLTC and the KLC and accused colonial commissioners of ignoring the unifying KLC testimony in favor of the divisive politics of the earlier NLTC. Using specific annotated references from the KLC report, the NKCA "protested against the Land of our heritance which is reserved for us and our descendants being given to Europeans."[22] The NKCA coordinated territorial defense against miners and used documents like the KLC evidence to present themselves as the inheritors of a patriotic territory.

The NKCA also used the results of the KLC to introduce itself to potential supporters. At public barazas, NKCA leaders performed dramatic readings of the KLC evidence and final report for local audiences. Brandishing the third volume of the KLC evidence at an open baraza in East Kakamega to great theatrical effect, NKCA leader Moses Muhanga proclaimed that the volume revealed the colonial government's intention to evict property owners from the mining lease areas and relocate them to Elgon Forest.[23] Rumors of such a removal and resettlement circulated widely across the district.[24] Forest rights were a hotly contested issue in local politics as farmers pushed the boundaries of the reserve into bordering forests. In East Kakamega and North Maragoli, a local campaign arose to refuse compensation for gold mining in land from Kakamega Forest.[25] Peasant farmers, who had fought for control of their forests throughout the colonial period, refused to participate when the warden of mines held meetings with chiefs and elders to select forest areas for inclusion in the reserve.[26] Muhanga, a former clerk in the district commissioner's office, used the threat of resettlement in Elgon Forest not only to bring farmers in the south in line with their political campaigns but also to reach out northward to the distant populations around Mount Elgon who would be equally affected by a resettlement plan. As in front of the KLC, the new NKCA leaders used such public performances to map an imagined space of common cause through a new geographic sensibility.

The district commissioner accused the NKCA of a "campaign of deliberate distortion," of reading its own version of the KLC to mislead illiterate populations.[27] Indeed, the KLC had concluded that fifteen hundred acres from Mount Elgon Forest Reserve should be added to the North Kavirondo Reserve "to compensate for any surface land excluded for mining leases in the future."[28] However, the NKCA misrepresented this recommendation in its public performances to mean eviction and forced resettlement when in reality it provided only a meager general compensation for lost lands. These performances proved effective: after such meetings in 1933 and 1934, the NKCA collected numerous subscriptions and increased its membership dramatically. As a result of the NKCA's vocal criticisms of the KLC report, the district commissioner in 1935 ordered chiefs to make the collection of funds by the association illegal.[29]

On 5 January 1936, a colonial court convicted five members of the NKCA for the illegal collection of subscriptions: Andrea Jumba, Reuben Muhati, Mudi Lisudza, Lumadede Kisala, and John Adala. Although the Supreme Court overturned the charges, the imprisonment of the NKCA leaders laid the foundation for "the association's mythical charter of origin."[30] While conducting research in western Kenya in 1965, John Lonsdale recorded this commonly circulated version of the NKCA's myth of origin:

> The district commissioners wished to impress the NKCA with British power, and so arranged for an aeroplane to make mock dive-bombing runs over Kakamega prison. The plane crashed and the European pilot was killed. The commissioner ordered their fellow prisoners to bury Jumba and Lumadede alive in the pilot's grave. Only by dancing on top of the growing pile of earth did the two escape; the disheartened commissioner then released them.[31]

Lonsdale traced the myth to a fatal airplane crash at Rosterman Gold Mines, which caused the deaths of the pilot and gold miner H. Bunting, who had been performing an aerial display for a European wedding party.[32] Most striking in this myth was the combination of modern symbols of resistance with biblical imagery. Planes often figured prominently in narratives of oppression and resistance in colonial Kenya. Lonsdale pointed to a similar event among the Nandi, when the government used an aerial assault with bags of flour at a baraza to warn Nandi prophets against their recent agitations.[33] The NKCA's myth of origin was further enriched with vivid biblical imagery: imprisonment, burial, and rebirth, themes found in stories like those of Shadrach, Meshach, and Abednego. The NKCA often used biblical imagery in their petitions and rallies, drawing upon a ready repository of narratives and parables to claim moral authority over the land and its people.

The "reborn" NKCA leaders used their newfound notoriety to promote themselves as the adjudicators of a moral community. In petitions and at public meetings, NKCA leaders began speaking about "our land," "our women," and "our rights." The novel innovation here was the call to a specifically ethnic and territorial "ours." In a petition to the colonial secretary, the NKCA presented the demands of European miners on their resources not as individual concerns but as a threat to the reproduction of their imagined people: miners would "take away or divide the water and various other matters connected therewith which would mean dragging us and our cattle etc. into starvation and ultimate death."[34] The colonial government worried the NKCA was gaining traction as the "new middlemen" in representing local grievances.[35] As the originators of a new ethnic community with their own story of oppression and rebirth, the NKCA presented itself as the rightful mouthpiece for the voicing of injustices and the birthing of a new nation.

In the courts, the NKCA filed numerous cases acting as the legal representatives of a corporate body. The NKCA took up the highly emotive question of compensation for life lost in the mines. Idakho and Isukha laborers spoke of underground minework as a "death trap."[36] Deaths in the mines led to spontaneous demonstrations often instigated when local women stormed mining compounds and demanded the right to bury their husbands and sons. The colonial administration responded by imprisoning the protesters for trespassing.[37] As deaths in the mines led to increasingly confrontational demonstrations, the NKCA brought forward numerous cases of compensation for mining accidents to local courts.[38] The NKCA openly questioned why in the case of death during mining operations, the mourning European family received 18,000 shillings, while the heirs of a native laborer killed in the mines received only 380 shillings.[39] Compensation, the district commissioner responded, was the equivalent of three years' wages and thus determined by the color bar. Compensation, both for land and life, reflected the rising tensions between European miners and local populations, fought increasingly in moral and racial terms. The official response to these cases was to demand by what authority the NKCA interjected into private family matters. Indeed, the NKCA did assume the right to present cases, at times without the consent of the families in question, that would in more traditional course have been handled by the elders of the deceased's clan. For the NKCA, those killed were not solely members of a family or the clan networks that still dominated local communal identities but moreover lost sons of a larger community.

The NKCA also took up the moral protest against the corruption of women witnessed during the gold rush and the danger these sexual politics posed for the social reproduction of its imagined community. The NKCA forwarded itself as the defenders of female virtue by bringing legal cases before local courts. In 1938, NKCA president Andrea Jumba stood before the district commissioner and charged a European miner with raping and impregnating a Tiriki girl.[40] The commissioner dismissed the charges on the grounds that there had never been a case of a "white raping a black, as the latter were usually willing to perform if paid" and suggested they "wait until the child is born and its colour seen." This unsatisfactory answer elicited countercharges of prostitution from the NKCA and demands of the moral obligations traditionally imposed when sex of any kind led to progeny. Matters of rape and children would traditionally have been handled within the family or extended kinship network, as they entailed issues of possible dowry refunds, custody of children, and the future marriage of the women in question.[41] Although still in its formative days, the control of women and their sexuality would become an increasingly central platform for ethnic patriotic work, as will be seen in later chapters. In filing these legal cases, the NKCA tentatively, and not without controversy, forwarded itself as the rightful legal adjudicators of a moral community, transforming private matters over land, women, and death into public patriotic concerns of territory, morality, and social reproduction.

THE POLITICS OF A NAME:
FROM KAVIRONDO TO LUYIA

As the immediate threats of the gold rush markedly declined from 1936, the NKCA set about the intellectual work of casting for their people a name and a past. Comparative patriotic work compelled NKCA leaders to call their constituents by name and in doing so draw them in line. This project necessitated a creative process of appropriation, consolidation, and reinvention—of history and of belonging.

From the outset of colonial contact, geographers and administrators struggled to name the stubbornly diverse peoples of western Kenya. In 1923 the provincial commissioner of Nyanza lamented the difficulty of finding a "name" for a people who spoke such "widely differing dialects of the same language."[42] The administration "promiscuously" named those resident in the district "Bantu of Kavirondo . . . for lack of a better term."[43] The term Kavirondo invoked a specific geographic history (see chapter 1), first appearing as a vague and distant mapped frontier on European maps near the end of the 1870s.[44] But locally, the term's origins and meanings proved subject to debate and adaptive to different historical currents. In 1928 the *East African Standard* ran a series of correspondence on the origin of Kavirondo and its various Luo and Bantu applications in western Kenya.[45] In the standard narrative, Arab and Swahili traders applied the term to the inhabitants they encountered around Lake Victoria. Makerere graduate A. J. Oyugi wrote an elaborate tale in the *Makerere Journal* linking the term to military instructions shouted by Mumia's forces and misinterpreted by Arab gun traders.[46] Howard Elphinstone, known for his work on Kiswahili, similarly argued the term most likely derived from the Luhanga word *murondo*, the sound of a rifle.[47] While translations varied according to the root language and the nature of the encounter in which the term emerged, these shifting ethnonyms revealed the deeply political history of naming practices in the region.

The two more common translations of the term, one often spoken and the other whispered in historical corners, revealed the gendered and moralizing readings of this colonial ethnonym. Oral narratives commonly located its origin in the Kiswahili term *rondo*, meaning the "heel," and translated Kavirondo as the people who "squatted on their heels." Many elders linked this term dismissively with the women in Kisumu who "squatted" along roads and in marketplaces. In 1966, Osogo recounted that "Nyanza women . . . both Luo and Baluyia, have a habit of sitting on their heels after putting both knees on the ground."[48] This gendered reading pictured "Kavirondo" as uncivilized, unmannered, and unmasculine.

In another less common translation, to be Kavirondo was to be uncircumcised. In her study of women in colonial Kenya, Tabitha Kanogo argued that in central Kenya, Kavirondo meant "the other," uncircumcised males who in Kikuyu culture represented a dangerous "other" outside social community control.[49] In 1946, E. V. Hippel wrote to the *Uganda Journal* that while Kavirondo had many meanings, it also contained "a second (hidden) meaning . . . that these inhabitants . . . do not practice circumcision."[50] When he asked uncircumcised Luo men about this translation, "their usual reaction has been a sheepish grin." Although male circumcision was far from universal, this usage would have deeply offended the honor and masculinity of many of the Bantu and Kalenjin communities in North Kavirondo.

In all these translations, Kavirondo was a foreign term, variously un-mannered, emasculating, and disempowering for the diverse communities of the region. The "origins" of Kavirondo, however defined, were distinctly rooted in this colonial encounter. The name Kavirondo itself presented a moral problem. In a rare demonstration of unity, local councillors from all the disparate communities represented in the colonial epithet Bantu of Kavirondo rejected the term and campaigned for a locally articulated name.

The campaign to abolish the Kavirondo name prompted heated debates over the selection of a new corporate name that revealed a dramatic shift in the political ethos of naming in the interwar period. District Commissioner Thompson viewed this movement as an assertive process by the largely Bantu communities of North Kavirondo to differentiate themselves from their Luo neighbors: "The point raised appeared to be that as their Nilotic brethren had a generic term Luo by which to call themselves, it behooved the Bantu to exhume from the past, or invent for the future, a name for themselves too."[51] The naming of political communities was always a complex and imaginative process. In 1931 a Banyore petition demanded their recognition "in name as well as in fact," as part of their anti-Wanga campaign against Chief Mulama.[52] Among the larger communities, such as the Logoli, the Wanga, and the Bukusu, naming derived from a founding father who had given birth to a new line of descendants. Although some argued this was the norm across the district, naming was a much more complicated process, particularly in the colonial era. Group names just as often referred to geographic relations and important features in the landscape (see chapter 1). Naming thus served as a crucial ground on which geographic and political imaginations of community and kinship were defined and debated.

In 1929 the NKTWA met to discuss replacing the contemptuous Kavirondo label and debate the relative value of alternative terms. The first suggested term, Abakwe, meaning the people of the east, raised obvious questions about the geographic orientation of this project and privileged the southeastern politicians that dominated the association: this option was abandoned early.[53] The most frequent proposal was Abalimi, derived from a common term for agriculturalist, cultivator, or later, "common peasant."[54] The first grammar book produced for the district qualified its translation of lima as "to dig," with the explanatory note that "the cultivation of the fields is a woman's work and responsibility and pride."[55] Communities throughout the district, however, differed on the relative importance of cultivation to their livelihoods and many found the term derogatory or even a term of "reproach" in its reference to the work of women.[56] With the NKTWA in serious disarray by this point, the issue of naming the communities of North Kavirondo remained dormant until the gold rush prompted local thinkers to imagine a new community out of the North Kavirondo map.

After the gold rush the NKCA seized the opportunity to be the originators of a name that would unite its constituents, present, future, and even past. In early 1935 the NKCA published a pamphlet entitled *Abaluhya—Kinship* and announced its candidate for a name.[57] In this pamphlet, the NKCA outlined the historical origins of this "kinship" and named the people of North Kavirondo "Luyia."[58] The term Luyia had appeared earlier in an NKTWA-published magazine entitled *Omulina wa Valuhya* (Friend of the Luhya). However, evidence of its use in this short-lived publication is limited, and the NKTWA likely used the term in its more literal translation of a council of elders or meeting place rather than as an ethnic appellation.[59] The term Luyia did not gain wide currency as an ethnic name until the publication of the NKCA's pamphlet. In this pamphlet, Andrea Jumba used his notorious proverbial flair to argue for integration:

> The father wanted to help his children to live happily. One day he called them all together. He gave a stick to each one and asked each one to break his stick. He again collected ten sticks of the same size as he had given to each child. He tied them together and asked the eldest boy to try and break them as he had broken the one he had at first. He tried but in vain. . . . Think about it yourselves.[60]

The Luyia name provided just such a string, tying together the disparate sticks of communities in North Kavirondo.

Although its meaning shifted over time, the NKCA evoked the term Luyia to reimagine kinship metaphors of community. In its most common usage the term *oluhia* referred to the "fire-place on a meadow," where the "old men of the clan community meet every morning."[61] In Günter Wagner's assessment, the "oluhia" served as an important communal site for political negotiations, initiation rituals, and the burial of clan heads.[62] Within the *Abaluhya—Kinship* pamphlet, NKCA writers reconfigured this space of public meeting as an appellation of common kinship. In 1949 prominent politician Philip Ingutia defined the word Abaluyia as the plural form of Omuluyia, meaning "a member of the clan . . . so the word Abaluyia, means the people of one clan or the same origin."[63] Luyia historian John Osogo, writing in the 1960s, defined Abaluyia as "fellow tribesmen," and as the oldest and most important of local customs. Thus,

Osogo asserted, "It is understandable . . . how the name *oluyia* came to mean tribe, especially as it was a common practice for people to ask, 'to which *oluyia* do you belong?'—meaning to which fire."[64] The oluyia so defined represented a physical location, posited at the "centre of the public life of the clan,"—a space where problems common to all were brought, discussed, and decided upon around the fire.[65]

Appropriating the term Luyia invoked the symbolic value attached to the precolonial locus of power and communion within the public sphere. In the nineteenth century the diverse communities of western Kenya organized their social and political relations heterarchically, allowing for multiple nodes of power and identification. Many elders and chiefs viewed the choice of this term as an affront to their power, an "assertive appellation" by the young, mission-educated NKCA leaders of their right to rule.[66] The emerging dual elite in the rural areas was a common trope in the colonial history of African polities.[67] Provincial Commissioner Sidney Fazan later recalled a heated discussion with several chiefs who warned "forcibly" against the use of the term Luyia, as it was "fraught with political import."[68] Debates in the LNC erupted in fierce shouting matches.[69] Some pointed to the "fatuity" of using a word that basically translated as clan to refer to groups that often intermarried. In meetings of the North Kavirondo LNC, councillors argued that no one term would be acceptable to all members and that an "entirely non-tribal word must be looked for."[70] Echoing the "radical rudeness" that Carol Summers has identified in the young Bataka Union activists of Buganda—who similarly reworked "the idea of *bataka* from a hierarchical collection of elders' clan leadership into something close to a concept of universal citizenship"—the young men of the NKCA noisily disrupted the traditional order of things and appropriated the term Luyia to claim authority and reconfigure kinship ideologies for their larger patriotic project.[71]

The choice of this name reflected a broader trend in the changing practices of naming under colonial rule and the thoroughly self-conscious patriotic work of the interwar period. Unlike Kikuyu, Luo, or Gusii cultural entrepreneurs who drew their constituents in direct descent from a mythic founding father, NKCA writers detached the name of this new ethnic identity from any founding father and instead privileged a horizontal drawing together of disparate, autonomous clans into one discursive and political space. Later ethnic projects would follow suit. The Mijikenda would, in the 1940s, chose a name that reflected a similar corporate impulse, though still reflecting an idiom of kinship.[72] Ethnic entrepreneurs along the coast chose their name with "the intention of uniting our tribes and bringing back the KINSHIP which existed in the time of our forefathers."[73] For the Kalenjin, naming revealed the centrality of an oral culture that would also prove crucial to Luyia ethnic imaginings. The name Kalenjin, popularized through radio broadcasts in the 1940s, literally called their constituent communities together by hailing, "I say to you."[74] While naming still reflected calls to tradition, kinship metaphors, and sites of power, the innovation in this period was the shifting of naming away from descent and genealogical depth and toward terms that obligated members within a discourse of place and communal belonging. For the NKCA, the Luyia ethnonym evoked a political ethos of heterarchical social and political relations joined together through a common appellation not only to kinship but moreover to space.

The Luyia name gained common currency throughout the 1930s. The NKCA relentlessly promoted its Luyia name, not waiting for official sanction by the colonial government or the LNC to insert the term into its petitions, organizational names, and public meetings. At a meeting of the KTWA in 1939, Paul Agoi and NKCA secretary John Adala led the vote to remove Kavirondo from the organization's name in favor of the "Luo-Abaluhiah Welfare Association."[75] Despite heated debates, in 1942 the North Kavirondo LNC voted to officially adopt Luyia, the term narrowly defeating Abalimi in a vote of twenty-three to twenty-two.[76] The closeness of this vote revealed yet again the tense, dissenting landscape of political thought across district, despite the seemingly unifying effects of the gold rush. The term seemed particularly unfavorable to Bukusu representatives, who lived on the periphery of the Luyia project at this moment and were wary of political domination from the south.[77] Despite Bukusu resistance and the objections of many elders, the energies and political work of NKCA members made the choice of a name appear predetermined. As mapped by KLC representatives and NKCA members, the people of North Kavirondo now had a name.

For Bethwell Ogot, the NKCA pamphlet marked the beginning of Luyia cultural nationalism and the "invention of the imagined Greater Luyia Community."[78] As a text of cultural nationalism, Ogot posited this pamphlet not only within the history of the Luyia people but also within the larger "untold story" of Kenyan nationalism. This pamphlet reflected the social and political work of cultural entrepreneurs in the interwar period and a new geographic imagination. John Nottingham and Carl Rosberg have located this pamphlet within a distinct political project, its role to publicize the existence of the Luyia while simultaneously inventing it in name.[79] The naming of the "Luyia" through this pamphlet marked a moment of genesis, of becoming, for the Luyia as a "tribe."

Alongside their promotion of the Luyia name, NKCA thinkers embarked on the cultural work of finding a usable past for this named ethnic community. As Derek Peterson and Giacomo Macola have argued, "The work of history writing was necessary because Africans did not, all at once, identify themselves as members of political communities."[80] Africa's diverse demography, complex political frontiers, and cultural plurality posed a problem for twentieth-century ethnic entrepreneurs, and writing histories provided one means of closing these frontiers and encouraging their constituents to see "themselves as cosharers of a patrimony."[81]

While their chosen name invoked the historical autonomy of clans who gathered in one space, the NKCA problematically chose to rewrite Wanga monarchical history as the source of "Luyia" tradition. Despite lingering anti-Wanga sentiment among many communities, the NKCA saw in Wanga monarchical history a tool of political representation. The NKCA filled its early petitions and pamphlets with narratives of a unified and centralized political past.[82] In a petition sent to the secretary of state entitled "Abaluhya," the NKCA traced the legitimacy of the Luyia ethnic identity through the royal precolonial history of the Wanga.[83] The NKCA asserted that in precolonial times, the Bantu communities of the region were part of a self-governing kingdom: "about 300 years ago before the white man['s] arrival in this country. We had our own tribal Government[,] the Bawanga[,] who originated the name 'Wange' [sic] from their ancestor." NKCA historians depicted this Wanga father as the progenitor of a territory where the "population was scarce." Recasting Luyia history in this monarchical tradition allowed NKCA historians to claim an invented precolonial unity and history of political sovereignty.

In defending a history of sovereignty and authority, the NKCA drew comparative legitimacy from the recognized monarchical traditions of the Great Lakes region: "It was a Kingdom not unlike that of Buganda, or Bunyoro."[84] As Peterson and Macola have further argued, "In colonial eastern Africa as in the Asante state, researchers wrote royalist histories in order to distinguish their people from the anonymous subjects of colonial and postcolonial governments. By this strategic ornamentalism-from-below, they . . . made the messy, pragmatic work of political organization look like a natural order."[85] Royalism provided an argument not only for community building but also for practicing sovereignty. Throughout the colonial period, North Kavirondo representatives submitted requests for amalgamation with Uganda, believing Ugandans benefited from greater autonomy and representation due to their protectorate status.[86] These appeals invoked the redrawing of the interterritorial boundary in 1902 and the severing of political communities across Hobley's boundary. Wanga nabongo Mumia spoke often of the interruption to the consolidation of his kingdom: had it not been for the establishment of colonial rule, Mumia would have expanded his kingdom to one "very much on the lines of King Mutesa of Uganda."[87] The year 1902 haunted early Luyia historians and contemporary oral narratives with a sense of lost opportunities and lost territories. Osogo argued in several texts that "if Mumia had not foolishly refused to go to England for the coronation of King Edward VII in 1902, he would have acquired the same status as that of the Kabaka of Buganda, whose regents went."[88] In eastern African history, and across the British Empire, monarchism and the "imperial ideology" of kingship provided a potent defense against colonial rule.[89] As Justin Willis argued in the case of the kingdom of Bunyoro, "The assumption of kingship became bound up with a degree of historical myth-making, which cast the 'kings' as descended from the creators of an 'ancient empire,' and colonial forerunners of the British."[90] In imagining a monarchical past, the NKCA reoriented its Luyia constituents westward, away from the mess of unrecognized stateless communities of Kenya and toward the stated kingdoms of the Great Lakes region.

It was precisely the movement against Wanga domination that prompted the reconfiguration of kinship networks and fostered smaller-scale, locational political imaginations. And yet the political usefulness of the Wanga's centralized royal tradition reemerged throughout the colonial period as a convenient source of historical narratives to legitimate larger ethnic projects. Despite the vigorous political work of the anti-Wanga campaigns, the movement had not extended to the figure of Paramount Chief Mumia. In 1931 representatives from across the district asked Ezekiel Apindi, the Nyanza representative to the Joint Select Committee on Closer Union in East Africa, to obtain recognition for Mumia as "protector of the land" and "guardian of the soil" on behalf of the natives of North Kavirondo.[91] Papering over historical disjuncture, the NKCA used its new "Luyia" history to petition for "a Sultan which was translated in Abaluhya language as NABONGO WA BALUHYA," or the king of the Luyia people.[92] As in the process of naming, finding a past could serve strategic and practical ends in the interwar period. This return of the Wanga for the political purpose of uniting the diverse constituents of the new Luyia polity was the ultimate historical irony.

The retirement of Mumia from active duty, in 1926, opened an opportunity for a campaign to elect a successor to the paramount chieftaincy. In 1937, Mumia wrote an open letter entitled "Paramount Chief Letter—Nabongo's letter," in which he argued his treaty with Frederick

Jackson guaranteed the protection of his kingdom and his heirs.[93] The NKCA enlisted Legislative Council member Mohamed Shams-ud-Deen, representative for the Indian community, to argue that the treaty signed by Jackson justified the reinstallation of paramountcy in North Kavirondo.[94] These treaties were presented as proof of the ability of Africans in western Kenya to negotiate with colonial powers and to govern themselves. In a 1935 petition to the secretary of state for the colonies, the NKCA outlined the reasons for electing a new paramount chief: to facilitate the representation of matters affecting "all tribes of North Kavirondo," to facilitate tax collection, and to maintain security within the district.[95] While Emma Hunter views such calls for a "paramount chief" among the Chagga as an affront to "modernity" and to the nationalist project of postwar Tanganyika, for the Luyia these claims reflected a complex and often contradictory marriage of reinvented tradition and modern governmentality.[96]

The historical narrative of lost sovereignty jump-started the NKCA's campaign to elect a paramount chief to succeed the retired Mumia. In 1935, Chief Mulama, central voice in both the NLTC and the KLC, emerged as the NKCA's chosen candidate for paramount chief of the newly imagined Luyia community. The anti-Wanga campaign against Chief Mulama's rule in Marama saw him excommunicated from his CMS church, sidelined by the young leaders of the NKTWA, and evicted from his home (see chapter 2). With the birth of the NKCA, Mulama recognized an opportunity to regain his lost political position. Rumors circulated throughout the district that Mulama had traveled to Uganda to see the kabaka and had "fortified himself with some sort of witchcraft."[97] While sensational, these rumors reflected a common strain of social thought in this era. In the 1930s court cases abounded over the trafficking of "medicines" and of people across the border to consult witch doctors in Tororo, Uganda, to gain leverage over their political opponents.[98] In the NKCA and the creation of a Luyia ethnic polity, Mulama saw occasion to merge his political and monarchical ambitions.

To consecrate the selection of a new leader, the NKCA created a political theater in which democratic and "ornamental" props were set uneasily before a public audience.[99] The NKCA advertised a baraza for 1 June 1935 in Mulama's North Marama location to select the next paramount chief, to be witnessed by district and provincial commissioners.[100] The NKCA created a magnificent stage, with a dramatic throne positioned before a large audience awaiting the chosen king. The invented royal ritual carefully staged for this coronation demonstrated the NKCA's "mastery of the public spectacles of monarchy."[101]

The large crowd received a shock when they discovered no official government representation at this meeting and a disorganized NKCA committee. When Mulama failed to arrive on time, the NKCA offered the seat to several chiefs and prominent people in attendance, namely Chief Sudi of South Kitosh, Chief Osundwa of North Wanga, and Paul Agoi of the NKTWA. All declined the position and left furious at being duped into the meeting. In interviews with the district commissioner, audience members likened the affair to the "fanatics" of the Dini ya Roho sect led by Rev. Alfayo Odongo Mango, who only a year earlier had been killed in riots in the Wanga locations and was further seen as a Luo partisan.[102] After this failed performance, the NKCA announced the official selection of Mulama as paramount chief, on 3 June 1935 by "public election."[103]

The NKCA was playing a careful, if messy, bureaucratic game, forwarding a form of governmentality that sat uneasily between a monarchical tradition resented by its stubbornly autonomous constituents and a democratic ethos witnessed by colonial procedures. Just as wily independent school leaders among the Kikuyu played bureaucratic games to trick the colonial administration into recognizing their illegal schools, NKCA members played with colonial bureaucratic methods and ornamental monarchism to force them into recognizing their chosen leader.[104] The NKCA forwarded itself as a democratic electorate: Jumba declared to the governor that by "universal agreement all over the country of 'Abaluhyia' . . . Mulama was elected by the District."[105] Mulama had been chosen, in progressive fashion, "by both the Elders and youngers."[106] This pretension no doubt drove many to condemn the association. Publicly aligning themselves with the government, chiefs throughout the district cracked down on the movement of NKCA members and the collection of subscriptions in their locations, which led to the arrest of NKCA leaders in 1936.[107] As in the small-scale parochial politics of the 1920s and choosing of their communal name, the NKCA's attempt to elect a paramount chief represented an affront to chiefly power and ordered succession.

The NKCA's reliance on Wanga history and leadership as a source of cultural nationalism proved contentious for many communities. The Wanga role in early pacification expeditions and subsequent extension of their rule remained a fresh and open wound in many locations. Despite consistent official rejection, the NKCA's demands for a paramount chief reemerged for public theatrical effect during the visits of high-ranking colonial officials, much to the embarrassment of the local administration.[108] While the position of paramount chief generated little opposition in theory, the selection of Mulama and the reification of Wanga history by NKCA writers revealed the deep fissures and contradictory uses of history within this ethnic project. Both narratives of historical monarchy and the campaign for a paramount chief sat uneasily with locational polities that refused to bend the knee.

BETWEEN NATION AND LOCATION: CONTRACTIONS AND CONTRADICTIONS OF THE INTERWAR ERA

During the late 1930s colonial policies of state simplification challenged the centralizing work of the NKCA and further entrenched the location as the space of native administration and political competition. While aggressive colonial policies allowed the NKCA to reach out to constituents farther afield and prompted ethnic patriots across Kenya to move tentatively from competition to common cause, the global politics of war and empire would interrupt the consolidation of both ethnic and national patriotic mandates.

Under the direction of Sidney Fazan, one of the longest-acting provincial commissioners in Nyanza (1936–42), North Kavirondo underwent a fundamental reorganization of land and authority in the late 1930s. Fazan's résumé as secretary on the KLC, district commissioner in the Central Province, and member of the Kenya Legislative Council heavily informed his philosophy of economic development and the role of the native administration within the colony.

Fazan's reorganization of the district further institutionalized the territorial delimitation of political competition and kinship already underway. The colonial administration increasingly expressed its frustration with what it saw as the anachronistic position of chiefs in the developing local political economy. Fazan paired economic development with a necessary transformation of chiefs into "a sort of chairman of committee" overseeing the native departmental staffs of bureaucratic bodies, such as agriculture, veterinary, and medical.[109] Fazan suggested that such a new understanding of chiefly power would require the territorialization of the position: "The problem of where the chief should be is then found to depend more on economic circumstances and trade than on historical accidents and memories of clan and family feuds." Fazan drew parallels with the system in Uganda, where *saza* chiefs were not clan leaders but rather territorial representatives. In 1937 the institution of the olugongo replaced headmen, or *mlangos*, and transformed the position into "territorial agents."[110] Olugongos often replaced up to four or five mlango representatives, 403 mlangos across the district being reduced to 76 olugongos and 60 mlangos. *Olugongo* translated as the territorial concept of a "ridge of land" and marked the boundaries of clan lands (see chapter 1).[111] The colonial appropriation of this term aimed to reconfigure the relationship between kinship networks, authority, and territorial boundaries.

Although the administration promoted the increased recognition of African elders in the spirit of indirect rule, it simultaneous repositioned these local authorities within bureaucratic hierarchies.[112] Clan elders were transformed from local expressions of authority into "arbitrators or expert witnesses."[113] Fazan had similarly worked to limit the power of elders, particularly in terms of land, in the Central Province a decade earlier.[114] Further limiting executive power, Fazan overhauled the judiciary system, shifting toward a divisional system outside the reach of individual chiefs. The North Kavirondo LNC sent a subcommittee to central Kenya to observe the workings of the divisional tribunal system already in place there.[115] In 1936, Fazan initiated the process of reducing native tribunals in North Kavirondo from twenty-five to twenty-six divisional courts.[116] Wagner pointed to the consolidation of the native tribunals as "one of the principal factors in the creation of larger political units."[117] Transforming clan elders and chiefs into bureaucratic committees and expert witnesses gave new meanings to the already rapidly changing local practices of authority.

While colonial officials worked to reinforce locational divisions, the NKCA embarked on a progressive expansion northward, mapping its constituency from its southern base to the distant northern reaches of the district. The campaign for paramount chief marked the NKCA's first foray out of its southern strongholds and into the central locations. However, the NKCA's reach still did not extend into the populous northern locations of the Bukusu, Tachoni, and Kabras, far removed from the direct effects of the gold rush, suspicious of the often better educated southern politicians, and still resentful of Wanga power. These northern communities lived on the frontiers, both geographical and cultural, of the Luyia ethnic project. The NKCA initially worked through FAM networks to expand its membership. Although headquartered in Kaimosi, in 1915 and 1919 FAM expanded its sphere of influence, establishing missions at Lugulu and Malava, in the northern locations. FAM used Logoli missionaries and teachers in these new missions, imposing the Luragoli language and creating links between the two largest populations in the district separated by the deep Kakamega Forest.[118] As the NKCA moved north, they used FAM's dispersed spheres of influence as breeding grounds for new members. For the first time, local politicians began to venture outside their home locations to gain wider support.

The NKCA traveled the contours of the district, holding meetings and open barazas from Mbale, in the far south, to Kimilili, in the north.

Driving this push north were the new threats of soil erosion and intrusive colonial agricultural policies. By the late 1930s soil erosion was the primary concern of British policymakers throughout their East African colonies.[119] Soil conservation projects were part of the "second colonial occupation," where, as David Anderson has argued, the colonial government's direct intervention in African agricultural practices "heightened political consciousness by giving African farmers something to complain about."[120] There were two main reasons for soil erosion in the reserves: overuse due to population pressures and soil degeneration caused by cattle-ranching practices such as overgrazing. In 1938 the North Kavirondo LNC passed a resolution enhancing the authority of chiefs and headmen to compel communal labor for soil conservation works including terracing, strip-cropping, contour plowing, stonewalling, and other protective measures.[121] In the same year, a land tenure survey conducted throughout the province recorded the complaints of farmers over the demands soil conservation put on their labor, their time, and their own land practices.[122] Soil conservation pushed many peasant farmers into what Steven Feierman has termed "the arms of resistance," creating a common set of grievances and political discontent.[123]

By the end of the 1930s soil conservation projects dominated the agendas of NKCA meetings.[124] The NKCA linked such projects with the encroachment of the White Highlands into North Kavirondo. Pegs and trenches used for terracing and land contouring bore suspicious resemblances to earlier mapping and mining projects. In a letter to the district commissioner, the NKCA questioned a "new rule" passed by the colonial government aimed at decreasing and dividing the land of "the Abaluhya people" through soil conservation programs.[125] Provincial Commissioner Fazan stressed the proper demarcation of boundaries and landholdings not only as part of soil conservation measures but also as a means of settling land disputes that clogged native courts.[126] One European settler from the Trans Nzoia encouraged farmers in the northern locations that through a complete system of trenches for soil conservation each "location could be fairly accurately mapped, showing every shamba [farm] in size and [type of] crops."[127] With such official language, it was unsurprising that local populations viewed the soil conservation projects as part of boundary processes aimed at limiting African landholdings.

Soil conservation was a particularly volatile issue in the northern locations. Destocking paralyzed this cattle-based economy while anti–soil erosion measures increased fears of the encroaching highlands. At a baraza in Kimilili, Fazan linked soil conservation projects with a threat to limit stock numbers if "excesses" were not controlled along the Elgon Forest boundaries.[128] Peasant farmers viewed terracing projects as part of a larger conspiracy to limit African land to make room for European settlers. The ranks of the soil conservation staff were filled with the sons of often-unpopular chiefs, leading to further coercion and conflict.[129]

The NKCA capitalized on this resentment and led campaigns against soil conservation methods and forced agricultural work. Intelligence reports linked the destruction of soil conservation beacons and projects with indiscipline in FAM schools in Kimilili, the main grounds of NKCA support.[130] In 1939 members of the NKCA were arrested for forcibly preventing an agricultural officer from entering a farm at Broderick Falls.[131] The encroachment of the White Highlands into the reserves reemerged as a central theme in the territorial consolidation of this new political community.[132] By 1940 the NKCA's efforts in the north proved fruitful, gaining strong membership numbers and successfully bringing a case of corruption against the infamous Chief Amutalla.[133] The NKCA had achieved more extensive districtwide support than any other African organization in North Kavirondo to date.

Colonywide policies of land consolidation and soil conservation also encouraged the tentative interethnic political contact and comparative patriotic work of the early 1930s to evolve into genuine cooperative action among the NKCA, KCA, and KTWA.[134] In a letter intercepted by the colonial government between the NKCA and the KTWA, Moses Muhanga inquired if the district commissioner of Central Kavirondo was "ordering shambas to be divided up, as is happening in North Kavirondo with great urgency."[135] KCA leaders, with Jesse Kariuki at the helm, visited Mulama in North Kavirondo in 1938 to discuss the recently released Crown Lands (Amendment) Ordinance defining the White Highlands.[136] Kariuki warned that the new amendment would further limit Native Reserves and cause more land alienation. Intelligence reports blamed Kikuyu influence for the persistent talk of the dispossession of native land at NKCA meetings.[137] In 1939 the colonial government intercepted letters from John Adala to George Ndegwa, secretary of the KCA, discussing the collection and movement of funds.[138] In response, the director of civil intelligence, B. W. D. Cochrane, wrote to the superintendent of police to inquire, "who are the 'abaLuhiya' referred to in the last paragraph" of these intercepted letters?[139] These communications culminated in a 1940 meeting in Nairobi where members of the KCA, NKCA, and KTWA discussed issues of land, agriculture, and education.[140] In these petitions and correspondence, regional associations drew parallel narratives of land alienation and discrimination to argue against colonywide policies of compulsory destocking and soil conservation, "for and on behalf of the Kenya Africans."[141]

With these national developments and the outbreak of World War II, the tone of NKCA petitions began to shift away from local historical injustices to a new international language of self-determination, rights, and citizenship within the nation of Kenya and as loyal subjects of the British Empire.[142] The NKCA increased its connections to wider pan-African movements, collecting funds to pay for a correspondence course offered by Marcus Garvey, the self-styled "Negro Emperor."[143] Pan-African ideas, talk of "UHURU," and appeals to African rights began to pervade their writings.[144] Welfare projects became more central to their platform as they aimed to produce tangible results for their fee-paying members. By 1940 the NKCA devoted much of its funding to improving water facilities throughout the district, the administration calculating they now constructed more facilities than the Medical Department.[145] The NKCA's increasing popularity and ability to collect illicit funds greatly worried the administration.[146] Fearful of the evident momentum of political consolidation within the district, across the colony, and even seemingly across the continent, the colonial administration adopted progressively more repressive tactics to rein in dissent.

Under the Defence Regulations implemented in Kenya during the war, the colonial administration proscribed the KCA, the Ukamba Members Association, and the Taita Hills Association in 1940.[147] The detention of prominent Kamba, Kikuyu, Meru, and Taita politicians in May 1940 dealt NKCA leaders a "severe jar to their nerves."[148] The NKCA was right to be scared. On 1 June 1940, the outgoing district commissioner of North Kavirondo asked Provincial Commissioner Fazan to declare the NKCA illegal and detain its leading members.[149] At this critical juncture, a new and more moderate district commissioner, Kenneth Hunter, took over the administration in North Kavirondo. Hunter decided to meet with the leaders of the NKCA before resorting to legal action, as he feared harsh and hasty treatment would only increase their popularity, as occurred after their arrest in 1936. In a private meeting Hunter warned Andrea Jumba of the fate of other political leaders and explained the need for the suspension of the NKCA, as "the war has come to the boundaries of Kenya."[150] After consultation with other NKCA members, Andrea Jumba and Mulama announced the voluntary dissolution of the NKCA at barazas across the district in June 1940.

Despite this closure, NKCA members continued to operate informally and later reformed as the Nyanza Central Association (NCA).

Rumors of unrest in North Kavirondo spread to Nairobi in August 1940. The Criminal Investigation Department suspected NKCA members Lumadede Kisala and John Adala of spreading wild rumors of troops being parachuted into the province.[151] However, protest during the war years had lost much of its bite and national momentum. Within a few months of the NKCA's voluntary dissolution, the local administration triumphantly noted improvements in soil conservation work, "even in Kitosh."[152] The colonial administration also began courting this young political leadership. Most dramatically, in 1940 early ethnic patriot and NKTWA president Paul Agoi was selected to replace Chief Mnubi as chief of Maragoli, the most densely populated and politically active location. As chief, Agoi convinced NKCA leader Andrea Jumba to observe the anti–soil erosion trenches in Maragoli. Upon seeing the projects, Jumba conceded that they were "quite a good idea" and ceased his campaigns against the measures in this NKCA stronghold.[153] The tide was indeed changing, but the political work of the NKCA was not lost.

⮌

THE ONSET of World War II marked a moment of crisis and interruption for the geographic work of ethnogenesis in North Kavirondo. Although the NKCA failed in its historical project and paramount-chief campaign, they succeeded in naming a new political community and in making ethnic patriotism in North Kavirondo imaginable. Geographic imagination proved key to this success, choosing a name that reflected the plural, self-conscious, and communal nature of political work among the Luyia: gathering together. The NKCA lamented that the official response to their political demands was always for the people of North Kavirondo to "go and unite."[154] In 1943 the district commissioner of North Kavirondo declared that, if successful, a united Luyia "would take their rightful place as the leading tribe of Kenya."[155] Here again the competitive and comparative patriotic work of ethnic entrepreneurs in eastern Africa reinforced the geographic work inaugurated in front of the KLC. While their past remained fragmented and their political thought multiple, their name proved remarkably durable and prompted others to envision a language, a political polity, and a homeland for this named community in the coming decades.

4 ⤳ Speaking Luyia

Linguistic Work and Political Imagination

"Luyia is a non-existent language."[1] So declared Rachel Kanyoro, with more than a hint of irony, at the outset of her 1983 linguistic study of the Luyia language. The title of her study was fitting: then as now, Luyia patriots insist on their linguistic "Unity in Diversity." Some claimed the very term Luyia translated as "those sharing the same language."[2] Throughout western Kenya, "speaking Luyia" was central to "being Luyia." The ability not only to speak well but also to speak with those from different groups was a highly regarded trait.[3] Language and an oral culture of interpellation were central to eighteenth- and nineteenth-century community formations and networks. Divergent migratory routes into the competitive and complementary ecological niches of western Kenya had both encouraged the development of diverse languages and political cultures, and built wider oral communities.

Writing in 1943, North Kavirondo district commissioner F. D. Hislop pondered the future of the Luyia ethnic project: "The greatest difficulty in the above consummation is probably that of language."[4] The linguistic diversity of this compact region overwhelmed missionaries and colonial administrators attempting to translate the Bible and to carve out governable units. With the foundation of the Luyia Language Committee, in 1941, local cultural entrepreneurs set themselves up as amateur linguists, seeing linguistic work as a cultural tool for advancing their political agendas. However, controversies over orthography, pronunciation, and translation revealed the competing interests of missionaries and African linguists. Land and territory were at the center of these struggles over the production of language. Linguistic competition prompted many to guard their linguistic autonomy as jealously as they had their political autonomy against externally imposed chiefs. Kanyoro's bold contradiction was then, in many ways, correct: a "Luyia" language never existed, but multiple spoken "Luyias" did.[5] Despite the failure of the protracted attempt to standardize one Luyia language, language work revealed a complex oral geography and the self-conscious and competitive linguistic cultures of colonial western Kenya.

THE MAKING AND UNMAKING OF AFRICAN LANGUAGES

Benedict Anderson's *Imagined Communities* foregrounded the importance of language, and in particular the technologies of writing and print capitalism, to the formation of political communities.[6] Although Anderson's model underestimated the importance of oral cultures and alternative forms of literacy, its attention to the written word encouraged historians to think more carefully about the role of the transcription of African languages in the making of ethnic identities. Whether through privileging missionary intervention or local patriotic work, much of this scholarship has insisted on the standardization of written vernaculars as a necessary ingredient in the emergence of moral ethnicities.[7]

This emphasis on language creation as central to the "invention of tradition" has allowed a form of script determinism in the imagining of African communities to creep in. Yet, as Dmitri van den Bersselaar found in the failure of the Union Ibo language in Nigeria, the creation of a written "ethnic" language was not always successful or particularly necessary for the construction of local patriotisms.[8] The rigid insistence on written vernaculars as a badge of ethnic legitimacy risked obscuring the dynamism, multiplicity, and cultural dissent of oral cultures. As Ruth Finnegan has argued in the case of the Limba of Sierra Leone, linguistic diversity could actually form the core of African communal identities: "Limba was in fact variously spoken, in a number of dialects, some of which were barely mutually intelligible . . . in spite of their habit of contrasting their own various dialects, they still assumed that one thing that they all shared together . . . was the Limba language."[9] For the Limba, comparative linguistic work generated a self-conscious oral tradition. Speakers compared terminologies, playfully mocked differences in pronunciation, and debated linguistic expressions. The dynamism of orality as social practice bred communities defined not by a singular common language, consecrated in the transcription of a standard written form by colonial missionaries, but rather by a cosmopolitan pluralism, by the ability of a multiplicity of people to communicate in person.[10] Such oral practices allowed communities of diverse origins to debate morality and define civility in ways that were mutually intelligible and yet constantly reiterated their diversity.

Like the Limba, Luyia patriots insisted on language as central to their formulations of community despite the diversity of their dialects. Though the flexibility and immediacy of orality proved difficult to reproduce in the new "world on paper," the technologies of writing created new contexts for linguistic and patriotic work.[11] While missionaries and African patriots alike worked to order their constituents through linguistic work, concerns over the creation of a standardized Luyia language revealed more the multiplicity of oral cultures, the diverse geographic imaginations contained within them, and the tensions between priorities of transcription and the dynamism of oral social ordering.

LINGUISTIC DIVERSITY IN WESTERN KENYA

The immense linguistic diversity among the communities northeast of Lake Victoria confounded early explorers, missionaries, and administrators. In 1906 one missionary linked this diversity to a perceived lack of political organization: "The multiplicity of territorial divisions, . . . the unsettled state of the country, have had their inevitable influence on the language. Bantu Kavirondo has *no common language*."[12] Missionaries encountered a vast array of local spiritual terminology. The terms for God were as varied as the religious systems: *Nyasaye* was common among southern dialects, *Khakaba* among the Wanga, while the northern Bukusu prayed to *Were*. Early administrators also noted the contrasting forms and terminologies of political authority, from the Wanga *nabongo* (king) and the strong military leadership of the Bukusu *omugasa*, to the more amorphous authority of Logoli clan elders, or "one of the drum" (*weng'oma*).[13] While colonial officials and missionaries interpreted this multiplicity as proof of an "unsettled" political landscape, this variety of languages and political cultures in western Kenya reflected more the complex migrations, niche settlements, and social exchanges necessitated by the varied environments.

Centuries of migrating settlers brought a plurality of linguistic influences to western Kenya.[14] Anthropologist Günter Wagner mapped the complex migratory routes into western Kenya through a depiction of the variety of Bantu, Dholuo, and Maa language stocks that penetrated the region from all sides (see fig. 1.4).[15] In his 1949 history, *Habari za Abaluyia*, Makerere graduate and teacher at the prestigious Alliance High School Joseph D. Otiende similarly used linguistic differences in pronunciation and vocabulary to support claims to divergent origins and patterns of interpenetration.[16]

In some cases, diverse terminologies reflected not different meanings but rather defensive cultural practices. While the various terms of *enyumba*, *eshiribwa*, and *indzu* all translated as both lineage and the physical enclosure of the homestead, local communities used their unique vocabularies to identify and call together members of their extended clan networks.[17] In other cases, common terms were found to contain different meanings or refer to entirely different concepts. *Laama* translated for many as "to pray," but for others as "to curse," a grave theological challenge for missionary standardizers.[18] Even concepts connected to the very act of speaking could vary dramatically: *sunga* translated as "to speak" among the Marach but as "to hang" among the Logoli. The list goes on and on, sometimes to amusing effect as we shall see, and was further complicated by elements of speech and pronunciation. In Kanyoro's analysis, the commonly held belief that closely related languages will share lexicons for the terms of fundamental importance—those related to kinship, the body, everyday items or features—was severely challenged by the Luyia example: "There are wide difference even in such basic terms such as 'day' and 'night.'"[19] Such linguistic differences revealed the diversity of political thought and of local moral economies in western Kenya.

But this is not to say that speakers in western Kenya were thus unable to understand each other. To the contrary, complementary niche ecological settlements and early patterns of economic specialization and interdependence had encouraged linguistic borrowing and common languages of exchange and interaction. Eighteenth- and nineteenth-century markets across the lakes region revealed how gestures, common terms, and the increasing use of Kiswahili into the nineteenth century facilitated transactions among Luyia groups and with their Nandi and Luo neighbors.[20] Jean Hay argued that similarities between Bantu and Dholuo economic terms testified "to a close and prolonged contact."[21] Multilingualism, code switching, and extralinguistic expressions all facilitated wider regions of mutual intelligibility without sacrificing cultural distinctiveness or political autonomy. While Kanyoro found that dialect intelligibility could range quite dramatically, as low as 20 percent for some dialect combinations, she nonetheless concluded that the Luyia should be regarded as a "speech community": as a community of speakers who share an ability to communicate and transmit knowledge based on their interactions as a social, rather than linguistic, group.[22]

Words in this linguistically plural region were the constant site of argument, political strategy, and reformulation. Linguistic culture was oral, discursive, and relational, adaptable to environmental, economic, and political pressures. Linguistic communities reformulated their words at times to defend their political autonomy and at others to adapt to the needs of mutual interdependence and comprehensibility.

MAPPING LANGUAGE:
MISSIONARIES AND EARLY LANGUAGE WORK

The colonial preoccupation with the scientific categorization and mapping of African peoples into primordial "tribes" relied heavily on linguistic perceptions. Colonial officials in western Kenya lamented the difficulty of finding a "name" for a people who spoke such "widely differing dialects of the same language" (see chapter 3).[23] Colonial administrators had mapped the district of North Kavirondo ostensibly to contain all Bantu speakers northeast of Lake Victoria and to separate them from their Dholuo-speaking southern neighbors. And yet territorial containment belied the complex linguistic scene created within the boundaries of North Kavirondo. Missionaries added a religious topography to colonial maps through their language work. Both missionaries and colonial administrators, often acting as amateur linguists, mapped culture onto language.

Within North Kavirondo, perceived dialect groupings guided early mappings of administrative divisions. Table 4.1, created by linguistic surveys taken in the late 1930s, demonstrates the colonial perception of linguistic breakdown.[24] Tables like these reduced the complicated spectrum of dialects into neat columns of speakers that corresponded to administrative units. Other linguistic studies, however, contested this ordering, extending the very number of dialects anywhere from fifteen to twenty-six.[25] Some colonial officials argued that the linguistic differences between Luidakho and Luisukha were insufficient to support claims to separate dialects. Other dialects, such as Tachoni, were completely elided by particular missionary groups, confused administrators, and competing local activists seeking to bolster demographic numbers, secure locations, and justify claims to political representation. What constituted a separate language or dialect was a deeply political question, complicated by the blurred and overlapping boundaries of communities.

The territorial distribution of these dialects heavily influenced the political and social geographies of community. As dialect boundaries were fluid and often blurred, many struggled to categorize different dialect groups in an effort to simplify the linguistic complexity of North Kavirondo (figs. 4.1, 4.2). One of the earliest linguistic consultants in the district, Wagner originally proposed to examine the correlations between linguistic change and cultural developments in North Kavirondo.[26] In his extensive study, however, linguistic analysis became much more limited,

Table 4.1 Linguistic breakdown in North Kavirondo		
Tribe	*Dialect*	*Population*
Bukusu or Kitosh (prob. including Tachoni)	Lubukusu	56,000
Logoli	Luragoli	49,000
Isukha	Luisukha	33,000
Banyore	Lunyole or Lunyore	32,000
Wanga	Luwanga	30,000
Marama	Lumarama	18,000
Hayo	Lukhayo	18,000
Tiriki	Lutiriki	17,000
Marachi	Lumarachi	14,000
Kisa	Lukisa	13,000
Kabras (prob. including Tachoni)	Lukabrasi	11,000
Batsotso	Lutsotso	10,000
Idakho	Luidakho	7,000
Banyala	Lunyala	5,000
Samia and Banyala in Central Kavirondo	Lusamia and Lunyala	22,000

programmatic, and technical. From a phonological standpoint Wagner categorized four dialect groups: Luidakho, Luisukha, Lunyore, Lutiriki, Lutsotso, and Luwanga in the first; Lunyala and Lusamia in the second; Lubukusu in the third; and Luragoli in the fourth.[27] Throughout his study, Wagner highlighted the great linguistic divide between the Bukusu and the Logoli at either extreme of the district, giving separate tables of their terminologies of authority, tradition, and land tenure. Later linguists similarly struggled to map dialect groups into geographic areas. Luyia linguist P. A. N. Itebete broke sixteen dialects into four geographic regions based on migrational patterns.[28] Kanyoro dedicated an entire chapter to the possible variations of linguistic classification, finally settling on a simplified geographical breakdown containing northern, central, and southern branches based not on linguistic features but rather on suggested "sharable" literary groups.[29] More recently, in a study of the interlacustrine zone of eastern Africa, Yvonne Bastin concluded simply that Luyia dialects were "more distinct and progressively different from north to south."[30] While African and European linguists continue to disagree on the terms of linguistic classification, all remark on the

FIGURE 4.1. Map of locations in North Kavirondo. Kanyoro, *Unity in Diversity*, 9.

influence of diverse migrations, the importance of speech, and the complex patterns of dialect distinctiveness and mutual comprehensibility.

Missionary "spheres of influence" superimposed another layer of mapping onto this complicated linguistic picture and created new geographies of exchange and community. The sheer number of different missionary groups operating in North Kavirondo, numbering as many as ten by the 1920s, spoke to the complex relationship between missionary

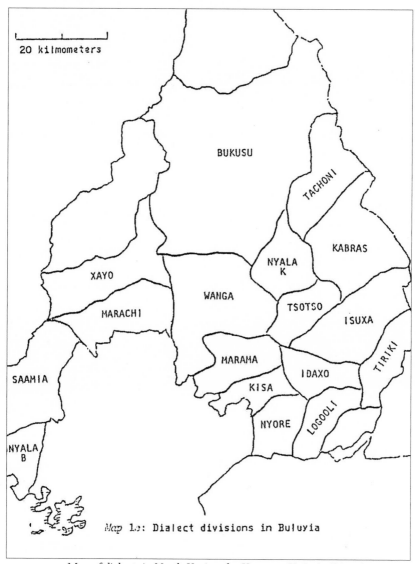

FIGURE 4.2. Map of dialects in North Kavirondo. Kanyoro, *Unity in Diversity*, 10.

work and language consolidation. Of the most important, the American Quakers of FAM, the Anglicans of the CMS, the Protestant Church of God, and the Catholic Mill Hill Missionaries all arrived in the region at the turn of the century and immediately commenced language work to carve out their religious communities.

FAM missionaries were the first to establish a mission station, at Kaimosi in 1902, and to begin work in a local language. Although based in a Lutiriki-speaking area, FAM focused on Luragoli as most of their early converts came from the populous Logoli region, publishing the first Luragoli reader in 1907.[31] By 1940, FAM had published over twenty educational and religious booklets in Luragoli. As FAM expanded its missions, it used Luragoli texts as means of conversion among Banyala, Bukusu, Kabras, and Tachoni populations. The geographically dispersed and noncontiguous nature of FAM missions created new religious topographies and lexicons of belonging.

Arriving from Uganda, CMS missionaries contrasted the relative ease they experienced implementing a standard Luganda language policy in Uganda with the complex linguistic picture in North Kavirondo. In 1912, Rev. Walter Chadwick began language work around the CMS mission stations at Butere and Maseno, creating a "union" language called Luhanga. Although predominantly formed from Luwanga, the CMS persistently asserted that Luhanga amalgamated elements of Lukhayo, Lukisa, Lumarachi, Lumarama, Lusamia, and Lutsotso. By 1938 the CMS had completed a Luhanga translation of the New Testament and sponsored the writing of folktales.[32] According to Reverend Kilgour, over sixty-three thousand copies of the Luhanga gospels circulated in the district.[33] The geographic position of CMS missions, right in the middle of the district surrounded by a sea of other missions, located Anglican evangelism within a particular historical discourse and encouraged CMS missionaries to see western Kenya from the vantage of their Wanga locations.

Although FAM and the CMS dominated missionary publications, two other missions also produced important translations during this period. The Church of God mission arrived in Bunyore in 1905 and quickly produced a Lunyore orthography for religious and instructional texts. By 1929 the Church of God completed their translation of the Lunyore New Testament. The Roman Catholic Mill Hill Missionaries, unlike the others, produced materials in various dialects as they extended their sphere of influence, though focusing mostly on Luwanga prayer books, catechisms, and hymnals. Both the Church of God and the Mill Hill mission maintained more isolationist policies, creating pockets or even islands of converts in the areas where they established missions. The lack of coordination, noncontiguous geographic spread, and outright competition among these mission societies led to an abundance of language work and multiple orthographic systems.

Language policy existed at the intersection of three colonial enterprises: administrative communication and propaganda, mission proselytizing, and education. In 1915 the CMS debated the relative value of choosing one dialect or promoting the use of Kiswahili as a lingua franca.[34] The vocal CMS archdeacon W. E. Owen advocated the use of Kiswahili for official and educational purposes.[35] Administrators hoped the promotion of Kiswahili would curtail conflicts over discrimination and educational advantages in mixed schools.[36] However, Kiswahili also presented certain disadvantages. Many local intellectuals in Kenya were wary of Kiswahili, seeing it as a "political threat" to their own linguistic and political work.[37] Many missionaries criticized Kiswahili for its connections to Islam. Islamic traders from the coast and pockets of Somali settlers led to the emergence of a small but influential Islamic community in western Kenya, particularly worrisome to missionaries as members of the Wanga royal family converted in the 1920s.[38] Students in North Kavirondo complained in 1925 that the Kiswahili used in in the local newspaper *Habari* was "too advanced."[39] Despite its wide use in multiethnic schools, in urban centers, and in social exchanges that predated colonial rule, Kiswahili proved too risky in the eyes of colonial officials, who privileged "vernacular" languages as part of theories of "adapted" education.[40]

With the rejection of Kiswahili, missionaries and administrators agreed in 1920 to work toward a "Union Version for the Bantu Kavirondo."[41] It would take another twenty years before the Luyia Language Committee would be formed. While missionaries and Kikuyu converts at the Tumutumu missions started work translating the Bible into standard Gikuyu as early as 1912 and the Luo Language Committee officially began its work in 1927, work on a standardized Luyia language did not gain momentum until well into the 1940s.[42] While the linguistic diversity of western Kenya certainly daunted missionaries, it was by no means unique. The CMS's Rev. Leonard Beecher, who gained a reputation for language work in central Kenya, pointed to similar levels of diversity in other parts of the colony: "as many and as varied forms exist in the *Kikuyu* tribal areas as appear to exist in Kavirondo."[43] The relatively late process of creating one language in North Kavirondo rather reflected the defensive yet overlapping linguistic traditions in the region, the profusion of competing missionary groups, and the particularities of indirect rule in western Kenya. Whether through debates over Kiswahili, the reformulation of names, or the defense of linguistic difference, language proved a site of argument and political strategy for forwarding claims to cultural distinctiveness and political sovereignty.

The founding of the NKCA and the political work of its young ethnic entrepreneurs gave renewed energies to the creation of one unified language. In 1940 the American Bible Society approached Reverend Beecher to conduct a "factual appraisal" of language in North Kavirondo.

Beecher was at the time charged with creating an African broadcast using vernacular languages for the Information Office in Nairobi. Radios were becoming increasingly popular not only as a means of government propaganda but also as a vehicle for local political projects.[44] By 1941 the Information Office regularly broadcasted in Kiswahili, Kikamba, Dholuo, and Gikuyu.[45] In 1942 the North Kavirondo LNC voted thirty-two to nine that all broadcasts should be in "Luluhya," a language as yet unwritten.[46]

THE LUYIA LANGUAGE COMMITTEE

The creation of the Luyia Language Committee in 1941 reflected not only missionary and colonial interests but moreover the social work of African cultural entrepreneurs. Language work in western Kenya was a site of contestation and creativity, where the different priorities of missionary linguists and African translators collided.

The strongest initial advocates of a standard Luyia language emerged from a new generation of African graduates. The first Luyia graduates from the important Makerere College in Uganda returned to the district in the 1930s to high-ranking posts in government schools and on local boards.[47] At Makerere, these men had written extensively in the *Makerere College Magazine* and other college periodicals on political developments and social change back in their home locations. After the disbanding of the NKCA, at the outset of World War II, Makerere graduates returned to take up the Luyia ethnic project and promoted language work as a central tool for uniting the compatriots they had imagined from afar.

Foremost among these young Makerere graduates, W. B. Akatsa was an accomplished writer and emerging educational leader in the district. At Makerere, Akatsa distinguished himself as a writer, winning numerous prizes for his poetry and essays in English and in Kiswahili.[48] In 1941 he sent an open letter to the newly convened Luyia Language Committee entitled "An Appeal for Linguistic Unity among the Abaluhya."[49] In this eloquent tract, Akatsa sketched an oral community of mutually intelligible speakers in western Kenya: "Go where a Muluhya may in North Kavirondo, he is understood, and is at home, and speaks to his fellow Abaluhya in no other medium than his own particular dialect." Rather than support any particular dialect, Akatsa appealed to the committee to call upon expert linguistic knowledge to settle the profusion of "Luwhatever languages" and create a "scientific" uniform language.

Fellow Makerere graduates and local teachers E. A. Andere and Solomon Adagala echoed this technocratic disposition. Andere pushed for the "complicated and delicate" work of linguistic consolidation to be conducted in conjunction with educational committees.[50] Adagala warned the committee not to rely on illiterate elders "who have no idea of the present day changes," but rather to privilege teachers and other "intelligent members of our Community."[51] The views of this small but influential cadre of teachers and leaders reflected a new political ethos that privileged technocratic skill, youth, and an urbane culture.

Throughout Kenya, language committees proved a common strategy for ethnic patriots and a training ground for burgeoning political leaders.[52] Well into the 1960s, Luyia politicians wrote of linguistic work as central to political development in the pages of the Abaluhya Makerere Students' Union's quarterly magazine, *Muluhya*, founded in the mid-1950s.[53] Written mostly in English with an occasional article in Kiswahili, articles in this magazine ranged in topics from education and land policies to customary practice and political history. The cover design reflected the discursive and plural nature of their political project as well as a projection of the role they claimed for themselves: two men greeting each other, one in little clothing holding a spear shaking hands with another with school uniform and pen in hand. In 1964, *Muluhya* would host a "history writing competition" to encourage its subscribers to write histories of the Luyia, ten years after historian J. E. G. Sutton had contributed an introductory paper, "Towards a Luyia History," in their inaugural issue.[54] For Luyia cultural entrepreneurs, linguistic work and print capitalism offered an opportunity to exercise their technocratic ethos and to forward their political agendas.

Although these Makerere graduates formed the avant-garde of Luyia language advocates, European missionaries provided the material backing and main personnel of the committee, positioning themselves as linguistic brokers in the consolidation of a Luyia language. Representatives of FAM, the Church of God, the Mill Hill mission, and the CMS all attended the committee's first meeting on 4 April 1941, with CMS archdeacon Owen at the helm.

CMS missionary Lee L. Appleby became the only member dedicated to full-time linguistic work. Appleby brought a particular sensibility and set of experiences to this work. Throughout the 1930s she had worked on Luhanga translations, passing her Luhanga exam in 1934.[55] As principal of the CMS girls' school in Butere, she experimented with Luhanga publications of folktales, concluding that previous Luhanga publications had failed to gain wide audience due to their "prosy style and Anglicised Luhanga."[56] For her new Luhanga folktale publication, Appleby enlisted a young Wanga woman with very little English to write in the "real Luhanga." As Patrick Harries and others have demonstrated, these missionary personalities often had a great influence on the direction and ethos of African linguistic work. For Appleby, linguistic work in Africa was about finding the "authentic" African voice, unspoiled by modern education and ripe for conversion.[57]

The Luyia Language Committee had a rocky beginning: their first meetings ended in the committee's resignation due to disagreements over orthography and the importance of each dialect.[58] Early discussions focused exclusively on Luhanga, Luragoli, and Lunyore. As Harries has argued for South-East Africa, standardization was often less the consolidating process missionaries claimed and more an exercise in creating linguistic hierarchies, elevating one dialect over others.[59] While each mission vigorously defended the wide intelligibility of their own particular dialect, the noncontiguous spread of missionary work in western Kenya created mission spheres that "now overlap in the dialect areas. The size of the respective spheres of influence of the three missions could only be assessed by a census of their Church membership."[60] Mission groups counted their numbers and mapped their converts to promote their own linguistic work and further their strategic positions within the district.

Other linguistic endeavors throughout Africa provided inspiration and direction. Beecher drew on his continuing work with the Gikuyu language to advocate the use of one central dialect: "In *Kikuyu* . . . we have refused to recognise any dialect but one."[61] Beecher recommended that Appleby consult the work of Ida Ward on "Union Ibo" in Nigeria as a blueprint for standardization. As in North Kavirondo, the profusion of Ibo dialects, according to Ward, reflected "the smaller unit organisation of the Ibo people."[62] She argued that "Union Ibo," created for Bible translation in the early 1900s, failed to become a locally relevant language as it was "too randomly mixed."[63] Ward recommended standardization around one central dialect to ensure consistency and comprehensibility. Appleby quoted Ward's work to defend the elevation of one central dialect in pursuit of a "living language with nothing artificial about it."[64]

With these examples in hand, Beecher and Appleby steered the committee toward Luhanga, much to the frustration of Church of God and FAM missionaries. In an open letter, retired paramount chief Mumia defended Luhanga as the language of the district: Mumia "unhesitatingly recommended Luhanga, as being the root and as it were mother language of all the rest."[65] He further argued that the inhabitants of North Kavirondo never required interpreters in public or private life, referencing a long history of cultural interpenetration: "These tribes also were in frequent communication . . . about such matters as Dowry and Case shauris, which were matters of discussion and settlement between them."

While echoing Akatsa's emphasis on spoken culture, movement, and mutual intelligibility, Mumia privileged Luhanga as the natural mother tongue of the diverse communities his Wanga chiefs had briefly ruled.

Despite continuing concerns, Appleby worked toward an orthographic system based largely on Luhanga. The committee adopted the 1930 IIAILC Bantu orthography, following the models of Luganda and Kiswahili and avoiding diacritical marks.[66] Wagner suggested orthography should follow the most "progressive drift": the unconscious change in natural language toward common usage.[67] The committee aimed to base their choices on the "actual pronunciation of the majority of people."[68] However, standardizing spelling proved controversial, as did pronunciation (for example, the "k" versus "kh" distinction), the use of noun class prefixes, and the sounding of plosives. Standardized spelling threatened the oral distinctiveness of dialects, glossing over the importance of pronunciation and patterns of speech to political and cultural meaning. Kanyoro sketched the problems encountered with "emotive" pronunciations: *omurwi*, a common term for "head," if pronounced by Luragoli speakers translated as "anus"; the Samia pronunciation of the term for "morsel" would mean "little penis" in the southern dialects.[69] Differences in pronunciation and what one scholar of Luyia linguistics describes as "sound realizations" were pervasive and self-conscious; speakers in western Kenya simultaneously drew together and set themselves apart through their "characteristic articulation" of sounds.[70]

In 1943 the committee produced a circular to test the appeal of their proposed orthography.[71] Written in Luhanga, the circular tabulated the differences among Luhanga, Lunyore, and Luragoli in pronunciation, spelling, and grammar, placing them alongside the proposed Luluyia orthography. Andere used his linguistically mixed students at Nyang'ori Primary School to test the committee's orthography against vernacular mission texts. Andere gave two Bukusu boys the Luragoli New Testament and the committee's circular to read. Despite being accustomed to Luragoli texts, both boys preferred the circular, finding they "understood it better and also it was easier to read."[72] These students unconsciously highlighted a central tension of Luyia linguistic work: their Lubukusu dialect was indeed closer to the Luhanga used in the circular as Lubukusu and Luragoli represented the most distant dialects in the district.[73] But for the Logoli and others, as will be seen, this orthography proved troubling, both linguistically and politically. Standardizing orthography imposed a linguistic hierarchy that threatened the flexibility of oral communications and revealed the instrumental use of language in competing political arguments. The committee accepted Appleby's orthography in March 1944 and publicized it widely through articles in the vernacular press, instructional booklets, and leaflets.[74] Luhanga, like Wanga political history, was thereby made "Luyia."

TRANSLATING GENDER, LAND, AND POWER

Despite this orthographic victory for Appleby and Luhanga, the work of translation revealed the complex bargaining between diverse local vocabularies and the priorities of missionaries, and the centrality of land and power within the formulation of the Luyia language. The Luyia Language Committee set to work translating grammars, dictionaries, and, most ambitious, a Luyia Old Testament. In the late 1940s the district social welfare officer headed a major literacy campaign, using pamphlets, articles, and film.[75] The CMS bookshop in Nairobi reported that of the 5,000 Luyia readers published, 4,964 had been sold and that the Luyia primers were very popular.[76]

To find the words of this new language, Appleby convened meetings with elders throughout the district.[77] Despite the controversy these meetings often entailed, Appleby maintained a romantic vision of the work of translation. In an article for *Bible Translator*, Appleby mused about the leisurely pace necessary for accessing African cultural life.[78] She idealized the lack of local terms for "neighbor," reminding "us of a society where people never just "happen" to live side by side." And yet, in the first vocabulary, Appleby defined the term *omurende* as a "foreigner" among most dialects, but as "neighbour" among the Logoli. Although Appleby repeated the necessity of a "large African contribution" in translation work, much of this contribution came from only six Marama and Wanga elders from the CMS base. While the committee occasionally included representatives from the Samia, Batsotso, and Banyore, their input was limited and representatives from the numerous Bukusu and Logoli were rarely invited to attend meetings. This method of linguistic investigation risked being incomprehensible to wider audiences. For the tricky translation of "pray," the Committee eventually settled on *saba*, despite its inadequate meaning of "to ask." In the same vein, for "curse" the committee ironically supported the use of *laama*, despite its translation as "to pray" in many dialects. With limited African input, translations often suppressed the divergent modes of thought that produced competing vocabularies. As Solomon Adagala had worried, the young intellectuals whose early political work had created the conditions for the consolidation of a Luyia language were now being sidelined in favor of the "illiterate elders" of Appleby's romantic vision.

Language work offered a window into the processes by which colonial and missionary agents reconfigured ideals of domesticity, morality, land, and community into local terms. Appleby clearly aimed the 1947 *First Luyia Grammar* at the European community, whether missionary, settler, or administrator. As Derek Peterson argued in his analysis of successive Kikuyu dictionaries, translators embedded ideas of gender roles, power, and colonial subject positioning in their lessons.[79] Translation exercises often focused on domestic values and moral conduct: texts instructed readers to translate such phrases as "that is a bad custom" and "bread is good food."[80] Appleby's translation exercises provided a glossary for missionaries to encode gendered domesticities and civilize their African converts through linguistic discipline.

While infusing grammar lessons with proper domestic behavior, local gender terms proved difficult to match with the committee's ideas of gender relations, labor, and movement. The committee used *omukhasi* for "woman," yet its Luwanga translation referred specifically to a married woman.[81] The term "concubine" also proved tricky as local words tended to imply the position of junior wife or a voluntary relationship In this case, the committee opted for the Kiswahili word. Similarly the term *omusumba* in the nineteenth century referred to a boy or man who had left his own people, whether voluntarily or by force, and had become the charge of a wealthy person. With that tradition fading, the term had begun to differentiate, meaning "servant" in some areas and "unmarried man" in others.[82] The committee, though, opted to translate the term simply as "bachelor."

While the committee struggled to translate terms that reflected gender, class, and social relations, many of their earliest publications focused on proper household conduct, nutrition, and childcare and encouraged African women to stay within the confines of the home.[83] The movement of women outside the district was a growing concern among missionaries, administrators, and African men seeking to control the social reproduction of the tribe. *Achendanga obubi*, translated as "she is living an evil life," linked the immoral behavior of *obubi*, often translated as "evil," with *chenda*, the term for traveling outside the home. The committee was thus creating a lexicon of morality that would later be mobilized by political associations in campaigns against errant women and runaway wives living in urban centers.[84] Through these translations, missionaries and African translators inscribed norms of domesticity and moral conduct into local vocabularies of gender and work.

A greater concern for Luyia standardizers emerged in the renderings of geography, territory, and political community. For a district so obsessed with land demarcation, this preoccupation was perhaps unsurprising. Translators and committee members faced challenges working local geographical concepts into Western "scientific" norms. The constantly adjusting compass points of north, south, east, and west, for example, had no corresponding terms in any of the dialects. *Masaba*, a common term for Mount Elgon, translated as "north" in the southern locations and "west" in Kitale.[85] Thus geographical terms were relational, shifting depending on the positioning of the subject and their relation to the surrounding environment.[86] The Committee decided no local terms would translate into these absolute directional terms. Through a strange process of pidginization, the Committee settled on modifying the English terms "north" and "south" to "notsi" and "sautsi."[87] This "phonological" adaptation proved quite common, particularly for terms related to the church, education, and government.[88] Geographic terms also revealed a distrust in the frontiers of political communities. As NKCA members and government officials before them had struggled to reach out to the Bukusu frontiersmen at the northern edges of the reserve, the Luyia Language Committee unknowingly revealed that central dialect terms with similar roots, *indulo* and *induli*, linked "horizons" and the edge of geographic vision with "rebellion or mutiny." These translations reconfigured local cognitive mapping beyond the relational field that guided precolonial understandings of geography.

Language work, like cartographic work before it, also aimed to peg people to particular tracts of land. Notions of land, ownership, and communal territory were actively reformulated in the process of translation. Appleby's *Luyia-English Vocabulary* presented a barrage of words for the demarcations of land while reformulating their meaning and context.[89] The *Vocabulary* defined *ara* not only as a break or cut but also as a demarcation of land and the driving out of people from their homes. These multiple meanings revealed the role boundaries played in histories of conflict and community formation. Further, these translations reinforced the practice of trenching as demarcation, defining boundary concepts as "digging the field on either side," despite the multiple local means of boundary demarcations. Later, the biblical translation of "owners" caused much debate.[90] Translations aligned conceptions of self with property by defining *omwene* as both self and owner. In these translations, the committee created a glossary of terms for the work of surveyors and local land courts as well as for ethnic patriots seeking to discipline their disputatious constituents.

The constant conflicts among local dialect advocates over such distinctions revealed the differing political systems of territory and authority. The translation of "king" caused problems, as members of the committee debated the distinction between a ruler of people and a ruler of land.[91]

Interestingly, the committee never considered the term *nabongo* for the translation of "king," perhaps being too loaded with local political meaning at the time. The translation of "nation," central to readings of the Proverbs, prompted debates over whether the term referred to a people or a territory.[92] Several translations considered implied vertical hierarchical understandings of community while others conflated tribe and nation and contained more fixed geographical references. In 1943, Appleby chose *lihanga* to translate "nation," defining the nation as those "taken collectively." Wagner, however, translated *lihanga* as "the community of clans organized under the political rule of the Wanga chiefs."[93] Choosing *lihanga* to render "nation" problematically positioned the concept of nationhood as an extension of Wanga political hierarchy. It is perhaps unsurprising that despite its adoption by the Luyia Language Committee, *lihanga* never appeared in Luyia political tracts or publications.

These translations further inscribed the local into biblical narratives. Adrian Hastings has argued that vernacular Bibles acted as primers by which Africans, and indeed Britons, came to see themselves as a part of a nation with a shared purpose.[94] As ethnic associations like the NKCA regularly invoked religious examples in their political imaginings, quoting biblical verses at the outset of petitions and narrating biblical proverbs in public meetings, these translations contained important implications for the languages of patriotism.

Translation work revealed not only the attempt to infuse local terms with British morals but also the competing values within divergent dialects. Standardizers, whether missionary or African, were divided by self-interest. For supporters of a Luyia language, linguistic work provided a vehicle for grounding their constituents and disciplining their neighbors. And yet Appleby's insistence on Luhanga and the committee's selective African membership alienated many of these early advocates. For dissenters, the Luyia language increasingly represented a threat not only to cultural distinctiveness and political sovereignty but also to the very oral community described by Akatsa and others as the essence of "being Luyia."

GROUNDS FOR DISSENT:
DEFENDING LINGUISTIC AUTONOMY

Despite the early support of Makerere graduates and other local political thinkers, the work of the Luyia Language Committee prompted the dissent and eventual departure of many key African leaders, missionaries, and whole dialect groups. From orthography to translation, dissent arose from local representatives who sought to defend their linguistic autonomy and protect their cultural distinctiveness. The predominance given to Luhanga raised concerns for those who had fought against Wanga political domination. The proposed orthography failed to account for the importance of pronunciation and patterns of speech: mutual oral intelligibility did not ensure mutual comprehensibility when translated to the page. The most fervent voices of dissent emerged from the two largest, and spatially distant, linguistic groups: the southern Logoli and the northern Bukusu.

Although the Logoli produced the founding fathers of the NKCA, Luyia language work ignored their political importance and pitted their Quaker missionaries against the Anglican leaders of the committee. The timing of the Luyia Language Committee was indeed conspicuous: the CMS vigorously campaigned to commence the committee's work before FAM completed its Luragoli Old Testament.[95] Luragoli was also a particularly distinctive dialect, especially in matters of pronunciation, and very early proved a challenge to the promotion of Luhanga as the dominant dialect.

When the committee's 1943 orthography sidelined Luragoli, Logoli teachers and politicians protested their cultural suppression under the weight of Luhanga. Although an early supporter of Luyia language consolidation, Solomon Adagala now denounced the committee's attempt "to force the whole of North Kavirondo . . . to turn to Luhanga."[96] Adagala complained that the committee had "taken no steps to invite a Logoli member to join the Committee."[97] A group of Logoli teachers from Kaimosi protested that the "majority system" for determining spelling and word usage unfairly disadvantaged the Logoli: "All dialects should be taken into account and difficulties shared."[98] In 1945 a Logoli soldier in the South East Asia Command wrote to the Information Office in Nairobi that Appleby was "trying to divide North Kavirondo."[99] These protesters blamed denominational biases for internal disunity and the severing of the Logoli from linguistic and political development in the district.

These protests came at a time of political integration as the two Logoli locations united under Chief Agoi, in 1940. In these letters, teachers and politicians positioned themselves not only as the guardians of a distinctive Logoli cultural heritage, but also as progressive, educated, and urbane representatives of a larger civil society. The Maragoli Society, formed in the early 1940s to defend and promote Logoli cultural and political work, petitioned for Luragoli to "form a greater part of the unified language," due to the numerical importance of the Logoli and FAM's reach across different dialect areas.[100] These were not protests against the principle of unification or the importance of vernacular literacy but rather were demands for a reassessment of linguistic hierarchies.

Logoli opposition prompted the committee to remap North Kavirondo based on a complicated linguistic arithmetic.[101] In 1943 the committee published a memorandum distancing Luragoli from Luluyia, claiming it was closer to Gikuyu than to any Luyia dialect.[102] Beecher's study of the dialects in North Kavirondo led him to believe it was "possible to draw a line across the map of Bantu Kavirondo dividing the Ragoli group from the rest."[103] In 1943, Appleby concurred that "a line can be drawn across the map, very easily separating" the Logoli from the rest of the Luyia.[104] In Appleby's linguistic map, Group One comprised the majority of dialects including Lunyore, Lubukusu, and Luwanga, while Group Two divided off Luragoli, Luidakho, Luisukha, and Lutiriki. Appleby argued that most people in both groups favored a common written form but that many missions and local leaders were unwilling to commit to the necessary sacrifices and adjustments. FAM missionary Reverend Hoyt complained that the new linguistic maps reduced the extent of their influence and use of Luragoli texts.[105] Hoyt argued that Kabras and Bukusu populations had used their Luragoli texts for decades, and they would "be happy to use it in the Old Testament, as well as the New Testament, which they have used for twenty years." In committee meetings, many African members refused Appleby's remapping on the opposite grounds, arguing Luragoli should stand alone. One Isukha member on the committee fought fervently for Luisukha to be included in Group One. These missionary remappings failed to suppress the linguistic geographies and political alignments of the African members on this committee.

The committee overtly favored excluding Luragoli to include the greatest number of dialects under their orthographic banner.[106] The linguistic map drawn in 1943 reflected the ambiguous and fluid nature of territorial identification in North Kavirondo. To assuage Logoli and FAM critics, the new map included shaded areas to indicate where "written" Luragoli extended into surrounding tribes.[107] Linguistic experts and missionaries lamented that it "may not be possible for *Ragoli* to become an integral part of *Standard Luyia*."[108] In 1946 the Kenya Advisory Committee of the British and Foreign Bible Society in Nairobi granted that Luragoli was "clearly in a different linguistic category."[109]

The Luyia Language Committee collaborated with government bodies to undermine and isolate Luragoli language work. In 1949 the LNC emphasized that their "orthography grant" was available only for the promotion of Luluyia and not "the Luragoli language which some people were trying to introduce as the lingua franca."[110] The director of the East African Literature Bureau firmly asserted they would sponsor only publications in Luluyia. By 1951 the LNC went a step further, refusing to fund Luragoli language work at all, giving financial support only to the Luyia Language Committee.[111] Appleby claimed this decision by the LNC clearly "indicated the attitude of leading Africans."[112] However such claims masked the intense internal debates within the committee and the LNC over language policy. The secretary of the Maragoli Education Board complained to the Department of Education that Logoli students were failing in school due to the imposition of the Luyia language.[113] Over protests from the board, the government insisted that "Luyia is suitable for use in Maragoli schools . . . and therefore school and adult development should not be retarded by the clamour of a Nationalistic minority."[114] Appleby believed that if the committee published "enough attractive literature, with carefully chosen vocabulary, we will have the whole of Bantu Kavirondo with us except for a handful of Maragoli extremists."[115] Despite this environment, FAM continued to publish in Luragoli, publishing the first complete Bible anywhere in the district in 1951, and the written form remains an important vehicle for the expression of Logoli political thought and cultural production.[116] There were a Luragoli magazine and orthography broadcasts hosted by the Maragoli People's Association.[117] The exclusion of the populous and politically active Logoli dealt a serious blow to the legitimacy of the committee's work and encouraged the growth of a competitive linguistic culture.

Among the populous Bukusu, controversy over language consolidation emerged only as the translation of Luyia texts reached into the northern territories. Despite their numbers, the Luyia Language Committee barely acknowledged the distinctive nature of the Lubukusu dialect before the 1950s. Since the Catholic Mill Hill mission used Luwanga texts in the area and FAM used their Luragoli texts, the committee assumed Bukusu readers would easily adapt to any new orthography. In 1952 the committee conducted its first serious investigations into Lubukusu and the comprehensibility of their Luyia translations in the northern locations. Investigations by Appleby and her assistant, Jared Isalu, quickly revealed differences in vocabulary were more significant than originally assumed.

Bukusu resistance to the Luyia Language Committee challenged colonial boundaries and forwarded Bukusu political campaigns of the 1940s. Like the Luyia language project itself, local concerns over the Lubukusu dialect first manifested in calls for an internally articulated name. In 1946 a committee of northern representatives sent a letter to the LNC demanding Kitosh, the name given to them by their Maasai neighbors and translating as "enemy," be replaced with their own term, Bukusu.[118]

Demands for new ethnonyms were often the first step in political campaigns for greater educational access and administrative representation. Bukusu elders petitioned both the Kenyan and Ugandan governments to join their linguistically similar Bagisu neighbors on the Ugandan side of Mount Elgon.[119] Administrators and missionaries who worked on and around the mountain reported Lubukusu was indeed closer to Lugisu than to any Luyia dialect. The BFBS had earlier published material in Lugisu but had replaced these publications with Luganda texts in 1937.[120] Appleby noted that these requests for the linguistic unification had their roots in Bukusu territorial and political campaigns.[121] As with the earlier mapping efforts, the committee seemed determined to maintain a contiguous Luyia territory outline. Despite repeated arguments by experts, missionaries and Bukusu elders that Lubukusu was closer to Lugisu, the interterritorial boundaries continually forced the Bukusu into the North Kavirondo map.

Lubukusu posed the greatest challenges to a Luyia vocabulary. The committee sought creative solutions to the translation problems illustrated in the previous section. On Appleby's second visit to Bukusu territory, the "Chief's Language Committee" submitted a list of terms that would require explanation. For the Book of Genesis, the committee addressed these issues by adding explanatory footnotes and providing Bukusu readers with alternative Lubukusu terms. These marginal notes and substitute terms made a mess of these texts, rendering them unpleasant for Bukusu readers, who were forced to constantly interrupt their readings and adjust their linguistic framework. In 1954 the Bukusu Locational Council at Sirisia refused to cooperate further with Appleby's work.[122] By 1957, Bukusu chiefs refused to use Luyia texts in their schools.[123] In 1958, Bukusu political leaders, helped by the Mill Hill mission, formed the Lubukusu Language Committee.[124] Bukusu politicians used language work as a declaration of their ethnic separateness from the Logoli who taught them in FAM schools, the Wanga who had ruled them, and the Luyia standardizers who ignored their cultural distinctiveness.

Competing linguistic projects challenged and, in the end, defeated the goals of Luyia standardizers. The four numerically dominant dialects— Luhanga, Lunyore, Luragoli, and Lubukusu—remained divided among the four dominant missionary bodies and highly dependent on their support, both financial and intellectual: when Father Rabanzer of the Catholic Mill Hill mission left Kenya in 1961, the Lubukusu Language Committee became all but defunct.[125] Although this lower-level ethnonationalism reflected patterns described in the historical scholarship on ethnic consolidation, missionary-led language work in western Kenya extended across noncontiguous territories and diverse linguistic groups, reflecting more the multilingual, self-conscious, and competitive nature of such work.

↜

ALTHOUGH THE Luyia Language Committee did standardize a language they called Luluyia, most viewed it as merely a variation of Luhanga, and the new language neither suppressed the multiplicity of linguistic cultures nor became a vernacular language of discourse and ethnic argument. Appleby continued to work on the Luyia Old Testament well into the postcolonial period, finally publishing the first official Luyia Bible in 1975 to great enthusiasm. However, only a year later, Bible House in Nairobi reported sales dropping to dangerous levels.[126] Complaints revolved around vocabulary and comprehension. Unsurprisingly, Wanga, Marama, and Kisa readers registered the fewest number of complaints. Bukusu readers suffered the greatest disadvantages, as reflected in complaints sent to the committee and in the text itself: "Over half of the indexed 'dictionary' at the back of the Bible . . . are in fact Bukusu words."[127] Linguistic work in western Kenya encouraged local communities to present themselves as speakers of distinct linguistic traditions, strategically emphasizing their uniqueness and difference, and even denying their very understanding of other dialects in the region.[128] Local communities in western Kenya adapted linguistic strategies to extend, defend, and define the limits of their political communities.

While the language work of the 1940s encouraged this competitive culture, linguistic plurality also informed new political values that emphasized the multilingualism and technocratic mastery envisioned by Makerere graduates. In 1947, Chief Agoi recommended J. D. Otiende to the Legislative Council for his "broadminded and cosmopolitan" nature, based on his mastery of several Luyia dialects, Dholuo, Kiswahili, and English.[129] In the late colonial period, urbane and federal-minded Luyia leaders would write their patriotic literature in the national languages of Kiswahili and English. In 1949, Otiende published the first history of the "Luyia" in Kiswahili.[130] The pages of *Muluhya* would switch between English and Kiswahili despite theoretical discussions on the importance of vernacular culture. The Abaluyia Peoples Association, founded in 1952 by many of the same young cultural entrepreneurs who supported language work in the 1940s, instituted a revealing linguistic policy: English would be their official language, Kiswahili would facilitate wider understanding, and any Luluyia dialect "would be optional."[131] Quotidian cultural exchanges, political meetings, and public rallies reflected this multiplicity of languages and a fiercely oral political tradition.[132]

Despite the failure of the Luyia language project, the idea of linguistic unity remained central to the political ethos of the Luyia community. Ethnic patriots promoted the idea that "speaking Luyia" was what constituted "being Luyia." And yet, the competitive linguistic environment witnessed throughout this project revealed the power and the potential threat of the locality to Luyia ethnic patriotism, a threat that would re-emerge throughout the 1940s in response to crises over land, gender, and customary belonging. Linguistic culture in western Kenya, while fragmented, defensive, and at times combative, retained the dynamism, plurality, and spatial dimensions that Luyia patriots sought to contain.

5 ∽ Mapping Gender

*Moral Crisis and the Limits of Cosmopolitan
Pluralism in the 1940s*

> Wives do not always agree.
> — "Mzee Mombasa" Batholomeo Munoko[1]

LUYIA ELDERS in western Kenya often depict the complicated relationship among their constituent communities in familial terms. *Luyia*,
they say, embodies a husband with seventeen wives: each wife represents
a different "tribe" and together they are "called the wives of one husband"[2] — and wives do not always agree.

Said another way, a Luyia proverb speaks to the dissent that living
together inevitably engenders: "'Come let us live together' soon results
in disagreements."[3] While the interwar years represented a high tide of
ethnic patriotic work, the 1940s brought a time of moral anxiety. Political
thinkers in eastern Africa saw their patriotic work threatened by colonial
policies that intervened into their households, by migrant labor that attracted young men and women to cities and settler farms further away
from their social control, and by the resurgence of the parochial politics
of the locality.

Without a past, without a language, the Luyia project fractured in
the 1940s as moral concerns over land tenure, customary practice, and
gender relations prompted a turn toward the locality. In the reserves,
new, small-scale locational institutions built demographic discipline
through the reformation of moral behavior and alternative models of
household respectability. In emerging urban centers, these associations
organized football matches and launched campaigns against prostitution
to bond and discipline their members through a gendered discourse of
male camaraderie and female deviancy. In the late 1940s a crisis over the
practice of female circumcision among one of the Luyia "wives" brought
this resurgence of the culturalist politics of the locality into sharp focus.[4]

Reflecting wider anxieties over mobility, gender, and moral discipline, the young Tachoni girls who crossed administrative and cultural borders in search of circumcision challenged colonial geographies and revealed the messy, local politics of gendered belonging.

While small-scale locational organizations followed a particular patriotic logic, a new generation of cosmopolitan, multilingual, and urbane Luyia entrepreneurs responded to these challenges with new forms of geographic and demographic work linking rural to urban, local to the nation. Active founders of the first national party, the Kenya African Union (KAU) in 1944, Luyia politicians remade local arguments over civic virtue, patriotism, and communal belonging in the nation's image. While a more minimalist ethnic project than the more centralized ambitions of the KCA or the Luo Union, Luyia architects buttressed their political work with gendered and geographic discourses. Through the technocratic tools afforded by electoral politics, customary law panels, and the first national census, Luyia cultural brokers disciplined the dissent among their competing "wives." In response to the moral panic over mobile women and the practice of female circumcision, Luyia political thinkers made the female body subject of their territorial control and demographic work. The Luyia home they constructed, now called North Nyanza with the successful removal of the hated "Kavirondo" moniker, proved spacious: a mere thirteen years after their naming, the Luyia emerged on the 1948 census full-grown, with 653,774 named and numbered constituents.[5] Through a discourse of cosmopolitan pluralism and demographic discipline, ethnic patriots in the late 1940s articulated a "Luyia" political body and mapped a space of gendered belonging.

THE POLITICS OF THE LOCALITY: BANDS OF BROTHERS AND ERRANT WOMEN

The 1940s brought a series of crises—in land, in livelihoods, and in morality—to eastern Africa that prompted political thinkers in western Kenya to turn inward. The years of World War II strained local economies, extracting manpower, cattle, and agricultural products from North Nyanza and exacerbating local conflicts over land and resources. Insufficient short rains in 1942 caused widespread crop failure and famine particularly in the densely populated southern locations of the district already stressed by the disruption of the gold rush.[6] Black market sales of maize sprang up at markets throughout the district and across the Ugandan border. Literate African farmers read newspapers with their neighbors and bemoaned the new terms of crop prices guaranteed to European farmers.[7] New forms of agrarian imperialism intervened into and threatened the autonomy of local household economies of land tenure and generational authority.

While land conflicts preoccupied local concerns, bleeding into disputes over marriage, authority, and customary law, increased economic pressures prompted many young African men to seek alternative routes to economic and personal advancement. At any time during the 1940s and 1950s, up to 60 percent of the able-bodied male population from North Nyanza worked outside the district.[8] The towns of Nairobi, Nakuru, Eldoret, and Mombasa presented alternative spaces of economic and social mobility. During World War II the African population in Nairobi swelled dramatically, by 25 percent, composed primarily of Luyia and Luo migrants.[9] By the 1948 census the Luyia represented 41 percent of Eldoret's population and around 10 percent of other major towns, numbers most likely on the conservative side, as they often did not reflect seasonal migrations and the shifting modes of identification, modes that were particularly complex in the urban setting.[10] As early as 1942 the provincial commissioner worried that the fully mobilized Nyanza labor force and strain on local resources would endanger "the native structure of society."[11]

Despite their seasonal migrations, these men faced difficulty in maintaining control over their land, wives, and households back in the reserves. In the overcrowded Maragoli and Bunyore locations, colonial administrators blamed rampant soil erosion and increasing land fragmentation on the "greed and jealousy" of women left to head their households.[12] Women heads of households often employed strategies such as digging furrows around their fragmented land to clearly demarcate their holdings and to protect against encroaching neighbors in their husbands' absence. Widows were particularly vulnerable, as they not only were in precarious positions in terms of their land rights but also saw challenges to the control of their sons and daughters.[13] Husbands and sons returned from labor contracts to find their land requisitioned and their wives and mothers imprisoned.

Husbands also worried about their wives unchecked sexuality in what Kenda Mutongi called an era of "moral panic."[14] In 1931 the LNC debated the necessity of holding women "individually responsible" in cases of adultery, a major shift in much of local custom that had positioned women as permanent minors in the perpetual care and responsibility of a male relative.[15] Accusations of adultery, reports of prostitution, and the emergence of brothels in the townships, first in Kakamega and Kisumu and later in urban centers further afield, multiplied in the years following the gold rush, with rumors circulating about the activities of "Kavirondo prostitutes."[16]

While this moral panic was not entirely new, driven as it was by earlier industrial changes, population shifts, and longer migrancy periods, into the 1940s an increased urgency over how to discipline these "wayward" women became apparent. As Mutongi recorded, stories of prostitution "were heard in the villages—by the hearths, by the water well, and in the *shambas*—as many of the older Maragoli women joined with African men and colonial officials in expressing growing anxiety about young women's morality."[17] The secretary of the Maragoli Locational Council described these sexual practices as "ugonjwa"—a disease that would infect the good character of rural homesteads and cause infidelity and immorality to spread.[18] The LNC empowered headmen to take "such action as such headman may consider necessary," on any dwelling or premises presumed to be a brothel, "house of ill fame," or in any way "prejudicial to morality."[19] Whether real or imagined, anxieties over the behavior of unsupervised wives reflected not only a moral panic but also a demographic panic over the reproduction, biological and social, of the community.

African men were not the only ones moving to the towns of eastern Africa. LNC members complained that towns were becoming escape routes for runaway wives and daughters, threatening the moral health of the community.[20] At the same time as Luyia linguists were associating the terms *achendanga* and *obubi* in their new exercise books to link female immoral or evil behavior to travel, local district bodies were working toward greater judicial control over the movements of their female constituents.[21] As early as 1938, chiefs and LNC members debated mechanisms for "direct action . . . for the return of girls who run away" and complained they had no legal means of controlling the movement of women.[22] In 1941, Luyia elders formally requested government action to bar young Luyia girls from traveling out of the district unaccompanied.[23] In the early 1940s the North Nyanza district commissioner noted the "widespread feeling" that "Kavirondo girls" were increasingly migrating into the towns "to live a freer life and eventually become prostitutes."[24] With no legal means of controlling this movement, LNC members opted to use public opinion, at home and in the towns, to enforce measures of moral respectability and communal shaming.[25] Chief Agoi went further, lauding the effectiveness of elders travelling to Kisumu to "recover erring daughters" in cases where the "sanctions of native law and custom were absent."[26] These debates often ignored or sidelined the multiple reasons that prompted African women to leave the reserves, some for the same economic opportunities as their brothers, others to escape forced marriages and domestic abuse. The categories of "runaway wives" and "errant daughters" underpinned patrilineal discourses of control and ignored deeper conflicts over gender, marriage, custom, and economics in the 1940s.[27]

While representing alternative spaces of economic opportunity, urban centers undermined the ability of elders and administrators alike to exert control over mobile African youth and threatened "to pervert both marriage and the process through which masculinity was fashioned and transmitted."[28] Editorial letters to vernacular newspapers decried the unchecked and immoral behavior of young men and women freed from tribal restraints. In letters to *Baraza*, members of the Eldoret Club marveled at the arrival of young women from North Nyanza without permission, supervision, or apparent direction: "If you asked them whom they have come to see, their reply is, 'We haven't come to see anybody, we've just come to Eldoret.'"[29] The authors warned that "the sort of things that are going on" would corrupt even the most respectable women who traveled alone. The authors blamed negligent fathers in North Nyanza, entreating them to "look after their girls . . . and not let [them] go astray." By the 1940s tales of these runaway women had reached a fever pitch, not just among Luyia men but also among male patriots across eastern Africa.[30] These independent women, whose movement and sexuality broke away from reserve controls, embarrassed their male urban counterparts, tarnished the reputation of their reserve-based fathers and husbands, and threatened to spread this "disease" back to rural households.

These closely connected moral concerns over land and gender prompted a young generation of politicians to create new institutions to defend their moral communities. Smaller-scale parochial institutions expressed a growing concern over locality and social control.[31] In their political work, they worked to reform manners, to curb delinquency, and to draw their constituents in line, at home and away.

Many of these new associations found their leadership within the ranks of voluntary associations and mission-educated teachers. The Bukusu Union formed in the wake of the proscribed Kitosh Education Society in 1940 with Pascal Nabwana and Philip Mwangale at the helm. The Maragoli Society brought together young Logoli mission teachers and Makerere graduates like Solomon Adagala. The Bunyore Welfare Society and the Bunyore Educated Peoples' Society, emerging later in the period, both stressed educational advancement, locational politics, and the preservation of Bunyore "traditional" values.[32] All these associations built illegal schools, resurrected "bush" education, and were on the frontlines of linguistic debates in the 1940s.[33] Their constitutions pledged to defend the moral character and cultural heritage of locational communities. Conceiving the locality as a territorially distinct space of obligation and belonging, they stressed good manners and moral discipline in their constructions of collective respectability.

The introduction of locational councils, in 1946, reinforced locational units as the site of administration and political imagination. The Maragoli Locational Council produced a Logoli history booklet, "Kitabu kya Mulogooli na Vana Veve," that illustrated precolonial customs and moral taboos as a model for its constituents.[34] Concurrently, Logoli men revived traditional group circumcision ceremonies, precipitating conflict between Christian converts and nonconverts, and between the Logoli and their neighbors.[35] The Maragoli Locational Council attempted to mediate these conflicts by establishing separate dates for Christian and traditional circumcisions. Other locational councils similarly wrote histories that separated them from their neighbors and embarked on their own linguistic and cultural projects.[36] These councils offered new avenues for the advancement of locational politicians as they transformed the more parochial institutions of elders and chiefs into professional technocracies.[37]

As sons and daughters left the district in ever-larger numbers, locational associations offered a more effective and intimate interface for defining kinship and defending household discipline outside the reserve. Although rarely permanent urban dwellers, Luyia men in Nairobi, Eldoret, Nakuru, and Mombasa established ethnic associations to anchor themselves within multiethnic urban scenes and maintain ties with their reserve-based compatriots. By 1949, no less than fifteen locational associations from North Nyanza operated in Nakuru. These locational associations served many functions. They organized dances, trading permits, and sporting events to socialize their new members. They provided care and support for sick members and facilitated burial services by transporting bodies back to the reserve, by far the largest expense on budget for most associations.[38] The emergence of this "urban citizenship" prompted locational associations to map urbanity into the locality, and vice versa.[39] In towns across eastern Africa, Luyia locational associations reproduced kinship networks to maintain the reach, however tenuous at times, of the reserves to these urban youths.

Foremost among these strategies, the colonial game of football provided a crucial new field for male competition and expressions of local patriotisms.[40] Football, in John Iliffe's words, "inherited the teamwork of group dancing, the language of warfare, and the *cachet* of modernity."[41] In the 1930s, Günter Wagner noted that the war customs he recorded from precolonial raidings in western Kenya were being adapted to the football field.[42] Rival footballers greeted each other as warriors. War songs challenged opposing teams and announced victors to villagers. Just as elders in the Comorian Association in Zanzibar promoted football over the *ngoma* dance traditions as an alternative forum for male competition, locational associations in North Nyanza sponsored football teams as an outlet for locational rivalries and as a rite of passage for young men who could no longer raid and war to prove their manhood.[43] Football also represented an important field of honor and a "political asset," with both local and colonial audiences.[44] When appealing to the colonial administration to become the next Bukusu chief, Jonathan Barasa listed his football accolades alongside his educational accomplishments.[45] Elijah Masinde, leader of the religious and anticolonial movement Dini ya Msambwa (see chapter 6), gained his reputation on the football field, propelling him to the national "chiefs" team. To this day, despite Masinde's many exploits as an anticolonial rebel, his most frequently recounted story tells of the football he kicked up to the sky that never returned to earth, foregrounding his prophetic future.[46]

But football was also about discipline and patriotism. In the 1940s locational associations transported football from the reserve to the towns to reinforce male fraternity in the face of urban "detribalization." Football became so popular among Luyia associations that in Nakuru eight out of twelve teams in the "tribal league" hailed from Luyia locations.[47] This type of leisure activity acted as a "socializing agency" for young migrant workers.[48] Through football, associations such as the Wanga Educated Men Association sought to "promote brotherliness among Ba-wanga youth" in Nairobi.[49] Locational football teams acted out the bonds of kinship and civic responsibilities lost in the towns.[50] When players from the North Kavirondo team were sent off the field for unsportsmanlike behavior at the Remington Cup football competition in 1938, the North Kavirondo LNC responded by orchestrating a public shaming and imposing a ban on playing football for a period of fifteen months on penalty of losing their jobs, a sentence the LNC had no power to enforce.[51] Football thus acted as a yardstick of civic responsibility that reflected the social reputations of both the players and their ethnic associations. On football pitches across urban centers, teammates became agemates and teams became tribes under their locational banners.

Brothers banded together in the towns also reproduced kinship networks as they worried about their unsupervised households back in the reserve. Across eastern Africa, prostitution became a flashpoint for the political and demographic dilemmas faced by ethnic patriots.[52] In Kenya ethnic patriots from divergent projects gathered in 1946 to discuss their common concerns over these "wayward women." In a report by the "Joint Tribal Committee of Nairobi," while the various organizations disagreed on the means of disciplining these women, all agreed that ethnic associations should have the power "to control the behaviour and lives of the various tribes, both men and women."[53] Colonial administrators noticed not only the potential danger but also the comparative patriotic work involved in these antiprostitution campaigns: on a letter from the Eldoret branch of the Marach Union suggesting they would purchase railway tickets for runaway girls, the Uasin Gishu district commissioner scribbled, "Dangerous! No girl or woman must be 'arrested' if she leaves her husband or family. The Kikuyu tried this."[54]

Throughout Rift Valley Province, branches of the Maragoli Society and the Bukusu Union put runaway wives and prostitution among their top priorities.[55] The Bunyore Welfare Society pledged to "stop Banyore ladies or women to leave home to go to any town with a view to roam about and practice brothel."[56] The "women's question" for these association was a matter not only of responsibility but also of demographic and household discipline. Colonial administrators and African men used the term *prostitute* to cover all manner of women demonstrating independent tendencies, be they wives escaping abuse or forced marriages, unmarried women seeking new opportunities, or business-minded entrepreneurs moving to the city to practice any number of trades. Further, prostitution itself masked a wide range of social, economic, and sexual arrangements.[57] Despite this variety, locational associations positioned women as the bearers of cultural reproduction and moral respectability, male members seeing their own honor threatened by the activities and movements of these women.

As early as 1944 the North Kavirondo Local Native Council abandoned earlier tactics of sending deputations of elders to urban centers to persuade African women to return home in favor of "forceable repatriation."[58] Urban locational associations sought the authority to arrest and deport errant women on behalf of their district-based countrymen. The Maragoli Association asked for women arrested within Kisumu to be handed over to them.[59] Underlying these claims was the belief that the proper place of women, whether married or not, was in the reserve, where customary law could regulate their behavior. While the colonial government refused to endow associations with the power to arrest and deport women, it encouraged them to "persuade women in a friendly manner" to return to their home locations.[60]

Persuasion amounted to forcible removals and theatrical, public repatriation rituals. Locational associations conducted these antiprostitution and repatriation campaigns with the consent and participation of chiefs, elders, and family members back in the reserves. Chiefs submitted to the associations lists of names of the women to be repatriated. Often these lists contained only the scantest of information on the first names or locations of these women: one listed three women named only Mary from Maragoli.[61] After Chief Jeremiah Ochieng heard that the daughter of one of his constituents, Nyangweso Esonga, had been discovered in Mombasa, he wrote to the district commissioner to have her returned, which she was, twelve days later.[62] Repatriation was key, but there was also a danger in these repatriations: petitions filled with language of disease, worried that returning "girls and women" would infect local men and women and spread the immorality of town life back into the borders of the reserve.[63] And so, as Mutongi vividly depicted in the case of Maragoli, these repatriations often involved humiliating public performances.[64] These performances served not so much as public shamings—many of the women so repatriated were viewed as beyond shaming—but as moral lessons on how to live a "respectable life" and warnings to other women of the consequences of transgressing these boundaries.[65]

Through these campaigns and popular discourses, urbanity was thus coded as male, and the removal of African women from urban centers amounted to a unifying, patriotic duty. Luyia organizations also got involved in the antiprostitution campaigns spearheaded by locational associations, though with less success and to a much more limited degree. While football often divided Luyia loyalties, the control of women united despite the divergent household politics of fathers at home. The impermanent nature of male Luyia urban residency meant locational associations experienced a great deal of flux and instability, disappearing and reappearing rapidly. In towns across eastern Africa, the Abaluyia Welfare Association (AWA), the Abaluhya Friendly Association, and later the Abaluyia Peoples Association (APA) provided a more constant presence within the towns. The AWA, for example, claimed to represent "the sons of the soils" but functioned more as an umbrella organization, a federation of locational associations.[66]

These federations had to limit their mandates in order to manage tricky locational politics: the AWA faced potential riots and struggled to maintain its members when particular locations went unrepresented in the Abaluyia Football Club.[67] But they all placed the moral control of urban young men and women atop their lists of priorities. In their constitution, the Abaluyia Association vowed "to stop the spread and infection of any bad character that may be noticed among members of the Association, particularly the desertion of women from the lawful husbands or girls who break loose from parents or guardians. Also men who cause women or girls to act contrary to the good family or parental life."[68] The Abaluyia Friendly Society of Eldoret held special meetings dedicated entirely to discussing the arrest and repatriation of any "Luyia" prostitutes to the reserves.[69] They bragged of their success in catching "people hiding other people's wives" and used "Society Askaris," or volunteers, to patrol the taxi parks and monitor people's homes in the towns.[70] Warnings from the colonial administration against such vigilante justice were often perfunctory and without teeth.[71] To further these causes, associations proposed to check young women's papers, police prostitution, file court cases, and recommend repatriation.

These claims to moral custodianship, however, did not go unchallenged. In 1950, Rosa Kadenge charged AWA president J. L. Mukholosi with abduction after AWA members attempted to forcibly remove her from her home in Eldoret.[72] Mukholosi had a checkered past, having earlier been forced to resign as president of the Abaluyia Friendly Society due to his own illegal residence in Eldoret.[73] AWA branches from across the colony sent letters of support to the court magistrate. Mukholosi demanded the case be dismissed, as "one of this Association's duties is to prevent Abaluhya women from running away from their district." He argued that without permission from chiefs or headmen to travel to urban centers, women were often turned away upon arrival, leading them to sell their clothing or engage in prostitution in order to return to their home locations. AWA members, Mukholosi argued, were providing a crucial service lacking in the native administration in defense of the honor of their women. The AWA asked for the release of Mukholosi and his "local policemen" and the immediate return of Rosa to her home location. Through such cases the AWA claimed the right to police any and all Luyia woman.

The court ruled in Rosa's favor, Mukholosi receiving six months' hard labor for abduction and for privately funding the askaris to enter farms and urban centers to arrest women.[74] The grounds for this decision remain obscure and the results were most likely uncommon. Courts more often dismissed such cases as family matters and simply returned these women to their families. Fragmented evidence suggests that Rosa, and others like her, continued to be harassed in Eldoret despite the courts ruling in her favor.[75]

Rosa's case did, however, signal the decline of the AWA and its limited success intervening in culturalist politics. While the issue of errant women and runaway wives provided common ground for these men to overcome their varied locational allegiances, the ability of Luyia cultural brokers to subsume women under a larger ethnic banner proved limited. High rates of intermarriage and the very transmutable ethnic identity of African women allowed locational leaders to imagine all women from the district, regardless of origin, as subject to their male authority: women labeled as Kavirondo or Luyia in the towns threatened the reputation of all men from western Kenya. Later, some would even accuse these women of providing money to Mau Mau rebels in defense of antiprostitution campaigns.[76] In 1955 the APA pictured "runaway wives" as a threat to the survival, both moral and physical, of their offspring, and thus of the tribe itself: "A few women have come to abide here are persons who have deserted their proper husbands in the reserve leaving poor children uncared behind full of misery and without education."[77] Such campaigns would continue well into the postcolonial period. While leaving the actual work of antiprostitution campaigns to locational associations and generally shying away from these culturalist projects, Luyia patriots harnessed these gendered discourses to feed a particular form of Luyia political consciousness and extend their demographic and geographic work into the towns of eastern Africa.

THE FEMALE CIRCUMCISION CRISIS IN NORTH NYANZA

While ethnic associations practiced the politics of the locality at home and in new urban centers, perhaps the largest threat to the demographic geography of the Luyia project came from within the district. In the late 1940s a conflict over the practice of female circumcision in western Kenya forced one group within this territory to choose between custom and patriotism. The crisis that ensued was both of identity and of administration, as local leaders and government officials were compelled to reformulate customary policy in ethnic, gendered, and territorial terms.

Circumcision, both male and female, was at the forefront of gendered debates within imperial and African circles over adulthood and the moral health of ethnic communities. As their Luo neighbors represented one of the few groups in Kenya who did not circumcise their men, many assumed, and continue to assume, that all Bantu communities to their north practiced the rite. Many early explorers noted the falsity of such assumptions, recording a variety of practices ranging from elaborate circumcision ceremonies to the absence of any form of circumcision.[78] Among the Bukusu, Tiriki, and Logoli, male circumcision was near universal and essential to notions of masculinity and community. For others, such as the Wanga, circumcision was expected only for the eldest son in a family.[79] Among others still, such as the Bakhayo, Banyala, Kisa, Marama, and Samia, male circumcision was optional and often not practiced at all. The importance of cultural interpenetration across perceived ethnic territories proved an important determining factor: those groups in closest proximity to Kalenjin and Maasai neighbors considered male circumcision as crucial to community membership, while groups nearer Nilotic neighbors took a more flexible approach to the rite.

This complex picture of customary relativity and plural cultural choice did not, however, mean that male circumcision was an unimportant social rite and sphere of moral debate. Male circumcision in North Nyanza did, at times, produced controversy. Tiriki converts clashed with nonconverts over taking male circumcisions out of the forest and into hospitals.[80] Kalenjin men in Nyang'ori complained that freshly circumcised Logoli men paraded in front of their women.[81] Male circumcision also sparked cross-border rivalries and insults over potency and maturity. Bukusu men taunted prospective boys during circumcision ceremonies with chants of "if you are a coward, go and live with the Luos."[82] Among the Tiriki and Logoli, circumcision songs similarly derided those who feared the knife as Luos.[83] As independence approached in the 1960s, cases of Luo men in South Wanga being forcibly circumcised in North Nyanza were taken up by Luo politicians to demand boundary changes.[84] Upon investigation, most cases were dropped due to insufficient evidence and many were found to involve mixed marriages of Wanga women and Luo fathers.[85] These were localized and limited conflicts over household virtue and intermarriage rather than any systematic population-building exercises within a Luyia ethnic project. Oral informants were near universal in their agreement that male circumcision neither defined Luyia community membership nor proved a barrier to intermarriage.[86] And surprisingly it would be female circumcision, a practice uncommon among the vast majority of communities in North Nyanza, that would spark a crisis of belonging.

As customary law remained largely unwritten in the 1940s, the enforcement of customary practice in North Nyanza proved an uneven and contradictory process. From their inception, LNCs used their power to institute districtwide legislation on cultural practices. At its first meeting, in 1925, under pressure from Protestant missions and colonial officials, the North Nyanza LNC used its second resolution to ban "the practice of Mutilation of females" throughout the district.[87] This resolution bears underlining: the North Nyanza LNC was unique as the only body in the entire colony to mandate a complete prohibition on female circumcision at this time.[88]

The female circumcision controversy of 1929 in central Kenya bore witness to the dramatic consequences of imperial and missionary incursions into cultural practice. Congregations of Kikuyu Christians refused to comply with missionary prohibitions on female circumcision, causing widespread desertion of churches and the entrenchment of the practice within the political discourse of Kikuyu nationalism.[89] Reeling from this controversy, the central government shifted course and opted to allow their men on the ground to determine policy within presumed ethnically defined regions.[90]

For most Luyia groups the bylaw against female circumcision served little purpose, as they did not historically practice the rite. But for those communities bordering Rift Valley Province, this ban galvanized new debates concerning cultural alignment and cross-border exchange with Kalenjin and Maasai neighbors, for whom the practice was common. The LNC empowered local headmen to undertake punitive actions against those permitting and performing the operations in their locations. In the mixed Tiriki location, headman Chweya used the ban to harass the local Nyang'ori population in his location.[91] Nyang'ori families often ignored the ban or crossed into Rift Valley Province to circumcise their girls where the colonial policy toward the practice was one of "masterly inactivity."[92] Pressured to check the uncontrolled movement of Nyang'ori girls crossing provincial and "ethnic" borders, the North Nyanza LNC amended their original ban to allow an exemption for the Nyang'ori living within the district.[93] This shift brought claims of nativism, cultural plurality, and legal accountability to the forefront of colonial ethnic and territorial politics. Those defined as Nyang'ori living within the limits of the North Nyanza District had the legal right to practice female circumcision, while it remained illegal for the rest of the district's population. But these legal gymnastics did not bring this story to an end. The political developments of the late 1930s and the birth of the Luyia ethnic project led to North Nyanza's own female circumcision crisis.

The female circumcision crisis in North Nyanza emerged in the context of debates around ethnic consolidation and the territorialization of the customary. The crisis first manifested in the northern Kabras and Bukusu locations that bordered Maasai and Kalenjin populations in the Trans Nzoia and Uasin Gishu. In 1935, the year the NKCA named the Luyia into existence, several cases of female circumcision surfaced in the Kimilili location. One of the girls was found to be the daughter of local headman Mayunga. All fathers involved were fined and Mayunga was dismissed from his post.[94] Reports of female circumcisions then spread, 1937 witnessing an increase in cases of illegal circumcisions of North Nyanza girls on settler farms in the Rift Valley.[95] Chief Amutalla struggled to exert control over the rush of "little ladies . . . having had the operation" on settler farms before returning to his location.[96] Whether in the Rift Valley or in North Nyanza, female circumcision operators mostly hailed from the Kalenjin, hired for their professional skill and paid in stock.[97] Enlisting specialized experts across ethnic lines was a common precolonial practice, from rainmakers to iron welders and circumcision experts. Local administrators targeted these Kalenjin operators through the courts, pass controls, and increased surveillance of the interdistrict movement of cattle.[98] Harsh prosecutions against fathers ensued and the LNC imposed legal restrictions on the movement of young women outside the district, a move that dovetailed with campaigns against errant, mobile women in the towns.[99]

Fresh from the Kikuyu female-circumcision controversy, both colonial administrators and missionary bodies in North Nyanza seemed eager to keep their distance from this emerging conflict.[100] In North Nyanza the female-circumcision crisis reflected not imperial efforts to legislate proper moral conduct and control female bodies but rather an internal crisis over respectability, belonging, and demographic discipline for the newly minted Luyia ethnic polity.

The majority of cases emerged among Tachoni girls. Local administrators, both African and British, struggled to comprehend the seemingly autochthonous emergence of this practice among a group thought to be firmly within the Luyia fold. The Tachoni, like many other communities in North Nyanza, had varied and mixed roots. Several Tachoni clans traced their origins to the Uasin Gishu Maasai and were among the earliest settlers around Mount Elgon.[101] As Bukusu and Kabras populations settled among them in the eighteenth and nineteenth century, the Tachoni progressively "bantuised."[102] By the arrival of C. W. Hobley, at the turn of the century, the Tachoni had dropped the use of the Maa language and regularly intermarried with surrounding Bantu communities. In the colonial mind, the Tachoni were merely a subsection of the larger Bukusu or Kabras populations.[103] The Luyia Language Committee did not recognize the Tachoni as a separate linguistic group, despite fervent protests from the Tachoni.[104] By the time of the female circumcision crisis, little was known about the Tachoni as a separate cultural community.

The appearance of female circumcision ceremonies in the 1940s prompted inquiries into the cultural history of the Tachoni. Despite gaps in the administration's ethnographic archives, Tachoni petitioners argued female circumcision was an ancient custom, practiced since "time immemorial" and essential to maintaining their identity and way of life.[105] In his historical study of circumcision, Pius Wanyonyi Kakai argued that the Tachoni began practicing both male and female circumcision at the their origin point in Misri (Egypt) and that according to oral accounts the first circumciser was "a woman who used a stone to circumcise."[106] In the 1940s many argued the silence in the historical and ethnographic records was due to the brutal suppression of this custom by the infamous Wanga chief Murunga. In their own anti-Wanga campaign, Tachoni and Bukusu activists successfully unseated Murunga in 1936. It is perhaps telling that the sudden increase in cases of female circumcision coincided with the demise of Wanga rule in the north.

It remains difficult to reconstruct the reasons why young Tachoni women crossed into foreign territories to be circumcised, due to a lack of archival sources documenting the perspectives of young African women and the contemporary resistance among Tachoni men and women to discussing this highly emotive and politicized issue. Despite these difficulties, colonial records of court cases and barazas held with illiterate Tachoni elder men and women revealed some of the underlying social and moral concerns involved in this practice.

Female circumcisions were far from the large, organized, and public spectacles pictured by administrators and political opponents; rather the rituals were organized largely along family lines, sporadic and individual in nature. Like among the Kikuyu, Tachoni men and women justified the practice in terms of community membership, passage into adulthood, and fecundity. Both male and female circumcisions were a "sign of maturity in thought, deed and word."[107] For both male and female initiates, circumcision symbolized the beginning of a new life. Initiates took on new names that reflected social values: Nabwera for neat and tidy, Murumba for strength, Sibuli for militancy and respectability.[108] Thus, as Tabitha Kanogo has argued, the prohibition on female circumcision could mean both "social and ethnic death."[109] While Tachoni elders publicly recognized that the practice had no contemporary relation to fertility, citing examples of uncircumcised Christian Tachoni women who had disproven this myth, they insisted their women remained committed to the importance of the rite. The defense and opposition to this rite thus revealed a greater concern with competing terms of respectability and belonging than with biological conceptions of fecundity or sexual control.

The most common justification centered on the role of this rite as a symbol of female exclusivity and respectability. Tachoni fathers prosecuted for the offense often argued their daughters sought circumcision without their knowledge or permission. As in Lynn Thomas's study of Meru girls who circumcised themselves in the 1950s in defiance of the ban, Tachoni girls were said to secretly cross into Rift Valley Province to undergo the procedure.[110] Provincial Commissioner Kenneth L. Hunter alleged he had evidence of married women with children submitting to the operation, "showing that there had been strong persuasion if not coercion."[111] Tachoni elders, however, argued these girls voluntarily underwent the operation to "preserve their customs" and to belong to an exclusive fellowship of circumcised women.[112] Uncircumcised women could not publicly abuse circumcised women, while the latter could not publicly joke with the former. Circumcised women would not drink beer or feast with the uncircumcised, creating public gendered hierarchies of respectability and spaces of belonging.[113] Many argued that fines imposed due to the ban actually added to the mystique and exclusivity of this rite of passage. For these Tachoni girls, circumcision represented entry into an exclusive fellowship of respectable, mature women.

As in other campaigns against female circumcision, the colonial administration identified women as the main instigators and perpetuators of the practice, thus rendering the practice "almost impossible to eradicate."[114] Tachoni men similarly shifted the ultimate responsibility for the continuation of the practice onto African women, arguing their daughters underwent these operations without their consent. Campaigns against such women buttressed colonial hierarchies and secured the position of LNC members and African patriotic men as the cultural and moral custodians of the tribe.[115]

In the late 1940s, locational associations took up the cause and transformed the numerous but sporadic cases against female circumcision into an outright political campaign. The Tachoni Union protested the over four hundred cases of illegal circumcision against Tachoni fathers pending in the local courts.[116] The union enlisted Indian lawyer A. Qadir Malik from Eldoret to defend their case. Writing on behalf for the Tachoni Union, Malik argued "from time immemorial the tribe has followed the Custom of Circumcision of Females."[117] Only in the 1940s, they argued, was the law being enforced by Bukusu and Kabras majorities to persecute and suppress Tachoni identity. "Time immemorial" became the constant refrain of petitions, marshaling historical narratives of entitlement and primordial customary rights, both crucial arguments to the exemption clause. Tachoni petitioners defended the practice as cultural nationalism, much as Jomo Kenyatta had during the Kikuyu circumcision controversy.[118] They repeatedly emphasized the practice was necessary to the social reproduction of their community and to guard against submersion under the numerically superior Bukusu and Kabras populations.[119] This campaign was thus part of the moral and demographic work of locational politics. The work of the Tachoni Union reinforced the locality as the space of customary practice and defended their autochthonous right to govern their women's bodies and ensure the reproduction of their community.

Local officials derided this campaign as purely political, "another pawn in the Tachoni game of tribalism."[120] Indeed, Tachoni petitions regarding female circumcision often accompanied petitions for separate representation and greater access to resources. While a minority of educated and Christian Tachoni opposed the operation in principle, they were equally opposed to Luyia cultural brokers' attempts to dictate customary practice.[121] The Tachoni Union, whose members drew from this educated minority, protested not in support of the practice but rather against its prosecution. They proposed either to be included in the exemption or to have the prohibition abolished entirely.[122] Petitioners argued that the custom would give way within a generation under the pressures of education and modernization. Tachoni campaigners presented the female circumcision crisis as part of larger territorial struggles over resources, political representation, and customary autonomy.

The female circumcision crisis transformed the question of whether to circumcise young girls from a private "family matter" into a public debate subject to the competing interests of the LNC, political associations, and African men from a variety of communities and political leanings.[123] For the Tachoni Union, the ban on female circumcision represented a threat to a patriotic identity, as they represented it, within a discourse of cultural and political autonomy; for the Tachoni girls who crossed borders, whether at the behest of fathers and mothers or of their own volition, this crisis embodied a threat to their gendered identity within a moral discourse of virtue, reputation, and social status. For Luyia ethnic patriots, however, the female circumcision crisis revealed the disjuncture between discourses of cultural pluralism and the coherence and progressive reputation of their larger patriotic project.

MAKING THE NATION RELEVANT: ELECTIONEERING AND DEMOGRAPHIC WORK

In the late 1940s a new generation of Luyia ethnic patriots, who moved in and out of local, ethnic, and national politicking, responded to these moral crises by taking up demographic work and crafting a careful cosmopolitan discourse of pluralism and gendered belonging. Through the technocratic tools of electioneering, census campaigns, and customary law, now nationally oriented Luyia patriots seeking to contain these gendered and deconstructive local politics worked to gain recognition for their "Luyia" body politic and make the national relevant in the local.

During the war years, the deaths of several historic chiefs—Paramount Chief Mumia, Chief Shivachi of Idakho, Chief Sore of Isukha, and Wanga Chief Murunga—signaled a generational shift.[124] As the early generation of chiefs passed or retired, many having ruled for an average of eighteen years, space opened up within the district for a reformulation of leadership.[125]

While precolonial political structures among these communities reflected diffuse and heterarchical patterns of authority, local leadership qualifications generally emphasized seniority, genealogical descent, wealth, and military leadership.[126] To this, the Abaluyia Customary Law Panel would add "politeness, generosity, ability, personality and good and wise judgment."[127] In the 1940s locational leaders reformulated chieftaincy to position themselves as the next generation of leaders. The NCA, the Bukusu Union, and the Maragoli Society all argued for chiefly requirements to include a high level of education, courses on "democratic governance," and advanced language skills in both Kiswahili and English.[128] Demobilized soldiers argued that the older generation lacked the knowledge and worldliness necessary for leadership in the postwar era and called for younger, more educated men to take these positions.[129] The professionalization of the native administration through locational councils and other bodies further emphasized technical competence and thus advantaged young, educated locational leaders in pursuit of colonial careers.

These new politics held a complex relationship with the past and "traditional" reservoirs of power. Peter Wafula, South Bukusu LNC member, questioned the logic of empowering chiefs to stop meetings like those held around the oluhia: "As an African was educated, he started to realize the benefit of the meetings which his grandfather was holding . . . the Government being full of jealousy tried his best in every corner to stop an African from holding a meeting."[130] However, Wafula's call to traditional measures of governance was unusual and those who called on the past as reservoir of moral authority often found themselves out of favor. While the promotion of Paul Agoi as chief of the Logoli, in 1940, signaled the integration of early ethnic patriots into the local administration, his later attempt to refashion himself along the lines of an invented royal tradition quickly raised suspicions and precipitated his downfall in 1950.[131] The project of this new generation was thus unlike young Kikuyu politicians, who merged modern education and print capitalism with self-promotion as the defenders of lost traditional orders, or Taita leaders, who married a progressivist ideology with notions of birthright and moral authority.[132] Locational leaders in North Nyanza instead fostered a progressive discourse of education and democratic governance less concerned with past qualifications of moral community than with modern technocratic competence.

These local postwar developments in the formulation of leadership reflected a larger transition in colonial policy toward limited African participation, welfare schemes, and social engineering.[133] Within this developmental ideology, the colonial government encouraged the growth of a "responsible" cadre of African politicians within officially sanctioned colonial channels. Many Luyia politicians in Nairobi were among the thirty-three founding members of the Kenya African Union (KAU), in 1944, the first national, multiethnic party.[134] While originally entering North Nyanza through the paramount chief debates, pointing to KAU's strategic alignment with "traditional" reservoirs of power in local contexts, KAU quickly grew in popularity among young political thinkers.[135] Although in existence for merely a decade, KAU's influence on the historical trajectories and language of territorial nationalism far outweighed its failings as a political pressure group.

None perhaps better exemplified the intricate marrying of ethnic patriotism and protonationalism among Luyia political leaders than J. D. Otiende. Otiende was one of the early "bookish liberals."[136] An accomplished Makerere graduate, Otiende taught at important Alliance High School during the war years, teaching returning ex-soldiers and elite African sons from across the colony.[137] From an early age, Otiende was a member of both the KCA and the NKCA.[138] A founding member of KAU, Otiende penned many of their petitions and worked as an editor on their newspaper, *Sauti ya Mwafrika*.[139] Otiende was responsible for transmitting KAU's message back to the reserve, convincing chiefs to join and collecting funds.[140] As KAU vice president, Otiende pushed for "safeguards for minorities," Crown land for African use, and the peaceful interpenetration of ethnic communities.[141]

Otiende incorporated these lessons in national leadership into his writing of Luyia history. In 1949, Otiende published the first academic history of the Luyia, *Habari za Abaluyia*.[142] This text was the first volume in a series entitled *Customs and Traditions in East Africa*, whose goal was to present "a balanced attitude to the complexities of modern life which a young nation must have."[143] In this text, written in the national language of Kiswahili, Otiende traced the diverse origins of North Nyanza's settlers.[144] Otiende ordered different linguistic and cultural practices into neat columns and locational sections. He filled sections on "the life of the people," "daily needs," and the "current state" of North Nyanza with culturally sensitive qualifications and differences in language and practice. Despite these qualifications, Otiende told his readers to look to their common values of charity, kinship, and progress. "Faults and Manners" were tabulated through a list of ten commandments of sorts, dealing with authority, respect, and the payment of cattle for sins.

The text gained great local standing and was often called up as evidence in local disputes. Kalenjin petitioners in the late 1950s, for example, would use Otiende's text to defend their own political campaigns within the Nyang'ori location: Kalenjin petitioners claimed "as it is quote by [J.] D. Otiende in Book name 'HABARI ZA BALUHYA' stating that Nyang'ori location belonged to people who are Terik in Nyang'ori location (Nandi speakers)."[145] Although potentially divisive, Otiende crafted these locational histories strategically to entrench the territory of North Nyanza as the space of Luyia ethnic identity. Otiende ended his text with a call to what being Luyia meant: "The people may work far away and forget they are Luyia. In the towns, they will unite under their proper names like Kisa, Bunyore, Maragoli, and say they are the people of North Nyanza—they are the *Abaluyia*."[146] In these history lessons, Otiende instructed his readers to focus not on divisive customary rights and myths of founding fathers but rather on thoroughly contemporary values. As opposed to the monarchical history writing of the NKCA, Otiende's partisan history provided a demographic and geographically constrained political vision that allowed the diversity of locational identities to define rather than defeat calls to contemporary Luyia unity.

In 1947 nominations for increased African seats in the Legislative Council gave new national Luyia leaders like Otiende the impetus to consolidate their electoral base and demographic numbers. Nominations reflected the ascension of the new qualifications for local authority. Some called for the nomination of accomplished locational leaders, like Solomon Adagala and Philip Ingutia, both well respected for their Makerere education, experience as schoolmasters, and service in the locational administration.[147] Others called for the nomination of the more cosmopolitan national Luyia politicians. W. W. W. Awori, prominent KAU member, editor of newspapers such as *Habari* and KAU's *Sauti ya Mwafrika* as well as the short-lived Luyia newspaper *Muluhia*, topped everyone's list for nomination.[148] Chief Agoi recommended Otiende for his "broadminded and cosmopolitan" nature and his mastery of multiple languages.[149] In Agoi's recommendation, Otiende was a "public man," a candidate whose learning and urbanity outweighed his young age. Otiende in turn recommended E. A. Andere, fellow Makerere graduate, AWA general secretary, and major figure in both Luyia language and customary law projects.[150] A new generation of leaders had emerged. The three top vote-getters—Awori, Andere, and Otiende—represented not narrow locational politicians but rather crucial figures in larger ethnic and national patriotic projects. The new brand of Luyia leadership was urbane, highly educated, multilingual, and cosmopolitan.

The first national census of 1948 provided these Luyia leaders with the opportunity to consolidate their constituents, prove their numbers, and literally put the Luyia on the national map. Census taking had long been a cornerstone of colonial governmentality and yet was a continually contested feature of colonial rule. Early administrators lamented constantly changing ethnonyms and other local strategies used to subvert the compilation of the "Census Book."[151] For the labor census of 1946, the North Nyanza administration restricted sampling areas to Isukha, Kakalelwa, Marama, and Itesio. This sampling effectively excluded the two most numerous and land-pressed groups, the Logoli and the Bukusu, who district officers felt would "not take kindly to being sampled," leaving labor figures uselessly overgeneralized.[152] The agricultural census of 1950 raised protest from the AWA and KAU, and many farmers refused access to their lands.[153] In Marama five men were convicted for refusing to answer the questions of the agricultural statistics officer, a case taken up by KAU vice president Tom Mbotela.[154] African communities often feared that these official censuses would translate into land alienation and further taxation: "The people of North Nyanza are entirely opposed to the idea of counting African land, and farm produce for the simple reason that they do not know the real motive behind this Agricultural Census."[155] While census taking proved a reductive and politically fraught endeavor, it also provided new grounds on which to define and debate political community.

As with the map, the census provided an opportunity for patriotic work. The first national census of 1948 supplied Luyia patriots a technocratic means to prove the success of their demographic work and to make legible to the colonial state a particular ethnic vision within the district and the nation. Under the direction of E. A. Andere, the AWA launched a campaign for the recognition and consolidation of Luyia numbers on the national census. The AWA aimed to subsume the complex ethnic diversity of the district under a centralized ethnic banner, so that "everybody may be counted and also to be counted under one name."[156] In barazas and pamphlets circulated throughout the district, the AWA instructed people as to how they should answer census takers: the "Tribe" should be "Omuluyia," and all other names should be reduced to "Clan" and "Sub-Clan" designations. In these meetings, Andere linked the census with concerns over Luyia men and women in the towns and campaigns for a Luyia representative on the Legislative Council. The AWA worked through its federated alliance of locational organizations across the country to align migrant laborers and urban dwellers with their reserve-based counterparts. Urban populations were crucial to proving overall Luyia numbers within the colony, to staking claims within urban settings, and to mapping Luyia networks outside the reserve. In this way the AWA could present a centralized political vision and minimalist ethnic map.

Population statistics also validated a particular form of political advocacy. The census provided a technocratic device for ongoing population-building exercises in areas of boundary disputes. The Bunyore branch of the AWA used the opportunity to voice concerns over their populations left in Central Nyanza. The branch argued that members who lived in Central Nyanza suffered discrimination under the Luo in terms of resources, local governance, and language policies. They campaigned to be counted separately and worked toward securing majorities in mixed locations.[157] In the Trans Nzoia and Uasin Gishu, the AWA and the Bukusu Union worked to consolidate and increase their numbers to lay claim to tracts of territories outside North Nyanza. While often divisive in local politics, these population-building campaigns in Central Nyanza and the Rift Valley aimed at renegotiating interdistrict boundaries and at proving the validity, and indeed the usefulness, of a Luyia polity.[158] The census also arrived at the height of the female circumcision crisis, opening an opportunity for Luyia proponents to demonstrate the political and social benefits of their census work: choose Luyia or face political and social oblivion. Census taking provided a quantifiable form of territorial community building.

Despite the colonial administration's skepticism as to whether all groups in North Nyanza had agreed to be "classified as Baluhya," the AWA succeeded in getting their name on the final report.[159] Throughout the census report, no other ethnic moniker from North Nyanza appeared, the AWA's campaign aided by colonial policies of ethnic simplification that limited the number of acceptable answers.[160] It remains difficult to assess whether Africans in North Nyanza chose to answer census takers using the AWA's consolidated hierarchical structure or whether census takers read the Luyia name into a multitude of answers.

The results of the census revealed the AWA's success not only in achieving recognition for their name but also in fulfilling the promise of their investment in the territorial idea. Luyia numbers shot to the top of the 1948 census table of the "main tribes of Kenya" (fig. 5.1). Geographic and demographic work went hand in hand: the patriotic investment in the map of the Luyia ethnic architects of the 1930s paid off in the census of 1948. North Nyanza represented the single largest population of any district throughout the colony, nearly doubling most other districts. As the administration divided statistics on ethnic populations by districts, the Luyia topped the national census list of tribes with 12.5 percent. Although the Kikuyu and the Luo maintained higher overall populations, their numbers were divided by district boundaries: the Kikuyu in Nyeri

EAST AFRICAN POPULATION CENSUS, 1948

MAIN TRIBES OF KENYA COLONY AND PROTECTORATE

Tribe	Male	Female	Total	Percentage of Grand Total %
Baluhya	323202	330572	653774	12.5
Luo (C.N.)	213628	229436	443064	8.4
Kamba (MKS)	186554	203223	389777	7.4
Kikuyu (KB)	199853	188309	388162	7.4
Kikuyu (F.H.)	188542	196309	384851	7.3
Meru	154284	170610	324894	6.2
Kisii	125002	130106	255108	4.9
Luo (S.N.)	124525	129962	254487	4.8
Kikuyu (NYI)	124613	128715	253328	4.8
Kamba (KTI)	108025	113923	221948	4.2
Embu	95244	108446	203690	3.9
Kipsigis	78999	80693	159692	3.0
Nyika (KFI)	62091	66107	128198	2.4
Nandi	59119	57562	116681	2.2
Nyika (VGA)	54886	57577	112463	2.2
Turkana[*]	38278	38652	76930	1.5
Masai	33455	33746	67201	1.3
Kamasia	33502	33348	66850	1.3
Teita	26738	30174	56912	1.1
All others	360602	332508	693110	13.2
TOTAL[ø]	2591142	2659978	5251120	100

[*] Estimated.

[ø] Excluding 1633 persons in transit.

FIGURE 5.1. Kenya population census, 1948. East Africa Statistical Department, Nairobi, 1950.

were counted as separate and distinct from those of Kiambu. The territorial concentration of the Luyia provided them with at least the official gloss of the largest homogeneous ethnic population in the entire colony. In less than thirteen years the Luyia population had grown from nonexistence to 653,774.

MAPPING THE CUSTOMARY:
THE ABALUYIA CUSTOMARY LAW PANEL

While Luyia leaders secured this national demographic victory, the politics of the locality and crisis of morality persisted. Commenting on the presence of Luyia women in Nairobi, the commissioner of the North Nyanza District recommended that "if the Abaluhya in Nairobi wish to continue to be regarded as Abaluhya, it behooves them to acquaint themselves with the well defined and time tested customary law."[161] For Luyia patriots, customary law proved an ideal technocratic tool to reinforce their demographic work and to delimit North Nyanza as an ethnic, if plural, homeland.

Throughout the 1940s and 1950s customary law panels across Kenya worked toward the abridgment of local practices into usable legal codes. Customary law and the African court system provided the "cornerstone of indirect rule," transforming chiefs into the authors and arbiters of "customary" justice.[162] In the "invention of tradition" school of thought, British officials conspired with African men to "invent" customary practice, just as missionaries "invented" African languages, to fit their own formulations of African traditions and privilege elder African men over women and junior men.[163] The practice of customary law was, however, never a simple exercise in governmentality.[164] Rather, customary law created a theater in which a wide array of Africans engaged in the creative intellectual work of debating the terms of respectability, customary responsibility, and membership in newly imagined political communities.[165]

The Abaluyia Customary Law Panel began its work near the end of the 1940s. Until the late colonial period, customary law in North Nyanza remained scattered, ill-defined, and subject to parochial contests between chiefs and their subjects.[166] The enormous local variations in practices of inheritance, marriage, landownership, and customary rites of passage caused local native courts to clog with competing claims to divergent historical traditions. As seen in the female circumcision crisis, long histories of intermarriage and inter-ethnic exchange further complicated the territorial limits of each group's reported practices and jurisdiction. Leaving customary law largely unwritten until the 1940s had allowed colonial officials a certain degree of latitude in the application of and interjection into "native" cases. While preparing his magnum opus on native administration, Lord Hailey further noted the peculiar trend in North Nyanza to "always quote section of Penal Code . . . they do not try cases under general terms of Native Law and custom."[167] But for Luyia cultural brokers in the late colonial period, creating a system of customary law provided an opportunity to order their disputatious constituents.

Customary law panels represented a novel approach to the institution of customary practice. Where earlier processes relied on the traditional authority of elders and a certain unwritten flexibility, the law panels of the 1940s and 1950s professionalized the written sanctification of customary practice.[168] To this end, the Abaluyia Customary Law Panel enlisted not elders but teachers and young politicians to head this committee. E. A. Andere took on the role of law panel secretary and became the leading expert on customary practice. For Andere, consolidating customary law was a natural extension of the demographic work he pioneered in the 1948 census campaign.

As secretary of the Abaluyia Customary Law Panel, Andere struggled, as others had before him, to rationalize the internal contradictions of Luyia customary practice. Having witnessed the collapse of the Luyia Language Committee under the weight of competing linguistic projects, Andere and the law panel played a careful game of ethnic arithmetic in the selection of its members. Locational associations such the Bukusu Union, the Bunyore Welfare Association, the Maragoli Society, and the Tachoni Union, whose constitutions contained mandates to record and defend tribal customs, all lobbied for the incorporation of their particular versions of customary practice. The success of the law panel in the 1950s depended on the careful balancing of the diversity and self-interest among its constituents. The law panel succeeded in attracting an admirably diverse committee, containing at least one representative from each of seventeen different locational communities.[169] Through this diversity, the law panel worked to tabulate, order, and discipline the territorial extent and terms of membership for an invented Luyia tradition.

The texts published by the Abaluyia Customary Law Panel reflected the creative work of Luyia cultural brokers confronted with the customary diversity of their imagined constituents in areas of land tenure, marriage, inheritance, and authority. In these publications, Andere and the law panel rationalized this ethnic diversity within neat secretarial lists indicating adherence to or rejection of particular practices for each group. Land law provided perhaps the greatest variability: for days, members debated inheritance rights and the relative importance of ancestral graves as they tested their publications against actual case law.[170] Complicated tables, sections on "local variations," and constant qualifications riddled these texts.[171] The law panel charted the great variety of bridewealth practices within ordered columns: among the Bunyore, Idakho, Isukha, Logoli, and Tiriki bridewealth called for an average of three head of cattle while among the Bukusu, Tachoni, and Wanga bridewealth amounted to upward of ten head of cattle.[172] In marriage, the law panel noted men from particular locations were permitted to marry their sisters-in-law, while for others this practice remained strictly forbidden. In Andere's masterful hands customary practice in transition was rendered within a distinctly Luyia trajectory: "For the Banyala marriage of a sister was also forbidden in the olden days but today things have changed and the Banyala are now beginning to follow the custom of those Abaluyia who recognize the marriage of a sister-in-law."[173]

Ideas of progress thus underwrote the terms of respectability. Andere had learned from J. D. Otiende's history and manner lessons to tabulate and order these differences. In the end product, cultural relativity allowed these Luyia ethnic architects to construct a larger picture of cultural cohesion with a sense of inevitable variation given to the significance and signification of each practice. Customary law as envisioned by colonial administrators provided Luyia cultural brokers with a unified template to manage plurality and dissent, to enforce normative cultural values, and to encode measures of progress and respectability in customary practice, fixing their constituents not only to a territory but moreover to a homeland.

CHOOSING PATRIOTISM: ENDING THE FEMALE CIRCUMCISION CRISIS AND THE LIMITS OF CULTURAL PLURALISM

Although Luyia customary law necessarily allowed multiple systems to coexist, the female circumcision crisis prompted Luyia ethnic architects to legislate the limits of customary conformity more directly than in any other case. The female circumcision crisis proved a test for Luyia patriotism and demonstrated the limits of cultural pluralism.

Luyia patriots argued that female circumcision among the Tachoni threatened not only their mannered and progressive patriotic discourse but also the respectability of all Luyia women. North Nyanza LNC members argued they tolerated the custom among other groups but feared its spread among their own girls: the ban over all Luyia groups was necessary to empower chiefs and headmen to exact "reprisals against the circumcising minorities for seducing and circumcising girls of other tribes."[174] Fears of the practice "spreading" to other Luyia groups were stoked when cases of female circumcisions cropped up in pockets of the Bukusu and Kabras in the late 1940s. It seems probable that some Bukusu clans had practiced female circumcision until 1925, though oral and anthropological sources remain conflicted on this point.[175] Bukusu locational councillors warned any removal of the prohibition would cause "a considerable recrudescence of the custom among their own girls."[176] Bukusu petitioners portrayed Tachoni female circumcision ceremonies as "primitive" displays of dance, excessive drinking, and prostitution. They feared "this evil deed," would infect the "whole community of Baluyia in the District."[177] This description of a very public performance of female circumcision rites conflicted with evidence that these procedures often occurred in private and with great secrecy. High rates of intermarriage and the territorial dispersal of the Tachoni throughout the district also blurred the lines of discrete tribal territories.[178] The respectability of all Luyia women was at stake. Luyia women in other locations linked female circumcision with a lack of virginity and the "purity required for marriage."[179] Some Luyia men indicated a resistance to marrying circumcised women.[180] While blame landed squarely on the Tachoni, the female circumcision crisis threatened the educated, Christian, and urbane reputation Luyia ethnic architects sought to promote.

In line with their concurrent census campaign, Luyia leaders framed the female circumcision crisis as a choice: they required a "clear declaration that the Tachoni are a section of the Baluhya people."[181] Bukusu petitioners called on the Tachoni to come before the LNC and prove either their historical lineage as Maasai descendants or their cultural membership within the Luyia community.[182] At a baraza held in Kabras in 1951, the African assistant administrative officer emphasized to a gathering of Tachoni that "if they want to call themselves Abaluhia and to be attended to by the Government as other Abaluhia Tribes in North Nyanza they should stop this practice."[183] Provincial Commissioner Kenneth Hunter, remarking on the uniqueness of North Nyanza's complete prohibition on female circumcision, warned that its imposition might have been unconstitutional and discriminatory toward minorities within the district.[184] The African District Council (ADC) easily passed new legislation providing further exemptions for members of the Maasai and Kalenjin, strangely given the blanket term Sabaot, but left the Tachoni liable to further prosecution.[185] This new legislation elevated ethnolinguistic affiliations to the determining factor of customary and legal accountability. While emerging national Tachoni leaders like Burudi Nabwera were able to convince the administration to allow an exemption period that would give Tachoni leaders time to persuade their community to give up this practice, others still doubted that the Tachoni would ever embrace "true patriotism."[186] Well into the 1960s meetings of the Tachoni Union still put the "position of MTachoni in Buluhya tribe" at the top of their agendas.[187] At the heart of these debates were the definitions of membership, in in gendered terms, within the Luyia ethnic project and the territorial frontiers of respectability and customary control.

As Lonsdale argued in the case of the Kikuyu female circumcision controversy, such conflicts over customary practice "marked the boundaries of a mutually intelligible ethnic language of class, gender and virtue."[188] Luyia ethnic architects used this crisis to territorialize community membership through an unprecedented call to cultural conformity. Proponents of a Luyia ethnic identity mandated that Luyia women must not be circumcised, though no similar stipulation existed for male membership. Tachoni men, who underwent circumcision facing the sun, in the manner of their Maasai neighbors, would not be forced to conform with the more common Luyia practice of turning their backs to the sun.[189] For Luyia women, it would seem, cosmopolitan pluralism had its limits. As in urban campaigns against errant women, men were able to maintain their personal, locational identities while women were forced to carry the Luyia banner and maintain its calls to progress, modernity and respectability. The circumcision of Tachoni girls undermined the practiced civility and mannered progress espoused by Luyia male patriots. In these debates, African leaders in North Nyanza marshaled Luyia-ness to draw deviants into their cultural fold. In no other case would a cultural practice be banned or mandated for membership within this plural ethnic community.

⤺

In the 1940s the politics of home and away, of men and women, and of locality and nation reflected the larger social transformations and the variety of politics debated throughout eastern Africa. Demographic work proved crucial to both the politics of the locality and the now national, comparative politics of ethnic patriotisms. When the first Luyia politician, Philip Ingutia, finally reached the Legislative Council, in 1949, he called for the official recognition of the Luyia name in terms that echoed Otiende's history lessons: "Those 'tribes' have been living together for such a long time, that there has been much interpenetration and intermarriage, that we can no longer speak of them as tribes, but sections of a larger tribe, the Abaluyia. They speak dialects of the same language, Luluyia. There has been a strong trend towards unity among the Abaluyia."[190] In general notice no. 34, in 1950, the name Abaluyia gained official recognition.[191] Through their geographic and demographic work, Luyia leaders had made national politics relevant to the local and transformed the little-known Luyia ethnic project from its parochial and fractured roots into a viable vehicle for politicking on the national scene.

But, as Derek Peterson has recently argued, "Demography was more than an academic project": it was also a moral project.[192] The moral crises of the 1940s proved the necessity of gendered discipline and the mapping of belonging. Football teams, antiprostitution campaigns, and the codification of customary law all served as population-building tactics meant to fix Luyia constituents to a particular mapped homeland. Errant women and the bodies of Tachoni girls presented a common ground for Luyia men of diverse locational loyalties to direct their demographic attentions and thus fed the development of particular Luyia discourse, limited in its culturalist agenda but robust in its geographic and demographic goals. In the 1950s this gendered discipline would turn progressivist discourse: Luyia organizations would be unique in their petitions for universal suffrage ahead of the first African election in 1957.[193] While more "conservative" communities like the Luo mobilized historical arguments against women's suffrage, Luyia organizations called for all eligible men and women to receive the vote.[194] Women like Perus Angaya Abura, a Church of God convert, trained teacher, health care provider, and prominent member of the elite women's movement Maendeleo ya Wanawake, embodied a form of domestic modernity that Luyia male leaders presented as qualifying for the privilege of the vote.[195] But while this plea for women's rights fit well with the progressive discourse of Luyia political thought, it also served a more pragmatic function, increasing the demographic weight of the North Nyanza constituency.

While their multiple "wives" did not always agree or behave as their "Luyia" husbands instructed them, Luyia ethnic patriots in the 1940s succeeded in crafting a common, domestic moral vocabulary and mapping a homeland in western Kenya in which husbands and wives, sons and daughters, members of locality and nation, could marry, fight, and live together.

6 ᔍ Between Loyalism and Dissent
Ethnic Geographies in the Era of Mau Mau

THE STORY of Gerald Masibayi, now the Marach elder on the Luyia Council of Elders, revealed the at times paradoxical benefits gained from espousing a Luyia ethnic identity in the politically polarizing time of the late colonial era in Kenya.[1] Born in 1924, Masibayi received an elite education typical of many Luyia cosmopolitans in the schools of western Kenya and Uganda, culminating in his completion of the Cambridge Certificate in 1947. After graduating from the engineering program at Entebbe, Masibayi returned to Nairobi to join the Public Works Department. Near the end of 1951, the department enlisted Masibayi to prepare a memorandum for the upcoming Flemming Commission on the conditions of African workers and civil servants. Masibayi traveled the country, interviewing African civil servants and witnessing their working conditions.

Masibayi believed one of the reasons he was chosen for this task was his Luyia identity, which colonial officials believed would allow him a level of objectivity and distance from the heightened political atmosphere of the Central Province where rumors of a secret, radical society were spreading and the name Mau Mau was beginning to be heard. Masibayi was shocked by the state of African labor, particularly in the Central Province. Detained Kikuyu civil servants reported massive abuses, lack of food, and arbitrary killings. In his report, submitted just after the colonial government had declared a state of emergency in October 1952, Masibayi petitioned for the end of racial pay scales and highlighted the problems of land and detention in the Central Province. In January 1953 the colonial government drew up detention orders and removed

Masibayi from his home in the Bahati estate. Part of the colonial government's "municipal housing experiment," Bahati was a hotbed of criminal activity. Colonial officials feared Mau Mau oath administrators were inducting workers from other ethnic groups within these mixed estates.[2] Masibayi was charged with supplying pipes, used to make homemade guns, to Mau Mau fighters and sent to the recently erected emergency detention camps. Then as now, Masibayi and his family denied the charges and accused the administration of framing him to prevent his report from becoming public. Masibayi never met with the Flemming Commission, nor was his report ever officially filed.[3]

In five years of detention, Masibayi worked his way down the pipeline of detention camps, from Athi River to Kapenguria.[4] Daily, colonial administrators interrogated and tortured him to confess that he had taken the Mau Mau oath. Throughout five years of interrogation, Masibayi maintained it was inconceivable for him to take a Kikuyu oath. Masibayi predicated his defense on his Luyia identity: "I am not a Kikuyu to take a Kikuyu oath." Suspected Luyia dissidents in the 1950s frequently asserted that as members of the Luyia community they could not take an oath of another community, least of all a "Kikuyu oath." Masibayi's espoused Luyia identity would, eventually, aid in his release when his "tribal particulars" led to questions surrounding the legitimacy of his detention. His father, olugongo for the Marach location, and his uncle, chief of the location, petitioned the colonial administration to review the circumstances of his detention.[5] Soon after, Masibayi was released, never having confessed. Upon his return to the North Nyanza District, he was integrated into the local administration, first as a tax revenue clerk and merely a few years later as chief.

The story of Gerald Masibayi reflects the different positions a Luyia identity afforded during the 1950s. For Masibayi, being "Luyia" was characterized not by genealogy or cultural practice but by a distinct moral geography and the articulation "of a certain common cause." These ironic twists, from loyal civil servant to dissident and back again as a chief, were actually quite common in the final decade of colonial rule and revealed the complex ethnic geographies of loyalism and dissent in the era of Mau Mau.

The deep moral anxiety of the 1940s gave way to a more broadly distributed, radical national crisis in the 1950s that polarized the political landscape of Kenya between ethnic and national, educated elite and worker, loyalist and dissident. While the Luyia leaders of the 1940s had taken up linguistic work, leveraged their demographic work onto census sheets, and defined a gendered homeland in western Kenya, the 1950s would require these ethnic patriots to reconfigure their political projects, both intellectually and territorially. Many, from colonial administrators to historians and contemporary popular media, have been quick to label anyone outside the borders of central Kenya as "loyal," as outside of the conflicts and moral debates of the Mau Mau rebellion. Yet the national geographies of loyalism and dissent were much more complex: positions of loyalists and militants were in their essence colonial categories that imposed moral orders on political communities in the making. That the reality on the ground was much more complicated seems self-evident, evinced even in the brief case of Gerald Masibayi, but remains unexamined in the historiography on anticolonial struggle and the politics of decolonization.

In western Kenya the politics of loyalism and dissent preexisted the declaration of the Emergency and prompted Luyia cultural brokers to develop a theory of ethnic belonging that allowed those who espoused it to maneuver within these colonial categories. Beginning in the 1940s, a religious and anticolonial movement emerged in North Nyanza, largely among the northern Bukusu community. Led by the charismatic, self-proclaimed prophet Elijah Masinde, the Dini ya Msambwa movement challenged both colonial and patriotic geographies. Through their religious pilgrimages, cultural reforms, and anticolonial activism, Msambwa followers threatened to unground the progressive discourse and civic reputation cultivated by Luyia patriots. By the late 1940s, both colonial officials and Luyia thinkers had come to organize law and culture territorially, fixing diverse communities to "tribal" territories and disciplining those who moved beyond these territorial confines. These frontier rebels, calling up the portable territorial spirits of their ancestors, revealed the porous and ambiguous bounds of community and raised questions for African political thinkers, migrant laborers, and colonial administrators alike regarding the movement of African peoples between ethnically defined territories. Unknowingly, the Dini ya Msambwa movement acted as antecedent for debates around closed colonial ethnic geographies and counterinsurgency tactics later perfected during the Mau Mau rebellion.

As the Mau Mau rebellion prompted a new kind of ethnic politicking, Luyia political thinkers fashioned a more flexible idea of Luyia identity in the 1950s, a form of territorial consciousness that would allow Luyia cosmopolitans, farmers, and workers to move more freely through Kenya's polarized political landscape. This Luyia idea, taken up in the context of dissent within their borders and systematic colonial discrimination against the Kikuyu during the Mau Mau rebellion, offered a means of exercising agency for its constituents: to stand for elections;

to take up urban employment; to provide a voice for political activism in multiethnic schools; to dissent against colonial policies; and, in rare cases, to navigate Mau Mau detention camps. In the 1950s political thinkers in North Nyanza marshaled a theory of ethnic pluralism and a moral geography of belonging to navigate the Emergency-era politics of loyalism and dissent and to remake the Luyia.

ANTECEDENTS OF LOYALISM AND DISSENT

While much has been written on the Mau Mau rebellion and the moral dimensions of Kikuyu political thought, loyalism has remained a highly undertheorized topic and a blanket expression over a wide range of political orientations.[6] Daniel Branch's recent intervention, the first study dedicated entirely to the history of loyalism, offers a sort of collective life history of the "loyalists," from their origins and motivations to their triumph in the postcolonial era.[7] While Branch effectively argued for the need to center loyalists within any understanding of the Mau Mau rebellion, his study still suffers from a myopic view on central Kenya and indeed on Mau Mau as the only form this debate took.

The moral crisis in the family and in household discipline evident in central Kenya was part of a broader social insecurity felt by communities across eastern Africa. African men struggled to maintain control over their land, their wives, and the means of production as young men and women, the "impatient" youths, moved away from the home and challenged the authority of older social orders.[8] While the Kikuyu were not unique in this, the Mau Mau rebellion created particular avenues for expressing dissent, a specific set of urgent political choices, and alternative routes for reestablishing order. Finding resonances with Brett Shadle's revisions on the cult of Mumbo, Branch demonstrated how a breakdown in lines of patronage and accountability made positions of loyalism not only viable but also attractive as a means of achieving self-mastery.[9] And yet most problematic for Branch was finding a definition to identify who actually was a loyalist. Loyalism did not, as Branch assumed, provide a crystallizing force capable of creating a defined social unit: it was instead at once a strategy, a colonial imposition, and a form of argument forwarding ongoing local debates and particular agendas.

In western Kenya the politics of loyalism and dissent were obviously not the same as in central Kenya, yet they were informed by similar local debates. Before the Mau Mau rebellion, it was Dini ya Msambwa that most terrified colonial officials and tested local partisan loyalties. The Msambwa movement created its own rhetoric of loyalism and dissent formulated, as in Mau Mau, in ethnic and antimodernist terms. Dini ya Msambwa threatened not only the territorial control and tribal geographies of colonial administrators but also the reputation, progressive values and moral geographies of Luyia ethnic architects.

ETHNIC GEOGRAPHIES AND FRONTIER REBELS: THE DINI YA MSAMBWA MOVEMENT

As its name implied, Dini ya Msambwa was, or rather is, a religious movement inspired by a return to the ancestors, a return to the social and moral order of precolonial eastern Africa. Leader Elijah Masinde marshaled a long lineage of Bukusu prophets and called on his followers to transform the private familial religious practices of Bukusu traditions into public political action, and to make encroaching white settlers from the highlands and African neighbors accountable to the ancestors and the oral code they invoked.[10] While calling for a pan-African religious revival, Masinde's rhetoric and practices were firmly rooted in Bukusu traditions. As their locations bordered the European settlements of the Trans Nzoia, the Bukusu had come under severe land pressure and were frequent laborers and squatters in neighboring territories. In its social reformism and political activism, Masinde's movement offered a radical alternative moral economy.

Elijah Masinde and his fellow leaders Samson Wafula and Benjamin Wekuke were all mission educated and trained in local administration. When fired from his position as a clerk at the Kavujai native tribunal, in 1943, Masinde led his growing followers in campaigns against soil conservation and forced agricultural work, regularly targeting agricultural officers, resisting cattle inoculations, and deliberately destroying agricultural projects.[11] After a dramatic series of arsons in 1945, which included FAM churches, African grain stores, and the home of the Assistant Agricultural Officer, colonial officials remitted Masinde to the Mathari Mental Hospital on charges of insanity.[12] His return to the district, in May 1947, cleared of the charges of insanity, reignited calls to reject European rule and return to traditional practices.[13] The administration linked the increased Msambwa activity with the concurrent rise in cases of female circumcision: in the words of Provincial Commissioner Kenneth Hunter, "The teachings of Elijah Masinde [called] upon all tribes to revert to tribal practices and custom and avoid all European control."[14]

These politically charged accusations came during a week of increasingly confrontational Dini ya Msambwa action. First, on 7 February 1948 hundreds of Msambwa followers occupied a Catholic mission at Kibabii, demanding the removal of the European priest. The scene was a dramatic one: Msambwa followers chanted, tore their cloths, and threw themselves on the ground. Three days later, a riot occurred in Malakisi over the jailing of Dini ya Msambwa leaders. During the Malakisi riot eleven Africans were killed and dozens injured when police opened fire on protesters. This event led to the proscription of the sect, an immediate crackdown on Dini ya Msambwa members, and a coordinated inter-territorial manhunt for Elijah Masinde, found hiding in the traditional refuges of the caves of Mount Elgon.[15]

Msambwa followers were, from the outset, territorial rebels.[16] They defied colonial boundaries through aggressive settlement campaigns, labor strikes in the Trans Nzoia and pilgrimages to Mount Elgon, their Mount Zion. Their very name invoked a tradition of mobility and frontier mentality: Bukusu frontiersmen in the nineteenth century transformed territorial *msambwa* ancestral spirits into "ancestral ghosts" so that they could inhabit the caves and springs of their new territories.[17] These portable spirits allowed for a kind of aterritorial political work, allowing settlers to expand into dangerous new territories.

Through their pilgrimages, their entrepreneurship in other territories, and their political philosophy, Msambwa followers did geographic work. As in earlier resistance, Dini ya Msambwa members counter-mapped the symbols of imperial cartographic control. In the investigation on the Malakisi riot, colonial officials identified the root cause as an ongoing conflict over survey beacons. An article in the *Standard* reported that the "first signs of trouble appeared when the people were told that the trigonometric (survey) beacons on the hills in Kimilili concealed 'medicine' . . . it is believed that the present trouble has its roots in the restoration of the beacons."[18] In November 1949 police discovered a Dini ya Msambwa flagpole planted along a new road from Kimilili to Kamakoiya. The compulsory labor used to construct this road was part of the communal punishment imposed on the generalized Bukusu population after the Malakisi riot. Two letters attached to the flag declared war on the British and urged Africans to refuse compulsory-labor demands.[19] Two days later officials found concrete beacons destroyed along the Kabras–Uasin Gishu boundary. Among the possessions confiscated from the three men arrested for destroying the beacon was a book listing all the beacons along the northern boundaries of the district.[20] This territorial activism reflected countermapping strategies dating back to the turn of the century. Bukusu frontiersmen had regularly destroyed beacons and crossed borders into the Trans Nzoia and Uganda to preserve their autonomy and reclaim land they viewed as their historic inheritance. In this same tradition, Msambwa followers sabotaged the symbols of land demarcation and countermapped a new, dangerously ungrounded geographic horizon.

These antiterritorial practices were made all the more dangerous as new colonial policies worked to further territorialize ethnic geographies. The project of enclosing "tribal" geographies was distinctly revved up in late 1940s, partly in response to the moral crises (see chapter 5), partly as a component of broader late colonial strategies. Colonial refusals to extend the limits of the Native Reserves or recognize African land claims in the White Highlands had encouraged African farmers in densely populated areas to engage in more aggressive land strategies.[21] The Nyanza provincial commissioner linked the extension of "tribal lands" through encroaching cultivation and overnight infiltration campaigns with population-building work ahead of the 1948 census.[22] Trespassing of people and stock became major offenses in the late 1940s, defined not in terms of private property but in terms of the sanctity of ethnic territories. Nandi and Luyia chiefs formed border committees to deal with stock theft, trespassing, and the infiltration of Nandi squatters into Kaimosi after being forced off European farms in Kapsabet.[23] Cases of encroaching cultivation and land infiltrations clogged local courts and prompted the colonial administration to harden its policies toward "alien" trespassers.

Harsher regulations on trespassing had particular consequences in areas bordering European settlement. Claims to large tracts of land to the north of the district in the Trans Nzoia had united local and national Luyia politicians since the Kenya Land Commission. During the 1948 Census, Luyia organizations worked to consolidate their numbers in these disputed territories and mixed borderlands. The census report revealed Luyia populations, largely Bukusu but also Kabras, Logoli, and Banyore, represented 50 percent of the Trans Nzoia population.[24] European settlers seeking to reduce the claims of Luyia squatters pressured the Trans Nzoia and Uasin Gishu LNCs to enact legislation aimed at reducing and eventually eliminating squatters' cattle in their districts. Echoing the earlier *kifagio* campaign against the Kikuyu, which "swept away" squatters' cattle in the 1920s, this legislation threatened the livelihood of Bukusu families and transformed Bukusu laborers, many of whom had labored in Trans Nzoia for upwards of twenty years, into trespassers.[25] No longer having claims to land in North Nyanza, Bukusu men returned to the district at night, erecting houses before dawn.[26] These overnight settlers became such a common occurrence that the administration outlawed any travel at night between the northern locations and the Trans Nzoia.[27] The Bukusu were not unique in these repatriation campaigns, but their geographic position on the edge of the reserve made them common targets. Repatriates threatened social disorder within the district, digging up old land claims and provoking familial disputes over inheritance and complicated lineages.

In the late 1940s colonial policy toward the problem of squatters and overcrowding took a distinct turn toward the draconian. In a reversal of the policy laid out by the Kenya Land Commission, which had recommended the maximum permeability of tribal boundaries, movements and settlements between Native Reserves were now vilified as creating "foreign enclaves in the tribal territories."[28] In 1946 the chief secretary of Kenya laid out new restrictions on these practices: "interpenetration" would require "settlement involving a change of tribe on the part of the interpenetrator, who becomes a member of the tribe among whom he settles and relinquishes that membership of the tribe into which he was born": those who settled among a different group without such "naturalization" would be classified as trespassers, settling through illegal "infiltration."[29] Immigrants would be required to amend their tribal particulars on their identity cards, register as a permanent member of the adoptive tribe, and "abandon any connection with his district of origin."[30] Any offense against local custom or refusal to undergo initiation rites rendered the immigrant liable to eviction. Offenses liable for expulsion included the importation of other "aliens," persistent demands for separate schools or services, contempt for local authorities, demands for alien-bride prices, and disregard of local land laws. Membership in separate ethnic associations was firmly prohibited: thus, a Bukusu farmer living in the Trans Nzoia was prohibited from being a member of the Bukusu Union or any Luyia association, effectively limiting ethnic political action to natal reserves. The distinction drawn between these two processes, interpenetration and infiltration, revealed the tensions inherent in colonial policy toward customary practice and the sanctity of "tribal geographies."[31]

Nyanza provincial commissioner C. H. Williams voiced his doubts regarding the feasibility of such policies. Although he stressed the importance of adoption ceremonies, "if a 'reasonable' one exists," his experiences in the Nyanza administration convinced him that complete absorption was unrealistic and in some cases impossible and undesirable.[32] Williams illustrated his doubt with numerous examples of refusals to undergo adoption ceremonies: the Chepkos Maasai in West Suk, the Kikuyu in Kisii, and the numerous communities from Nyanza Province concurrently being expelled from the Trans Mara. Even more compelling, Williams argued the "impossibility" of expecting Logoli immigrants in Luo territory, for example, to become "good Luo . . . in a lifetime," as this would require the Logoli to forego their important rites of male circumcision. Such population movements pointed to the multiple "ways of being" in colonial Kenya and challenged both colonial "tribal geographies" and historical interpretations based on primordial or constructivist models of ethnic identity.[33]

Colonial policies of interpenetration encouraged a distinctly nativist politics to develop. The new policies sparked widespread panic over mass evictions and instigated secretive and increasingly aggressive infiltration campaigns. In 1949 the colonial government evicted thirty-six families of Logoli settlers from the Trans Mara.[34] Many of these Logoli evictees subsequently sought settlement in the Kanyamkago location of South Nyanza, where a large number of Logoli settlers had already established residence. As Williams had predicted, the incompatibility of Logoli and Luo customs placed these Logoli settlers again at risk for eviction. Logoli immigrants attempted to circumvent local authorities by moving at night and settling in Kanyamkago in secret. When discovered, the ten-shilling fine did little to deter their return.[35] Luo inhabitants petitioned to evict all Logoli settlers from the location, citing colonial policy on interpenetration and incompatible customary practices. With no room at home and the restrictions on cultural practice in new lands, Logoli migrants suffered a vicious cycle of landlessness and conflict. The Logoli were not alone in these practices: across Kenya the initiative of ordinary people revealed the more complex choices and multiple levels of identification operating outside the control of both colonial officials and ethnic patriots.[36]

Such hardening of ethnic geographies came as a response to what colonial officials saw as the threat of "contamination" and ambiguous belonging—dissent crossing borders on the backs of immigrants who by their very movements challenged colonial geographies. Officials worried that Bukusu squatters spreading throughout Rift Valley Province carried with them the contagion of rebellion.[37] The Malakisi riot, in February 1948, precipitated the large-scale repression and eviction of Bukusu squatters from the Trans Nzoia. Bukusu evictees, finding no more room in North Nyanza, were forced to migrate further north to the arid region of West Suk. The discovery of a Msambwa "cell" in Keringet in West Suk stoked these fears and accelerated calls for mass evictions of Bukusu settlers. And it was here, miles away from the territorial birthplace of the msambwa movement, that the most violent and destructive episode in Dini ya Msambwa's history would take place.

The Kolloa Affray, as it came to be known, sent shockwaves through the European settler community, baffled local administrators, and led to the abrupt enforcement of interpenetration policies.[38] Kolloa, located in the Rift Valley district of Baringo, was a sleepy backwater of Pokot traditional pastoralists. Unlike the Bukusu, the Pokot were neither a major source of colonial labor nor the victims of land alienation. These pastoralists maintained much of their precolonial way of life, resisting colonial attempts to introduce education and Christianity and demonstrating "no desire for advancement."[39] These factors contributed to the shock triggered by the events of April 1950.

On 24 April 1950, a contingent of four European administrators, forty armed African police, two chiefs, and their assistants traveled to Kolloa to arrest Lucas Pkech, a Pokot leader who was rumored to be leading frenzied meetings and spreading the "seditious teachings" of Dini ya Msambwa.[40] Upon arrival, the colonial command discovered Pkech leading five hundred armed Pokot singing and dancing on a pilgrimage to their "Zion"—Mount Elgon.[41] While the exact order of the events that followed remains disputed, the result was a dramatic confrontation between these two forces. In the battle that ensued, African policemen and European officers opened fire killing Pkech and thirty-two followers and wounding another fifty.[42] Three European officers and one African police corporal also lost their lives.

Although the two Msambwa movements differed in almost every element save their name, the Kolloa Affray stoked colonial anxieties over the spread of rebellion and accelerated the urgency of implementing stricter controls on interpenetration.[43] While the Pokot suffered the most direct and severe punishments meted out by the colonial government—seven hangings, hundreds of arrests, and severe collective punishments in cattle, fines, and labor—the administration blamed the "infection of West Suk" on Bukusu immigrants from the Trans Nzoia and called for the wholesale repatriation of the Bukusu "originators."[44]

Despite the near total removal of Dini ya Msambwa elements from West Suk and Baringo by the end of 1950, the Pokot administration used the Kolloa Affray to give Bukusu settlers an ultimatum: undergo Pokot initiation or vacate their lands.[45] The initiation ceremony mandated by the West Suk LNC included smearing mud on the initiate's hair, a common practice among the Pokot more important than circumcision in marking the transition to adulthood during the *sapana* ceremony, and that was further connected to marriage and a warrior male cultural identity.[46] Initiates were also required to consume the "warriors' drink," a mixture of milk and the blood from a freshly slaughtered goat.[47] After this ceremony, initiates were expected to reject their connections to previous traditional beliefs and practices and fully adopt Pokot customs.

Many Bukusu residents in West Suk refused to submit to initiation.[48] In protesting these ceremonies, Bukusu petitioners pictured Pokot practices as "primitive," "against Western Civilization," and "repugnant" to Bukusu values, fitting their protests into the colonial administration's exemption clause: initiation ceremonies could not be enforced if "repugnant to morality."[49] Petitioners outlined the "improvements" brought by the Bukusu to the Pokot areas in terms of education, Christianity, and modern farming practices.[50] Petitioners further feared these initiations would mean the loss of hereditary rights to Bukusu landholdings in Pokot areas.

Backed into a corner, Bukusu elders traveled to the West Suk ADC and agreed to repatriate Bukusu settlers who refused to be initiated.[51] In 1952 dozens of Bukusu settlers joined the hundreds of evictees already being forcibly repatriated in North Nyanza.[52] Farmers in North Nyanza complained of the added hardships these repatriations produced: "We were surprised to see thousands of Africans being repatriated from Trans Nzoia, Suk and Uganda back into North Nyanza this year. This act has caused considerable hardship and trouble to the natives of Kitosh."[53] North Nyanza chiefs, seeking greater punitive powers, complained of the shame Dini ya Msambwa brought to their locations with their "uncivilised and anti-social" behavior.[54] Non-Bukusu farmers worried they would be forced to move to make room for returning Bukusu farmers.[55] These Bukusu farmers had settled more permanently in these foreign territories than previous labor migrants, and thus returnees experienced a greater degree of social dislocation and dispossession, both in terms of land and familial relations.

The antiterritorial politics of Msambwa rebels reflected much broader strategies and anxieties. Squeezed by colonial land policies and encroaching European settlements, Africans across Kenya moved into new territories and mobilized flexible forms of identification that threatened both colonial and patriotic constructions of ethnic geographies. While colonial policies buttressed ongoing Luyia projects to construct a territorially defined homeland, they also created endless cycles of interpenetration and repatriation and promoted an aggressive form of nativist politics that threatened the civility, cosmopolitanism, and discourse of pluralism promoted by Luyia cultural brokers.

DINI YA MSAMBWA IN THE ERA OF MAU MAU

As an anticolonial, religious, and political movement, Dini ya Msambwa sprang from similar moral roots as did its later and more violent counterpart and would serve as an important antecedent for both colonial counterinsurgency practices and patriotic debates around loyalism and dissent. John Lonsdale and Derek Peterson have understood Mau Mau as essentially a moral reform movement, an internal struggle within Kikuyu society to redefine self-mastery and moral authority as traditional reservoirs of community accountability came under threat.[56] Indeed those deemed loyalist or rebel emerged from the same wellspring of intellectual work and concerns over household discipline and social reproduction.[57]

Elijah Masinde and his followers shared many of these same concerns. They saw their land and routes to achieving adulthood and self-mastery squeezed by European settlers from the encroaching highlands. They saw their religious traditions and ancestors desecrated through Christian derision and the proscription of their practices. Msambwa followers preached of returning to older notions of moral discipline in domestic gender relations, in religious worship, and in the use of their land.[58]

However, the political ethos behind this movement differed significantly from Mau Mau thought. Although secrecy played an important socializing role in traditional Bukusu society, Dini ya Msambwa proved much nosier.[59] A self-declared prophet, Masinde marshaled a long tradition of Bukusu prophets in support of his messianic and anticolonial message.[60] As Michael Adas argued, prophets throughout eastern Africa often prompted rebellions through their calls to moral restoration and social reform.[61] In the late eighteenth century, the prophet Maina wa Nalukale prophesized that the Bukusu "will keep on migrating and fighting with aliens. You will not circumcise your children in one place. You will trek round mount Masaaba [Mount Elgon] twice, and on the third round, you will meet with a snake called *Ya-Bebe* which will stop you from drifting further. You will soon be engulfed in wars of dispersal."[62] Later prophet Mutonnyi wa Nabukelembe predicted that strangers would come from the east, defeat the Bukusu in battle, and force them into servitude.[63] Several Bukusu prophets echoed prophecies heard across eastern Africa in the late nineteenth century of a snake that would weave its way through the region and bring with it oppression, referring to the coming of the railway and European colonizers. These prophets offered a public and secular, rather than religious, form of social critique, and performed multiple functions as healers, "war-prophets," and community leaders.[64]

Masinde used the grammar of prophecy to critique colonial interventions into Bukusu practices and reclaim a usable past. Through calls to their prophetic past, Masinde positioned himself as a cultural nationalist: "I went on praying and instructing my people to unite together and not separate . . . to live in harmony."[65] According to the Kenya Intelligence Committee, Masinde had effectively remade Bukusu religiosity from a "family to a tribal level . . . before long the cult became a militant form of African nationalism."[66] In his classic nationalist text *Not Yet Uhuru*, Luo leader Oginga Odinga captured the complex relationship between politics and religion in Kenya's nationalist histories: "In fact, Masinde started as a political organizer not a religionist . . . his 'amens' alone are a national anthem."[67] Msambwa followers reinvigorated traditional forms of worship that had fallen out of practice among the Bukusu, such as sacrificial shrines, wooden sticks used for prayer, and warrior dress.[68] A popular Msambwa hymn called upon the great Bukusu prophets of the past to "help us so that these Europeans may be driven away."[69] Yet, Msambwa also incorporated religious influences that had penetrated the district in the past fifty years: the drums of the Salvation Army, the hymns of the Quakers' Friends African Mission, the crosses of the Roman Catholics and the dress of Islamic traditions.

Masinde transformed the private familial religious practices of Bukusu traditions into public political action, hosting public prayer meetings, making public sacrifices, and encouraging the noisy disruption of colonial life.[70] He combined the open and public nature of secular prophecy with these reinvented religious practices, transposing rituals from the shrines placed in household doorways to sites of public and historic resonance. The most famous of these meetings was held at Chetambe's Fort, the location of the last great stand of resistance by the Bukusu against the British, in 1895. In front of a crowd of five thousand people, many dressed in traditional warrior attire, Masinde marshaled this history of resistance and made symbolic sacrifices, killing a black ram and burying its head as a symbol of the lost warriors of the battle at Chetambe.

Without weapons, Masinde told his followers to "use their tongues" to fight colonial authorities, European settlers, and Asian traders.[71] Masinde and his followers preached on the streets of the need to regain their honor. Msambwa adherents would follow agricultural officials, African headmen, and Asian shopkeepers, hurling accusations at them, making loud denunciations of their practices and presence in the community. Masinde's noisy transformation of private familial ancestral worship into public spectacle offended many Bukusu sensibilities. Even in his deportation trial, in 1948, Masinde was able to harness his reputation for prophecy to subvert colonial antiinsurgency tactics. During the trial, Masinde represented himself and provided a compelling defense, predicated on hearsay and the oral, undocumented nature of prophetic movements. Aware of the futility of this legal exercise, Masinde prophesized that when deported to Lamu he would not remain there long.[72] His prophecy was, for many, confirmed when the colonial administration moved him to Marsebet soon after his arrival in Lamu.[73] The colonial administration banned news of his football exploits on the coast and even felt it necessary to make "daily changes of his guards in order to avoid their being contaminated by Masinde's vituperative tongue."[74]

Unlike Mau Mau oaths of secrecy, Msambwa followers readily admitted their membership as an assertion of their religiosity. In their violence, Msambwa followers targeted the symbols of colonial power, settler expropriation, and religious imposition rather than attack private individuals. As a moral reform movement, Dini ya Msambwa sat somewhere between the noisy East African Revivalists, who promoted an open and accountable religious culture without calls to the past, and the Mau Mau forest fighters, who enforced a code of secrecy and moral conduct taken from representations of a traditional past.[75] Through their social critiques and religious innovations, such prophetic movements upset colonial order and tested local patriotic loyalties.

Colonial officials, however, failed to recognize these differences in political ethos. Dini ya Msambwa unknowingly acted as the testing ground for the territorial and counterinsurgency tactics later perfected during Mau Mau and then redoubled on Msambwa followers. Colonial administrators worked to close borders and territorially isolate Msambwa followers from surrounding populations—vilifying Msambwa adherents in the same ethnic terms that would later be used against Mau Mau rebels. After the Kolloa Affray, the colonial administration extended the power of local officials, granting district commissioners in North Nyanza and the Trans Nzoia the power to prosecute Dini ya Msambwa cases directly.[76] By August 1952, despite the low incidence of any Msambwa activities and the continued exile of its leadership, prosecutions still received the maximum penalties of three years imprisonment with hard labor. Colonial officials admitted the difficulty in differentiating between Msambwa activities and those connected solely with Bukusu customs or individual acts of criminality. As one official wrote, "The nature of D.Y.M. meeting is not dis-similar from certain Msambwa customs which are of course, still permitted."[77] Wechulia Nahiti and Khaemisa Mayari were detained merely for possessing two "DYM sticks," wooden sticks used for multiple Bukusu religious practices, and for discussing the death of Chief Waruhiu at the hands of the Mau Mau.[78] Further, the acts of arson often associated with Msambwa adherents were a common form of retribution practiced by the general Bukusu public, a way to declare a previous land right or punish deviations from social norms or obligations. But in the colonial mind, arson was associated with mental instability and criminality, thus deepening the anxiety over the psychological instability of Msambwa adherents.[79]

Convicted Msambwa members were sent to prisons and detention camps for "rehabilitation." The language of rehabilitation and reeducation pervaded colonial approaches to the detention of Dini ya Msambwa prisoners well before these terms took on their more notorious implications within the Mau Mau detention camps.[80] As early as 1950 administrators in North Nyanza stressed that "rehabilitation of releasees must be the biggest problem of the future."[81] In explaining the lengthy sentences meted out to Dini ya Msambwa prisoners, the district officer of Bungoma disclosed that these measures served not so much a punitive function but rather allowed "the Prison Department (ill equipped as they are to do so) to try and effect a change of mind."[82]

The infamous detention camps established during the Mau Mau rebellion have recently been the subject of intense debate in the scholarly community after the publication of Caroline Elkins's Pulitzer Prize–winning *British Gulags*. Debate has centered on methodological practice, on the use and misuse of sources, and on the narrow and at times sensationalized depictions of camp life presented by Elkins.[83] The heated historiographical debate has revealed that more complex and nuanced readings of detention and camp life are necessary.

As evident in Gerald Masibayi's story, confession was a staple, highly ritualized aspect of camp life. Louis Leakey, in his text *Defeating Mau Mau*, and Thomas Askwith, key architect of the Mau Mau "rehabilitation" policy, both argued that traditional oathing among the Kikuyu was reversible only through confession.[84] Rehabilitation for Dini ya Msambwa convicts similarly began with confession. Dini ya Msambwa convicts were then classified using the same system applied to Mau Mau detainees, ranking from confessed and cooperative, marked with an X, to hardcore, marked with a Z.[85] However, unlike Mau Mau prisoners, Msambwa adherents readily admitted their membership in this religious community. During Masinde's 1948 deportation trial, presided over by Judge M. C. Nageon de Lestang, who would later preside over the trial of the infamous Mau Mau general Kaleba, Masinde readily admitted leading Msambwa followers but denied founding the movement: "Msambwa is an old religion so it was not started by me."[86] Many in the colonial government and psychiatric community saw the willingness of Msambwa followers to "confess" their faith as proof of their mental instability. After an interview with a suspected Msambwa follower, Kavujai district officer C. Campbell noted, "Eriya is mentally unbalanced and made no effort to withhold information about his beliefs and actions."[87] Rehabilitation for Msambwa prisoners thus had to be predicated on a different set of priorities.

For Msambwa adherents, rehabilitation required not only confession but moreover conversion, both of religion and of lifestyle. Convicts labored on various work projects during the day and at night participated in "rehabilitation" exercises, trade training, and classes in Christianity.

Educational courses included simple arithmetic, spelling, hygiene, and geography.[88] Football matches in the camps were a particularly popular event, pitting detainees against prison staff three times a week. This use of football is ironic, as Masinde gained local measures of honor and indeed his reputation as a prophet through his prowess on the football pitch. As Dini ya Msambwa adherents linked their membership in this movement with traditional systems of belief, a change of religion, and not just of mind, was necessary: as Bishop L. C. Usher-Wilson argued, "The cure must lie in religion."[89] Proving their abandonment of Msambwa practices through religious conversion was central to their release. While for most this meant conversion to Christianity, for many prisoners deported to Lamu conversion to Islam still aided their return.[90] Rehabilitation for Msambwa adherents entailed a process of acculturation through work, leisure, and conversion.

The successful release of Dini ya Msambwa prisoners required further performances of their reformation in their home locations. Dini ya Msambwa prisoners returned within the continuing waves of repatriations following the Kolloa Affray and suffered similar social dislocation. Proof of renunciation and rehabilitation amounted to public performances. Dini ya Msambwa convicts were paraded in front of barazas of "Village Elders" and onlookers. Former prisoners were then impelled to take an "indigenous oath" by standing naked in front of a tree and striking the "murembe" stick, renouncing Dini ya Msambwa before these witnesses. Those who did not fulfill these demonstrations were immediately returned to police custody and reconvicted.[91] So-called murembe oaths were also used in the detention camps and for screening purposes in locational barazas.[92] Such "oaths" aped local customs of conflict resolution: in several traditions, a person accused of a crime against the community would "swear to his innocence or his veracity by stepping over a piece of 'Murembe' tree placed between him and his challenger, and saying, 'If I am guilty,' or, 'do not speak the truth, may this tree rise and kill me.'"[93] Returning prisoners who refused to perform this oath highlighted the ongoing internal debates around civic virtue, community membership, and moral authority within the district.

Into the 1950s the two movements, Msambwa and Mau Mau, began to overlap and inform each other, particularly in the colonial mind. In the Trans Nzoia, where administrators saw Dini ya Msambwa as a "greater threat to law and order than Mau Mau," the colonial administration took on an almost paranoiac fear of the possible "alliance . . . in subversive and militant activities" between "Mau Mau–infected" Kikuyu farmers and Msambwa adherents working on settler farms in the area.[94] Mau

Mau activities were discovered around the Mount Elgon Forest Reserve, the symbolic Zion of Msambwa devotees. Although by the end of 1953 officials felt confident no connection had occurred, Emergency Regulations allowed for a massive crackdown on suspected Msambwa followers, even though their public political activism had been all but halted by the early 1950s.[95] When prosecutions faltered "due to the circumstantial nature of evidence," the local administration simply applied for detention orders under the Emergency Regulations.[96] For those already serving prison sentences, failure to provide proof of their complete abandonment of the principles of Dini ya Msambwa resulted in their continued detention, now under Emergency Regulations.[97] The "blitz" on Dini ya Msambwa during the Emergency had important consequences for policies of interpenetration and territorial integration in western Kenya.[98]

In response to the threat of mobile Msambwa rebels and unsettled "interpenetrators" crossing colonial boundaries in search of new lands, the colonial administration launched a project of territorial reordering in western Kenya. In 1956 colonial officials opted to divide the North Nyanza District. For the colonial administration, the territorial division of the district would allow for closer administration and "surveillance" of Dini ya Msambwa and of labor movements into the Rift Valley.[99]

Deliberations over the partitioning of North Nyanza renewed local debates around ethnic alignment, resource distribution, and territorial identification in western Kenya. The main proponents of the division emerged unsurprisingly from the Bukusu, whose motivations were both economic and political. Bukusu advocates claimed they produced the greater proportion of the maize-based prosperity in the district and contributed more to the communal levy for maize yet saw the least benefits in terms of resource distribution and development projects.[100] Alongside economic arguments, the Bukusu argued that though "generally Abaluyia" in their ethnic alignment, their significant differences in language and custom justified separate territory and institutions.[101] Young politicians in the south claimed the partition was merely an "attempt by the government to divide the Abaluhya people."[102] The exact placement of the new boundary was cause for heated debate and in the end satisfied few: it would "take a whole page of the Laws of Kenya to describe it [the new boundary] accurately" (fig. 6.1).[103] In 1956 the district of Elgon Nyanza was born with its own boundaries, administrators, and bureaucratic trappings.

Throughout the 1950s, then, western Kenya was faced with not one but two rebellions. For both the colonial administration and Luyia patriotic thinkers, the answer was territorial. As the end of the Emergency

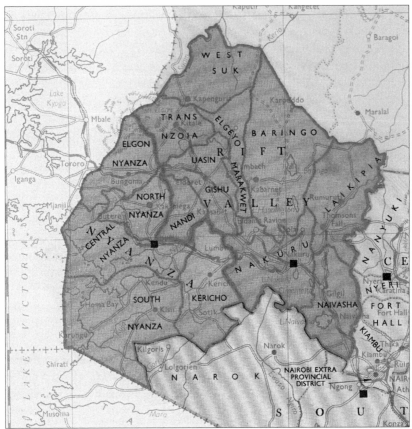

FIGURE 6.1. New district boundaries; Elgon and North Nyanza, Kenya political map. Survey of Kenya, Nairobi, 1958.

approached, petitioners complained that more-dangerous Mau Mau detainees were being released ahead of many Dini ya Msambwa prisoners.[104] The pace of release of Dini ya Msambwa prisoners finally increased after the rescinding of the Emergency Regulations, in 1960.[105] Elijah Masinde would remain in exile well into 1962, ultimately spending longer in detention than Jomo Kenyatta. As president, Kenyatta would go on to reimprison Masinde several times in the postcolonial era, reflecting the threat posed to both colonial and postcolonial governance by Masinde's particular brand of social critique and prophetic politics.

NAVIGATING NATIONAL CRISIS: THE NEW LUYIA IDEA

The nationalist discourse that emerged in the 1940s and 1950s required African political thinkers, busy consolidating their own patriotic work, to espouse a multiethnic platform and reorient their projects toward the nation. From the inception of the Kenya African Union (KAU), ambitious, urban Luyia leaders provided the party with access to rural constituents outside the Central Province.[106] Into the 1950s the colonial administration began suspecting KAU of acting as a front for radical and increasingly violent politics. Amid circulating rumors of a radical takeover of its leadership, KAU extended its base in western Kenya to reinforce its multiethnic appearance and counteract government suspicions of illegal KCA activities under the guise of nationalism. The history of nationalism and the politics of the Mau Mau rebellion prompted Luyia political thinkers to craft a flexible ethnic idea that would allow their constituents to navigate the politics of loyalism and dissent.

The Luyia leaders of the 1940s provided a crucial voice in the making of a multiethnic nationalist discourse. W. W. W. Awori first rose to national prominence when the KAU executive selected the young Luyia treasurer to deliver their memorandum to London in 1946.[107] Although plagued with a series of disasters, from lost luggage to massive travel debts, Awori's trip to London foregrounded the growing conflict between himself and the soon-to-be KAU president Jomo Kenyatta and his later move into trade unionism and Luyia ethnic politics.

Suspicious of Kenyatta's intention to use KAU as a front for Kikuyu interests, Awori refused to include Kenyatta in the presenting of KAU's memorandum.[108] Despite these concerns, Awori worked with his father, the influential Canon Jeremiah Awori, and fellow KAU leader Joseph Otiende to collect funds from North Nyanza for Kenyatta's return and accepted the vice presidency of KAU under the newly elected President Kenyatta.[109] When the two leaders came head to head over government proposals on African registration and East African federation, Kenyatta drew a line in the sand and forced Awori's resignation.[110] Awori began speculating in private meetings that "the fortunes of K.A.U. are declining and that its interests are being sacrificed to those of the K.C.A."[111] Awori then flirted with the leadership of the African Workers' Federation (AWF), an organization that emerged in a spontaneous manner on the first day of the Mombasa general strike in January 1947.[112] Workers and trade union movements have long held an uneasy position within the history of African nationalisms.[113] Awori predicated his acceptance of the leadership on the mandate of the AWF acting as a true federation of unions rather than as a single union.[114] But young radical Kikuyu workers in Nairobi, members of the militant Forty Group, disenchanted with the slow pace of constitutional reform, blocked Awori's nomination, believing the educated leaders of KAU would "not hesitate 'to sell the workers down the river.'"[115]

A classic constitutional reformer sidelined in the national historiography, Awori's career with KAU and the trade unionist movement revealed his frustration with the divisive politics he saw in Kenyatta's KAU. Indeed, Arthur Moody Awori, brother to Awori and future vice president of Kenya (2002–7), explained his older brother's abrupt departure from politics later in the 1950s through the common dialectic of tribe and nation: "Our family has had the history, sometimes to our own undoing, the history of looking at things nationally as opposed to tribally."[116] Awori saw the horizontal mass mobilization of workers and the language of federation as a possible antidote to parochial national politics.

Kenyatta's strategic choice of Otiende to replace Awori as KAU vice president reaffirmed the place of western Kenya in the ethnic arithmetic of national politics. With Kikuyu support dangerously divided, the administration feared KAU planned a "determined attack to establish itself in North Nyanza."[117] John Adala, outspoken Banyore politician, became the chairman of the Nyanza KAU branch.[118] In November 1951, Kenyatta addressed two meetings in North Nyanza, at Mbale and Chwere, hoping to shore up support, to great local effect.[119] To these audiences, Kenyatta articulated the national project as a political, rather than culturalist, project for *uhuru* through the practice of self-help and mutual respect.[120] Kenyatta drew together Kenya's different localities through a discourse of cultural relativism that resonated with local Luyia projects: "We need to decorate ourselves as well, we need to respect each other and then speak in one voice."[121] However, a controversial KAU meeting at Nyeri turned unruly in July 1952 would prompt the banning of KAU meetings throughout the colony.[122]

Fearing the influence of these "radical" politics in the national project, the colonial administration courted moderate politicians with increased African seats on the Legislative Council. Awori used this opportunity to advance his own political ambitions. In 1952, Awori set out on a successful publicity campaign for the Legislative Council, posting advertisements promising, among other things, to "negotiate ceaselessly the subject of North Nyanza District becoming a Province."[123] The declaration of the Emergency, on 20 October 1952, and the arrest of Jomo Kenyatta and much of KAU's leadership in Operation Jock Scott prompted Awori and Luo Legislative Council member Walter Odede to step into the executive branch of KAU. Awori then worked to secure the legal team to defend Kenyatta at his trial.[124] When the colonial administration also detained Odede early in 1953 for allegedly spreading Mau Mau among the Luo in Nyanza, Awori officially became the president of KAU.[125]

Awori's return to KAU leadership was not greeted with universal support. In 1953, Nyanza chiefs passed a resolution of no confidence in Awori and Odede and called for their resignation from KAU. Nyanza chiefs argued Awori and Odede had taken over KAU "without reference to [their] Nyanza constituents."[126] The chief of Idakho personally wrote to Awori warning that he "should not be a member of KAU, since Baluhya only selected you to be their representative in the Legislative Council."[127] For this chief, Awori represented an ambassador of the Luyia people on the Legislative Council and not a national political leader. Others, however, applauded Awori's move. The Nyanza African Union in Nakuru passed resolutions in full support of Awori and Odede and accused members of the native administration of "a gross abuse to public dignity," in their attempts to force Awori and Odede out of KAU.[128] Nyanza provincial commissioner R. D. F. Ryland commented on the tension and ironies between local and national politics for Luyia leaders: "Though this unwise opportunism afforded great satisfaction to the small minority of local politicians it alienated the sympathies of the natural and accepted leaders of the tribes."[129]

With the banning of KAU, in June 1953, as a subversive society, those national political leaders left were detained, deported, or restricted to their home locations. KAU Nyanza branch chairman John Adala was detained on charges of "participating in a proscribed secret society."[130] Although denouncing Mau Mau violence and escaping full detention, Awori continued to publish tracts on the national movement and letters by the infamous Mau Mau field marshal Dedan Kimathi in his new publication *Habari za dunia*, which was later banned in 1954.[131] The administration now viewed Awori as "the most dangerous man in the Province."[132] J. D. Otiende walked a similarly dangerous line between colonial service and political dissent. In Operation Cowslip, police seized stacks of papers from Otiende, from personal correspondence to newspapers, and from the minutes of KAU meetings.[133] When Otiende returned to the district in 1952 for the funeral of his brother, conspicuously escaping Operation Jock Scott in Nairobi, the colonial administration placed him under home arrest with constant police surveillance for the next few years.[134] However, he continued to work in the ADC, the Agricultural Betterment Fund, and various local associations. He angered the administration when he spoke at public gatherings in 1954 of racial segregation and the hypocrisy of the British press showing only Mau Mau killings and not those perpetrated by government forces.[135] Otiende later claimed to have harbored Dedan Kimathi during this period: led by leopards in the Kaimosi forests, Otiende housed and provided supplies to Kimathi and his forest fighters under the cloak of night.[136] Although unlikely, Otiende related these tales of Mau Mau complicity to reinsert Luyia support into the national narrative of anticolonial struggle, "gikuyuized" in postcolonial histories.[137]

With national politics effectively prohibited, Luyia political leaders found a new way of practicing national politics through ethnic patriotism. While Luyia architects had secured a recognized name and delimited territory by the late 1940s, their political and cultural content of for this project remained scattered and divisive. Responding to growing political polarization, Awori and Otiende united Luyia leaders from across the district in the founding of the Abaluyia Peoples Association (APA). W. B. Akatsa warned that "this organization should not lead us to become narrow minded so that we prefer it to national bodies e.g. K.A.U."[138] With the other hand, ex-chief Mulama proclaimed that the "Abaluhya should take over the political leadership of Africans in the Colony from the Kikuyu who had shown themselves unworthy."[139] Leaders of the APA worked to make national politics consequential for local constituents and to craft a new Luyia idea, one capable of providing its constituents with the flexibility to navigate the spaces between and around the colonial politics of loyalism and dissent.

The ethnic homeland defined and defended by the end of the 1940s provided the territorial starting point for the APA's reformulation of Luyia-ness. The naming of this new political body raised concerns over territorial representation and ethnic exclusivity. At its first meeting, in 1952, one APA member complained that "the word 'Abaluyia' was discriminatory against minority groups."[140] First president C. N. W. Siganga defended the use of the term by defining Abaluyia within a discourse of territorial consciousness: Abaluyia meant "all persons resident in the *present* district of North Nyanza whether they were originally Bantu or Tesio, Nyang'ori, Elgonyi and Luo."[141] Awori, too, framed North Nyanza as a diverse and integrative space, "famous for its financial strength, its progress and its football." The inclusion of Elgonyi, Nyang'ori, Luo, and Teso inhabitants of the district naturalized this space of ethnic plurality. This federated, territorialized Luyia idea allowed for a particular kind of political activism based not on shared language or ethnic origin but rather on territorial belonging.[142] The diverse and integrative histories of North Nyanza influenced a civic-minded construction of a regional "public": in the words of Siganga, "as long as North Nyanza people spoke with different voices . . . government would not know what the public think." In a time of increasingly instrumentalist and culturalist discourses around the primordial character of ethnic identities, this de-ethnicized and territorial orientation was notable, locking the constituents of the APA into a particular geographic vision based on transnational ideas of federated plurality, civic virtue, and territorial integration.

The APA thus forwarded themselves as a political vehicle for Luyia ambitions rather than a watchdog of culturalist politics. Unlike other ethnic parties across Kenya, the cultural work of the APA was limited. While the Luo Union continued to write histories and hunt down urban women, and KCA members radicalized traditional oaths to discipline their constituents, the APA, in the manner of KAU, established itself as the political voice of disparate, autonomous parts of a corporate body.[143] Although their constitution called for "intensive research into the history, laws and customs of the Abaluyia," the organization never produced any tracts or treaties on these issues.[144] Otiende had written their history in 1949. Andere was busy publishing their customary practices. In a sense, the APA left these culturalist projects to the "professionals," to the historians, linguists, and customary law panelists among its members. The cultural work of disciplining moral behavior and debating marriage and land was left largely to their constituent locational branches. The APA's reformulation of a Luyia ethnic identity without a unified history, language, or genealogical grounding was a strategically limited project that allowed these new political leaders to espouse a vision of geographic commonality within North Nyanza.

The APA's ideology arose out of challenges of loyalism and dissent that threatened to unground their projected territorial and ethnic mandate. The declaration of the Emergency proved both impetus and threat to this project. After the banning of KAU, local officials deemed that any political meetings at this time "only mean talking hate," banning all APA meetings.[145] The APA's leadership came under close scrutiny. Awori and Otiende remained under strict surveillance and Siganga was accused of having come under communist influence during his time at university in the UK.[146] However, the APA's promotion of a Luyia idea based on territorial nationalism afforded its constituents opportunities and a means of exercising agency in the morally uncertain and politically polarizing time of the Emergency.

MORAL UNCERTAINTY AND THE POLITICS OF LOYALISM AND DISSENT

While the Emergency radically polarized African communities into colonial categories of progressive loyalism or retrograde rebellion, the deep moral uncertainty of the era reinforced the need to work in the in-between spaces of the nation and the local, of loyalism and dissent.

Within North Nyanza, this time of moral uncertainty reflected the social pressures and conflicts that began in the 1940s and extended far beyond central Kenya. Luyia laborers watched as Kikuyu laborers in Nyanza were rounded up and the Kikuyu wives of Luyia husbands were photographed and registered.[147] African farmers in the south pushed into forest reserves from overflowing locations only to receive eviction notices and face prosecution.[148] Local groups sabotaged afforestation projects, uprooted borderline trees, and set brush fires along boundaries.[149] Opposition to afforestation projects in Maragoli and Bunyore fueled fears of spreading discontent and posed the "greatest threat to internal security."[150] These southern locations also suffered more acutely from what came to be known as the "Mau Mau hunger."[151] Letters to the vernacular press forecasted famine due to the diversion of grain for Emergency efforts.[152]

Colonial officials worried that such unrest foreshadowed new Mau Maus in the making. Chiefs in the southern locations of Idakho, Isukha, Maragoli, and Bunyore and the northern locations of Kimilili, Malakisi, and Teso all received anonymous letters threatening personal violence after the declaration of the Emergency.[153] Retired chief Mukudi of Samia and Bunyala, a central figure in anti-Wanga protests, for which he was detained in 1917, was reported to have taken the Mau Mau oath in 1953 and to be recruiting among the Banyala. Oathing ceremonies were discovered in the Sesenye forest and as many as fifty Banyala and Samia members were detained and sent to detention along with Mukudi.[154] In 1957 the Bunyala Association seized on this polarizing discourse to demand mandatory membership for their constituents: "Some members of this tribe were implicated in the subversive movements . . . due to misguidance and/or being disunited, we feel that time has come when every Munyala ought to join the Association."[155] When the *Daily Telegraph* reported in 1953 that "thirty Maragoli tribesmen from Nyanza province of Kenya were among 180 Africans identified by hooded informers as Mau Mau in a screening operation," colonial anxieties regarding these locational threats seemed to be confirmed.[156]

At APA meetings in January 1954, Banyore members drew parallels between their own land shortages in the overpopulated locations of Bunyore and Maragoli and the Kikuyu land grievances: "Those Kikuyu were fighting for their lands just as the Baluhya people would one day have to fight."[157] Banyore men and women were being moved all over eastern Africa as their numbers continued to grow and they pushed into surrounding locations and forests. Throughout the 1940s the Bunyore Welfare Society in Central Nyanza protested the Luo-dominated LNC for not

allowing Banyore residents to build churches or schools, be accountable
to their own customs, or use their own language.[158] As Banyore families and migrant workers moved farther away, concerns over language,
culture, and marriage became even more acute. In March 1951 the executive officer of African land utilization and settlement approved the
settlement of Banyore families in the Olenguruone settlement, where
Kikuyu squatters had radicalized oath taking in the early 1940s as a form
of mass resistance.[159] Farther afield, Banyore settlers faced difficulties in
the Kigumba settlement of Bunyoro in Uganda, lands that Luyia leaders protested as "unhealthy and where the security of land tenure is not
guaranteed."[160] Banyore families were either locked in untenable land
congestion in their own location or left adrift across eastern Africa in
government-run land settlements notorious for their inadequate soils
and harsh local administrations.

In the 1950s, Banyore members of the APA began to compare their
situation to the plight of the Mau Mau fighters. Young Banyore members
of the Bunyore Welfare Society formed their own internal committee
called the Babukha, literally translated as "they have moved" and further
denoting concepts of "youth" and "virility."[161] This discourse of mobility
and youth underscored a new disposition among these frustrated young
political actors seeking to re-establish lines of community and discipline.
The Babukha saw the strategies of Mau Mau fighters as a possible antidote to their social and economic uncertainty.

By the end of 1954 this committee had taken over the leadership
of the Bunyore Welfare Society. The colonial administration read the
takeover by a radicalized youth movement as a repetition of the fate
of KAU's Nairobi branch at the outbreak of the Mau Mau rebellion.
President of the Bunyore Welfare Society, Aggrey Minya, was hailed at
meetings as their "own Kenyatta."[162] Minya, like Awori, was a Nairobi-
based trade unionist and played a leading role in the formation of the
Kenya Federation of Registered Trade Unions, successor to the AWF.[163]
After Tom Mboya took over leadership of the federation, in 1953, Minya
returned to his base in the Bunyore Welfare Association. Informers reported that Minya was speaking at meetings across North Nyanza of the
support Nairobi-dwelling Luyia provided to Mau Mau fighters in food
and supplies.[164] With Minya's return to the district, members of the Babukha debated the introduction of oathing among their members, the
collection of funds for detained leaders such as Banyore politician John
Adala, and the nature of their support for Mau Mau.[165] Makate Otiato,
recently returned from Nakuru, argued that "if Mau Mau had not commenced killing their own people . . . every tribe in Kenya would have

joined them by now."[166] Five North Nyanza inhabitants detained in 1954 professed sympathy for the principles and aims of Mau Mau, but not its methods.[167] This common refrain, from APA members to Elijah Masinde's followers, haunted colonial officials and pointed to the intellectual debates and tensions around the means and methods of gaining independence. These were serious moral and intellectual critiques and not solely the self-advancing strategies of instrumental loyalists.

In response, the acting governor proposed that the whole membership of the Babukha be detained under Emergency Regulations. Fearing the possibly radicalizing repercussions of such drastic actions, the Nyanza provincial commissioner proposed the detention of two leaders, later increasing that number to six, with the outspoken Makate Otiato topping their list.[168] Indeed, of the few Luyia in detention during the Emergency the majority hailed from Bunyore.[169] Although the Babukha dissolved after the detention of its leaders, colonial administrators worried the committee's activities were symptomatic of larger trends within the locations.

Despite the banning of the APA and the moral uncertainty reflected in these kinds of locational politics, the Luyia idea fashioned by the APA proved useful in navigating these polarizing politics. Many Luyia leaders used the Emergency to position themselves as loyal, progressive, and moderate citizens. Abaluyia Association president Musa Amalemba maneuvered through these politics to replace Nairobi city councillor Ambrose Ofafa after his murder by Mau Mau assassins, in November 1952. In 1954, Pascal Nabwana and C. N. W. Siganga proposed that the North Nyanza ADC fully endorse multiracial government in Kenya with the caveat that the loyal inhabitants of North Nyanza "be considered for a share in the new Government of Kenya."[170] When the colony was granted its first African election, in 1957, Luyia candidates and the Luyia electorate benefited from this loyalist image. For the Coutts Commission, whose task it was to determine the qualifications of franchise, proven loyalty to the colonial administration was key to prospective electoral participation.[171] In theory, any criminal conviction or detention without conviction over the past two years would mean disqualification for potential voters or candidates. And yet Otiende managed to petition to have his years of house arrest discounted and to stand, though unsuccessfully, for this election. The politics of loyalism and dissent, while still dogging patriotic work, did not, as some have argued, altogether translate into the production of the late colonial, and postcolonial, elite.[172]

Luyia laborers, too, benefited from this loyalist image. European farmers in the Trans Nzoia complained that their Luyia labor force was greatly reduced by the enlistment of young laborers into the security forces.[173] The infamous Operation Anvil, which cleared Nairobi of nearly half its total Kikuyu population by May 1954, decimated Nairobi's labor force.[174] The administration filled these gaps with "loyal tribes."[175] By 1955 the "Nyanza population," both Luo and Luyia, in Nairobi had risen from well under 30 percent before the Emergency to almost half the African population of the city. The Abaluyia Association used this increase in its Nairobi constituents to extend its influence and protest against Luo favoritism in city employment.

Alongside these expanded opportunities for loyal government service, the Luyia identity also provided flexibility in relations with other ethnic groups and occasions for subversion of colonial authority. Men like Awori, Otiende, and even Masibayi were able to strategically invoke these identities for their own purposes. The same Luyia identity that prompted Masibayi's enlistment in the Flemming Commission afforded him certain advantages within the detention camps. First suspected as an informer, Masibayi's fellow Kikuyu detainees soon elevated him to camp teacher. Masibayi instructed fellow detainees on such subjects as English, math, and handwriting. His work as a camp teacher reflected the intellectual life of the detention camps that Derek Peterson unearthed in his recent work.[176] He became a popular figure and his Luyia identity allowed him to avoid the some of the inter-Kikuyu politics of the camp, such as forced oathing among Kikuyu detainees.[177]

James Osogo, brother to Luyia historian John Osogo, similarly spoke of how his Luyia identity gained him the trust of both the British staff and his fellow Kikuyu classmates at the famous Kagumo Teachers College. When the Kagumo staff enlisted students to patrol their campus against Mau Mau fighters, with "blunt pangas" (machetes) their only weapons, the students chose Osogo to front their protests.[178] Politics was a taboo subject among the Kikuyu students, many of whom had fathers and brothers engaged on either side of the rebellion. Osogo's Luyia identity afforded him the opportunity to defend the students' interests without being accused of Mau Mau loyalties.

Luyia students at Makerere used the pages of their magazine, *Muluhya*, to recount stories of Luyia detainees tortured and yet released, like Masibayi, due to pressure from prominent Luyia politicians. In one case, a prominent member of the Nairobi City Council had used his position to get a group of Luyia detainees released: "Among them was a woman who had been subjected to brutal torture, to induce her to accept having taken the oath. She claimed to have been tortured by sharp broken bottles in the most un-Christian manner."[179] Luyia Makerere student and author S. D. Wayo recounted this story in contrast to the massive settler demonstrations after the murder of the son of a white settler in January 1953 that forced the leader of the European members, Michael Blundell, out to negotiate with the near riotous crowd: "What," Wayo mused, "would have happened . . . if the demonstrators had been Africans?" Many such stories exist across western Kenya: in some, Luyia farmers provided food to passing rebels; others used their positions as teachers or civil servants to abet Mau Mau activities; still others collected funds for the schooling of the sons of Mau Mau fighters; often, these roles overlapped.[180] Within and outside the reserve, the Luyia idea provided flexibility and opportunities within the polarizing colonial politics of loyalism and dissent.

᠍

IN ALL these stories, it was the particular nature of the Luyia identity that provided for a new kind of politics in the 1950s. From the grounds of western Kenya, there clearly existed no neat dividing line between loyalism and dissent: indeed in each of these narratives they overlapped and informed each other, just as they did in central Kenya. And while texts like Daniel Branch's have acknowledged this, they have often failed to adequately account for the ways people moved in and out of these "identities" and made strategic, and intellectually informed, uses of these colonial categories to maneuver during the Emergency. The Mau Mau rebellion and the coming construction of postcolonial Kenya informed but also were informed by these ongoing constructions of ethnic patriotism, of political thought, and of territorial nationalism developing across eastern Africa during the 1950s.

While the APA fashioned a Luyia idea around territorial consciousness, the messy, ambiguous, border-crossing politics of the late colonial era threatened local moral economies and prompted colonial territorial strategies that dismembered the territory of Luyia political thought. For Luyia political thinkers, the division of the district in 1956 threatened to sever the geographic imagination of their political community. In his weekly column in *Baraza*, entitled "Behind the Headlines," Awori denounced the division of the district as "detrimental to the people and progress of this area."[181] Indeed the division realigned Awori's own home location in Bukhayo into the new district. Awori blamed the division for fostering "tribalism" between the two districts, citing the refusal of one team to play football in the other district.[182] But despite this division, the first African election in 1957 maintained North Nyanza and Elgon Nyanza as one constituency and late colonial politics would give ample reason for Luyia patriots to continue mapping them together. The federal vision of Luyia political leaders provided structural and ideological tools capable not of overcoming but rather of incorporating the plural nature of its constituents in the face of the reductive colonial politics of ethnic identity. With elections, boundary commissions, and the politics of decolonization on the horizon, Luyia patriots would work to transform these late colonial politics of loyalism and dissent into capital for debates around postcolonial belonging and regional sovereignty.

7 ⌁ Mapping Decolonization

AT A heated debate in the Kenya Legislative Council on 19 July 1962, Dome Budohi put forward a motion for the creation of a region "exclusively for the Abaluyia, by the Abaluyia, of the Abaluyia in an independent Kenya."[1] Invoking the guiding mantra of the upcoming Kenya Regional Boundaries Commission, Budohi appealed to the council "to let those who want to live together live together." Prominent Luo lawyer and parliamentary secretary for lands, surveys, and town planning C. M. G. Argwings-Kodhek then took the floor, denouncing the very term Luyia as a fabrication: "It never existed before. We do not know who these Abaluyia are." A lengthy and impassioned exchange ensued, pitting Luyia politicians against their Luo neighbors in Nyanza, both vying to secure important resources and constituents ahead of decolonization. While Argwings-Kodhek mobilized genealogical arguments against historical invention, centralizing nationalist leaders Tom Mboya and Jomo Kenyatta undermined Luyia efforts through a modernist discourse of civic nationalism: "The people of this country should regard themselves not as tribal groups, or national groups, but as one nation." Echoing Ernest Renan's classic national-amnesia theory, both Mboya and Kenyatta argued throughout decolonization that tribal differences and historical divides must be forgotten for the nation to exist.[2]

As decolonization neared, commissions like the Kenya Regional Boundaries Commission called upon African communities to map their political communities into emerging independent nations. Cartographic literacy had grown throughout the colonial period. Into the 1950s land consolidation programs created incentives for the low partisan work of mapmaking that encouraged a competitive culture of mapping and high-lighted class and gender cleavages. Electoral politics further prompted locational activists to defend the bounds of their political communities through the mapping of electoral constituencies. Despite these competitive mappings, Luyia groups forwarded a deluge of maps to the 1962 boundaries commission that visualized a united and autonomous Luyia region, much as they had thirty years earlier before the Kenya Land Commission. Census-taking and population-building exercises fitted the smaller maps of competitive local polities into larger ethnic imaginings to defend majority rights over contiguous territories and envelop dissenting neighbors. Luyia leaders further presented a form of historical cartography as political activism. They told histories of monarchical traditions and lost territories to envision alternative polities, defend their ability to practice sovereignty, and encourage their constituents to expand their geographic imagination to a "Greater Luyia." As centralizing nationalists fought to maintain colonial boundaries as their rightful inheritance, mapping—or countermapping—the nation became a strategy of dissent. Luyia partisans in western Kenya drew maps and engineered borders to debate the terms of state formation, to naturalize the diversity of their plural constituents, and to defend alternative models of sovereignty and political community.

DECOLONIZATION AND THE
MAKING OF AFRICAN NATIONS

The decolonization of Africa occurred only decades after European colonizers partitioned and mapped colonial possessions that would transform into independent African nations. In the heady postindependence years, liberal interpretations of decolonization saw African nationalism as the fruits of progressive colonial projects.[3] In this view, whether through violent uprising or orderly constitutional reform, the transfer of power from colonial rulers to African leaders fulfilled the prophecy of African nationalism and gave birth to new nation-states.[4] For John Iliffe, "nationalism (as distinct from anti-colonialism) in West Africa was chiefly a response to elections."[5] John Lonsdale, however, rewrote this view of nationalism for eastern Africa: while the constitutional reforms debated around the bargaining table at the Lancaster House conferences epitomized the managed project of decolonization, nationalism in East Africa, according to Lonsdale, "was chiefly a response to gender conflict and class formation."[6] In either case, African nationalism was rarely as coherent or predestined as nationalists or liberal commentators would have liked. More often, the project of nationalism was staggered, contested, and filled with frustrated political imaginaries and contradictory claims to the postcolony.

Recent research in eastern Africa has begun to redress the narrowness of this liberal interpretation of African nationalism and inject a necessary element of doubt and dissent into the process of decolonization.[7] Outside the walls of Lancaster House, activists throughout eastern Africa appropriated the tools of mapping to envision alternative polities in the face of self-fulfilling nationalist projects. Along a ten-mile strip of the Kenyan coastline, "Mwambao" separatists staked claims to sovereignty or integration into the Zanzibari sultanate based on their protectorate status and the legal anomalies of nineteenth-century treaties.[8] Mwambao activists flew the sultanate's flag in the face of Kenyan nationalists.[9] To the north, Somali secessionists in the Northern Frontier District pushed the limits of this ill-defined border and through their movements and activism mapped irredentist claims to a Greater Somalia.[10] Maasai pastoralists across the Kenya-Tanganyika border called for the removal of interterritorial borders and restrictions on their grazing rights.[11] Further west in Uganda, Banyoro and Toro activists mapped historic kingdoms to demand the return of lost lands.[12] In the Rwenzori Mountains, partisans of the Rwenzururu kingdom built alternative parliaments, wrote histories, and "elaborated a discourse of ornamentalism as a defense against the homogenizing power of national governments."[13] Throughout the late 1950s and early 1960s, local partisans engineered borders and told cartographic histories to defend alternative claims to sovereignty. At the other extreme, African leaders from Tanganyika, Kenya, and Uganda proposed the dissolution of the artificial "boundaries which now divide our countries" through the creation of an East African Federation.[14] But as Tanganyikan leader Julius Nyerere predicted, once raised, the flags of independent nations were difficult to lower. The fixed boundaries of African nations, as Fred Cooper has argued, were the product of decolonization, not colonization.[15] Buried under the triumphant national histories of the postcolonial era was a moment during decolonization when the imagining of alternative nations was not just possible but prevalent.

A CULTURE OF COMPETITIVE MAPMAKING

The making and unmaking of boundaries in western Kenya was a continuously contested and unfinished process. The introduction of cartography and colonial governance imposed new geographic visions of land and community. While previous chapters have examined the variety of this geographic work, from language work to mapping the frontiers of gendered belonging and patriotic loyalty, here the attention turns to the more literal, pictorial mapping practices, to the incentivization of cartographic literacy and the role of mapping in representations not only of land but moreover of self, community, and nation.

In the 1950s colonial policies increased the incentives for earlier colonial lessons in the drawing of maps as a tool in the defense of property, patriarchy, and political community. Soil conservation and land consolidation programs spurred political activism throughout eastern Africa, linking the mapping of private landholdings with political authority, gender privilege, class differentiation, and the defense of moral communities.[16] In the 1955 "Terrace War" in Uluguru, Walunguru activists in eastern Tanganyika launched a large-scale rebellion against soil conservation work and forwarded an alternative model of state structure and community membership.[17] In Kenya the colonial government responded to dramatic land deterioration, population growth, and social dissent in the 1950s with a new approach to African agricultural and landownership. The Swynnerton Plan, which became official state policy in 1954, understood these problems as chronic to colonial policies of landownership in the reserves and to African land practices.[18] The plan called for the removal of restrictions on African farmers toward capitalist forms of cash cropping and the consolidation of African landholdings.[19] Land consolidation, enclosure policies, registration, and the granting of individual land titles all intervened into the private and social practices of African landownership and promoted the mapping of competitive land claims.

Land consolidation policies were modernist exercises in state legibility, to use James Scott's terms, obsessed with the creation of "visible units" and the "straightening [of] boundaries."[20] Colonial officials employed aerial photography to track the progress of land consolidation programs.[21] Areas of successful land consolidation produced images of ordered, clearly indented grids of geometrical spaces. As Raymond Craib argued in the case of nineteenth-century Mexico, "Social order and capitalist progress rested on the imposition of a new spatial order with its own moral, political, and economic modalities . . . rational grid plans were mirrors of modernity itself."[22] In 1962, Legislative Council member for Taita-Taveta D. M. Wannyumba would complain that these aerial maps were supplanting local geographic realities: "Many maps of Taita Taveta District, even those recently drawn are very misleading. They are merely photographs from the air and to us mean very little."[23] Across the colony, state-led practices of spatial ordering lifted mapped perspectives off the ground and privileged top-down, geometric rationalizations of local geographies. These new mappings did not so much create these changes as produce the terms and visual markers through which ongoing competitions over land would be articulated. Land consolidation mapping saw a transition away from the complex mappings of earlier court cases toward a privileging of straight lines on the page.

Land consolidation brought about a dramatic increase in land cases and fostered a competitive mapmaking culture differentiated along gender, class, and ethnic lines.[24] In North Nyanza, and indeed across the colony, land consolidation privileged male heads of households who formed committees responsible for determining "individual rights, gathering and exchanging of fragments and demarcating on the ground under the supervision of the administration along the lines of customary law."[25] African farmers who achieved these ordered quadrates were rewarded with grants from the Agricultural Betterment Fund and access to valuable cash crops. The colonial administration sent Luyia elders and councillors to Kikuyu farms and promoted Kikuyu land consolidation as a model for the entire colony.[26] As Fiona Mackenzie has argued in regards to the Central Province, these land policies effectively privileged elder men over both women and junior men as they invoked only recently formulated "customary" laws "to legitimate land claims, within strategies of land accumulation."[27]

In an oft-quoted passage, Swynnerton also underlined the class implications of his plan: "able, energetic or rich Africans will be able to acquire land and bad or poor farmers less, creating a landed and a landless class. This is a normal step in the evolution of a country."[28] Wealthy African men who could prove their historical residence in a given area could consolidate large tracts of land, dispossessing tenants, absent migrant laborers, and junior men along the way. As argued by Steven Feierman, land consolidation was a means by which rural capitalists were able to extend and formalize their control over property and attenuate the access of dependents, clients, and junior kinsmen to their gardens.[29] Reporting on the southern locations of North Nyanza, P. G. Fullerton noted a "radical change. . . . Land is now being subdivided amongst sons not merely as shamba-land but as 'Residential Plots' . . . the present pattern is one of 'suburbanization of the reserve'; not villagization."[30] Young male migrant laborers, absent from North Nyanza in numbers that reached 80 percent of the able-bodied male population by the late 1950s, struggled to maintain land and inheritance rights in the reserve.[31] In Mombasa and Nairobi, Luyia and Luo men led riots in May 1956 protesting the consolidation of their lands back in the reserves in their absence.[32] The class privilege involved in these programs further encouraged wealthy men to take up the geographic work to sustain and in some cases manufacture their power, as will be seen in the distribution of voting rights. In North

Nyanza, so-called kinship groups did bulk of work "straightening present boundaries."[33] And yet, with overlapping committees operating in multiple locations and rarely corresponding to any workable notion of kinship or clan, the work of land consolidation proved laborious, continuing well into the 1960s and 1970s, and served to create new rural power structures.

Beyond the gender and class debates over rights of ownership and tenant farmers, competitive mapping projects further opened up nativist arguments over insiders and outsiders, indigenes and migrant settlers. Baraza discussions filled with fears of dispossession and forced removals in the face of land consolidation.[34] Land consolidation projects became embroiled in the continuing evictions of minority "interpenetrators" (see chapter 6). Luo farmers struggled to maintain land claims in North Nyanza and often faced harassment and threats of forced removal. On the other side of the border, Samia farmers in Central Nyanza found themselves landless as Luo landholders consolidated their own tracts. Tenant farmers, called "strangers," or *abamenya*, fell into a precarious legal category: only those who could prove their place on the land over several generations, from the time of their great-grandfathers, could enjoy the privileges of ownership.[35] Tenants who could not prove such genealogical depth were subject to the whims of male heads of households busily consolidating their properties. In all of these cases a tension existed between historic claims to lost lands and more recent proofs of length of residence. Such programs thus incentivized, in western Kenya as much as across the colony, the elaboration of a "discourse of indigeneity."[36] As Derek Peterson has argued, land consolidation programs intersected with and furthered the patriotic and demographic work of antiprostitution campaigns, census engineering, loyalist positioning, and electoral politicking.[37] Land consolidation produced a competitive culture of mapmaking that not only pitted landowners against tenants, husbands against wives, and fathers against sons but also defined communities as either indigenes or outsiders.

While African farmers consolidated their landholdings into the 1950s, colonial officials called upon these individual households to align themselves within electoral constituencies in an ever-increasing geographic scale. Land consolidation programs complicated the registration and qualifications of voters for the first African election, in 1957. The qualified "fancy" franchise for this first election catalogued and ranked potential voters by education, colonial service, and property.[38] Voting rights were tied not only to landownership but moreover to the amount of land owned: wealthy landowners could expect to receive up to three votes while poorer, landless peasants might only qualify for one, or none.

One editorial in *Baraza* heralded the qualifications for leaving space for uneducated elders and "the most poverty-stricken peasants."[39] In reality, this graded citizenship acted as a pedagogical tool, rewarding class privilege and loyal service while imposing arbitrary bureaucratic measures on the rights of political participation. Many feared that voter registration, which entailed a declaration of property holdings, would have consequences for pending land consolidation cases and for taxation.[40] The final "Voters Roll" for Elgon and North Nyanza, posted on the walls of district offices and sold for twelve shillings, publicly displayed the electoral rights earned by qualified voters.[41] In arguments over status, local debaters would often call upon this document as proof of their modernity, rank, and political position.[42] Debates over electoral rights and constituencies prompted locational partisans to map their political separateness from their neighbors.

Awaiting the arrival of the Regional Boundaries Commission in 1962, locational organizations produced maps for the concurrent Constituencies Delimitation Commission, which visualized their right to political representation and deconstructed the homogeneous space of Luyia ethnic architects. As in anti-Wanga campaigns, local communities produced censuses and promoted their customary differences in pursuit of electoral recognition. Logoli petitioners argued that their numbers and distinct cultural heritage justified the creation of two Logoli constituencies: only Logoli representatives with sound knowledge of their customs and historical entitlements could properly represent them on the national level.[43] Isukha petitioners drew competing maps that parsed land between themselves and their Idakho and Nandi neighbors.[44] In 1961 these conflicts led to several armed attacks on the borders of Nandi and Isukha farms.[45] To defend electoral claims, locational associations drew maps and bulked up their numbers against their neighbors.

In the north, Tachoni and Bukusu petitioners parsed land within their mixed locations. The Tachoni Union petitioned the local administration for "all Tachoni men who have Kipande [identity cards] . . . certifying the bearer to be Bukusu or Kabras should be changed by your authority."[46] Still struggling with the aftermath of the female circumcision crisis and the division of their home locations across the new district boundaries, Tachoni politicians sought to secure the identity of their constituents on colonial documentation to buttress their campaign for separate political recognition. The Tachoni Union urged all Tachoni people living in North and Elgon Nyanza to "send their Identity cards to the registration offices in order that they should have their names of tribes changed to the proper tribe, which is Tachoni."[47]

Before the Constituencies Delimitation Commission, the Tachoni Welfare Association Fund remapped locational lines across Elgon Nyanza, North Nyanza, the Trans Nzoia, and Uasin Gishu, filling this amorphous space with Tachoni clan names and population statistics (fig. 7.1).[48] This map revealed the cognitive mapping of Tachoni political thought, inverting the geographic perspective from the north-south orientation of British surveyors to an east-west orientation that centered Tachoni communities. Tachoni petitioners contested the colonial logic of using rivers as "natural" boundaries, sketching their populations and economies around these natural resources: in the words of the Tachoni Union, the "Nzoia River was put there by God. And so it could not be a barrier to our request."[49] Tachoni petitioners complained of the discrimination and administrative neglect caused by the division of their populations across multiple locations. They referenced the female circumcision crisis and their rejection of the Luyia and Bukusu Language Committees as examples of their cultural difference and oppression by Bukusu or Kabras native administrators. Tachoni demands for the remapping of their locations rested on calls to political, linguistic, and cultural distinctiveness that crossed locational and district boundaries.

To these repeated requests for a Tachoni location, the colonial administration responded, "It is not . . . considered that the numbers of your tribe justify the formation of a separate location."[50] The Nyanza provincial commissioner suggested that the interests of the Tachoni would be better served by "identifying themselves with the larger community in which they live." On the other side, the Bukusu Union mobilized the language "democratic majorities" to defend their right to

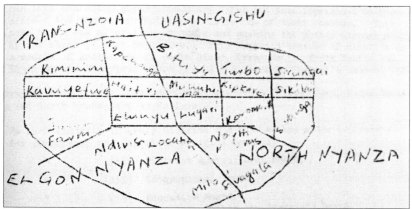

FIGURE 7.1. Map of Tachoni locations by the Tachoni Welfare Association Fund. Petition to the Constituencies Delimitation Commission, 1962, KNA, GO/3/1/16.

rule: it was "undemocratic" for the Tachoni to rule in areas where the Bukusu composed the obvious majority.[51] The Bukusu Union protested any arrangement that would transform their populations into a minority in any location. The Bukusu Welfare Association blinded the Constituencies Delimitation Commission with numbers and percentages to defend their majoritarian claims.[52] A Bukusu delegation presented a long history of "pure Bukusu leadership" as proof of their right to rule their constituencies.[53] In these petitions, Tachoni and Bukusu representatives produced competing maps and numbers that internally fractured the contiguous territory of Luyia political thought.

The spread of cartographic literacy and practice in western Kenya led to a competitive mapmaking culture and the adoption of cartographic metaphors and symbols in ongoing contestations over land and community. With memorandums sent to the Constituencies Delimitation Commission also finding their way to the Regional Boundaries Commission, the mapping of electoral constituencies threatened to deconstruct Luyia claims to a homogenous territory. As in the 1930s, the arrival of a national commission provided the grounds for Luyia patriots to compress these low partisan debates and envision a unified Luyia territory.

THE KENYA REGIONAL BOUNDARIES COMMISSION

The Kenya Regional Boundaries Commission of 1962 emerged out of the constitutional negotiations for independence between the Kenya African National Union (KANU) and the Kenya African Democratic Union (KADU). Boundary commissions such as this held throughout eastern Africa prompted African communities to defend alternative models of sovereignty and political community through drawing maps, enumerating named constituents, and telling cartographic histories.

The Luyia position in the battle between KANU and KADU has been greatly oversimplified. In the dominant narrative, KANU was the superalliance of the Kikuyu and the Luo, while KADU's support rested on precarious partnerships among political communities in Kenya who felt marginalized from the Kikuyu-Luo leadership of KANU. The majority of KADU's support came from the pastoralist Kalenjin, Maasai, and Somali groups along with coastal populations that were at the center of the above-listed separatist movements.[54]

The Luyia have been depicted as a KADU stronghold. The party's first vice president did hail from the region: Bukusu politician Masinde Muliro, who had won the legislative seat for North Nyanza in the tightly fought first African election, in 1957. Narrowly defeating the popular W. W. W. Awori, Muliro secured this victory through cultivating personal networks of patronage through the Catholic Church and the Bukusu Union and capitalizing on the complex voting geography and plurality of political loyalties in western Kenya.[55] While Muliro claimed the Luyia for KADU, the picture on the ground was much more complicated. While most district associations across Kenya merged as local branches into either KADU or KANU in the 1960s, in North Nyanza "the Baluyia people retained their independence of outlook" and represented "very much a mixture" of political parties.[56] This "independence" was reflected in the formation of the Buluhya Political Union (BPU) in 1960. Refusing to align with either KANU or KADU, the BPU brought together Luyia politicians from all parties into their numerous public meetings. Founder Musa Amalemba invited KADU's Muliro, KANU politician J. D. Otiende, and other locational leaders to give speeches at these meetings on topics such as "the case for Buluhya unity," "Abaluhya leadership—past and present," and "the Abaluhya in an Independent Kenya."[57]

The 1961 election revealed the depth of partisan politics and the defiant plurality of voters in North Nyanza. The North Nyanza constituency registered the highest number of voters of any district in the entire country: 142,458 voters representing nearly 95 percent of the estimated potential electorate. Given additional seats in the Legislative Council, Muliro easily recaptured his seat in Elgon Nyanza for KADU, while nine candidates ran for election in the new two-member North Nyanza constituency, representing KANU, KADU, the BPU, and a host of independents. As George Bennett and Carl Rosberg noted, soon after the election the diversity of political parties in North Nyanza was unique as compared to the five other dominant ethnic groups who participated in this election.[58] BPU candidate Amalemba won the first seat with 28,817 votes, capitalizing on local anti-colonial politics by campaigning to have Msambwa leader Elijah Masinde returned to the district, emphasizing that he had been "sent away earlier than Kenyatta."[59] Amalemba's victory catapulted the BPU to the third-ranked party on the national scene, behind the overwhelming national victory of KANU and the second place standing of KADU. KADU-supported candidate Eric Khasakhala took the closely fought second seat, after a campaign boost from Muliro. While Khasakhala's victory in North Nyanza secured an important win for KADU, when the votes for KADU and KANU-associated candidates are tallied together, this KADU victory among the Luyia appeared less convincing. All told, the KADU-affiliated candidates in North Nyanza, even if including the still independent BPU, totaled 55,242 voters against the KANU-affiliated total of 58,844.

Although the Luyia political landscape should be understood more in terms of its pluralism than the polarity of the KANU-KADU contest, Luyia support did provide KADU with important numbers and an agriculturalist base in western Kenya and also reflected broader intellectual convergences. David Anderson has called KADU's political program "defensive in character," glossing over the multiple intellectual debates and interests among its varied supporters.[60] In reality, KADU's political objectives, of balancing competing minority interests and remapping political power within the nation, resonated strongly with Luyia political thought.

After Kenya's first Lancaster House Constitutional Conference, in 1960, the policy of *majimbo*, variously understood as regionalism, federalism, or decentralization, became KADU's central platform, and the distinguishing policy difference between the two parties. Although derided in nationalist historiography as the brainchild of European settlers, the intellectual work of majimbo remains understudied despite its continuing political salience.[61] As Oginga Odinga often pointed out, the Kiswahili term *majimbo* covered a myriad of territorial ideas, including "province," "region," and even "district."[62] In KADU's rhetoric the centralized nation-state structure favored by KANU threatened cultural, financial, and political autonomy and transformed strong regional communities into a nation of minorities. KADU argued that federalism, as embodied in the majimbo plan, provided the "basis for a devolved constitutional arrangement that would protect smaller 'minority' communities from the dominance of larger communities."[63] The first regionalist map drawn by KADU was a complicated puzzle of thirteen pieces.[64] KADU listed economic viability, political amity, and ethnic amiability as the criteria for regional polities.[65] KADU's political program reenvisioned the internal demarcation of the Kenyan nation and forwarded an alternative model of state building.

For many, majimbo already existed: in policies of customary law and interpenetration; in the financial distribution of resources through self-funded LNCs; and in the decentralized form of local governance that had endowed colonial provincial and district commissioners with extensive discretionary powers. But more than simply a "bargaining counter," majimbo was, and for many still is, a potent argument against the continuation of colonial forms of governance under the guise of postcolonial independence.[66]

Debates over regionalism dominated the political campaigns of the 1961 election and subsequent constitutional conferences. For KADU supporters, federation guaranteed regional political communities "their identity and the powers they retain unto themselves."[67] In response, Tom Mboya penned KANU's "alternative to regionalism," discrediting KADU's regional program by associating it with coastal separatists and Somali secessionists.[68] KANU contradictorily argued both that there existed no tradition of regionalism in local cultures and that KADU's plan threatened a "reversion to old tribal concepts of land." KANU petitioned to maintain the status quo, defending a centralized state and the current provincial boundaries as administratively sensible and historically valid. As a result of debates over a federal constitution at the second Lancaster House conference, in 1962, Secretary of State for the Colonies Reginald Maudling appointed the Kenya Regional Boundaries Commission to determine the boundaries of six regional assemblies to effect the "decentralization of the powers of government."[69] These debates over regionalism in the Legislative Council and at Lancaster House were not mere parochial partisan issues but rather revealed the competing models of sovereignty and political community debated ahead of decolonization.

Into this political context, the Regional Boundaries Commission of 1962 called upon ethnic patriots to defend their political projects through the mapping of territory. Mapping became a veritable pastime throughout the colony, with local groups from school children to women's organizations mastering mapmaking skills to argue for political representation, ethnic patriotism, and resource redistribution.[70] An itinerant theater, the Regional Boundaries Commission traveled the country holding well-publicized public meetings at each stop that collected testimonies, petitions, and maps from African communities who gathered to participate in this drama of cultural production. It was perhaps unsurprising that the areas that sent in the majority of the hundreds of maps collected by the commission represented the stronghold of KADU's regional support. Petitions from KANU strongholds rarely contained maps, any slight boundary change being seen as potentially subversive and deconstructive to its centralized platform. KANU supporters petitioned to maintain the current provincial boundaries, accusing those who remapped the nation of divisive "tribal" politics. Thus mapping became a strategy of dissent, a symbol of alternative sovereignties, and a weapon of defense against centralizing African nationalists. As French geographer Claire Médard has argued, the Kenya Regional Boundaries Commission mapped the colonial "politics of territoriality" into the political and social fabric of postcolonial Kenya.[71]

Dome Budohi's motion to the Legislative Council in July 1962 inaugurated the campaign for a Luyia polity in western Kenya to become one of the rather arbitrarily designated six regions in the new Kenya. Supported by Luyia politicians from across the political spectrum, Budohi's motion called for the integration of all Luyia populations currently residing outside its colonial boundaries in Central Nyanza, the Rift Valley, and Uganda into one territorial polity. Budohi argued these Luyia minorities outside their borders suffered discrimination in education, language, employment, health care, and natural resources. Mapping the borders of a Luyia region served pragmatic political objectives: to secure resources, to ensure national representation, and to justify regional autonomy. More than that, however, Luyia leaders imagined an alternative polity in western Kenya in the face of national centralizers who sought to maintain colonial boundaries. Luyia leaders drew maps, built up demographic arguments, and told histories of lost sovereignty to further the objectives of their ongoing ethnic project. Urban branches of the BPU and the Abaluyia Association expressed their support for a Luyia region and voiced their opposition "to any suggestion that a MULUHYA in Kenya should be divided as the past time."[72] Despite the competitive culture of mapping in North Nyanza, the mapping of a Luyia region provided a common objective. With very few exceptions, representatives from North and Elgon Nyanza petitioned the boundaries commission to recognize a Luyia region.

In August and September of 1962, the commission traveled the country collecting oral evidence and petitions. Luyia-related groups presented an overwhelming number of memorandums and testimony to the commission and by far produced the largest collection of maps. In their abstract cartographic representations appended to petitions and carried into local meetings, Luyia representatives acted as amateur surveyors. Their maps used all the tools and symbols available to surveyors, including legends, color coding, topographical features, and ethnographic details. In their petitions, Luyia representatives forwarded their own definitions of boundaries, be they historic, linguistic, geographic, or political. Against colonial surveyors, Luyia representatives challenged the so-called natural boundaries imposed on them, instead visualizing communities that lived in and around the forests, rivers, and mountains that had been used to divide them (figs. 7.2, 7.3). Maps ranged from incredibly detailed descriptions of group distribution over amorphous spaces to simple territorial outlines representing naturalized spaces of ethnic homogeneity. Some took detailed survey and administrative maps and drew their own lines on top of colonial boundaries.[73] As in local land courts, representatives often interacted and performed their mapping practices, pointing out particular sites, drawing boundaries in the air, and calling on commissioners and audience members to "examine early maps."[74] Against a culture of competitive mapping in North Nyanza, Luyia representatives emptied the map of deconstructive land claims and minimally outlined their political geography. Mapmaking provided Luyia political actors with a visual means of contesting the historic legitimacy of colonial divisions and of envisioning a bird's-eye view of a homogenized Luyia territory.

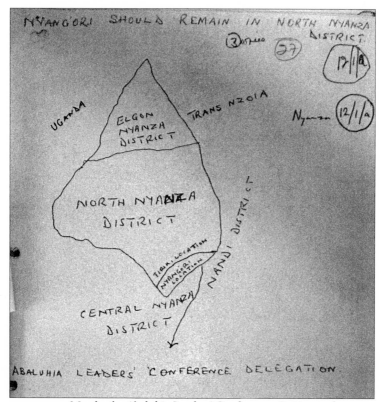

FIGURE 7.2. Map by the Abaluhia Leaders' Conference. Petition to the Regional Boundaries Commission, 1962, KNA, GO/3/1/16.

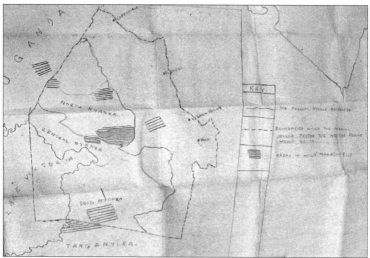

FIGURE 7.3. Map by the Maragoli Association. Petition to the Regional Boundaries Commission, 1962, KNA, GO/3/1/16.

The Regional Boundaries Commission's limited mandate prompted petitioners to map their districts within a larger imagining of the Kenya nation. Petitioners snaked six regional lines through the colonial outline and provided magnified insets of their particular claims. In their memorandums, Luyia representatives mapped a new geographical orientation for western Kenya. The most common shape of this new regional contour stretched northward to include Elgon Nyanza, North Nyanza, and disputed areas of Central Nyanza, Nandi, Uasin Gishu, Trans Nzoia, Elgeyo Marakwet, West Pokot, Karasuk, and Turkana (figure 7.4). This northerly stretch reoriented the Luyia away from their historical association with Lake Victoria and repositioned the northern locations at the center of the new region. Petitioners supported the incorporation of the northern expanses in terms of friendly association, economic

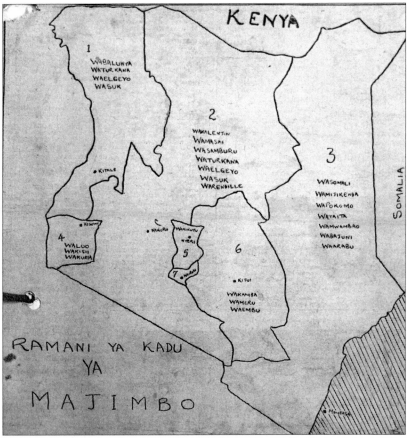

FIGURE 7.4. Map by the Luyia branch of KADU. Petition to the Regional Boundaries Commission, 1962, KNA, GO/3/1/16.

development, and topographical features. The imagining of a territorial homeland that stretched north built on the claims put before the Kenya Land Commission in the 1930s and attempts to bridge southern and northern ambitions among the Luyia in the 1940s and 1950s.

This northern mapping centered on claims to a town that existed only on the periphery of most other petitioners' maps. At the edge of the Trans Nzoia, Kitale was an underdeveloped urban backwater until the politics of decolonization thrust it onto center stage. Luyia petitioners mapped Kitale as their new capital. Before the boundaries commission commenced its work, in 1962, Masinde Muliro laid a symbolic "foundation stone" in the middle of the sports stadium at Kitale.[75] Bukusu claims on Kitale and on surrounding settler farms had served as a uniting point for Luyia leaders from the time of the gold rush. As validated the 1948 census, Luyia populations made up to 90 percent of the population in Kitale and counted majorities in most Trans Nzoia locations. The majority of Luyia maps positioned Kitale at the center of their claims to a new region, effectively shifting the balance of power in the district north.

Kitale became a space of contestation on competing national maps, its position between the lines often directly correlating to the party affiliation of the cartographer. Yet KADU's claims on Kitale threatened the tenuous alliance between its Luyia and Kalenjin politicians. As a competing neighbor, the history of Kalenjin politics shared much with the Luyia. As a concerted ethnic project in language and in politics, the Kalenjin identity similarly arose in the 1940s as a defense against neighbors and colonial policies.[76] Comprising mainly pastoralist groups, the Kalenjin had a more mobile sense of territoriality that bumped up against the expanding agriculturalist populations of the Luyia. With Luyia and Kalenjin partisans mapping claims to this remote township, Kitale became the "rock on which KADU's regionalism could founder."[77] The fate of Kitale, as will be assessed further on, revealed the centrality of shifting boundaries and geographical alignment to the politics of decolonization.

There was one strong voice of dissent in the Luyia demands for a northerly extending district. Select Logoli representatives presented an alternative mapping of western Kenya that maintained their southern orientation within Nyanza Province (fig. 7.5). Through detailed inserts, Logoli cartographers mapped Kisumu at the center of a region that extended down to Tanzania and up past Mount Elgon to the Cherangani foothills. This alternative mapping thus strategically centered the Logoli within a new political region, a bridge between the south and the north over which commerce and resources would travel. These Logoli petitioners sketched their historic and economic ties to Kisumu. The

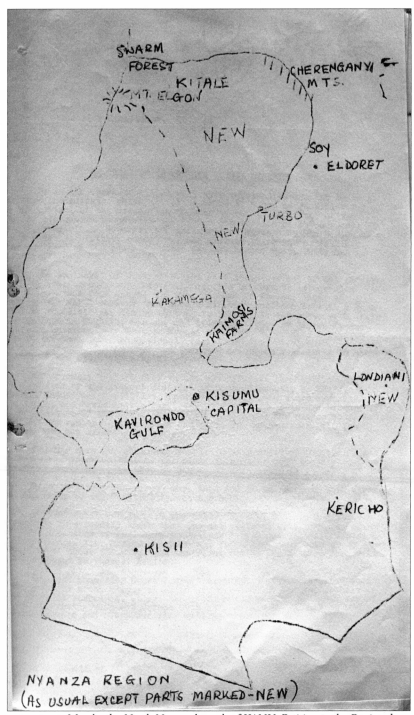

FIGURE 7.5. Map by the North Nyanza branch of KANU. Petition to the Regional Boundaries Commission, 1962, KNA, GO/3/1/16.

Maragoli Association claimed the very name *nyanza* was a Maragoli term meaning the sea, thus linguistically linking them to the lake basin.[78] The Uholo and Wanga Joint Committee similarly argued *inyanza* was a Luyia term.[79] Many influential Samia politicians in Elgon Nyanza argued that "the proposed new KADU boundaries were invented by small-hearted people who are afraid of the Kikuyu and the Luo . . . we in the District are a mixture of Abaluyia, Luo, Teso, Kalenjin, etc."[80] Southern politicians worried the northern mapping of the district would shift the balance of power among the Luyia even further toward the Bukusu following Muliro's victory at the polls in 1957. KANU politicians exploited this geopolitical power struggle to encourage the party's supporters to demand the retention of the Nyanza provincial boundaries.

This alternative mapping, however, had its limits. Most southern petitioners still called for the inclusion of northern expanses outside Nyanza. These northern lands had, since the 1930s, provided a unifying reference point for the diverse interests of Luyia politicians. In 1960, Luyia politicians from across KANU, KADU, and independent parties came together to demand unused Crown land in Kaimosi and in Uasin Gishu.[81] The BPU stressed the history of unifying calls for the Trans Nzoia, from the efforts of Paramount Chief Mumia to Legislative Council member W. W. W. Awori and religious leader Elijah Masinde.[82] Land in the north would provide "much needed expansion areas" for the land-pressed Logoli despite their resistance to separation from Nyanza.[83] Logoli and Samia representatives habitually finished their petitions with a call to Luyia unity: "If the other Abaluhya wish to go to another region the majority must prevail and the Maragoli would follow."[84] In the other direction, Jared Akatsa, representing the "non-partisan" Luyia inhabitants of Kisumu, petitioned that "Kisumu town is built of Buluhya wealth" and therefore should be part of a northern-stretching Luyia region.[85] Despite these alternative mappings, the physical mapping of a separate Luyia region provided a territorial reference that united the divergent interests of Luyia political leaders.

At stake in these two competing mappings was not only the alignment of political communities and resources but also the regional heart and geography of power in western Kenya. In a Nyanza region centered on Kisumu, the Luyia would have to compete for a majority with their more politically integrated Luo neighbors. A northerly remapping centered on Kitale would integrate the Luyia with the sparser Kalenjin and Maasai populations in the north and ensured their majority rule. The majority ideology that guided the boundaries commission's mandate impelled petitioners to mobilize such population arguments in defense of political and territorial claims. Larger political goals, too, were at stake in the drawing of these constituencies. KANU, KADU, and the colonial state kept a close eye on these numbers and how voter percentages would affect the regional success of competing national parties. This dramatic remapping of western Kenya aimed not only at integrating Luyia populations and land claims outside district boundaries but also at creating a Luyia majority and thus a powerful political bloc.

A GREATER LUYIA: POPULATION-BUILDING, PRECOLONIAL MONARCHIES, AND CARTOGRAPHIC HISTORIES

In mapping an expanded Luyia territory, petitioners sketched historical cartographies that told of territorially inclusive populations, lost monarchical sovereignties, and traditions of migration and interpenetration that defied colonial boundaries and imagined a "Greater Luyia" carved out of eastern Africa.

Alongside their maps, Luyia petitioners forwarded a barrage of numbers and percentages to the boundaries commission. Like processes of mapping, historians have reflected on colonial census taking as a "powerful instrument of modern territoriality."[86] In the words of Benedict Anderson, "Map and census thus shaped the grammar which would in due course make possible" the imagining of new ethnic and national identities.[87] However, as with mapping, census taking was not the sole domain of modernist state builders. Census taking provided ethnic patriots and subaltern activists a quantitative supplement to mapped arguments that grafted its own order onto existing maps.

In their petitions, Luyia representatives anchored their constituents to the map through census charts and population-building arguments. Luyia petitioners demanded national representation proportional to their population. Luyia politician Musa Amalemba argued linguistic mutual comprehensibility revealed the proper boundaries of the Luyia territory: throughout the region, "they do not need an interpreter: that is why the word Luhya is used."[88] The naturalization of the Luyia as a discrete ethnic category through the 1948 census allowed political organizations to claim simplified and consolidated numbers that ranked high on national ethnic percentages.

While overall numbers legitimized Luyia claims to greater national representation, the competitive population-building work of locational polities also provided leverage in disputes over mixed areas and borderlands. Mixed borderlands around Nyang'ori, the Trans Nzoia, and the Luo border represented the most contentious boundary conflicts facing the commission. On the Nyang'ori border with Rift Valley Province, Luyia associations claimed 75 percent of the population was Luyia.[89] They argued that not only were the Luyia populations in Nyang'ori in the majority, but "moreover, among the people calling themselves as Kalenjin, there are those who are Luyia by origin."[90] Recounting histories of interpenetration and clan absorption, petitioners claimed many Kalenjin settlers in Nyang'ori had been integrated into the Luyia community. The elaborate numbers created by Tachoni organizations in defense of their electoral position were turned here to justify claims on northern expanses. The geographical distribution of Tachoni members across provincial boundaries allowed them to claim the Trans Nzoia as their "real homeland."[91] Along the border with Central Nyanza, Luo and Luyia representatives battled over the numbers. In the North Gem location, consolidated numbers of Logoli, Banyore, and other Bantu settlers far outweighed those of the Luo; in South Gem these numbers were in a dead heat. The Gem Bantu Association petitioned for "a dividing line to be drawn between themselves and the Luo. Their aim is to have their own constituency: but first they must be joined in a region with their brother Abaluhya."[92] In this way, the association layered mappings of political communities as they petitioned for political recognition within larger remappings of the nation. Consolidated numbers provided Luyia representatives with a quantitative measure for their claims to geographic integration.

Alongside percentages, Luyia leaders constructed population-building arguments that reached into the territories of competing Luo and Kalenjin neighbors. While some conceded that no region could be "entirely Luhya since:—we have been living with members of other tribes for a long time," they also warned that the pervasiveness of intermarriage and mixed settlement would lead to great difficulty and possible violence if the government attempted to draw a line dividing these communities along ethnic lines.[93] The United Maragoli of East Africa argued that long histories of intermarriage and interpenetration had produced a territory in which all tribes were of "mixed blood."[94] They further argued that this regional mixing was a "very encouraging sign to a natural process to the growth of nationhood." The language of territorial nationalism allowed Luyia politicians to claim large tracts of land outside district boundaries and forcibly absorb other ethnic groups into Luyia plurality across an expanding contiguous territory. By drawing a strict distinction between Luo and Luyia numbers and enfolding Kalenjin and Maasai numbers into their own, petitioners aligned Luyia constituents with their northern neighbors. As with the maps they drew, Luyia ethnic architects sought to submerge the potentially divisive locational population-building work and secure majorities against their neighbors on the national map.

Despite the divisive history of monarchical politics in North Nyanza, petitioners before the boundaries commission invoked and mythicized the territorial extent of the Wanga kingdom. Monarchism provided a particularly potent alternative to nationalist projects, much as it had served as argument against colonial projects decades before. In Ghana the Asante kingdom asserted a historic right to self-determination and sovereignty apart from a decolonized Ghana.[95] In Uganda monarchical arguments traced alternative polities and buttressed secessionary claims, from the Rwenzori Mountains to the expansive kingdoms of Bunyoro and Buganda. However, monarchical claims had less legal weight in Kenya than in the recognized kingdoms of West Africa and the Uganda Protectorate. Kenya's status as a colony denied the existence of previously autonomous or stated peoples. The Lancaster House constitutional conferences did hold special debates on the complicated constitutional positions of regions that came under colonial rule by various means, such as in the Maasai treaty and the coastal protectorate. But for most the historical arguments forwarded by Kenya's decentralized communities sketched genealogies of migration and settlement to defend their right to land and representation. As David Anderson has shown, history was central to the territorial claims forwarded by competing groups before the boundaries commission: "The lineages of chiefs were set out as evidence of the source of political power, and ethnographies written by Europeans held up as definitive sources on ethnicity and cultural affinity."[96] However, as they had before the Kenya Land Commission in the 1930s, Luyia representatives avoided the contentious lineages and ethnographic evidence so central to the petitions of the Kikuyu, Luo, and Maasai. Luyia petitioners instead mobilized an alternative historical argument, that of monarchy and historical sovereignty, to map a separate polity in western Kenya.

Luyia leaders petitioned for their own questions of sovereignty to receive such special consideration.[97] At Lancaster House, Luyia members referenced treaties signed by "Abaluyia chieftains" and rejected the handing over of their "sovereignty . . . to the Government of Kenya."[98] The BPU repeatedly argued, "We of the Abaluyia were ruling from Busoga in Uganda to Naivasha in Kenya and our Chief was the first and only Paramount Chief to be named."[99] On 26 November 1962, Sitawa Mumia, grandson to Paramount Chief Mumia, wrote to the *Daily Mail* to demand the British government honor the treaty signed by Mumia and defend the sovereign rights of the Luyia upon their departure.[100] Elijah Masinde, writing under the auspices of the "Abaluhia at Coast," where he remained under deportation, demanded Luyia land "from Busoga to Naivasha be handed to us in accordance with the history of our monarchy government."[101] Yet, in contrast to monarchical claims elsewhere in Africa, Luyia politicians were not seeking the reestablishment of a lost kingdom. Their monarchical histories were not of lengthy royal successions and victorious battles. Luyia representatives instead used this royalist history to defend their ability to practice sovereignty and to validate a history of statehood apart from the Kenyan nation.

Not truly royalists, Luyia petitioners presented a pared-down historical narrative that focused more on colonial mapping projects and administrative changes. Bringing this narrative full circle, the 1902 boundary alteration that situated this new political community firmly within the boundaries of Kenya now became a rallying call for lost territories and sovereignty in the remapping of decolonization.

Luyia representatives engaged in a form of historical cartography. They sketched a series of colonial mappings in their memorandums, documenting the arbitrary division of families and the disregard of local sovereignties by capricious colonial administrators. Musa Amalemba argued Luyia unity had been disintegrated "by a stroke of a pen on a map."[102] Claims to a mapped precolonial kingdom ran along the lines of the original demarcation of the Uganda Protectorate, extending around Lake Victoria to Lake Naivasha: "We therefore demand that when the Boundaries Commissioners [delimit] the boundary that they should follow the oldest boundary."[103] Colonial conquest disrupted the expansion of this kingdom, and the 1902 boundary alteration further divided its subjects, reducing the numerical strength and territorial integrity of this precolonial polity. The Samia Union and others argued that if united with their kinsmen in Uganda, their numbers could no longer be ignored.[104] The BPU aimed to "unite all peoples living in Buluhya as well as those residing elsewhere but whose origin is in Buluhya."[105] This origin relied not on kinship networks and blood relations but rather on a territorial and imaginative space; and that space had emerged not only out of colonial constructions but moreover out of the creative reimagining of precolonial belonging. The constitutions of the BPU, the Abaluyia Association, and the Abaluyia Peoples Association all pledged to unite the Luyia "in Kenya and other adjacent territories."[106] The constitution of the Abaluyia Association of East Africa proclaimed to "promote unity and understanding among members of the Abaluyia tribesmen in East Africa."[107] Echoing campaigns in Bunyoro to reclaim lost counties, Luyia politicians demanded the "immediate return of our lost Districts."[108] These campaigns to reintegrate lost land and the "lost Luyia tribes" reached into the borders of Central Nyanza, Rift Valley Province, and across the 1902 boundary with Uganda (fig. 7.6).[109]

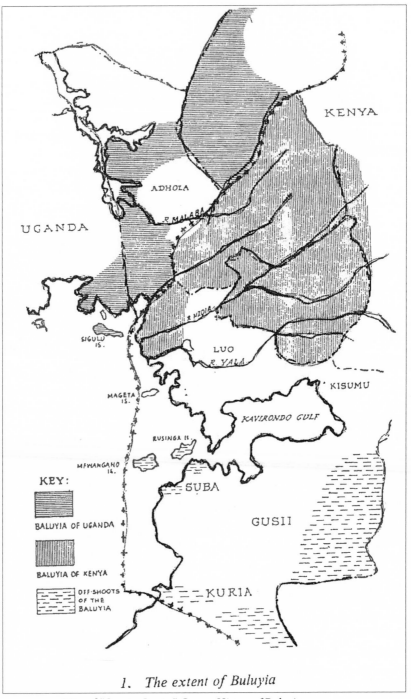

1. *The extent of Buluyia*

FIGURE 7.6. Map of "Greater Luyia." Osogo, *History of Baluyia*, 10.

In petitions throughout the 1960s, political activists on either side of the 1902 boundary used historical cartography to remap political community in the region. Luyia historian John Osogo asserted that for related communities left over the border in eastern Uganda the "only reason they are not recognized generally as Baluyia is that they live in a different territory."[110] In July 1961 the "Abaluyia of Mumbo," or Luyia of the west, from the Busia location of Uganda, petitioned both colonial governments to bring "the Abaluyia of Mumbo . . . under one independent district as before, before the declaration of independence in either Kenya or Uganda."[111] These petitioners argued that colonial rule had divided their territory, "against the wishes of the governed," and that their divided numbers put them at a disadvantage in both countries. As people of the "same language (Luluyia), same culture and the same traditional customs," petitioners demanded the recognition of their sovereignty and independence before the departure of the British. In 1962 the Abaluyia of Mumbo petitioners mapped a Greater Luyia territory, "carved out" around the current interterritorial boundary in a letter to the Ugandan governor, W. F. Coutts.[112] Petitioners spelled out the boundaries of this new territory through rivers, ancestral forts, and hills. On both sides of the border, Luyia partisans mapped an alternative polity carved out of the colonial boundaries of eastern Africa.

Luyia leaders positioned these seemingly irredentist arguments, both ethnic and historical, as central to the decolonization of colonial boundaries. Amalemba called for the "long overdue" settlement of interterritorial boundary.[113] The different pace of decolonization between Kenya and Uganda complicated negotiations on the interterritorial boundary between the two territories. While Uganda prepared for its own independence, in 1962, and the Joint Boundary Commission on the Kenya-Uganda border debated the nature of colonial boundaries, groups on either side questioned the legitimacy of the 1902 interterritorial boundary.[114] The Legislative Council of Uganda seemed eager to incorporate at least the Teso locations divided by the Kenya-Uganda border into their independent boundaries in 1962.[115] The Teso National Political Union argued they could no longer be considered a minority anywhere if they were allowed to join with "their brothers in Uganda as from River Malakisi, Bukhayo, in Kenya to Soroti in Uganda."[116] Many argued it was necessary to wait until Kenya received its independence and had recognized African leaders before moving into these negotiations. Other petitioners, however, spoke of the "moral obligation" of the British government to rectify colonial borders before its departure. Luyia groups in Kenya warned of the dangers of maintaining artificial colonial boundaries by drawing a comparison to the concurrent crisis caused by the secession of the Katanga region of the Congo after its independence in 1960: "We beseech thee in God's name not to plunge Kenya into chaos like those of Congo by adhering to artificial boundaries."[117]

Luyia representatives promoted the creation of this Luyia region as a step in the direction of an East African federation. Nationalists like Jomo Kenyatta proposed the East Africa Federation as a solution to the secessionist claims emanating from the Luyia in the west to Mwambao separatists on the coast and Somali irredentists the north. KADU Legislative Council members from North and Elgon Nanza, Khasakhala, Muliro, Peter Okondo, and Wafule Wabuge, petitioned that "the Abaluhya peoples are divided between Kenya and Uganda. The first step is to unite those in Kenya in one Region."[118] KANU leaders from Samia argued that although amalgamation with Uganda was preferred, a Luyia region was the only alternative within the purview of the boundaries commission.[119] After his return to the district during the height of the commission, Elijah Masinde made clear that his support of the Luyia history of monarchical sovereignty did not mean he supported regionalism. A staunch KANU supporter, Masinde positioned his view of territorial sovereignty within an East African federal vision: "about regionalism I refuse complete [sic]. I know three Majimbo in Africa only, Kenya, Uganda and Tanganyika."[120] Although these interterritorial arguments fit well within the federal discourse promulgated by Luyia leaders, altering state boundaries was beyond the mandate of the boundaries commission and so remained an unsolved problem for future postcolonial states.

While defending their ability to practice sovereignty through monarchical histories, Luyia petitioners kept the divisive local histories of their constituents at bay. From the anti-Wanga campaign to the failed monarchical history projects of the NKCA, Luyia partisans refused to bend the knee. In place of lengthy lineages and ethnographic evidence, Luyia politicians mapped their ethnic territorial claims through appeals to a history of ethnic diversity, cultural interaction, and territorial integration. Bantu associations along the Luo border told of their historical residence in the region: "Historically, all the land along Lake Victoria from Kisumu township was originally Abaluhya land."[121] A delegation calling themselves the Abaluyia of Uasin Gishu preempted claims that they had only recently emigrated to these regions for employment or as squatters by calling upon historical narratives of migration to prove that "this was their land originally."[122] The varied migratory patterns and precolonial "trek northward" of Luyia populations away from the lake supported their claims to a regional remapping of political community.[123]

Petitioners touted their long tradition of democratic values: "We the Abaluyia like democracy."[124] Civic virtues and the flags of state building—tax paying, the rights of citizens, and social security—ran throughout these petitions. Luyia petitioners called on the commission to "respect our ancestry [sic] custom of immigration" and protested that their claims to a separate region aimed not at "tribal hatred, but for social security."[125] A delegation of Samia women charged themselves with rousing "the conscience of our compatriots to the preservation of their human values and dignity in an independent Kenya."[126] For these female petitioners, safeguarding this dignity necessitated territorial recognition and cultural autonomy. Petitioners wrote of their cosmopolitan "obligation to strangers" and openness to welcome others to join the region, as long as these outsiders respected the customs of others and did not demonstrate "bad manners." Logoli representatives from KADU railed against integration with the "undemocratic" Luo, as suggested by the Maragoli Society: "We Baluhya cannot favour the Luo's communist influence."[127] Others pointed to the "balance" and mix of political parties in the region as evidence of their democratic spirit. This was not to be an exclusive and purely ethnically defined territory, but rather the Luyia identity rested on the absorption of others in a territorially contiguous space. Backed by a history of migration and interpenetration, Luyia leaders strategically claimed others became Luyia by living in their territory a practicing their form of cosmopolitan, civic patriotism. In a pragmatic formulation of a territorial and plural Luyia community, Luyia representatives justified their right to a separate region and visually documented complex processes of historical change, interpenetration, and territorial settlements.

As presented before this boundaries commission, mapping and the practices of territoriality proved to be the determining and defining doctrine of the Luyia ethnic project. Luyia leaders took up the map to dissent against encroaching neighbors and centralizing nationalists, to suppress deconstructive mappings land disputes and customary claims, and to remap the very meaning of "nation" ahead of independence.

REMAPPING THE NATION

In the end, the new national map envisioned by the Regional Boundaries Commission bore little resemblance to the colonial map (figs. 7.7, 7.8). The six new regions, which replaced former provinces, reordered political space in Kenya. Luyia representatives were successful in their campaign to be mapped separately. The boundaries of the Western Region truncated Luyia land claims to essentially the original boundaries of the

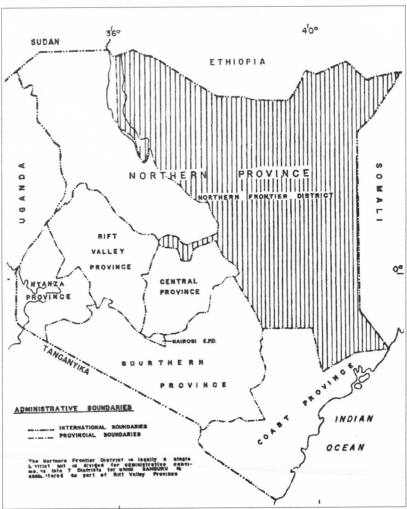

FIGURE 7.7. Map of administrative boundaries, 1961. Bogonko, *Kenya*, 300.

district with only a few additions. This new Western Region contained the Elgon and North Nyanza Districts, the Bantu-dominated Samia and Banyala locations of Central Nyanza, and small portions of the Trans Nzoia and Uasin Gishu. The Western Region defined by the commission covered the smallest geographic space and the fewest constituents of any region, comparable numerically to the vast Coast Region but over 35 percent less than the Nyanza, Rift Valley, Central, or Eastern Regions on average. This new mapping announced the Luyia as a formidable regional and ethnic bloc, no longer to be confused with or submerged under their Luo neighbors.

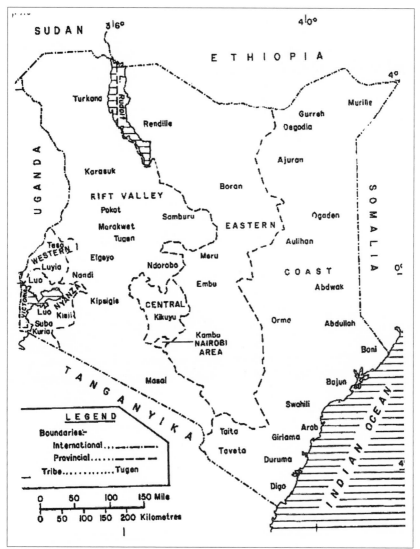

FIGURE 7.8. Map of new regions of Kenya, 1962. Bogonko, *Kenya*, 301.

In the official report of the Regional Boundaries Commission, the first of its maps depicted the "Luo-Luhya Border" as one of the most administratively problematic sites of demarcation. The commission lamented that intermingling along this border made it "impossible to draw a regional boundary between them without leaving substantial minorities of one or the other in a region separated from their brothers."[128] This border map blinded readers with Luo and Luyia population numbers along a borderline that jutted and contorted around these populations.

At the end of 1962, J. W. Howard was charged with demarcating the new Western Region. Borderlands became flashpoints of conflict, and local protests complicated Howard's work in these densely populated and ethnically mixed areas.[129] Although the Luyia gained many important concessions, disputed areas like Maseno and Kitale continued to make their way into national debates. Maseno, a predominantly Banyore town where early missionaries had established important schools, witnessed various violent flare-ups throughout the colonial period. In 1963 these tensions threatened to spark again. Banyore politician John Adala produced a press release on a spate of house burnings in Maseno and called upon all residents, be they Luyia or Luo, to trust in the system and respect the historic place of Maseno within North Nyanza and now within the Western Region.[130] Maseno represented a flashpoint in the power struggle between the Luo and Luyia partisans and, just as in the battle over Kitale, threatened the KANU alliance between Luo and southern Luyia politicians.

Despite moderate territorial gains, Luyia petitioners lost their claims to the northern expanses of the Trans Nzoia and to Kitale as their regional headquarters. In fact, the Western Region became the only region not to inherit a provincial headquarters from the former provincial boundaries. Luyia petitioners had mobilized all the multiple means of mapping behind the Kitale campaign: a remapping of space in western Kenya northward, an accounting of the numerical and economic significance of Luyia populations in Kitale, and a history of ethnic plurality and territorial integration. The boundaries commission, however, opted to leave Kitale within the Trans Nzoia, fearful of conflict between KADU supporters on either side of the debate. The Luyia won their own region but lost their claims to the northern reaches or to any urbanized center.

The fate of Kitale, however, was far from settled and revealed the central role boundaries played in the politics of decolonization. After the loss of Kitale, the BPU called on its Luyia constituents to "resign from their posts in Government . . . to boycott taxes, to destroy the voting cards, to break from KADU and wait and see."[131] Kitale became a wedge issue in the political power brokering between KADU and KANU. Luo politicians seemed particularly intent on preventing this realignment. When Muliro took this battle to the press, in 1962, advertising Mboya's opposition to the incorporation of Kitale in the Western Region, Mboya fired back that all KANU ministers and even KADU Kalenjin leaders opposed the plan. The secretary of state taxed Muliro with a breach of cabinet secrecy and "gave him a fairly robust tick off."[132] Governor Patrick Renison felt most KANU leaders were prepared to cede Kitale but that Mboya had made the issue a personal crusade to embarrass KADU and exacerbate the already tenuous relations between the Luyia and the Kalenjin.[133] Further, Mboya argued KANU required some tangible concessions to sell the new boundaries to their constituents.[134]

KADU heavyweight and symbolic figurehead of the Kalenjin ethnic project Daniel arap Moi walked a dangerous line in negotiations with Muliro over Kitale. Moi eventually agreed in private that the Rift Valley Regional Assembly would use its constitutional powers at independence to transfer Kitale to the Western Region, tempering the debate for a time.[135] Muliro staked his political career on the fate of Kitale, leaving his unopposed constituency in Elgon Nyanza to run for office in Kitale in the May 1963 election. In what David Anderson calls "the most dramatic demonstration of the power of central government," at independence, Minister of Home Affairs Oginga Odinga effectively blocked the order transferring Kitale to the Western Region.[136] Odinga also managed to procure the transfer of Maseno to his Nyanza constituency. This dramatic turn sounded the death knell for KADU as it exposed the impotence of the constitutional power held by opposition leaders.[137] With the flag of independence raised on 12 December 1963, KADU members began crossing the floor and postcolonial Kenya rapidly transformed into a one-party state. During its first year of independence, threats of a coming civil war reverberated from multiple corners, ringing with nativist claims and demands for territorial restitution.[138] The foundational stone laid by Muliro in the Kitale stadium had become the tombstone of regionalism, but the dream of federalism would remain a constant faultline in the political landscape of postcolonial Kenya.

While Luyia patriots succeeded in their quest for a mapped territorial identity within postcolonial Kenya, the loss of Kitale underscored the limits of cosmopolitan pluralism and their ability to transform more radical geographic imaginations into mapped realities. Ethnic patriots in western Kenya were left frustrated, these battles exposing their impotence on the national level and their compromised position locally. Like other failed projects of remapping sovereignty ahead of decolonization, the fate of the Luyia revealed a deeper tension between nativism and cosmopolitanism in late colonial Africa, between calls to past sovereignties and modern nation-state building, tensions that would continue and have often violent consequences in the postcolonial era.

⤻

THE FATE of the dissenting maps of Luyia patriots reflected a much broader trend. In 1958, a year after the independence of Ghana heralded that the "wind of change" was beginning to blow across the African continent, delegates at the first All-African Peoples' Conference had resolved to denounce "artificial frontiers drawn by imperialist Powers to divide the peoples of Africa" and called for the "the abolition or adjustment of such frontiers."[139] During these early years of decolonization, the discourse of artificial African boundaries became almost axiomatic. Pan-African thinkers lamented the arbitrary division of African communities by colonial powers. However, the crisis in the Congo, caused by the secession of the Katanga region in 1960 and the fear of further secessionist movements gaining traction, forced African nationalists to reconsider the consequences of throwing off colonial boundaries. Into the immediate postcolonial era, African governments and pan-African organizations worked to suppress the multiple alternative mappings imagined during decolonization. The final blow would come during the July 1964 meeting of the Organization of African Unity (OAU). At this meeting, Kenyan nationalists, facing the multiple threats of civil war mentioned above and already engaged in major military operations against Somali secessionists in the northeast, played a critical role in pushing through the "Resolution on the Intangibility of Frontiers," which recognized the "tangible reality" and respect for the borders gained by African nations "on the day of their independence."[140] Kenyan nationalists had a lot to lose if colonial boundaries were up for debate. The very fabric of "Kenyan" sovereignty was hemmed with colonial thread: pull that thread at any point and the whole thing could unravel. For the Luyia, as for African partisans across eastern Africa, the 1964 OAU boundaries resolution retroactively suppressed their dissenting maps and served to delegitimize and discipline any future dissident claims to alternative sovereignties.

As I argued at the outset of this study, tracing the contested genealogy of cartographic practice in western Kenya reveals one important constant: where land divided, territory united. Where the politics of land pitted neighbor against neighbor, landed against the landless, and men against women, the politics of territory bonded an imagined political community in western Kenya that proved resilient. With maps, numbers, and a history of sovereignty in hand, Luyia leaders had petitioned for their geographic imagination to be matched in cartographic expression. In response to Dome Budohi's impassioned call for a Luyia region, Luo politician Tom Mboya warned of the competing nationalisms that emerged from such ethnic arguments: "Kenya cannot develop into a nation if all that the leaders do is to harp on and magnify the differences that may exist among us . . . we are not going to progress if we are going to have hundreds of nations within the nation."[141] But Luyia patriots imagined just such a "nation of nations" within their own ethnic project. In mapping a territorial space "for the Abaluyia, by the Abaluyia, of the Abaluyia," Luyia patriots appropriated the technologies of mapmaking and the tools of territoriality to challenge colonial boundaries, to produce new geographic imaginations of community, and to renegotiate the meanings of decolonization, postcolonial citizenship, and sovereignty.

Beyond the Ethnos and the Nation

BACK IN 2007, while traveling around western Kenya collecting oral testimonies for this project, I interviewed an elder named Samuel Onyango whose farm bordered the Sio River. At the conclusion of the interview, Mzee Onyango asked if I would like to visit the "other side" of his family: his Ugandan family "across the river," he said with a smile. Henry, my research aide, and I climbed into a long wooden boat, paddled for a few minutes, and, without visas or border guards, landed in Uganda. In the river I notice charred posts sticking out of the water—remnants, I was told, of a bridge that former Ugandan president Idi Amin's soldiers had burned in 1976.

In 1976, Amin published a book entitled "The Shaping of Modern Uganda" in which he traced a history of imperial cartography in eastern Africa.[1] On the cover, Amin redrew the borders of Uganda using an amalgam of old colonial maps and planted the Ugandan flag firmly in neighboring countries (fig. A.1). The largest swath of territory Amin claimed was that of western Kenya, extending all the way to Nairobi, using as justification the same "stroke of a pen on a map" in 1902 that Musa Amalemba had appealed to before the Kenya Regional Boundaries Commission in 1962. Amin's historical cartography sparked border blockades, trade barriers, and violent demonstrations throughout Kenya. A war of words and of maps ensued, with both countries publishing competing national maps and forwarding conflicting narratives of historical sovereignty.[2] For Kenya, Amin's historical maps threatened the territorial sovereignty of the Kenyan nation achieved at decolonization. Amin's claims were made all the more ironic as he was at the time president of

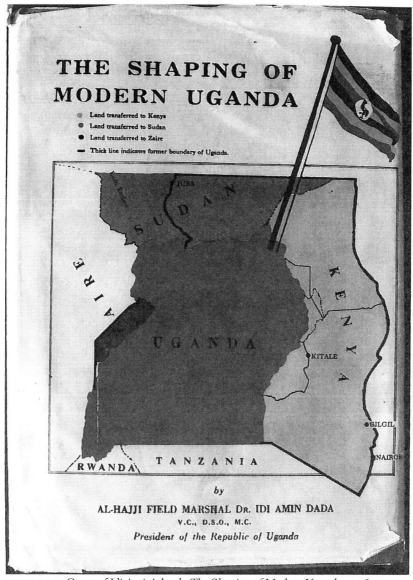

FIGURE A.1. Cover of Idi Amin's book, *The Shaping of Modern Uganda*, 1976.

the OAU, whose now infamous 1964 resolution on the inviolability of the boundaries of independent African nations made such boundary redrawings politically impossible.

While postcolonial discourses around the sanctity of colonial borders suppressed claims to alternative sovereignties, the practices of mapping dissent remained a prominent feature of African political and geographic work. Kenya secured its colonial boundaries at independence despite the numerous alternative mappings put forward by partisans inside and outside its territorial outline; and yet recent years have seen several of these claims resurface. Although Amin eventually backed down, reframing the whole exercise as purely "academic" in intent, the boundary between Kenya and Uganda has remained contentious. The two countries have engaged in a drawn-out battle over tiny and relatively desolate Migingo Island, in Lake Victoria.[3] Cross-border conflicts have plagued the Karamoja borderlands across Uganda, Kenya, South Sudan, and Ethiopia for decades. On the Kenyan coast, the reemergence of the Mombasa Republican Council in 2008, heir to the Mwambao separatist movement of the 1960s, has prompted new geographic activism along the coast and a retelling of history that waivers between claims to autochthony and to colonial treaties with cosmopolitan sovereigns of the recent past.[4]

Perhaps the most persistent case, and the one that not only provided the largest challenge to Kenyan sovereignty but also proved to be the motivation behind Kenya's vocal support of the OAU's boundaries resolution, emerged from the long history of Somali secessionism in Kenya's northern frontier. While seemingly remote from the geographic imaginations of western Kenya, the northern frontier actually shared an intimate connection with the region: the man who found western Kenya a perfect training ground for his imperial cartographic surveying techniques, Sir Geoffrey Archer, would be rewarded for his impressive work there with the task of demarcating the most difficult terrain in the colony, that of the Somali-dominated northern frontier.[5] In the northern frontier, Archer would not enjoy the same success he had in western Kenya. The northern frontier would remain a classic colonial frontier: an ill-defined zone of exception filled with defiantly mobile and racially ambiguous Somali pastoralists. As Archer put it, "just miles and miles of bloody Africa."[6]

In the era of decolonization, Somali partisans would transform this colonial history of racial othering and territorial ambiguity into a call for secession and the mapping of a Greater Somalia.[7] They refused to participate in the mapping of the Kenyan nation before the Regional Boundaries Commission. While their own Northern Frontier District Commission in 1962 reported that 85 percent of petitioners supported secession, the Regional Boundaries Commission ignored these findings and mapped Somali futures in the northern frontier into Kenya's postcolony.[8] Violent confrontations began almost immediately and threatened to derail Kenya's smooth transition to independence. A few days after Christmas 1963, Kenya inaugurated its independence by declaring a state of emergency in the new North Eastern Region, no small statement in a country where the colonial enactment of Emergency Regulations throughout the 1950s was a fresh and bitter wound. Kenyan nationalists labeled Somali secessionists with the doubly insulting Amharic-derived term *shifta*, bandits or raiders. Only days before independence, Kenyan newspaper headlines quoted Kenyatta calling on Kenyan patriots to "bring me a Somali raider—dead or alive."[9] Ironically, the Somali shifta, an ascription often taken up by participants themselves, were perhaps closer to the original Amharic use of the term, acting as "rebels" or "social bandits" working outside legal parameters to redress moral obligations of leaders to their constituents.[10] Kenyan nationalists, however, transformed Somali partisans into "dissident citizens" of a multiethnic polity.[11] The overwhelming violence of this frontier war allowed Kenyan nationalists not only to perform their newfound sovereignty but also to make an example of Somali secessionists and to warn current and future "dissidents" against such alternative mappings.

The Shifta War (1963–67), which persisted well into Kenya's first years of independence, and in many ways was regenerated with Kenya's invasion and continued occupation of southern Somalia, beginning in 2011, was not a material battle over strategic resources but rather a symbolic war over another kind of resource—the very meaning of boundaries, sovereignty, and citizenship in the postcolony.[12] As Ann Stoler has argued, these postcolonial practices, inherited from imperial formations, should not be understood as exceptional; rather these practices of sovereignty thrived on "the production of exceptions and their uneven and changing proliferations . . . on harboring and building on territorial ambiguity, redefining legal categories of belonging and quasi membership, and shifting the geographic and demographic zones of *partially* suspended rights."[13] This conflict has taken on ever more bizarre forms with the suggested solution of creating a "buffer zone" in Kenya's not quite "forgotten province" of Jubaland, transferred from the Kenya colony by the British to Italian rule in 1924.[14] Jubaland has, in many ways, become a "suspended space" carved out of postcolonial sovereignties.[15] This borderland, both geographically and ideologically, has served not only as an anomic space in which to define notions of belonging and obligation, alienness and exception, but also as a site of refuge from state powers and for the imagining alternative sovereignties.

Ultimately, while violent contestations over the terms of territory, citizenship, and sovereignty have proven a constant feature of postcolonial life, these numerous, largely frustrated alternative political imaginaries have attracted little historical scholarship. This absence proves true not only for eastern Africa but also for dissenting projects across Africa: for Katangan secessionists in the Congo, for Biafran nationalists in Nigeria, and for Tuareg pastoralists across multiple countries, among others.[16] Tracing a disparate geography of conflict across Africa, these alternative political imaginaries reflect the variety and geographic energies of postcolonial thinkers. At the other extreme, the continually frustrated move toward integration, as in the case of the East African Federation, offered as possible antidotes to these deconstructive conflicts, has similarly suffered from a lack of scholarly engagement.[17] Fred Cooper's new book on the failed attempt at federation in West Africa makes a compelling case for why these frustrated political projects need to be part of the scholarly agenda: "We need to set aside our assumptions of what a story of national liberation should be in order to understand the openings, closures and new possibilities as people perceived them and in terms of which they sought to act."[18] The same could, and should, be said about how we study ethnic imaginations and their relationship to nationalist thought. These cases have a lot to teach us not only about how Africans imagined, dissented, and made viable their political imaginations but also about why debates continue to rage over the meanings of governance and sovereignty, over citizenship and nativism, and over pluralism and dissent. While frustrated, these failed projects reveal the contingent nature of African nationalisms and the alternative geographic imaginations that continue to inform political and social formations in postcolonial Africa.

This book has, in large part, traced a genealogy of cartographic thought and geographic imagination in western Kenya. Perhaps most ironically, varied cases from across the continent speak to the fetishization of the map in postcolonial Africa. Colonial boundaries are often lazily blamed for the woes that haunt the African continent: imperial mapping created artificial nations; ethnic communities were invented and pitted against one another. And yet, mapping also served a generative purpose. For Luyia patriots, mapping provided a minimalist geographic imagination capable of containing their plural and dissenting bodies, of which the Luyia had many. Indeed, the colonial map seems to have provided the very material proof of the ability of African sovereignties to exist—claims to the "postcolony" requiring the "colony" to be articulated—for nationalists and their dissenters all the same. Kenya nationalists produced pamphlets, flags, symbols, and T-shirts, all exalting the mapped logo of the nation, cleared of any internal boundaries and lifted out of Africa as if existing it some idealized historical void. In 1968, Biafran nationalists produced postage stamps that lifted their colonial boundaries out of postcolonial Nigeria and claimed a separate independence: one such stamp, produced for their second anniversary, displayed Biafran child biting a chain circling over a faded colonial map of Africa. In the unrecognized breakaway state of Somaliland, established in 1991 and based on the colonial borders of British Somaliland, public monuments scattered throughout the capital depict an upheld hand gripping the mapped geo-body of Somaliland. South Sudan has perhaps ironically provided the clearest example of the fetishitic heights colonial maps have reached in recent years. When South Sudan achieved independence in 2011 by breaking away from the Sudan, the African Union withheld support until the very last minute, citing their policy on boundaries and secession since the 1964 resolution. Since then, there has been a frenzied search by South Sudan supporters to retrieve the supposedly missing 1956 colonial map of the Sudan's internal borders.[19] While some still await the feared opening of the Pandora's box of secession across Africa in the wake of South Sudan's "success," the geographic imaginations of these alternative polities still seem to find their inspiration and legitimation within colonial maps.[20] There is much more work to be done here. Colonial-mapped outlines, whether for recognized nations or their dissenters, have become the fetish of the postcolony, overvaluing the nation at the same time as disavowing the plural histories within and outside its borders.

The "triumph" of the map and the African nationalisms of independence may have succeeded in burying alternative claims at independence, but the grave has proven to be a shallow one. Since before independence, political communities mapped alternative spaces of sovereignty and patriotism against the self-fulfilling prophecy of the nation-state. Mapping provided an important tool of dissent and of political imagination. From the imaginative mapping of a Greater Luyia or a Greater Somalia to the erasure of national boundaries in debates over the proposed East African Federation, competing mappings of independence highlighted the creative processes by which African communities debated and defended alternative visions of sovereignty and political community. Taking seriously the mappings of alternative polities ahead of decolonization injects a necessary measure of uncertainty into the primacy of the nation-state as the legitimate category of analysis. Shifting focus away from the nation-state and toward these alternative cartographic political imaginations opens new pathways for studying the multiple and dissenting constructions of the past, present, and future of African political polities.

This shift in focus also offers a challenge to contemporary understandings of political life and conflict in postcolonial Africa. The horrific violence that engulfed Kenya after the 2007 elections is too easily explained away by the media, by politicians, and by many academics as just another case of ethnic violence. Some blame the "arbitrary" borders of colonialism; others blame rampant "political tribalism." Such explanations cheapen the serious critiques of power and deep social anxieties expressed during the elections and witnessed in its aftermath. Examining the history of Luyia cartographic imaginations provides a particularly good counterargument to these reactive claims. This study has argued not only that the making and meanings of these ethnic identities are more complex and contradictory than these charges allow—and thus that the roots of political violence are equally more complex and contradictory—but moreover that pluralism and diverse moral geographies can and often do sustain these imaginations.

This history of political pluralism among the Luyia provides a different twist to the common understandings of Kenya's political landscape, and in particular their often violent election seasons. From the first African election, in 1957, the Luyia confounded electoral expectations and inaugurated an almost defiant tradition of political pluralism.[21] In the run up to this election, W. W. W. Awori warned Luyia constituents of the dangers of a narrow political outlook: "Here in Kenya our tragedy is that tribalism is still rampant. People think in terms of tribes and not of personalities. We can hardly create leaders responsible for our destiny when ideas of this nature run amok in our heads."[22] And Luyia voters into the postcolonial era have consistently borne this suspicion out: as noted by Charles Hornsby and David Throup in their study of postcolonial politics in Kenya, "in 1963, as in 1992, the Luhya split three ways, some voting with the Kalenjin, some with the Kikuyu, others remaining independent."[23] Even in 2013, which many saw as the first election with a viable Luyia candidate on the ballot in Musalia Mudavadi, the Luyia vote remained defiantly split. The limits of invention and imagination were clear: many of the constituent communities that make up the Luyia refused and continue to refuse to be incorporated or subsumed, be they the more distant related Teso and Sabaot or the more central Bukusu and Logoli. Commenting on a political contest between prominent Logoli politician Moses Mudavadi and Marama politician Martin Shikuku in the 1980s, linguist Rachel Kanyoro argued that people in western Kenya decided "to understand or not to understand one another by interpreting the political scene of the time."[24] The calls of political tribalism—in its ability to subsume the debates of moral ethnicity to promote homogenized ethnic bargaining positions and maximize access to material accumulation and control of state power—thus never fully consolidated within the Luyia political project.[25]

But what Hornsby and Throup, along with many others, have missed in their instrumental readings of Luyia political failure was the cosmopolitan patriotism of this political history. Pluralism was, in many ways, a choice, though a choice constrained and conditioned by a particular geographic landscape and situated colonial histories. While the patriotic work of imagining a Luyia political community was an invention thoroughly situated within the colonial era, it was the geographic practices and cultures of accommodation and interdependence of the eighteenth and nineteenth centuries that gave this project its durability. Lines on the page proved insufficient for inculcating map-mindedness in either colonial subjects or ethnic constituents. African farmers uprooted the pegs of British bureaucrats and gold miners. Urban migrants, young Tachoni girls, and mobile Msambwa rebels pushed the frontiers of colonial and patriotic geographies. Squatters and borderland farmers worked their way into forest reserves and penetrated new settlements, blazing new paths beyond the borders of the reserve and creating new "ways of being." And yet the map did provide for a new kind of geographic imagination in western Kenya. The map provided the tangible pictorial representation to make the political work of Luyia patriots legible. The vision of Luyia ethnic patriots was made possible not only through their own patriotic work but moreover through the social energies of their wide, and vocal, constituents. Formed by the late colonial politics witnessed throughout this study, Luyia ethnic patriotism stuck precisely because it built on deeper geographic histories, and it continues to provide Luyia political thought a theory of common citizenship that offers a way through Kenya's aggressive political landscape.

This study hints at much larger implications: of the generative possibilities of interethnic relations, of regional and federal solutions, and of the value of pluralism and diversity. While cosmopolitan patriotism may not be a particularly appealing label for many, when reframed within this longer history it becomes not a foreign, elitist concept of a globalized world but an indigenous, intensely local philosophy of "living together." To echo John Lonsdale, such rooted and yet imaginative moral ethnicities, with their calls to personal accountability, cosmopolitan plurality, and civic virtues, might actually be the most fruitful sources of future formulations of citizenship and peaceful, multiethnic nationalisms.[26]

Despite its self-consciously articulated genesis, the "Luyia" idea has proven remarkably durable if unpredictable. Indeed plurality and dissent have come to form the most resilient features of Luyia processes of identification, helping explain not only their long and unique history of political pluralism—their "intricate" and "elusive" sense of unity—but also their continued dismissal and denial of access to the capital of political tribalism in modern Kenya.[27] This book has argued that restrictive models of ethnic identity that insist on the consolidation of vernacular cultures, customary authority, and imagined ancestral moral communities have become trapped in their own logic. While recognizing the plural, multiple, and comparative work that has long characterized the political imagination of ethnic patriotisms, such models still seem hell-bent on reproducing this coherence and dismissing those that do not achieve these measures of ethnic legitimacy. This study has been less concerned with saying what the Luyia are, or were, than with exploring what they imagined they could be: less concerned with some essential essence than with their multiple ways of being. There is a much larger story to be told here, a story that would take up Cooper's call to shed the expectations of what African identities, be they ethnic, national, or regional, should look like and would instead examine the diverse ways African imagined, debated, and dissented over what they could be. This kind of study would privilege a social history of geographic imaginations, of the ways people conceived of and used space, as much as the political work they engaged in to manage the pluralism and dissent within and outside the confines of their imagined communities and territorial bodies.

Although Idi Amin's attempt to "recover" western Kenya for his "modern Uganda" fit well within late colonial imaginings of a Greater Luyia and boundary engineering work among Luyia patriots themselves, by 1976 the Luyia had firmly thrown their lot in with the Kenyan post-colonial state. For Mzee Onyango, however, this border also reflected a broader set of histories: histories of his family crossing back and forth over the river for generations; histories of colonial intervention and post-colonial nation building; histories of drought and plenty, violence and security; histories of resistance, negotiation, and political imagination, of lines drawn and undrawn in the beds of the river. In an ever more global-ized world, these borderlands remind us of the rich geographic imaginations of community, exchange, and dissent contained within and outside the map of these contested terrains.

While the Luyia are often viewed as an exceptional case of political community continually made and unmade, this study suggests the arguments, debates, and mappings of the Luyia were not as unique as they may seem. As Henry and I crossed boundaries, and as Perus Abura faced the dilemma of the 2009 census, perhaps the geographic imaginations that made the Luyia possible also suggest a possible way forward: a way out of the bounded confines of the ethnos and the nation; a way to "gather together," to be "of the same village," to speak with the same moral vocabulary without imposing consensus; and a way of seeing and embracing the plurality and dissent inherent in all mappings of political communities.

Notes

INTRODUCTION: MAPPING POLITICAL COMMUNITIES IN AFRICA

1. Perus Angaya Abura was born 29 March 1930 in the Kisa location, North Kavirondo, Kenya. Perus Angaya Abura, interviews by author, Kakamega, 9 July 2008, 6 October 2009.

2. Kenya Colony and Protectorate, *Population Census 1948* (Nairobi: East Africa Statistical Department, 1950). Throughout the colonial period the spelling of "Luyia" varied greatly. The spelling chosen here, Luyia, with the collective variation Abaluyia, was determined by a vote of the North Kavirondo Local Native Council in 1942, accepted by the Luyia Language Committee, and adopted by the postcolonial Kenyan government, though Luhya and Abaluhya remain common, particularly in the popular media, and others including Abaluhia and Abaluhiya also appear in various sources.

3. Nic Cheeseman, "Introduction: Political Linkage and Political Space in the Era of Decolonization," *Africa Today* 53, no. 2 (Winter 2006): 4; Bård Anders Andreassen and Arne Tostensen, "Of Oranges and Bananas: The 2005 Kenya Referendum on the Constitution," Chr. Michelsen Institute Working Paper 13, 2006, http://aceproject.org/ero-en/regions/africa/KE/http___www-cmi-no_pdf__file-_publications_2006_wp_wp2006-13.pdf. For a fuller discussion of these political developments see Daniel Branch, *Kenya: Between Hope and Despair, 1963–2011* (New Haven: Yale University Press, 2011).

4. Julie MacArthur, "How the West Was Won: Regional Politics and Prophetic Promises in the 2007 Kenya Elections," *Journal of Eastern African Studies* 2, no. 2 (2008): 227–41.

5. See the special issue on the 2007 Kenya elections, *Journal of Eastern African Studies* 2, no. 2 (2008).

6. Otuma Ongalo, "As for Me and My Household, We Shall Not Declare Our Tribe to Census Officials," *Standard*, 8 August 2009.

7. Ted Malanda, "Exchanging Goats for the Tribe," *Standard*, 31 August 2009.

8. Alphonce Shiundu, "Respond to All Queries, Answers PM," *Nation*, 25 August 2009.

9. Malanda, "Exchanging Goats."

10. Peter Leftie, "Kenyans Free to Identify with 114 Tribes," *Nation*, 14 August 2009.

11. Justin Willis and George Gona, "Tradition, Tribe, and State in Kenya: The Mijikenda Union, 1945–1980," *Comparative Studies in Society and History* 55, no. 2 (2013): 452–54; Willis, *Mombasa, the Swahili, and the Making of the Mijikenda* (Oxford: Clarendon Press, 1993); Gabrielle Lynch, *I Say To You: Ethnic Politics and the Kalenjin in Kenya* (Chicago: University of Chicago Press, 2011).

12. Willis, *Mombasa*, 202.

13. Alphonce Shiundu, "Govt Targets 97 Percent Census Success Rate," *Nation*, 28 August 2009.

14. Mutahi Ngunyi, "What Kibaki Should Consider in Picking New VP," *Nation*, 31 August 2003; Wafula Buke, "Raila to Fulfil Luhya Dream of Ascending to Presidency," *Nation*, 21 September 2007; "Mudavadi Asks Luhya Not to Split Vote," *Standard*, 26 February 2013; Yusuf Masibo, "Wamalwa Urges Luhya Leaders to Unite Community, Shun Differences," *People*, 3 September 2013.

15. See special issue on the 2013 Kenya elections, *Journal of Eastern African Studies* 8, no. 1 (2014).

16. Collins Mabinda, "Why the Luhya Vote Will Split along Sub-ethnic Lines," *Star*, 23 June 2012.

17. Mutahi Ngunyi, "What Kibaki Should Consider in Picking New VP," *Nation*, 31 August 2003.

18. Julie MacArthur, "When Did the Luyia (or Any Other Group) Become a Tribe?," *Canadian Journal of African Studies* 47, no. 3 (2013): 351–63.

19. William Okwemba, interview by author, Kima, 19 October 2007; Moody Awori, interview by author, Nairobi, 21 July 2008; Paul Wamatuba, interview by author, Bungoma, 25 September 2007; Arthur Ochwada, interview by author, Funyala, 12 October 2007. For a fuller study of Luyia self-definitions, see Rachel Angogo Kanyoro, *Unity in Diversity: A Linguistic Survey of the Abaluyia of Western Kenya* (Vienna: AFRO-PUB, 1983), 194–201.

20. Benedict Anderson, *Imagined Communities* (London: Verso, 1983).

21. Partha Chatterjee, *Nationalist Thought and the Colonial World: A Derivative Discourse?* (London: Zed Books, 1986).

22. Fredrik Barth, *Ethnic Groups and Boundaries: The Social Organization of Culture Difference* (Long Grove, IL: Waveland Press, 1969). For a discussion of the historiography of ethnicity in Africa, see Thomas Spear, "Neo-traditionalism and the Limits of Invention in British Colonial Africa," *Journal of African History* 44, no. 1 (2003): 3–27.

23. John Iliffe, *A Modern History of Tanganyika* (Cambridge: Cambridge University Press, 1979), 324; Leroy Vail, ed., *The Creation of Tribalism in Southern Africa* (Berkeley: University of California Press, 1989); Terence Ranger, "The Invention of Tradition in Colonial Africa," in *The Invention of Tradition*, ed. Eric Hobsbawm and Ranger (Cambridge: Cambridge University Press, 1983), 211–62.

24. Jean-François Bayart, *The State in Africa: The Politics of the Belly* (London: Longman, 1993), 41–59; John L. Comaroff and Jean Comaroff, *Ethnicity,*

Inc. (Chicago: University of Chicago Press, 2009); Mahmood Mamdani, "Political Violence and State Formation in Post-colonial Africa," International Development Centre Working Paper 1, 2007; Mamdani, *When Victims Become Killers: Colonialism, Nativism, and the Genocide in Rwanda* (Princeton: Princeton University Press, 2002); Bruce Berman, Dickson Eyoh, and Will Kymlicka, eds., *Ethnicity and Democracy in Africa* (Athens: Ohio University Press, 2004).

25. Jonathan Glassman, *War of Words, War of Stones: Racial Thought and Violence in Colonial Zanzibar* (Bloomington: Indiana University Press, 2011).

26. Barbara L. Voss, *The Archaeology of Ethnogenesis: Race and Sexuality in Colonial San Francisco* (Berkeley: University of California, 2008), 33.

27. James C. Scott, *The Art of Not Being Governed: An Anarchist History of Upland Southeast Asia* (New Haven: Yale University Press, 2009); Jonathan D. Hill, ed., *History, Power and Identity: Ethnogenesis in the Americas, 1492–1992* (Iowa City: University of Iowa Press, 1996); David Zeitlyn and Bruce Connell, "Ethnogenesis and Fractal History on an African Frontier: Mambila-Njerep-Mandulu," *Journal of African History* 44 (2003): 117–38.

28. Richard Werbner and Terence Ranger, eds, *Postcolonial Identities in Africa* (Atlantic Highlands, NJ: Zed Books, 1997), 1; Julie MacArthur, "The Perils of Ethnic History," review of *I Say to You: Ethnic Politics and the Kalenjin in Kenya*, by Gabrielle Lynch, *Journal of African History* 53, no. 1 (March 2012): 122–23.

29. John Lonsdale, "Moral Ethnicity, Ethnic Nationalism and Political Tribalism: The Case of the Kikuyu," in *Staat und Gesellschaft in Afrika*, ed. Peter Meyns (Hamburg: Lit Verlag, 1995), 95.

30. Terence Ranger, "The Invention of Tradition Revisited: The Case of Colonial Africa," in *Legitimacy and the State in Twentieth-Century Africa*, ed. Ranger and Olufemi Vaughan (London: Macmillan, 1993), 62–111.

31. John Lonsdale, "The Moral Economy of Mau Mau: Wealth, Poverty, and Civic Virtue in Kikuyu Political Thought," in *Unhappy Valley: Conflict in Kenya and Africa. Book Two: Violence and Ethnicity*, ed. Bruce Berman and Lonsdale (Athens: Ohio University Press, 1992), 315–504; Lonsdale, "The Prayers of Waiyaki: Political Uses of the Kikuyu Past," in *Revealing Prophets: Prophecy in Eastern African History*, ed. David M. Anderson and Douglas H. Johnson (London: James Currey, 1995), 240–91; Lonsdale, "Listen While I Read: The Orality of Christian Literacy in the Young Kenyatta's Making of the Kikuyu," in *Ethnicity in Africa: Roots, Meanings and Implications*, ed. Louise de la Gorgendière, Kenneth King, and Sarah Vaughan (Edinburgh: Centre of African Studies, University of Edinburgh, 1996), 17–53; Lonsdale, "Kikuyu Christianities," *Journal of Religion in Africa* 29, no. 2 (May 1999): 206–29.

32. John Lonsdale, "Moral and Political Argument in Kenya" in *Ethnicity and Democracy in Africa*, ed. Bruce Berman, Dickson Eyoh, and Will Kymlicka (Athens: Ohio University Press, 2004), 268.

33. Spear, "Neo-traditionalism," 26.

34. MacArthur, "When Did the Luyia Become a Tribe?"

35. Tim Parsons, "Being Kikuyu in Meru: Challenging the Tribal Geography of Colonial Kenya," *Journal of African History* 53, no. 1 (March 2012): 65, 68.

36. Rogers Brubaker and Frederick Cooper, "Beyond 'Identity,'" *Theory and Society* 29, no. 1 (2000): 1–47. I am grateful to Fred Cooper for our discussions on the reception of this article.

37. Paul Richards, *Fighting for the Rain Forest: War, Youth and Resources in Sierra Leone* (Oxford: James Currey, 1996), 79.

38. I owe much of my thinking on "ethnic patriotism" to the work of Derek Peterson, John Lonsdale and Steven Feierman.

39. John Lonsdale, "Comparative Patriotisms and Ethno-history in Eastern Africa" in *Recasting the Past: History Writing and Political Work in Modern Africa*, ed. Derek R. Peterson and Giacomo Macola (Athens: Ohio University Press, 2008), 251–67.

40. In addition to those already mentioned, see Myles Osborne, *Ethnicity and Empire in Kenya: Loyalty and Martial Race among the Kamba, c. 1800 to the Present* (Cambridge; Cambridge University Press, 2014); Derek Peterson, *Creative Writing: Translation, Bookkeeping, and the Work of Imagination in Colonial Kenya* (Portsmouth, NH: Heinemann, 2004); Thomas Spear and Richard Waller, eds., *Being Maasai: Ethnicity and Identity in East Africa* (Athens: Ohio University Press, 1993); John Lonsdale, "When Did the Gusii (or Any Other Group) Become a Tribe?," *Kenya Historical Review* 5, no. 1 (1977): 123–35; Aidan W. Southall, "The Illusion of the Tribe," in *Perspectives on Africa: A Reader in Culture, History and Representation*, ed. Roy Richard Grinker and Christopher B. Steiner (Oxford: Oxford University Press, 1997), 38–51; Justin Willis, "The Makings of a Tribe: Bondei Identities and Histories," *Journal of African History* 33, no. 2 (1992): 191–208; Bill Bravman, *Making Ethnic Ways: Communities and Their Transformations in Taita, Kenya, 1800–1950* (Portsmouth, NH: Heinemann, 1998); Bethwell A. Ogot, "The Construction of Luo Identity and History" in *African Words, African Voices: Critical Practices in Oral History*, ed. Luise White, Stephan F. Miescher, and David William Cohen (Bloomington: Indiana University Press, 2001), 31–52; David William Cohen and E. S. Atieno Odhiambo, *Siaya: The Historical Anthropology of an African Landscape* (Athens: Ohio University Press, 1989); Matthew Carotenuto, "Riwruok e teko: Cultivating Identity in Colonial and Postcolonial Kenya," *Africa Today* 53, no. 2 (Winter 2006): 53–73; Bruce Berman, "Ethnography as Politics, Politics as Ethnography: Kenyatta, Malinowski and the Making of *Facing Mount Kenya*," *Canadian Journal of African Studies* 30, no. 3 (1996): 313–44.

41. J. D. Otiende, *Habari za Abaluyia* (Nairobi: Eagle Press, 1949); John Osogo, *A History of the Baluyia* (Nairobi: Oxford University Press, 1966); Gideon Were, *A History of the Abaluyia of Western Kenya, 1500–1930* (Nairobi: East African Publishing House, 1967); Gideon Were, *Western Kenya Historical Texts: Abaluyia, Teso, and Elgon Kalenjin* (Nairobi: East African Publishing

House, 1967); Were, "Ethnic Interaction in Western Kenya: The Emergence of the Abaluyia up to 1850," *Kenya Historical Review* 2 (1974): 39–44. For other history-writing projects of this era, see Derek R. Peterson and Giacomo Macola, eds., *Recasting the Past* (Athens: Ohio University Press, 2008). For more recent versions of this kind of production, see Shadrack Amakoye Bulimo, *Luyia Nation: Origins, Clans and Taboos* (Bloomington, IN: Trafford Publishing, 2013); Bulimo, *Luyia of Kenya: A Cultural Profile* (Bloomington, IN: Trafford Publishing, 2013).

42. Walter H. Sangree, *Age, Prayer and Politics in Tiriki, Kenya* (London: Oxford University Press, 1966); Jan J. de Wolf, *Differentiation and Integration in Western Kenya: A Study of Religious Innovation and Social Change among the Bukusu* (The Hague: Mouton, 1977); F. E. Makila, *An Outline History of the Babukusu of Western Kenya* (Nairobi: Kenya Literature Bureau, 1978); Kenda Mutongi, *Worries of the Heart: Widows, Family, and Community* (Chicago: University of Chicago Press, 2007); Simiyu Wandibba, "Notes on the Oral History of Abatachoni," in *History and Culture in Western Kenya: The People of Bungoma through Time*, ed. Wandibba (Nairobi: Gideon S. Were Press, 1985), 18–33; V. G. Simiyu, "The Emergence of a Sub-nation: A History of Babukusu to 1900," *Transafrican Journal of History* 20 (1991):125–44.

43. Judith M. Abwunza, "Ethnonationalism and Nationalism Strategies: The Case of the Avalogoli in Western Kenya," in *Ethnicity and Aboriginality*, ed. Michael Levin (Toronto: University of Toronto Press, 1993), 127–54; Francis Bode, "Leadership and Politics among the Abaluyia of Kenya, 1894–1963" (PhD diss., Yale University, 1978); Francis Bode, "Anti-colonial Politics within a Tribe: A Case of the Abaluyia of Western Kenya," in *Politics and Leadership in Africa*, ed. Aloo Ojuka and William Ochieng' (Kampala: East African Literature Bureau, 1975), 85–138; John Lonsdale, "Political Associations in Western Kenya," in *Protest and Power in Black Africa*, ed. Robert I. Rotberg and Ali Mazrui (New York: Oxford University Press, 1970), 589–638; Samuel S. Thomas, "Transforming the Gospel of Domesticity: Luhya Girls and the Friends Africa Mission, 1917–1926," *African Studies Review* 43, no. 2 (September 2000): 1–27; Hannington Ochwada, "Negotiating Difference: The Church Missionary Society, Colonial Education, and Gender among Abaluyia and Joluo Communities of Kenya, 1900–60" (PhD diss., Indiana University, 2008); Watson Omulokoli, "The Historical Development of the Anglican Church among Abaluyia, 1905–1955" (PhD diss., University of Aberdeen, 1981); Clifford Gilpin, "The Church and the Community: Quakers in Western Kenya, 1902–1963" (PhD diss., Columbia University, 1976); Stafford Kay, "Local Pressures on Educational Plans in Colonial Kenya: Post–Second World War Activity among the Southern Abaluyia," *International Journal of African Historical Studies* 11, no. 4 (1978): 689–710.

44. "Baganda" refers to the people of the kingdom of Buganda. Paul Bohannan, "Homicide and Suicide in North Kavirondo," in *African Homicide and Suicide*, ed. Bohannan (Princeton: Princeton University Press, 1960), 154.

45. E. G. Wilson, ed., *Who's Who in East Africa, 1965–66* (Nairobi: Marco Publishers [Africa], 1966), 7; J. S. Smith, *A History of Alliance High School* (Nairobi: Heinemann Educational Books, 1976).

46. North Nyanza District Commissioner to Nyanza Provincial Commissioner, 10 March 1947, Kenya National Archives (hereafter, KNA), Nairobi, DC/KMG/1/1/73; Matthew Carotenuto, "Cultivating an African Community: The Luo Union in 20th Century East Africa" (PhD diss., Indiana University, 2006), 201.

47. Lynch, *I Say to You*, 38.

48. Luyia Civil Law Panel, [1954], KNA, RR/8/24; meeting of Abaluyia Customary Law Panel, 16 May 1962, Kakamega Provincial Archives (hereafter, KPA), Kakamega, ATW/4/62.

49. E. A. Andere, "The Abaluyia Customary Law Relating to Marriage and Inheritance," [1952], KNA, DC/NN/7/1/1; Andere, "Abaluyia Land Law and Custom," [1952], KPA, DX/21/2/17; meeting of Abaluyia Customary Law Panel, 16 May 1962, KPA, ATW/4/62.

50. J .D. Otiende to editor, *Baraza*, 10 February 1948, KNA, DC/KMG/1/1/73.

51. *Report of the Commissioner Appointed to Enquire into the Methods for the Selection of African Representatives to the Legislative Council* (Nairobi, 1955).

52. "Before the Commission at Mumias: Evidence Taken at a Baraza of Natives of the North Kavirondo District," 12 September 1932, *Kenya Land Commission Evidence*, vol. 3 (Nairobi, 1955), 2222.

53. *North Kavirondo News*, August 1943, KNA, PC/NZA/2/2/82; Samuel Onyango, interview by author, Matayos, 21 September 2007.

54. "Re: Owuluyali," letter to editor, *Habari* [1944], KNA, DC/KMGA/1/16/12.

55. Here I am in dialogue with Kwame Anthony Appiah's extensive work on cosmopolitanism, including "Cosmopolitan Patriots," *Critical Inquiry* 23, no. 3 (Spring 1977): 617–39; *Cosmopolitanism: Ethics in a World of Strangers* (New York: Norton, 2006).

56. Mahmood Mamdani, *Define and Rule: Native as Political Identity* (Cambridge, MA: Harvard University Press, 2012); Christopher J. Lee, *Unreasonable Histories: Nativism, Multiracial Lives, and the Imagination in British Africa* (Durham, Duke University Press, 2014). For a critical approach to the complexities and multiplication of postcolonial nativist discourses, see Dorothy L. Hodgson, *Being Maasai, Becoming Indigenous: Postcolonial Politics in a Neoliberal World* (Bloomington: Indiana University Press, 2011).

57. Appiah, *Cosmopolitanism*, 144–53.

58. Harry Wamubeyi, interview by author, Butere, 5 October 2007. When meeting Luyia actor and prominent media figure Oliver Litondo in Toronto while he was promoting his new film *The First Grader*, my "mulembe" greeting was met at first with shock that quickly evolved into a warm, familial embrace; the term *mulembe* now appears in many Luyia events and popular culture forums, including the Luyia radio channel, Mulembe FM, and the popular Luyia musical series in Nairobi, *Mulembe Nights*.

59. Shem Musee, interview by author, Kona Mbaya, 22 October 2007; L. L. Appleby, *Luyia-English Vocabulary* (Nairobi: CMS, 1943); R. A. Snoxall, *Luganda-English Dictionary* (Oxford: Oxford University Press, 1967).

60. Helen Oronga A. Mwanzi, "Reflections on Orality and Cultural Expression: Orality as a Peace Culture," *Journal des Africanistes* 80, nos. 1–2 (2010): 63–74.

61. See for example Chike Jeffers, "Appiah's Cosmopolitanism," *Southern Journal of Philosophy* 51, no. 4 (December 2013): 488–510.

62. Jonathan Glassman, "Creole Nationalists and the Search for Nativist Authenticity in Twentieth-Century Zanzibar: The Limits of Cosmopolitanism?," *Journal of African History* 55, no. 2 (2014): 245.

63. Appiah, *Cosmopolitanism*, 60; Daniel M. Wako, *The Western Abaluyia and Their Proverbs* (Nairobi: Kenya Literature Bureau, 1954).

64. Lonsdale, "Comparative Patriotisms," 261.

65. Leroy Vail, "Ethnicity in Southern African History," introduction to *The Creation of Tribalism in Southern Africa*, ed. Vail (Berkeley: University of California Press, 1989), 15.

66. Tabitha Kanogo, *African Womanhood in Colonial Kenya, 1900–50* (Athens: Ohio University Press, 2005); Grace Bantebya Kyomuhendo and Marjorie Keniston McIntosh, *Women, Work and Domestic Virtue in Uganda, 1900–2003* (Athens: Ohio University Press, 2006); Susan Geiger, *TANU Women: Gender and Culture in the Making of Tanganyikan Nationalism, 1955–1965* (Portsmouth, NH: Heinemann, 1997); Luise White, *The Comforts of Home: Prostitution in Colonial Nairobi* (Chicago: University of Chicago Press, 1990); Dorothy L. Hodgson and Sheryl A. McCurdy, eds., *"Wicked" Women and the Reconfiguration of Gender in Africa* (Portsmouth, NH: Heinemann, 2001); Jean Allman, Susan Geiger and Nakanyike Musisi, eds., *Women in African Colonial Histories* (Bloomington: Indiana University Press, 2002). There are a few important exceptions to this statement, including Lynn M. Thomas, *Politics of the Womb: Women, Reproduction, and the State in Kenya* (Berkeley: University of California Press, 2003); Heidi Gengenbach, "'I'll Bury You in the Border!': Women's Land Struggles in Post-war Facazisse (Magude District), Mozambique," *Journal of Southern African Studies* 24, no. 1 (March 1998): 7–36.

67. Henrietta L. Moore, *Space, Text, and Gender: An Anthropological Study of the Marakwet of Kenya* (Cambridge: Cambridge University Press, 1986), 188.

68. This issue has also been pointed out in Allen F. Isaacman and Barbara S. Isaacman, *Slavery and Beyond: The Making of Men and Chikunda Ethnic Identities in the Unstable World of South-Central Africa, 1750–1920* (Portsmouth, NH: Heinemann, 2004), 324. Jan Bender Shetler's upcoming edited volume should provide a much needed redress to this hole in the scholarship. Shetler, *Gendering Ethnicity in African Women's Lives* (Madison: University of Wisconsin Press, 2015).

69. Charles H. Ambler, *Kenyan Communities in the Age of Imperialism: The Central Region in the Late Nineteenth Century* (New Haven: Yale University Press, 1988), 44.

70. Mama Wangamati, interview by author, Webuye, 17 October 2007; Perus Angaya Abura, interview by author, Kakamega, 9 July 2008; H. Moore, *Space, Text*, 171.

71. Appiah, "Cosmopolitan Patriots," 618; for an example of the tensions and contradictions of cosmopolitanism in Kenyan discourses, see David William Cohen and E. S. Atieno Odhiambo, *Burying SM: The Politics of Knowledge and the Sociology of Power in Africa* (Portsmouth, NH: Heinemann, 1992), 29. This debate has taken a new twist in recent years in the heated exchanges over "Afropolitanism." See, for example, Stephanie Santana, "Exorcizing Afropolitanism: Binyavanga Wainaina Explains Why 'I Am a Pan-Africanist, Not an Afropolitan' at ASAUK 2012," http://africainwords.com/2013/02/08/exorcizing-afropolitanism-binyavanga-wainaina-explains-why-i-am-a-pan-africanist-not-an-afropolitan-at-asauk-2012/, February, 2013.

72. Lynch, *I Say to You*, 32.

73. Steven Feierman, *Peasant Intellectuals: Anthropology and History in Tanzania* (Madison: University of Wisconsin Press, 1990); Peterson, *Creative Writing*, 23.

74. Michel Foucault, "Questions on Geography," in *Power/Knowledge: Selected Interviews and Other Writings, 1972–1977*, ed. Colin Gordon (New York: Pantheon, 1980), 63–77.

75. For one example of the prominent use of geographic metaphors with very little subsequent analysis, see Ben Wisner, Camilla Toulmin, and Rutendo Chitiga, eds., *Towards a New Map Of Africa* (London: Earthscan, 2005). Despite its title and the two maps printed on the opening page, the book contains almost no mention of actual mapping practices, construction of boundaries, or geographic conceptions.

76. Jan B. Shetler, "'Regions' as Historical Production," in *The Spatial Factor in African History: The Relationship of the Social, Material, and Perceptual*, ed. Allen M. Howard and Richard M. Shain (Leiden: Brill, 2005), 143. For more on the "spatial turn" in African studies see also Ulf Engel and Paul Nugent, eds., *Respacing Africa* (Leiden: Brill, 2010).

77. Achille Mbembe, "At the Edge of the World: Boundaries, Territoriality, and Sovereignty in Africa," *Public Culture* 12, no. 1 (2000): 262.

78. Ibid., 263.

79. Lynch, *I Say to You*, 15.

80. Denis Wood, *Rethinking the Power of Maps*, with John Fels and John Krygier (New York: Guilford Press, 2010).

81. George Curzon, Lord of Kedleston, "Text of the 1907 Romanes Lecture on the Subject of Frontiers," https://www.dur.ac.uk/resources/ibru/resources/links/curzon.pdf.

82. Matthew H. Edney, *Mapping an Empire: The Geographical Construction of British India* (Chicago: University of Chicago Press, 1997), 1, 3; David

Gilbert, David Matless, and Brian Short, eds., *Geographies of British Modernity: Space and Society in the Twentieth Century*, RGS-IBG Book Series (Oxford: Blackwell, 2003).

83. Robert David Sack, *Human Territoriality: Its Theory and History* (Cambridge: Cambridge University Press, 1986), 26.

84. See James Scott, *Seeing Like a State* (New Haven: Yale University Press, 1998).

85. Thongchai Winichakul, *Siam Mapped: A History of the Geo-body of a Nation* (Honolulu: University of Hawaii Press, 1994); Christopher Gray, *Colonial Rule and Crisis in Equatorial Africa: Southern Gabon ca. 1850–1940* (Rochester: University of Rochester Press, 2002).

86. For the theories of cognitive mapping see Ervin Laszlo and Ignacio Masulli, eds., *The Evolution of Cognitive Maps: New Paradigms for the Twenty-First Century* (New York: CRC Press, 1993); Fredric Jameson, "Cognitive Mapping," in *Marxism and the Interpretation of Culture*, ed. Cary Nelson and Lawrence Grossberg (Urbana: University of Illinois Press, 1988), 347–57.

87. Winichakul, *Siam Mapped*, 33.

88. Jan Vansina, *Habitat, Economy and Society in the Central African Rainforest* (Providence: Bloomsbury Academic, 1992), 5; Gray, *Colonial Rule*, 18.

89. Gray, *Colonial Rule*, 73–83.

90. Heidi Gengenbach, *Binding Memories: Women as Makers and Tellers of History in Magunde, Mozambique*, http://www.gutenberg-e.org/geho1/, 2005; Christopher Goscha, *Vietnam or Indochina? Contesting Concepts of Space in Vietnamese Nationalism, 1887–1954* (Copenhagen: NIAS Books, 1995); Sean Hawkins, *Writing and Colonialism in Northern Ghana: The Encounter between the LoDagaa and "the World on Paper," 1892–1991* (Toronto: University of Toronto Press, 2002); Allen M. Howard and Richard M. Shain, eds., *The Spatial Factor in African History* (Leiden: Brill, 2005); Paul Nugent, *Smugglers, Secessionists and Loyal Citizens on the Ghana-Togo Frontier: The Lie of the Borderlands since 1914* (Athens: Ohio University Press, 2002); Donald S. Moore, *Suffering for Territory: Race, Place, and Power in Zimbabwe* (Durham: Duke University Press, 2005); Sumathi Ramaswamy, "Maps, Mother/Goddesses and Martyrdom in Modern India," *Journal of Asian Studies* 67, no. 3 (2008): 1–35.

91. Paul Nugent and A. I. Asiwaju, eds., *African Boundaries: Barriers, Conduits and Opportunities* (London: Frances Pinter, 1996); Sara Dorman, Daniel Hammett, and Paul Nugent, eds., *Making Nations, Creating Strangers: States and Citizenship in Africa* (Leiden: Brill, 2007).

92. Derek Gregory, *Geographical Imaginations* (Cambridge: Blackwell, 1993).

93. Raymond B. Craib, *Cartographic Mexico: A History of State Fixations and Fugitive Landscapes* (Durham: Duke University Press 2004), 11.

94. Timothy Mitchell, *Rule of Experts: Egypt, Techno-politics, Modernity* (Berkeley: University of California Press, 2002); Scott, *Seeing Like a State*.

95. *North Nyanza Annual Report*, 1948.

96. Gengenbach, *Binding Memories*, 45.

97. Case of Jeremiah Nabifwo, 19 January 1959, KPA, WD/4/5.

98. Minutes of North Kavirondo LNC meeting, 14–16 April 1941, KNA, PC/NZA/4/7/7.

99. Hawkins, *Writing and Colonialism*, 47.

100. Chiteri land case, [1956], KNA, PC/NZA/3/15/68.

101. Chief Barasa to District Officer, Courts, 30 October 1958, KPA, ATW/4/50.

102. Günter Wagner, Records of Court Cases in North Kavirondo, 1933–35, International African Institute Archives (hereafter, IAI), London, England, IAI 1/123.

103. Martin Brückner, *The Geographic Revolution in Early America: Maps, Literacy, and National Identity* (Chapel Hill: University of North Carolina Press, 2006), 3.

104. Wood, *Power of Maps*, 1.

105. Ibid., 7.

106. Joel Wainwright and Joe Bryan, "Cartography, Territory, Property: Postcolonial Reflections on Indigenous Counter-mapping in Nicaragua and Belize," *Cultural Geographies* 16, no. 2 (2009): 153–54.

107. Dorothy L. Hodgson and Richard A. Schroeder, "Dilemmas of Counter-mapping Community Resources in Tanzania," *Development and Change* 33, no. 1 (2002): 80.

108. Scott, *Not Being Governed*.

109. Allen M. Howard, "Nodes, Networks, Landscapes and Regions: Reading the Social History of Tropical Africa, 1700s–1920," in *The Spatial Factor in African History: The Relationship of the Social, Material, and Perceptual*, ed. Howard and Richard M. Shain (Leiden: Brill, 2005), 81.

110. Roderick J. McIntosh, "Clustered Cities of the Middle Niger: Alternative Routes to Authority in Prehistory," in *Africa's Urban Past*, ed. David M. Anderson and Richard Rathbone (Oxford: James Currey, 2000), 22; Holly Hanson, "Mapping Conflict: Heterarchy and Accountability in the Ancient Capital of Buganda," *Journal of African History* 50, no. 2 (2009): 180–81.

111. Hanson, "Mapping Conflict," 202.

112. Neil Kodesh, *Beyond the Royal Gaze: Clanship and Public Healing in Buganda* (Charlottesville: University of Virginia Press, 2010).

113. Sumathi Ramaswamy, *The Goddess and the Nation: Mapping Mother India* (Durham: Duke University Press, 2010), 34–36.

114. Ibid., 291.

115. Howard and Shain, *Spatial Factor*, 10.

116. P. D. A. Harvey, *Maps in Tudor England* (Chicago: University of Chicago, 1993).

117. Binyavanga Wainaina, "Wangechi Mutu Wonders Why Butterfly Wings Leave Powder on the Fingers, There Was a Coup Today in Kenya," http://jalada.org/tag/wangechi-mutu/, 2014.

118. The archives of the American Friends African Mission (FAM) are located at Earlham College in Richmond, Indiana. As western Kenya claims the largest number of American-style Quakers anywhere in the world, research in the FAM archives was critical to my study.

119. White, Miescher, and Cohen, *African Words*, 5.

120. Karin Barber, ed., *Africa's Hidden Histories: Everyday Literacy and Making the Self* (Bloomington: Indiana University Press, 2006).

121. Sharon E. Hutchinson, *Nuer Dilemmas: Coping with Money, War, and the State* (Berkeley: University of California Press, 1996), 284–5.

122. Jan Vansina, *Oral Tradition: A Study in Historical Methodology* (Chicago: Aldine, 1965); Vansina, *Oral Tradition as History* (Madison: University of Wisconsin Press, 1985).

123. For a summary of this historiographical debate, see Barbara Cooper, "Oral Sources and the Challenge of African History," in *Writing African History*, ed. John Edward Philips (Rochester: University of Rochester, 2005), 191–215; Neil Kodesh, "History from the Healer's Shrine: Genre, Historical Imagination, and Early Ganda History," *Comparative Studies in Society and History* 49, no. 3 (2007): 527–31. For studies within this new trend, see Elizabeth Tonkin, *Narrating Our Pasts: The Social Construction of Oral History* (Cambridge: Cambridge University Press, 1992); White, Miescher, and Cohen, *African Words*; Gregory H. Maddox and Ernest M. Kongola, *Practicing History in Central Tanzania: Writing, Memory, and Performance* (Portsmouth, NH: Heinemann, 2006); Luise White, *Speaking with Vampires: Rumor and History in Colonial Africa* (Berkeley: University of California Press, 1990).

124. Audrey Wipper, *Rural Rebels: A Study of Two Protest Movements in Kenya* (London: Oxford University Press, 1977); Elijah Masinde's family and former Dini ya Msambwa members, group interviews by author, Kimilili, 10, 11 October 2007.

125. Batholemeo Munoko, "Mzee Mombasa," interview by author, Kiminini, 16 March 2007.

126. MacArthur, "How the West Was Won."

127. Arthur Ochwada, interview by author, Funyala, 12 October 2007.

128. Anderson Ojwang and Oscar Obonyo, "Scrambling to be Recognised by Dini Ya Msambwa," *African Press International*, 15 October 2007. For the importance of Elijah Masinde as a prophet of electoral victories, see MacArthur, "How the West was Won."

129. Willis, *Mombasa*; Lynch, *I Say to You*; Peterson and Macola, *Recasting the Past*.

130. Edward W. Said pioneered the study of "imaginative geographies" and the ability of space to take on emotional meanings. See Said, *Orientalism* (New York: Vintage, 1979), 55.

131. James R. Brennan, *Taifa: Making Nation and Race in Urban Tanzania* (Athens: Ohio University Press, 2012); James L. Giblin with Blandian Kaduma Giblin, *A History of the Excluded: Making Family a Refuge from the*

State in Twentieth-Century Tanzania (Athens: Ohio University Press, 2006); Giblin and Gregory H. Maddox, eds., In Search of a Nation: Histories of Authority and Dissidence in Tanzania (Athens: Ohio University Press, 2005); Emma Hunter, "Languages of Politics in Twentieth Century Kilimanjaro" (PhD diss., University of Cambridge, 2008).

132. Derek Peterson, Ethnic Patriotism and the East African Revival: A History of Dissent, c. 1935–72 (Cambridge: Cambridge University Press, 2012), 16.

133. John Lonsdale, "KAU's Cultures: Imaginations of Community and Constructions of Leadership in Kenya after the Second World War," Journal of African Cultural Studies 13, no. 1 (2000): 107–24; John Spencer, The Kenya African Union (London: KPI, 1985); John Nottingham and Carl G. Rosberg Jr., The Myth of "Mau Mau": Nationalism in Kenya (New York: F. A. Praeger, 1966); E. S. Atieno Odhiambo and John Lonsdale, eds., Mau Mau and Nationhood: Arms, Authority and Narration (Athens: Ohio University Press, 2003); Bruce Berman, "Nationalism, Ethnicity and Modernity: The Paradox of Mau Mau," Canadian Journal of African Studies 25, no. 2 (1991): 181–206.

134. Myles Osborne, "The Historiography in Mau Mau," in The Life and Times of General China: Mau Mau and the End of Empire in Kenya, ed. Osborne (Princeton: Markus Wiener, 2015), 255–61.

135. Brubaker and Cooper, "Beyond 'Identity'," 1–47.

CHAPTER 1: THE GEOGRAPHIES OF WESTERN KENYA

1. Wako, Western Abaluyia, 50.

2. Harry Wamubeyi, interview by author, Butere, 5 October 2007; Shem Musee, interview by author, Kona Mbaya, 22 October 2007.

3. R. A. Snoxall, Luganda-English Dictionary (Oxford: Oxford University Press, 1967).

4. C. W. Hobley, "British East Africa: Anthropological Studies in Kavirondo and Nandi," Journal of the Anthropological Institute of Great Britain and Ireland 33 (July–December 1903): 343–44.

5. Harry Wamubeyi, interview by author, Butere, 5 October 2007.

6. Bethwell A. Ogot, History of the Southern Luo (Nairobi: East African Publishing House, 1967), 70.

7. Margaret Jean Hay, "Local Trade and Ethnicity in Western Kenya," African Economic History Review 2, no. 1 (Spring 1975): 7–12; Gideon Were, "The Masai and Kalenjin Factor in the Settlement of Western Kenya: A Study in Ethnic Interaction and Evolution," Journal of Eastern African Research and Development 2, no. 1 (1972): 1–11; Were, "Ethnic Interaction," 39–44.

8. The term Kavirondo most likely first appeared on maps drawn by E. G. Ravenstein in the 1870s from information given to him by Mombasa missionaries. For full analysis of the origins and meaning of the term see chapter 4.

9. John Iliffe, Africans: The History of a Continent (Cambridge: Cambridge University Press, 1995). For a concise introduction to environmental history in Africa, see James C. McCann, Green Land, Brown Land, Black

Land: An Environmental History of Africa, 1800–1990 (Portsmouth, NH: Heinemann, 1999).

10. Bill Bravman, *Making Ethnic Ways: Communities and Their Transformations in Taita, Kenya, 1800–1950* (Portsmouth, NH: Heinemann, 1998), 21.

11. James L. Giblin, *The Politics of Environmental Control in Northeastern Tanzania, 1840–1940* (Philadelphia: University of Pennsylvania Press, 1992); David L. Schoenbrun, *A Green Place, A Good Place: Agrarian Change, Gender, and Social Identity in the Great Lakes Region to the Fifteenth Century* (Portsmouth, NH: Heinemann, 1998); Schoenbrun, "Conjuring the Modern in Africa: Durability and Rupture in Histories of Public Healing between the Great Lakes of East Africa," *American Historical Review* 111, no. 5 (December 2006): 1403–39; Jan Vansina, *Paths in the Rainforests: Toward a History of Political Tradition in Equatorial Africa* (Madison: University of Wisconsin Press, 1990).

12. Günter Wagner, *The Bantu of North Kavirondo*, 2 vols. (London: Oxford University Press, 1949), 1:5.

13. George M. Onyango, "The Geographic Setting of Western Kenya," in *Historical Studies and Social Change in Western Kenya*, ed. William R. Ochieng' (Nairobi: East African Literature Bureau, 2002), 6; Richard Waller, "Ecology, Migration and Expansion in East Africa," *African Affairs* 84, no. 336 (July 1985): 348.

14. Christopher Ehret, *An African Classical Age: Eastern and Southern Africa in World History, 1000 B.C. to A.D. 400* (Charlottesville: University Press of Virginia, 1998), 290–91.

15. Ogot, *History of the Southern Luo*; William R. Ochieng', *An Outline History of Nyanza up to 1914* (Nairobi: East African Literature Bureau, 1974); Schoenbrun, *Green Place*; Were, *History of the Abaluyia*; Were, "Ethnic Interaction," 39–44.

16. For a concise introduction to the debates around the "Bantu Expansions" in eastern Africa see David William Cohen, "The Cultural Topography of a 'Bantu Borderland': Busoga, 1500–1850," *Journal of African History* 29, no. 1 (1988): 57–79; Ogot, *History of the Southern Luo*; Ochieng', *Outline History of Nyanza*.

17. Simiyu, "Emergence of a Sub-nation," 125–44.

18. Peterson and Macola, *Recasting the Past*, 5–6.

19. Ibid., 6.

20. David William Cohen and E. S. Atieno Odhiambo, "Ayany, Malo, and Ogot: Historians in Search of a Luo Nation," *Cahiers d'Études Africaines* 27, nos. 3–4 (1987): 283.

21. Lonsdale, "When Did the Gusii Become a Tribe?," 123–35; Willis, "Makings of a Tribe," 191–208; Lynch, *I Say to You*, 40.

22. Were, *Western Kenya Historical Texts*.

23. Were, *History of the Abaluyia*, 149.

24. Cohen and Atieno Odhiambo, "Ayany, Malo," 283; Cohen and Atieno Odhiambo, *Burying SM*.

25. Osogo, *A History of the Baluyia*; Were, *Western Kenya Historical Texts*; Harry Wamubeyi, interview by author, Butere, 6 October 2007; J. D. Otiende, interview by author, Mbale, 9 October 2007.

26. Shetler, "'Regions' as Historical Production," 141–43; Osogo, *History of the Baluyia*.

27. Were, "Ethnic Interaction," 44.

28. Were, "Masai and Kalenjin Factor"; Moses Shiroko Atsolo, interview by author, Khwisero, 5 October 2007; Harry Wamubeyi, interview by author, Butere, 6 October 2007; Dunston Makalu, interview by author, Kaptegi, 21 October 2007.

29. Wandibba, "Oral History of Abatachoni," 18–33; Were, *Western Kenya Historical Texts*, 91–95; Administrative Note, "The Tachoni," [1955], KNA, ARC(MAA) 2/5/2/274I.

30. Osogo, *History of the Baluyia*, 1; Osogo, "The Significance of Clans in the History of East Africa," *Hadith* 2 (1970): 30–41. For a similar argument on the Ugandan side, see Justin Willis, "Clan and History in Western Uganda: A New Perspective on the Origins of Pastoral Dominance," *International Journal of African Historical Studies* 30, no. 3 (1997): 583.

31. Hay, "Local Trade"; Were, "Masai and Kalenjin Factor"; Were, "Ethnic Interaction"; N. Thomas Hakansson, "Grain, Cattle, and Power: Social Processes of Intensive Cultivation and Exchange in Precolonial Western Kenya," *Journal of Anthropological Research* 50, no. 3 (Autumn 1994): 249–76.

32. Wagner, *Bantu of North Kavirondo*, 2:162–65.

33. Bethwell A. Ogot, "Historical Portrait of Western Kenya up to 1985," in *Historical Studies and Social Change in Western Kenya*, ed. William R. Ochieng' (Nairobi: East African Educational Publishers, 2002), 25.

34. Hay, "Local Trade," 7.

35. Tiriki elders, group interview by author, Kaptegi, 21 October 2007; Walter H. Sangree, "The Social Functions of Beer Drinking among the Bantu Tiriki," in *Society, Culture and Drinking Patterns*, ed. David J. Pittman and Charles R. Snyder (London: Wiley, 1962), 12.

36. Günter Wagner, "Warfare," field notes, n.d., IAI, Malinowski/7/18.

37. C. W. Hobley, *Eastern Uganda: An Ethnological Survey* (London: Anthropological Institute of Great Britain and Ireland, 1902).

38. Wako, *Western Abaluyia*, 50.

39. Waller, "Ecology, Migration," 349–50; Ambler, *Kenyan Communities*.

40. Vansina, *Paths in the Rainforests*, 258.

41. Cohen and Atieno Odhiambo, *Siaya*, 124.

42. Suzette Heald, *Controlling Anger: The Sociology of Gisu Violence* (Manchester: Manchester University Press, 1989), 158–59.

43. Gray, *Colonial Rule*, 13–18; Schoenbrun, *Green Place*, 97–100.

44. Günter Wagner, "The Abaluyia of Kavirondo," in *African Worlds: Studies in the Cosmological Ideas and Social Values of African Peoples*, ed. Daryll Forde (Oxford: Oxford University Press, 1954), 35.

45. Neil Kodesh, "Networks of Knowledge: Clanship and Collective Well-Being in Buganda," *Journal of African History* 49, no. 2 (2008): 201n11.

46. Appleby, *Luyia-English Vocabulary*; record of evidence given before North Kavirondo Native Land Tenure Committee (hereafter, NLTC), 1 July 1930, KNA, DC/NN/8/1; Daniel M. Wako, "Principles and Procedures of Conflict Resolution and Settlement of Disputes among the Luyia of Kenya" (master's diss., Makerere University, 1976).

47. Sangree, *Age, Prayer*, 27.

48. Bukusu elders, group interview by author, Bokoli, 13 March 2007; Günter Wagner, "The Political Organization of the Bantu of Kavirondo," in *African Political Systems*, ed. Meyer Fortes and E. E. Evans-Pritchard (London: Oxford University Press, 1940), 232; Kodesh, "Networks of Knowledge," 210; Holly Hanson, *Landed Obligation: The Practice of Power in Buganda* (Portsmouth, NH: Heinemann, 2003); Schoenbrun, "Conjuring the Modern," 19–20; R. Wesonga, "Pre-colonial Military Organisation of Babukusu," in *History and Culture in Western Kenya: The People of Bungoma through Time*, ed. Simiyu Wandibba (Nairobi: Gideon S. Were Press, 1985), 42–50.

49. Shetler, "'Regions' as Historical Production," 158.

50. Wagner, *Bantu of North Kavirondo*, 1:76–81.

51. Were, *Western Kenya Historical Texts*; oral evidence given by Simioni Jumba, author of *The Mulogoli History and Family*, as well as other Logoli interviewees, 9.

52. Wagner, "Political Organization," 235.

53. Harry Johnston, *The Uganda Protectorate*, 2 vols. (London: Hutchinson, 1902), 2:743.

54. Bill Bravman made a similar argument in regard to the influence of the interlocking system of hills in southeastern Kenya on the decentralized political systems of the Taita. Bravman, *Making Ethnic Ways*.

55. Were, *History of the Abaluyia*; Simon Kenyanchui, *Nabongo Mumia* (Nairobi: Heinemann Kenya, 1992); James Dealing, "Politics in Wanga, Kenya, c. 1650–1914" (PhD diss., Northwestern University, 1974).

56. K. Dundas, "Ethnology of North Kavirondo," 1910, KNA, PC/NZA/3/31/8/1.

57. Kenyanchui, *Nabongo Mumia*, 19.

58. Record of evidence given before North Kavirondo NLTC, 1 July 1930, KNA, DC/NN/8/1.

59. Were, *History of the Abaluyia*.

60. McIntosh, "Clustered Cities of the Niger," 22.

61. Hanson, "Mapping Conflict."

62. Were, *Western Kenya Historical Texts*; Chief Ali Wamukoya, interview by author, Mumias, 19 September 2007.

63. Marama elders, group interview by author, Butere, 5 October 2007.

64. Wagner, *Bantu of North Kavirondo*, 1:55.

65. Ibid., 1:55, 343, 377; Osaak A. Olumwullah, *Dis-ease in the Colonial State: Medicine, Society and Social Change among the AbaNyole of Western Kenya* (London: Praeger, 2002), 71.

66. Osogo, *History of the Baluyia*, 34.

67. Günter Wagner to Bronislaw Malinowski, 1 December 1936, IAI, Malinowski/7/7.

68. Record of evidence given before North Kavirondo NLTC, 1 July 1930, KNA, DC/NN/8/1; Osogo, *History of the Baluyia*, 7.

69. Record of evidence given before North Kavirondo NLTC, 1 July 1930, KNA, DC/NN/8/1.

70. Wagner, *Bantu of North Kavirondo*, 2:77.

71. Record of evidence given before North Kavirondo NLTC, 1 July 1930, KNA, DC/NN/8/1.

72. Special meeting of the Bureau of the IAI, 8 March 1938, IAI_2/17.

73. Igor Kopytoff, "The Internal African Frontier: The Making of African Political Culture," in *The African Frontier*, ed. Kopytoff (Bloomington: Indiana University Press, 1989), 3–86.

74. Olumwullah, *Dis-ease in the Colonial State*, 50.

75. Osogo, *History of the Baluyia*, 49.

76. Wagner, *Bantu of North Kavirondo*, 1:55; "Wanga-English Dictionary" http://www.academia.edu/9346974/Wanga-English_Dictionary, 2008; Appleby, *Luyia-English Vocabulary*.

77. Wagner, *Bantu of North Kavirondo*, 1:64.

78. Gray, *Colonial Rule*, 15.

79. Ibid., 35.

80. Wagner, *Bantu of North Kavirondo*, 1:34.

81. J. D. Otiende, interview by author, Mbale, 7 July 2008.

82. Were, *History of the Abaluyia*, 131–52.

83. Frederick Jackson, *Early Days in East Africa* (London: Edward Arnold, 1930), 196–99; Were, *History of the Abaluyia*, 143–44.

84. Waller, "Ecology, Migration," 370.

85. John Ford, *The Role of Trypanosomiases in African Ecology: A Study of the Tsetse Fly Problem* (London: Oxford University Press, 1971); Shane Doyle, *Crisis and Decline in Bunyoro: Population and Environment in Western Uganda, 1860–1955* (Athens: Ohio University Press, 2006), 11–41; Giblin, *Politics of Environmental Control*, 121–32.

86. Robert M. Maxon, "Colonial Conquest and Administration," in *Historical Studies and Social Change in Western Kenya*, ed. William R. Ochieng' (Nairobi: East African Educational Publishers, 2002), 94; Gerald W. Hartwig, "Demographic Considerations in East Africa during the Nineteenth Century," *International Journal of African Historical Studies* 12, no. 4 (1979): 653–72; Waller, "Ecology, Migration"; Ambler, *Kenyan Communities*.

87. Henry Morton Stanley, "Letters of Mr. H. M. Stanley on his Journey to Victoria Nyanza, and His Circumnavigation of the Lake," *Royal Geographical*

Society Proceedings 20 (1875–76): 134–61; Joseph Thomson, "Through the Masai Country to Victoria Nyanza," *Proceedings of the Royal Geographical Society and Monthly Record of Geography*, n.s., 6, no. 12 (1884): 690–712; C. W. Hobley, "Kavirondo," *Geographical Journal* 12, no. 4 (1896): 361–72; Johnston, *Uganda Protectorate*, 2:722–55; C. W. Hobley, *Kenya: From Chartered Company to Crown Colony; Thirty Years of Exploration and Administration in British East Africa* (London: Frank Cass, 1970); J. Ainsworth, "Special Report 1909," 31 December 1909, *North Kavirondo Annual Report*, 1909; W. E. Owen, "The Bantu of Kavirondo," *Journal of the East Africa and Uganda Natural History Society* 44–45 (1932): 57–77; G. W. B. Huntingford, *The Eastern Tribes of the Bantu Kavirondo* (Nairobi: CMS, 1944).

88. Joseph Thomson, *Through Masai Land: A Journey of Exploration among the Snowclad Volcanic Mountains and Strange Tribes of Eastern Equatorial Africa* (Boston: Sampson Low, Marston, Searle, and Rivington, 1885), 487.

89. Charles Eliot, *The East African Protectorate* (London: E. Arnold, 1905), 44.

90. Margaret Jean Hay, "Changes in Clothing and Struggles over Identity in Colonial Western Kenya," in *Fashioning Africa: Power and the Politics of Dress*, ed. Jean Marie Allman (Bloomington: Indiana University Press, 2004), 68.

91. Photographic collection, "Roosevelt and Africa; A Brilliant Panorama of the Mysterious and Wonderful Dark Continent," 1909–1910, Library of Congress, Washington, DC, LOT 7349.

92. Johnston, *Uganda Protectorate*, 2:722.

93. Thomson, *Through Masai Land*, 484.

94. Johnston, *Uganda Protectorate*, 2:745, 43.

95. Treaties 71 and 72, 1890, National Archives: Public Records Office (hereafter, TNA:PRO), London, FO84/2166.

96. John Lonsdale, "The Politics of Conquest in Western Kenya 1894–1908" in *Unhappy Valley: Conflict in Kenya and Africa, Book One: State and Class*, ed. Bruce Berman and Lonsdale (Athens: Ohio University Press, 1992), 69.

97. Hobley, *Kenya*, 80.

98. C. W. Hobley, "A General Report by Mr. Hobley on Kavirondo District," 1896, TNA:PRO, FO1/122.

99. Hawkins, *Writing and Colonialism*, 60.

100. Minutes of Luyia Old Testament Translation Committee, 6th sess., April 1952, Nairobi, Anglican Church of Kenya (hereafter, ACK), Luyia Old Testament Genesis file.

101. Minutes of Luyia Old Testament Translation Committee, 5th sess., April 1952, ACK, Luyia Old Testament, Genesis file.

102. Osogo, *History of the Baluyia*, 58; Bode, "Leadership and Politics," 34.

103. Olumwullah, *Dis-ease in the Colonial State*, 50.

104. Lonsdale, "Politics of Conquest," 60–61.

105. Were, *History of the Abaluyia*, 163–69.

106. Lonsdale, "Politics of Conquest," 55; Bukusu elders, group interview by author, Bokoli, 13 March 2007.

107. Christopher Vaughan, "Violence and Regulation in the Darfur-Chad Borderland c. 1909–56: Policing a Colonial Boundary," *Journal of African History* 54, no. 2 (2013): 177–98.

108. Bukusu elders, group interview by author, Bokoli, 13 March 2007; Hobley, *Kenya*, 82–88.

109. Lonsdale, "Politics of Conquest," 60–61.

110. Jackson to Crewe, 20 October 1908, TNA:PRO, CO 533/47/513; *Mbale Monthly Reports*, 1911, Uganda National Archives (hereafter, UNA), Entebbe, A46/49.

111. John Lonsdale, "A Political History of Nyanza: 1883–1945" (PhD diss., University of Cambridge, 1964), 117.

112. *Kavirondo Province Annual Report*, 1906–7.

113. John Roscoe, Acting Secretary, CMS Uganda, to Acting Commissioner, 8 August 1900, UNA, A22/1; Report of Inspection, Mumias Station, North Kavirondo, 19 January 1916, KNA, PC/NZA/2/2.

114. Kenneth Ingham, "Uganda's Old Eastern Province: The Transfer to East Africa Protectorate in 1902," *Uganda Journal* 21, no. 1 (March 1957): 41–6; A. T. Mason, "Uganda's Old Eastern Province and East Africa's Federal Capital," *Uganda Journal* 22, no. 1 (March 1958): 43–53; A. C. McEwen, *International Boundaries of East Africa* (Oxford: Clarendon Press, 1971).

115. C. Eliot to British Foreign Secretary Marquess of Lansdowne, 25 January 1902, UNA, A46/1981.

116. Director of Surveys Raymond Alan to Chief Secretary, 3 March 1917, UNA, A46/870.

117. Correspondence File, Entebbe to London, 1901, UNA, A22/1.

118. Ingham, "Uganda's Old Eastern Province," 46; D. A. Low, *Fabrication of Empire: The British and the Uganda Kingdoms, 1890–1902* (Cambridge: Cambridge University Press, 2009), 126.

119. Hugh Fearn, *An African Economy: A Study of the Economic Development of the Nyanza Province of Kenya, 1903–1959* (London: Oxford University Press, 1961), 15.

120. C. Eliot to the Marquess of Lansdowne, 25 January 1902, UNA, A46/1981; Jinja District Officer to Commissioner, Entebbe, 3 February 1902, UNA, A11/2.

121. In 2009 conflict between Uganda and Kenya over control of the islands in Lake Victoria again sparked questions regarding the boundary between the two nations.

122. North Kavirondo Boundaries Schedule, 2 June 1927, KNA, PC/NZA/3/7/4.

123. Kisumu Province Boundaries Report, 1907, UNA, A45/94.

124. S. N. S. Maxwell, "Demarcation of Native Reserve Boundaries," 8 September 1927, KNA, PC/NZA/3/7/7/4.

125. *Nyanza Province Annual Report*, 1913. For the growth of maize production and export, see Fearn, *African Economy*, 79.

126. Fearn, *African Economy*, 80.

127. Report of Inspection, Mumias Station, North Kavirondo, 27 March 1912, KNA, PC/NZA/2/2.

128. *North Kavirondo Annual Report*, 1923.

129. North Kavirondo Handing Over Report, 16 September 1909, KNA, PC/NZA/3/45/1/1.

130. Jinja District Commissioner to Chief Secretary, 4 November 1908, UNA, A44/343; *Kisumu Province Annual Report*, 1910; Provincial Commissioner, Jinja Monthly Report, November 1910, UNA, A46/49.

131. *Nyanza Province Annual Report*, 1917; Sharon B. Stichter, *Migrant Labour in Kenya: Capitalism and African Response, 1895–1975* (London: Longman, 1982), 56.

132. Report on the Eastern Boundary, North Kavirondo Reserve, 1 October 1912, KNA, PC/NZA/3/7/2/2; Chief Native Commissioner to Nyanza Province Senior Commissioner, 26 October 1927, KNA, PC/NZA/3/7/2/3.

133. Kakamega District Commissioner to Nyanza Province Senior Commissioner, 27 March 1925, KNA, PC/NZA/3/17/2.

134. North Kavirondo Handing Over Report, 16 September 1909, KNA, PC/NZA/3/45/1/1.

135. *North Nyanza Political Record Book*, vol. 1, 1900–1916.

136. Geoffrey Archer, *Personal and Historical Memoirs of an East African Administrator* (Edinburgh: Oliver and Boyd, 1963), 34.

137. Mr. Boyle, Jinja District Commissioner, to Chief Secretary, Uganda, 4 November 1908, UNA, A44/303; Archer was responsible for the 1908 capture of the infamous Chief Dunga, who had escaped colonial custody in Uganda by hiding with extended clan networks in the East African Protectorate—anonymous to Chief Secretary, Uganda, 7 December 1908, UNA, A44/303; Geoffrey Archer, *Personal and Historical Memoirs*, 35–129. Archer later served as governor of Uganda (1923–24) and governor general of Anglo-Egyptian Sudan (1925–26).

138. *Nyanza Province Annual Report*, 1910.

139. Geoffrey Archer to Nyanza Provincial Commissioner, 14 April 1909, John Lonsdale Personal Archives, University of Cambridge.

140. Geoffrey Archer, Elgon District Intelligence Report, 14 April 1909, KNA, PC/NZA/3/45/1/1.

141. Sara S. Berry, *Chiefs Know Their Boundaries: Essays on Property, Power, and the Past in Asante, 1896–1996* (Portsmouth, NH: Heinemann, 2001), 13; Nyanza Provincial Commissioner Ainsworth's map book, KNA, PC/NZA/2/1.

142. Were, *History of the Abaluyia*, 175.

143. C. M. Dobbs, "History of Wanga Domination," 23 June 1930, Rhodes House Library, Oxford, Dobbs Papers, MSS.Afr.s.665/2.

144. "Native Authority Ordinance of 1912," no. 22, Papers of Archdeacon Owen, Church Missionary Society Archives (hereafter, CMS), Birmingham, England, ACC/83 01.

145. Jinga Provincial Commissioner to Chief Secretary, Entebbe, 12 May 1915, UNA, A46/842.

146. *North Kavirondo Annual Report*, 1918–20.

147. Archer's field notes; Bukusu elders, group interview by author, Bokoli, 13 March 2007.

148. Paul Wamatuba, interview by author, Bungoma, 25 September 2007.

149. *Nyanza Province Annual Report*, 1913.

150. North Kavirondo District Commissioner to Nyanza Provincial Commissioner, 11 October 1909, KNA, PC/NZA/3/31/1/1.

151. Acting Crown Advocate Stanley Packer, 16 February 1911, UNA, A46/630.

152. North Kavirondo Boundaries Schedule, 2 June 1927, KNA, PC/NZA/3/7/7/4; Chief Native Commissioner, "Demarcation of Native Reserve Boundaries," 8 September 1927, KNA, PC/NZA/3/7/7/4.

153. Craib, *Cartographic Mexico*, 12.

154. Berry, *Chiefs Know Their Boundaries*, 15.

CHAPTER 2: LAND, GOLD, AND COMMISSIONING THE "TRIBE"

1. Wagner, *Bantu of North Kavirondo*, 1:314.

2. "Report of Committee on Native Land Tenure in the North Kavirondo Reserve," October 1930, CMS, G3X A5/25. For population densities, see fig. 2.1.

3. Mahmood Mamdani, *Citizen and Subject: Contemporary Africa and the Legacy of Late Colonialism* (Princeton: Princeton University Press, 1996), 52.

4. Lonsdale, "Political History of Nyanza," 30.

5. C. M. Dobbs, "History of Wanga Domination," 23 June 1930, Rhodes House Library, Dobbs Papers, MSS.Afr.s.665/2.

6. Bukusu elders, group interview by author, Bokoli, 13 March 2007.

7. *Nyanza Province Annual Report*, 1930.

8. The term "Marama" originated from a battle in the late nineteenth century, when retreating Batsotso forces called the alliance of clans they fought *Marama*: "the people who have defeated us." James Otala Opuka, interview by author, Butere, 5 October 2007. For the clan composition of the Marama location, see Osogo, *A History of Baluyia*, 88; Were, *Western Kenya Historical Texts*, 121–56; Otiende, *Habari za Abaluyia*, 4.

9. Record of evidence given before North Kavirondo NLTC, 1 July 1930, KNA, DC/NN/8/1.

10. Record of evidence given before North Kavirondo NLTC, 1 July 1930, KNA, DC/NN/8/1.

11. FAM Annual Report, 11 February 1931, Friends United Mission Archives (hereafter, FUM), Earlham College, Richmond, Indiana.

12. Kenneth P. Lorhentz, "The Campaign to Depose Chief Mulama in Marama Location: A Case Study in Politics of Kinship," *Kenya Historical Review* 4, no. 2 (1976): 249–57.

13. Harry Wamubeyi, interview by author, Butere, 5 October 2007; *North Kavirondo Annual Report*, 1928.

14. For a fuller history of political associations in western Kenya in the interwar period, see Lonsdale, "Political Associations," 589–638.

15. *North Kavirondo Annual Report*, 1928.

16. *North Kavirondo Annual Report*, 1930.

17. Bravman, *Making Ethnic Ways*, 139.

18. "Committee to Investigate the System or Systems of Native Land Tenure within the North Kavirondo Native Reserve," 1930, KNA, DC/NN 8/1.

19. Lonsdale, "Prayers of Waiyaki," 280.

20. Olumwullah, *Dis-ease in the Colonial State*, 40.

21. Lonsdale, "Prayers of Waiyaki," 243.

22. Record of evidence given before North Kavirondo NLTC, 1 July 1930, KNA, DC/NN/8/1.

23. "Report of Committee on Native Land Tenure in the North Kavirondo Reserve," October 1930, CMS, G3X A5/25.

24. Special Meeting of the Bureau, Günter Wagner's proposed book, "The Bantu of Kavirondo: Westernization of a Bantu People," 8 March 1938, IAI_2/17.

25. "The Use of Anthropology to Colonial Administrators: Native Land Problems Arising at Kakamega," 16 January 1933, IAI, Malinowski/32/6.

26. Iliffe, *History of Tanganyika*, 324.

27. "Report of Committee on Native Land Tenure in the North Kavirondo Reserve," October 1930, CMS, G3X A5/25.

28. *North Kavirondo Annual Report*, 1932.

29. *North Kavirondo Annual Report*, 1931.

30. W. M. McGregor-Ross, "Gold in Kenya: Our 'Scrap of Paper,'" *Labour Magazine* 6, no. 10 (February 1933): 468–71.

31. J. Austen Bancroft, "Report on Kenya Colony," 1933, TNA:PRO, CO533/429/12.

32. A. D. Roberts, "The Gold Boom of the 1930s in East Africa," *African Affairs* 85, no. 341 (October 1986): 545–62.

33. Nyanza Province Intelligence Report, December 1931, KNA, PC/NZA/3/1/414.

34. *Kenya Mines Department Annual Reports*, 1930–34; Fearn, *African Economy*, 125–27.

35. *North Kavirondo Annual Reports*, 1934–35.

36. For a full discussion on the genesis of the Native Lands Trust Ordinance, see Priscilla Shilaro, *A Failed Eldorado: Colonial Capitalism, Rural Industrialization, African Land Rights in Kenya, and the Kakamega Gold Rush, 1930–52* (Lanham, MD: University Press of America, 2008).

37. Official Report, 5th ser., Parliamentary Debates, House of Commons, 8 February 1933.

38. Official Report, 5th ser., Parliamentary Debates, House of Lords, 8 February 1933.

39. T. Dunbar Moodie, *Going for Gold: Men, Mines, and Migration* (Berkeley: University of California Press, 1994); Alan H. Jeeves, *Migrant Labour in South Africa's Mining Economy: The Struggle for the Gold Mines' Labour Supply 1890–1920* (Montreal: McGill-Queen's University Press, 1985); Laurie Flynn, *Studded with Diamonds and Paved with Gold: Miners, Mining Companies and Human Rights in Southern Africa* (London: Bloomsbury, 1992); Brian Siegel, "Bomas, Missions and Mines: The Making of Centers on the Zambian Copperbelt," *African Studies Review* 31, no. 3 (December 1988): 61-84.

40. Nottingham and Rosberg, *Myth of "Mau Mau,"* 161; Roberts, "Gold Boom," 545–62; Bode, "Anti-Colonial Politics," 85–138; Lonsdale, "Political Associations," 589–638; Fearn, *African Economy*.

41. Shilaro, *Failed Eldorado*.

42. Ibid., 5.

43. Official Report, 5th ser., Parliamentary Debates, House of Lords, 8 February 1933.

44. Official Report, 5th ser., Parliamentary Debates, House of Commons, 14 July 1933.

45. *North Kavirondo Annual Report*, 1932.

46. E. L. B. Anderson and F. D. Hislop, District Officers, "The Kakamega Goldfields," memorandum, in *Kenya Land Commission Evidence*, 3 vols. (Nairobi, 1934), 3:2317.

47. For the market town of Gbagi, near Ibadan, the process of pegging translated directly into the name of the town, "Gbagi which, in the vernacular, meant 'to peg.'" Moreover, this pegging represented a "space-consuming and fairly permanent," reorganization of space. Akin L. Mabogunje, *Urbanization in Nigeria* (London: University of London Press, 1968), 194, 210.

48. FAM Secretary Emrys Rees to Commissioner of Lands, 1923, FAM East African Yearly Meetings Archives, Kaimosi, Kenya, Land Office Correspondence, 1902–33.

49. Chief Native Commissioner Maxwell, "Demarcation of Native Reserve Boundaries," 8 September 1927, KNA, PC/NZA/3/7/7/4.

50. David M. Anderson, "Depression, Dust Bowl, Demography, and Drought: The Colonial State and Soil Conservation in East Africa during the 1930s," *African Affairs* 83, no. 332 (July 1984): 322.

51. E. L. B. Anderson and F. D. Hislop, District Officers, "The Kakamega Goldfields," *Kenya Land Commission Evidence*, 3:2317.

52. Official Report, 5th ser., Parliamentary Debates, House of Lords, 8 February 1933.

53. North Kavirondo District Commissioner to Nyanza Provincial Commissioner, 13 January 1932, KNA, PC/NZA/3/14/374.

54. Shilaro, *Failed Eldorado*, 147.

55. Owen to Hooper, 3 May 1933, Papers of Archdeacon Owen, CMS, ACC/83.

56. North Kavirondo Intelligence Reports, 1934–39, KNA, PC/NZA/4/5/1.

57. Wagner, *Bantu of North Kavirondo*, 2:84.

58. Ibid., 2:84.

59. Chief Native Commissioner of Kenya, "Why Is Mining Allowed in Native Reserves?," 17 October 1932, KNA, PC/NZA/3/14/359.

60. *North Kavirondo Annual Report*, 1933.

61. Mutongi, *Worries of the Heart*, 70.

62. Agenda for Rally of Native Catholic Union at Yala, 14 February 1933, KNA, PC/NZA/2/562.

63. Personal report of F. N. Hoyt, 1933, FUM Archives; FAM to Commissioner of Mines, 5 January 1934, FAM East African Yearly Meetings Archives, Land Office Correspondence.

64. Mutongi, *Worries of the Heart*, 77.

65. North Kavirondo District Commissioner to Nyanza Provincial Commissioner, 13 January 1932, KNA, PC/NZA/3/14/374.

66. Personal report of F. N. Hoyt, 1933, FUM Archives.

67. Points from barazas held in East and West Kakamega and in North and South Maragoli on mining between 27 February 1933–6 March 1933, KNA, PC/NZA/3/14/359.

68. Shilaro, *Failed Eldorado*, 211.

69. Petition presented to House of Commons by Robert Hamilton, signed by Ezekiel Apindi, 9 May 1933, KNA, PC/NZA/2/2/44.

70. Notes of a baraza held at Milimu's camp, North Kavirondo, 11 January 1935, KNA, PC/NZA/3/14/359.

71. Warden of Mines Intelligence Report, September 1933, KNA, PC/NZA/3/14/372.

72. White, *Comforts of Home*, 38.

73. Minutes of North Kavirondo LNC meeting, 21–22 August 1933, KNA, PC/NZA/4/7/7.

74. Minutes of North Kavirondo LNC meeting, 21–22 August 1933, KNA, PC/NZA/4/7/7.

75. DC Kakamega to all prospectors, 27 January 1932, KNA, PC/NZA/2/7/38.

76. "Goldfields in the Kavirondo Districts," 1933, TNA:PRO, CO533/429/6.

77. Shilaro, *Failed Eldorado*, 211–12.

78. Minutes of North Kavirondo LNC meeting, 18 June 1934, KNA, PC/NZA/4/7/7.

79. Minutes of North Kavirondo LNC meeting, 28 October 1931, KNA, PC/NZA/2/1/36.

80. Minutes of North Kavirondo LNC meeting, 6–7 August 1931, KNA, PC/NZA/2/1/36.

81. Minutes of North Kavirondo LNC meeting, 15 May 1933, KNA, PC/NZA/2/1/36.

82. *Report of the Kenya Land Commission* (London, 1934), 434.

83. "Before the Commission at Mumias: Evidence Taken at a Baraza of Natives of the North Kavirondo District," 12 September 1932, *Kenya Land Commission Evidence*, 3:2221–23.

84. Minutes of North Kavirondo LNC meeting, 15–16 August 1932, KNA, PC/NZA/2/1/36.

85. Fiona Mackenzie, *Land, Ecology and Resistance in Kenya, 1880–1952* (Edinburgh: Edinburgh University Press, 1998), 83, 86.

86. "Report of the Committee on Native Land Tenure in the North Kavirondo Reserve," October 1930, CMS, G3X A5/25.

87 "Kikuyu" and "Gikuyu" are alternate terms for the same people, the largest ethnic community in Kenya. As quoted in Derek Peterson, "'Be Like Firm Soldiers to Develop the Country': Political Imagination and the Geography of Gikuyuland," *International Journal of African Historical Studies* 37, no. 1 (2004): 93.

88. Minutes of North Kavirondo LNC meeting, 30 May 1932, KNA, PC/NZA/2/1/36.

89. "Before the Commission at Mumias: Evidence Taken at a Baraza of Natives of the North Kavirondo District," 12 September1932, *Kenya Land Commission Evidence*, 3:2221–23.

90. Captain Hislop to North Nyanza District Commissioner, 12 August 1925, KNA, PC/NZA/3/23/3.

91. "Statements made on Affirmation by Two Natives to the District Commissioner, North Kavirondo, on 4 October, 1932, on Question of Land near Kipkarren River," *Kenya Land Commission Evidence*, 3:2223–25.

92. Peterson, "Be Like Firm Soldiers," 93.

93. *Report of the Kenya Land Commission*; Nottingham and Rosberg, *Myth of "Mau Mau,"* 95.

94. "Before the Commission at Mumias: Evidence Taken at a Baraza of Natives of the North Kavirondo District," 12 September 1932, *Kenya Land Commission Evidence*, 3:2222.

95. *North Kavirondo Annual Report*, 1932.

96. Ibid.

97. Nyanza Province Intelligence Report, September 1932, KNA, PC/NZA/3/1/414.

98. Lonsdale, "When Did the Gusii Become a Tribe?," 127; MacArthur, "When Did the Luyia Become a Tribe?"

99. *North Kavirondo Annual Report*, 1934.

CHAPTER 3: ETHNIC PATRIOTISM
IN THE INTERWAR YEARS

1. Peterson, *Ethnic Patriotism*.

2. Lonsdale, "Comparative Patriotisms," 251–67.

3. Willis, *Mombasa*; Lynch, *I Say to You*; Peterson and Macola, *Recasting the Past*.

4. Andrea Jumba claimed the NKCA formed secretly in 1931. Andrea Jumba, interview by John Spencer, 23 February 1973, Lonsdale Personal Archives.

5. Nyanza Province Intelligence Report, 1933, KNA, PC/NZA/3/14/374.

6. *North Kavirondo Annual Report*, 1930.

7. Nyanza Province Intelligence Report, June 1933, KNA, PC/NZA/3/1/414.

8. Personal report, F. N. Hoyt, 1934, FUM Archives.

9. FAM report from Kitosh Station, 26 June 1933, Jefferson W. Ford Papers, FUM Archives.

10. Lonsdale, "Moral Economy," 315–504; Peterson, *Creative Writing*, 103–13; Jocelyn Murray, "The Church Missionary Society and the 'Female Circumcision' Issue in Kenya," *Journal of Religion in Africa* 8, no. 2 (1976): 92–104; Kanogo, *African Womanhood*, 73–103.

11. Berman, "Ethnography as Politics," 323.

12. *Nyanza Province Annual Report*, 1936.

13. Warden of Mines Intelligence Report, August 1934, KNA, PC/NZA/3/14/359.

14. Warden of Mines, Intelligence Report, February 1934; Warden of Mines, Intelligence Report, August 1934, both in KNA, PC/NZA/3/14/372; Lonsdale, "Political Associations," 625.

15. J. D. Otiende, interview by author, Mbale, 9 October 2007.

16. Lonsdale, "Political Associations," 625.

17. Spencer, *Kenya African Union*, 112, fn. 144.

18. Andrea Jumba, interview by John Spencer, 23 February 1973, Lonsdale Personal Archives.

19. For the KCA, see the extensive work of John Lonsdale and Derek Peterson.

20. North Kavirondo Monthly Intelligence Report, April 1934, KNA, PC/NZA/4/5/1.

21. NKCA, petition, "Kavirondo Objections in the KLC's Report," 20 December 1934, Rhodes House Library, Papers of Charles Roden Buxton, MSS. Brit.Emp.s.405.

22. NKCA, petition to Honourable Colonial Secretary, 14 February 1936, KNA, PC/NZA/3/1/398.

23. North Kavirondo Monthly Intelligence Report, August 1934, KNA, PC/NZA/3/14/374.

24. Minutes of North Kavirondo LNC meeting, 16–17 August 1934, KNA, PC.NZA/2/1/36; Joshua Odango, interview by author, Musingu, 24 September 2007.

25. Warden of Mines, Intelligence Report, September 1933, KNA, PC/NZA/3/14/372.

26. North Kavirondo Monthly Intelligence Report, August 1934, KNA, PC/NZA/3/14/374.

27. North Kavirondo District Commissioner to Nyanza Provincial Commissioner, "NKCA," 31 August 1934, KNA, PC/NZA/3/1/552.

28. "Summary of Conclusions reached by His Majesty's Government," *Kenya Land Commission Report*, 2.

29. North Kavirondo Monthly Intelligence Report, August 1934, KNA, PC/NZA/4/5/1.

30. Lonsdale, "History of Nyanza," 544.

31. Ibid., 544n73.

32. Ibid., 544; North Nyanza Intelligence Report, 10 April 1936, KNA, PC/NZA/4/5/6.

33. Lonsdale, "History of Nyanza," 544n73.

34. NKCA, petition to Honourable Colonial Secretary, 14 February 1936, KNA, PC/NZA/3/1/398.

35. North Kavirondo Monthly Intelligence Report, August 1937, KNA, PC/NZA/4/5/3.

36. Shilaro, *Failed Eldorado*, 174.

37. Monthly Mining Police Report, February 1939, KNA, PC/NZA/2/4/5.

38. Minutes of North Kavirondo LNC meeting, 1935, IAI, Malinowski/7/18.

39. Minutes of meeting between NKCA and District Commissioner, 29 April 1937, KNA, PC/NZA/4/5/6.

40. North Kavirondo District Commissioner to Nyanza Provincial Commissioner, 24 January 1938, KNA, PC/NZA/3/1/345.

41. For a provocative account of the prosecution of rape cases in South Nyanza, see Brett L. Shadle, "Rape in the Courts of Gusiiland, Kenya, 1940s–1960s," *African Studies Review* 51, no. 2 (September 2008): 27–50.

42. *Nyanza Province Annual Report*, 1923.

43. *North Kavirondo Annual Report*, 1928.

44. Johnston, *Uganda Protectorate*, 2:722, fig. 1.6.

45. "The Origin of Kavirondo" article series, *East African Standard*, November 1928.

46. A. J. Oyugi, "The Origin of the Name Kavirondo," *Makerere Journal* 2, no. 1 (April 1938): 157–58.

47. Howard Elphinstone, "The Origin of 'Kavirondo,'" *East African Standard*, 20 November 1928.

48. Osogo, *History of the Baluyia*, 9.

49. Kanogo, *African Womanhood*, 74.

50. E. V. Hippel, "Kavirondo," *Uganda Journal* 10, no. 2 (September 1946): 167.

51. North Kavirondo District Commissioner C. B. Thompson to Field Jones, "KTWA," 1 May 1929, KNA, DC/NN/10/1/2.

52. *North Kavirondo Annual Report*, 1931.

53. North Kavirondo District Commissioner C. B. Thompson to Field Jones, "KTWA," 1 May 1929, KNA, DC/NN/10/1/2.

54. "Wanga-English Dictionary."

55. L. L. Appleby, *A First Luyia Grammar, with Exercises* (Nairobi: CMS, 1947).

56. Minutes of North Kavirondo LNC meeting, 5–6 November 1936, KNA, PC/NZA/4/7/7.

57. NKCA, "Avaluyha—Kinship" (pamphlet, 1935), as quoted in Lonsdale, "History of Nyanza," 539n59. The original copy of this important document has disappeared from every archival holding referenced by other historians and consulted by me.

58. See note 2 to the introduction regarding the spelling chosen for this study, "Luyia," determined by an LNC vote in 1942.

59. NKTWA, "Omulina wa Valuhya," August 1931, Lonsdale Personal Archives.

60. Historical introduction in NKCA pamphlet, "Avaluyha" (1935), quoted in Lonsdale, "History of Nyanza," 545.

61. Wagner, *Bantu of North Kavirondo*, 1:55.

62. Ibid., 1:55, 343, 377.

63. F. Ingutia "Meaning of the Term Abaluyia," November 1949, KNA, PC/NZA/2/1/158.

64. Osogo, *History of the Baluyia*, 7.

65. Wagner, *Bantu of North Kavirondo*, 1:477.

66. Lonsdale, "History of Nyanza," 545.

67. Marshall S. Clough, *Fighting Two Sides: Kenyan Chiefs and Politicians, 1918–1940* (Niwot: University Press of Colorado, 1990).

68. Nyanza Provincial Commissioner to North Kavirondo District Commissioner, "Luluhya," 14 October 1942, KNA, PC/NZA/2/1/158.

69. Minutes of North Kavirondo LNC meeting, 5–6 November 1936, KNA, PC/NZA/4/7/7.

70. Minutes of North Kavirondo LNC meeting, 15–17 September 1942, KNA, PC/NZA/2/1/158.

71. Carol Summers, "Young Buganda and Old Boys: Youth, Generational Transition, and Ideas of Leadership in Buganda, 1920–1949," *Africa Today* 51, no. 3 (2005): 111; see also Summers, "Grandfathers, Grandsons, Morality, and Radical Politics in Late Colonial Buganda," *International Journal of African Historical Studies* 38, no. 3 (2005): 427–47; Summers, "Radical Rudeness: Ugandan Social Critiques in the 1940s," *Journal of Social History* 39, no. 3 (2006): 741–70.

72. Willis, *Mombasa*.

73. Willis and Gona, "Tradition, Tribe," 452–54.

74. Lynch, *I Say to You*; Peterson and Macola, *Recasting the Past*.

75. Meeting of KTWA, Maseno, 9 December 1939, KNA, PC/NZA/2/1/43.

76. Minutes of North Kavirondo LNC meeting, 16 April 1942, KNA, PC/NZA/4/7/7.

77. North Kavirondo District Commissioner to Nyanza Provincial Commissioner, "Luluhya," 15 October 1942, KNA, PC/NZA/2/1/158.

78. Bethwell A. Ogot, "Mau Mau and Nationhood: The Untold Story," in *Mau Mau and Nationhood: Arms, Authority and Narration*, ed. E. S. Atieno Odhiambo and John Lonsdale (Athens: Ohio University Press, 2003), 13.

79. Nottingham and Rosberg, *Myth of "Mau Mau,"* 163.

80. Peterson and Macola, *Recasting the Past*, 9.

81. Ibid., 9.

82. NKCA, "Avaluyha—Kinship," pamphlet, 1935, quoted in Lonsdale, "History of Nyanza," 539n59; NKCA, petition to Secretary of State, 18 June 1936, TNA:PRO, CO533/473/5.

83. NKCA, petition to Secretary of State, 18 June 1936, TNA:PRO, CO533/473/5.

84. Ibid.

85. Peterson and Macola, *Recasting the Past*, 10.

86. *North Kavirondo Annual Report*, 1945; NKCA, petition to Secretary of State, 18 June 1936, TNA:PRO, CO533/473/5; KTWA, "Memorandum on Native Taxation," 1922, Papers of Archdeacon Owen, CMS, ACC/83.

87. Paramount Chief Mumia to Nyanza Provincial Commissioner, 3 April 1939, KNA, PC/NZA/3/27/99B.

88. Osogo, *History of the Baluyia*, 77.

89. Terence Ranger, "Making Northern Rhodesia Imperial: Variations on a Royal Theme, 1924–38," *African Affairs* 79, no. 316 (1980): 373.

90. Justin Willis, "A Portrait for the Mukama: Monarchy and Empire in Colonial Bunyoro, Uganda," *Journal of Imperial and Commonwealth History* 34, no. 1 (March 2006): 113.

91. *North Kavirondo Annual Report*, 1931; minutes of North Kavirondo Local Native Council (hereafter, LNC) meeting, 23–24 March 1931, KNA, PC/NZA/2/1/36.

92. NKCA, petition to Chief Native Commissioner, 11 December 1939, KNA, PC/NZA/3/27/99B.

93. "Paramount Chief Letter—Nabongo's Letter," 10 April 1937, KNA, PC/NZA/3/27/99B.

94. *Kenya Legislative Council Debates*, 9 March 1937, 179–83.

95. NKCA, petition Regarding the Appointment of Paramount Chief, 25 July 1935, TNA:PRO, CO533/461/5.

96. Emma Hunter, "In Pursuit of the 'Higher Medievalism': Local History and Politics in Kilimanjaro," in *Recasting the Past: History Writing and Political Work in Modern Africa*, ed. Derek R. Peterson and Giacomo Macola (Athens: Ohio University Press, 2009), 149.

97. North Kavirondo District Commissioner to Superintendent of Police, "Present Activities of the NKCA," 9 October 1935, KNA, DC/NN/10/1/2.

98. North Kavirondo District Commissioner to Tororo District Commissioner, Uganda, 24 June 1936, KNA, DC/KMG/2/1/132.

99. David Cannadine has explored the exportation of British royal obsessions and class hierarchies. Cannadine, *Ornamentalism: How the British Saw Their Empire* (Oxford: Oxford University Press, 2001).

100. North Kavirondo District Commissioner to Nyanza Provincial Commissioner, "NKCA and a Paramount Chief," 6 June 1935, KNA, PC/NZA/3/1/345.

101. Willis, "Portrait for the Mukama," 106.

102. North Kavirondo District Commissioner to Nyanza Provincial Commissioner, "NKCA and a Paramount Chief," 6 June 1935, KNA, PC/NZA/3/1/345; Cynthia Hoehler-Fatton, *Women of Fire and Spirit: History, Faith, and Gender in Roho Religion in Western Kenya* (Oxford: Oxford University Press, 1996); Thomas Spear, "Toward the History of African Christianity," in *East African Expressions of Christianity*, ed. Spear and Isaria N. Kimambo (Athens: Ohio University Press, 1999), 16–17.

103. Abaluhiya Ba NKCA, North Kavirondo Central Association, to North Kavirondo District Commissioner, 7 June 1935, KNA, DC/NN/10/1/2.

104. Derek Peterson, "Writing in Revolution: Independent Schooling and Mau Mau in Nyeri," in *Mau Mau and Nationhood: Arms, Authority and Narration*, ed. E.S. Atieno Odhiambo and John Lonsdale (Athens: Ohio University Press, 2003), 82–83.

105. Minutes of meeting at Government African School, Kakamega, 15 July 1935, KNA, DC/NN/3/2/16.

106. NKCA, petition to Governor, 9 July 1935, KNA, PC/NZA/3/1/598; NKCA, "Abaluhya" memorandum to Imperial Parliament through Right Honourable Secretary of State for the Colonies, 18 June 1936, KNA, PC/NZA/2/655.

107. Minutes of meeting at Government African School, Kakamega, 15 July 1935, KNA, DC/NN/3/2/16.

108. *North Kavirondo Annual Report*, 1937.

109. Nyanza Provincial Commissioner to Colonial Secretary, "Amalgamation of Locations," 24 April 1937, KNA, DC/NN/3/6/1.

110. *Nyanza Province Annual Report*, 1937.

111. Record of evidence given before North Kavirondo NLTC, 1 July 1930, KNA, DC/NN/8/1.

112. Nyanza Provincial Commissioner to North Kavirondo District Commissioner, 18 January 1937, KNA, DC/NN/3/6/1.

113. *Nyanza Province Annual Report*, 1938.

114. Lonsdale, "Moral Economy," 376.

115. *Nyanza Province Annual Report*, 1936.

116. Nyanza Provincial Commissioner to North Kavirondo District Commissioner, "Amalgamation of Tribunals," 8 October 1936, KNA, DC/NN/3/6/1.

117. Wagner, "Abaluyia of Kavirondo," 35.

118. Shem Musee, interview by author, Kona Mbaya, 22 October 2007; Ane Marie Bak Rasmussen, *A History of the Quaker Movement in Africa* (London: British Academic Press, 1994).

119. For a thorough accounting of the politics of colonial land policies in the 1930s and 1940s in western Kenya, see Martin Shidende Shanguhyia, "The State, Ecology, and Society in Western Kenya: Politics of Soil Conservation

and Land Management in Vihiga, 1930–1950" (PhD diss., West Virginia University, 2007).

120. D. Anderson, "Depression, Dust Bowl," 321.

121. Shilaro, *Failed Eldorado*, 116.

122. Native Land Tenure Nyanza Province Report, 29 December 1938, KNA, PC/NZA/4/2/1.

123. Feierman, *Peasant Intellectuals*, 178.

124. Nyanza Province Monthly Intelligence Report, July 1939, KNA, PC/NZA/4/5/3.

125. NKCA to North Kavirondo District Commissioner, 27 March 1940, KNA, PC/NZA/3/1/345.

126. Nyanza Province Monthly Intelligence Report, May 1940, KNA, PC/NZA/4/5/3.

127. North Kavirondo District Commissioner to Nyanza Provincial Commissioner, 21 August 1943, KNA, DC/KMG/1/1/157.

128. Nyanza Province Monthly Intelligence Report, May 1940, KNA, PC/NZA/4/5/3.

129. Chief Ali Wamukoya, interview by author, Panyako, 19 September 2007.

130. Nyanza Province Monthly Intelligence Report, April 1940, KNA, PC/NZA/4/5/3.

131. Nyanza Province Monthly Intelligence Report, February 1939, KNA, PC/NZA/4/5/3.

132. NKCA meeting agenda, 15 May 1940, KNA, PC/NZA/4/5/3.

133. Nyanza Province Monthly Intelligence Report, March 1940, KNA, PC/NZA/4/5/3.

134. Lonsdale, "Political Associations," 637.

135. Letters intercepted between NKCA and KTWA in censorship by Civil Intelligence Department, 10 April 1940, KNA, PC/NZA/3/1/345.

136. Nyanza Province Monthly Intelligence Report, October 1938, KNA, PC/NZA/4/5/2.

137. Nyanza Province Monthly Intelligence Report, July 1939, KNA, PC/NZA/4/5/3.

138. Kikuyu Central Association Correspondence, December 1938, KNA, PC/NZA/3/1/345.

139. Director of Civil Intelligence to Nyanza Provincial Commissioner and Superintendent of Police, 23 December 1939, KNA, PC/NZA/3/1/345.

140. Meeting of KCA, NKCA, and KTWA, 1940, KNA, DC/NN/10/1/2; Lonsdale, "Political Associations," 636.

141. Memorandum submitted by the members of KCA and KTWA in Kenya to Secretary of State for the Colonies on "Native Lands Ordinance," 1938, KNA, PC/NZA/3/1/398.

142. NKCA, petition to Secretary of State for the Colonies, 17 February 1938, TNA:PRO, CO533/496/6.

143. Nyanza Province Monthly Intelligence Report, April, May 1939, KNA, PC/NZA/4/5/3.

144. NCA to Honourable Chief Native Commissioner, 13 March 1944, KNA, DC/KMG/1/1/153.

145. Nyanza Province Monthly Intelligence Report, January 1940, KNA, PC/NZA/4/5/3.

146. Ibid.

147. Nottingham and Rosberg, *Myth of "Mau Mau,"* 186.

148. Nyanza Provincial Commissioner to Chief Secretary, "KCA (1938) and other Associations," 1 July 1940, KNA, OP/1/1323.

149. North Kavirondo District Commissioner to Nyanza Provincial Commissioner, "Abaluhya Association," 17 June 1940, KNA, DC/NN/10/1/2.

150. North Kavirondo District Commissioner to Nyanza Provincial Commissioner, 17 June 1940, KNA, DC/NN/10/1/2.

151. Criminal Investigation Department to R. Pedraza, Kakamega, 10 August 1940, KNA, DC/NN/10/1/2.

152. Nyanza Province Monthly Intelligence Report, December 1940, KNA, PC/NZA/4/5/3.

153. North Kavirondo District Commissioner to Nyanza Provincial Commissioner, 21 August 1943, KNA, DC/KMGA/1/1/157.

154. NKCA to Secretary of State for the Colonies, 13 June 1936, KNA, PC/NZA/2/655.

155. *North Kavirondo Annual Report*, 1943.

CHAPTER 4: SPEAKING LUYIA

1. Kanyoro, *Unity in Diversity*, i. An earlier version of this chapter was published as Julie MacArthur, "The Making and Unmaking of African Languages: Oral Communities and Competitive Linguistic Work in Western Kenya," *Journal of African History* 53, no. 2 (July 2012): 151–72.

2. Mark Udoto, interview by author, Ambundo, 23 September 2007.

3. Wagner, "Political Organization," 232.

4. *North Kavirondo Annual Report*, 1943.

5. Rachel Angogo Kanyoro, "The Abaluyia of Kenya: One People, One Language: What Can Be Learned from the Luyia Project," *Proceedings of the Round Table on the Assuring the Feasibility of Standardization within Dialect Chains* (1988): 87.

6. B. Anderson, *Imagined Communities.*

7. Lonsdale, "'Listen While I Read,'"; Paul Stuart Landau, *The Realm of the Word: Language, Gender, and Christianity in a Southern African Kingdom* (Portsmouth, NH: Heinemann, 1995); Patrick Harries, "Exclusion, Classification and Internal Colonialism: The Emergence of Ethnicity among the Tsonga-Speakers of South Africa." in *The Creation of Tribalism in Southern Africa*, ed. Leroy Vail (Berkeley: University of California Press, 1989): 82–117; Harries, "The Roots of Ethnicity: Discourse and the Politics of Language

Construction in South-East Africa," *African Affairs* 87, no. 346 (January 1988): 25–52; Harries, *Butterflies and Barbarians: Swiss Missionaries and Systems of Knowledge in South-East Africa* (Athens: Ohio University Press, 2007).

8. Dmitri van den Bersselaar, "Creating "Union Ibo": Missionaries and the Igbo Language," *Africa* 67, no. 2 (1997): 273–95; John Peel has similarly argued that African communities should not be seen as a "tabula rasa" on which cultural nationalism was imposed. Peel, "The Cultural work of Yoruba Ethnogenesis," in *History and Ethnicity*, ed. Elizabeth Tonkin, Malcolm Chapman, and Maryon McDonald (London: Routledge, 1989), 198–215.

9. Ruth Finnegan, *The Oral and Beyond: Doing Things with Words in Africa* (Oxford: James Currey, 2007), 18.

10. For a similar argument among the Asante, see Tom McCaskie, *Asante Identities: History and Modernity in an African Village, 1850–1950* (Edinburgh: Edinburgh University Press, 2000), 236.

11. Hawkins, *Writing and Colonialism*, 10; see also Jonathan Draper, ed., *Orality, Literacy, and Colonialism in Southern Africa* (Atlanta: Society of Biblical Literature, 2003).

12. "Kavirondo, a Comparison and a Contrast," *Uganda Notes* 4 (January 1906): UNA, A22/1.

13. Were, *Western Kenya Historical Texts*, 9.

14. Were, "Ethnic Interaction," 39–44.

15. Wagner, *Bantu of North Kavirondo Vol. 1*, 23.

16. Otiende, *Habari za Abaluyia*.

17. Wagner, *Bantu of North Kavirondo*, 1:55; "Wanga-English Dictionary"; Appleby, *Luyia-English Vocabulary*.

18. L. L. Appleby, "Luyia Old Testament Translation, Part I: Unifying the Written Form of the Language," *Bible Translator* 6, no. 4 (1955): 180–85.

19. Kanyoro, *Unity in Diversity*, 138–89.

20. Günter Wagner, Field Notes, September 1934, IAI, Malinowski_7/18.

21. Hay, "Local Trade," 7.

22. Kanyoro, *Unity in Diversity*, 151, 159.

23. *Nyanza Province Annual Report*, 1923.

24. L. L. Appleby, Sketch of Dialect Groups in North Nyanza, [1942], British and Foreign Bible Society (hereafter, BFBS), University of Cambridge, Luyia Language file, BSA/E3/3/324; North Kavirondo District Commissioner Anderson to Nyanza Provincial Commissioner, 1 July 1935, KNA, DC/KMGA/1/4/29.

25. L. L. Appleby's linguistic breakdown, [1942], BFBS, BSA/E3/3/324; Kanyoro, *Unity in Diversity*, 4.

26. Günter Wagner, "Plan of Study," 17 May 1934, IAI_1/19.

27. Wagner, *Bantu of North Kavirondo*, 1:26.

28. P. A. N. Itebete, "Language Standardization in Western Kenya," in *Language in Kenya*, ed. W. H. Whiteley (Nairobi: Oxford University Press, 1974), 93.

29. Kanyoro, *Unity in Diversity*, 79–80.

30. Yvonne Bastin, "The Interlacustrine Zone (Zone J)," in *The Bantu Languages*, ed. Derek Nurse and Gérard Philippson (London: Routledge, 2003), 510.

31. Language and Translation Committee Report, 1923, FUM Archives.

32. Minutes of Kavirondo District Missionary Committee, 1935–45, CMS, G3/A5/3.

33. R. Kilgour, "Bantu Kavirondo Languages," 1936, ACK, CMO/BSK/3.

34. Editorial Sub-Committee minutes, 3 November 1915, BFBS, BSA/E3/3/246.

35. W. E. Owen, "Laws into Swahili," 1922–27, CMS, G3/A5/o G1.

36. Butere Meeting Notes, 1934–53, CMS, G3/A5/o G1.

37. Peterson, "Writing in Revolution," 80; Derek Peterson, "Language Work and Colonial Politics in Eastern Africa: The Making of Standard Swahili and 'School Kikuyu,'" in *The Study of Language and the Politics of Community in Global Context*, ed. D. L. Hoyt and K. Oslund (Lanham, MD: Lexington Books, 2006), 185–214.

38. J. E. Chadwick to Miss Magowan, 4 July 1918, CMS, G3X A5/25.

39. *North Kavirondo Annual Report*, 1925.

40. Tim Parsons, *Race, Resistance, and the Boy Scout Movement in British Colonial Africa* (Athens: Ohio University Press, 2004), 41–49.

41. Editorial Sub-Committee minutes, Kampala, 7 January 1920, BFBS, BSA/E3/3/246.

42. Peterson, *Creative Writing*, 65–85; Carotenuto, "Cultivating an African Community," 200–202.

43. Beecher to Smith, 8 August 1941, ACK, CMO/BSK/3.

44. Lynch, *I Say to You*, 35.

45. "Broadcasting to the Bantu-Speaking People of Kavirondo," [1941], BFBS, BSA/E3/3/324.

46. Minutes of North Kavirondo LNC meeting, 17 September 1942, KNA, PC/NZA/2/1/158.

47. Luyia students ranked third among Makerere graduates from Kenya throughout the colonial period. J. E. Goldthorpe, *An African Elite: Makerere College Students 1922–1960* (Nairobi: Oxford University Press, 1965).

48. *Makerere College Magazine* 1, no.7 (May 1940).

49. W. B. Akatsa, "An Appeal for Linguistic Unity among the Abaluhya" (1941), BFBS, BSA/E3/3/324.

50. E. A. Andere to Secretary of African Education Board, 7 March 1951, ACK, ACSO/CPN/1.

51. Letters in response to proposed orthography, August–October 1943, ACK, CMO/BSK/3.

52. North Nyanza District Commissioner to Nyanza Provincial Commissioner, 10 March 1947, KNA, DC/KMG/1/1/73; Carotenuto, "Cultivating an African Community," 201; Lynch, *I Say to You*, 38; Peterson, *Creative Writing*.

53. Articles in *Muluhya*, 1954–64.

54. J. E. G. Sutton, "Towards a Luyia History," *Muluhya* 1, no. 1 (September 1954).

55. Kavirondo Ruridecanal Council, 31 August 1938, ACK, ACSO/CP/2.

56. L. L. Appleby to Richards, 9 November 1938, ACK, CMO/BSK/3.

57. L. L. Appleby, "Luyia Old Testament Translation, Part IV: Translation and People," *Bible Translator* 7, no. 3 (1956): 101–4.

58. Meeting of the Sub-committee on Bantu Orthography, 13 April 1942, KNA, DC/KMG/1/4/29; Owen to the District Education Board, 4 October 1942, KNA, DC/KMG/1/4/29.

59. Harries, *Butterflies and Barbarians*, 168.

60. Beecher to Dr. North, 3 December 1941, ACK, CMO/BSK/3.

61. Beecher to Smith, 8 August 1941, ACK, CMO/BSK/3.

62. Ida Ward, *Ibo Dialects and the Development of a Common Language* (Cambridge: W. Heffer and Sons, 1941), 8.

63. Ibid., 10; Ben Fulford, "An Igbo Esperanto: A History of the Union Ibo Bible 1900–1950," *Journal of Religion in Africa* 32, no. 4 (November 2002): 457–501.

64. L. L. Appleby to Hoyt, 23 October 1943, ACK, CMO/BSK/3.

65. Paramount Chief Mumia, "Common Language," 7 April 1942, ACK, CMO/BSK/3.

66. International Institute of African Languages and Cultures, *Practical Orthography of African Languages* (London: the Institute, 1930).

67. Günter Wagner, "Bantu Orthography," [1941?], ACK, CMO/BSK/3; Edward Sapir, *Language: An Introduction to the Study of Speech* (New York: Harcourt, Brace, 1921).

68. Appleby, "Luyia Old Testament, Part I," 183.

69. Kanyoro, *Unity in Diversity*, 135.

70. Evelyne Kisembe, "Dahl's Law and the Luyia Law in Luyia Dialects Spoken in Western Kenya," *Lwati: A Journal of Contemporary Research* 7, no. 4 (2010).

71. "Obuhandichi Bwa Oluluhya," 19 July 1943, KNA, DC/KMG/1/4/29.

72. E. A. Andere to LLC, [1943], ACK, CMO/BSK/3.

73. See Wagner, *Bantu of North Kavirondo*, 1:26.

74. L. L. Appleby, draft article on history of the Language Committee, ACK, BFBS, Correspondence file.

75. *North Kavirondo Annual Reports*, 1945–60; L. L. Appleby, "Luyia Old Testament Translation, Part II: The Work of the Translation Committee," *Bible Translator* 7, no. 1 (1956): 25–30; Appleby, "Luyia Old Testament Translation, Part III; Some Problems in Translation," *Bible Translator* 7, no. 2 (1956): 85–90.

76. CMS Bookshop Nairobi, Literature Report, 1945–46, CMS, G3/A5/o E11/1.

77. L. L. Appleby to Beecher, 11 November 1943, ACK, CMO/BSK/3.

78. Appleby, "Luyia Old Testament, Part IV," 101–4.

79. Derek Peterson, "Colonizing Language? Missionaries and Gikuyu Dictionaries, 1904 and 1914," *History in Africa* 24 (1997): 257–72; see also Keletso Atkins, *The Moon Is Dead! Give Us Our Money! The Cultural Origins of an African Work Ethic, Natal, South Africa, 1843–1900* (Portsmouth, NH: Heinemann, 1993).

80. Appleby, *First Luyia Grammar.*

81. Minutes of Luyia Old Testament Translation Committee (hereafter, LOTTC), 5th session, April 1952, ACK, Genesis file.

82. Kanyoro, *Unity in Diversity,* 135.

83. Luyia publications to August 1957, KNA, DC/KMG/2/8/42.

84. Mutongi, *Worries of the Heart,* 139–48.

85. Minutes of LOTTC, 5th sess., April 1952, ACK, Luyia Old Testament file.

86. Minutes of LOTTC, 6th sess., April 1952, ACK, Luyia Old Testament file.

87. Minutes of LOTTC, 10th sess., September 1952, ACK, Luyia Old Testament file.

88. Evelyne Kisembe, "Linguistic Effects of English on Luyia Languages," *Estudios de Lingüística Aplicada* 21, no. 37 (2003): 53–70.

89. Appleby, *Luyia-English Vocabulary.*

90. Minutes of LOTTC, 12th sess., February 1954, BFBS, Luyia Language file, BSA/E3/3/324.

91. Ibid.

92. Ibid.

93. Wagner, *Bantu of North Kavirondo,* 1:55.

94. Adrian Hastings, *The Construction of Nationhood: Ethnicity, Religion, and Nationalism* (Cambridge: Cambridge University Press, 1997).

95. Beecher to Owen, 12 October 1942, ACK, CMO/BSK/3.

96. Letters in response to circular on orthography, August–October 1943, ACK, CMO/BSK/3.

97. Minutes of North Kavirondo LNC meeting, 22 November 1944, KNA, PC/NZA/3/1/79.

98. Letters in response to proposed orthography, August–October 1943, ACK, CMO/BSK/3.

99. South East Asia Command to Kenya Information Office, 8 October 1945, KNA, DC/KMG/1/4/29.

100. Luyia Language Committee, draft reply to Maragoli Society, [1943], ACK, CMO/BSK/3.

101. "Luhya Orthography and Ragoli," [1943], ACK, CMO/BSK/3.

102. "A Further Memorandum on Luhya Orthography," [1943], ACK, CMO/BSK/3.

103. Beecher to Appleby, 10 October 1943, ACK, CMO/BSK/3.

104. Luyia Language Committee, "Luhya Orthography and Ragoli," [1943], ACK, CMO/BSK/3.

105. Hoyt to Beecher, 10 November 1943, ACK, CMO/BSK/3.

106. Luyia Language Committee, "Luhya Orthography and Ragoli," [1943], ACK, CMO/BSK/3.

107. Beecher to Appleby, 11 November 1943, ACK CMO/BSK/3.

108. C. G. Richards, "North Kavirondo Languages," 24 June 1946, ACK, CMO/BSK/3.

109. Kenya Advisory Committee of BFBS, 29 November 1946, BFBS, BSA/E3/3/246.

110. Minutes of North Kavirondo LNC meeting, 16–19 August 1949, KNA, PC/NZA/3/1/80.

111. Frank Bedford to Bradnock, Translation Editor of BFBS, 21 February 1951, BFBS, Luyia Language file, BSA/E3/3/324.

112. L. L. Appleby to Bedford, 25 October 1950, ACK, CMO/BSK/3.

113. Secretary, Maragoli Education Board, to Chair, DEB, 3 February 1946, KNA, DC/KMG/1/4/29.

114. Bedford to Bradnock, 21 February 1951, BFBS, BSA/E3/3/324.

115. L. L. Appleby to Beecher, 23 October 1943, ACK, ACSO/CPN/1.

116. J. D. Otiende, interview by author, Mbale, 9 October 2007.

117. President of the Maragoli Peoples Association, Eli Ogola, to the North Nyanza District Commissioner, 29 March 1960, KNA, DC/KMG/2/1/150.

118. Minutes of North Kavirondo LNC meeting, 28 February 1946, KNA, PC/NZA/3/1/80; Paul Wamatuba, interview by author, Musikoma, 25 September 2007.

119. L. L. Appleby to Bradnock, 25 February 1953, BFBS, BSA/E3/3/324.

120. BFBS Editorial Sub-committee minutes, 7 July 1952, BFBS, BSA/E3/3/246; ACK Minutes of 8th sess. of Luyia Old Testament Translation Committee, 6 August 1952, ACK, Luyia Old Testament file.

121. L. L. Appleby to Bradnock, 25 February 1953, BFBS, Luyia Language file, BSA/E3/3/324.

122. Meeting of Luyia Language Committee, 12 March 1954, KPA, DH/1/1.

123. Meeting of the Luyia Language Committee, 23 February 1957, KPA, DH/1/1.

124. *Nyanza Province Annual Report*, 1958.

125. Bungoma DEO to Educational Materials Adviser, 5 January 1961, KPA, DH/1/2.

126. Kanyoro, *Unity in Diversity*, 52.

127. Ibid., 52.

128. Rachel Angogo Kanyoro, "Post-research Experience: The Abaluyia of Western Kenya," *Proceedings of the Round Table on the Assuring the Feasibility of Standardization within Dialect Chains* (1988): 103–4.

129. Agoi to Nyanza Provincial Commissioner, 15 March 1947, KNA, DC/KMG/1/1/73.

130. Otiende, *Habari za Abaluyia*.

131. APA meeting minutes, 4 December 1955, KNA, DC/KMG/2/1/147.

132. W. H. Whiteley, "The Classification and Distribution of Kenya's African Languages" in *Language in Kenya*, ed. Whiteley (Oxford: Oxford University Press, 1974), 38–47; see also W. A. Foley, *Anthropological Linguistics* (Oxford: Wiley, 1997), 338–39.

CHAPTER 5: MAPPING GENDER

1. "Mzee Mombasa" Batholomeo Munoko, interview by author, Kiminini, 16 March 2007.

2. Jackton Simbuku Nyakuri, interview by author, Kitale, 16 March 2007.

3. Tim Wambunya, *Luyia Proverbs from Kisa, Marama, Tsotso and Wanga* (London: Luyia Publishing, 2005), 27.

4. Debates rage in the historiography over the proper terminology to apply to the practice of cutting or excising female genitals. In recent years the term *female genital mutilation* has gained prominence as part campaigns by NGOs against the practice. Lynn M. Thomas opted against *female circumcision*, the term most common in written and oral sources, as it implied an "equivalency between the genital cuttings performed on women and male circumcision." L. Thomas, *Politics of the Womb*, 187. However, this imposition of terms foreign to specific historical contexts masked many of the beliefs and motivations underpinning these debates. The Tachoni Union in western Kenya argued for such equivalency between male and female circumcision: "a person having only girls also circumcised at the time of circumcision of boys and therefore this wiped out the idea of girls. Such girls were considered by men as boys and so they both were equally important." Tachoni Union to District Commissioner North Kavirondo, 23 May 1951, KPA, DX/1/6. Here I've used the term *female circumcision* to allow the sources to speak for themselves and to avoid the moralizing effect of foreign and loaded terms. For more on these debates, see Bettina Shell-Duncan and Ylva Hernlund, eds., *Female "Circumcision" in Africa: Culture, Controversy and Change* (Boulder: Lynne Reiner, 2001).

5. In 1942 the North Kavirondo LNC officially adopted the term Luyia, and by 1948 Kavirondo was replaced by Nyanza in all official forms. To avoid unnecessary confusion, the term North Nyanza will be used for the remainder of this study.

6. Nyanza Province Intelligence Reports, May–June 1943, KNA, PC/NZA/3/1/413.

7. Senior Agricultural Officer to Director of Agriculture, 16 March 1942, KNA, PC/3/1/355; Robert M. Maxon, "'Fantastic Prices' in the Midst of 'an Acute Food Shortage': Market, Environment and the Colonial State in the 1943 Vihiga (Western Kenya) Famine," *African Economic History* 28 (2000): 27–52.

8. *North Nyanza Annual Report*, 1945–55.

9. *Nairobi Municipal Native Affairs Office Annual Report*, 1941, KNA, ARC(MAA) 2/3/8 III.

10. Kenya Colony and Protectorate, *Population Census 1948*, East Africa Statistical Department (Nairobi, 1950).

11. *Nyanza Province Annual Report*, 1942.

12. North Nyanza to the Nyanza Provincial Commissioner, 7 June 1955, KPA, DA/3/32.

13. Mutongi, *Worries of the Heart*.

14. Ibid., 139–48.

15. Minutes of North Kavirondo LNC meeting, 23–24 March 1931, KNA, PC/NZA/2/1/36.

16. Minutes of North Kavirondo LNC meeting, 30–31 March 1937, KNA, PC/NZA/4/7/7.

17. Mutongi, *Worries of the Heart*, 140–41.

18. Secretary of the Maragoli Locational Advisory Council to the Maragoli Society, Kitale Branch, 7 August 1946, KNA, DC/KMG/2/1/133.

19. North Kavirondo LNC, Resolution no. 5 of 1945, 6 June 1945, KNA, PC/NZA/3/18/21.

20. North Nyanza Marriage files, 1940–55, KNA, DC/KMG/1/1/152.

21. Appleby, *Luyia-English Vocabulary*. For debates around the translation of *obubi* as "evil" or "body/flesh," see the minutes of LOTT, 12th sess., February 1954, BFBS, Luyia Language file, BSA/E3/3/324.

22. Minutes of North Kavirondo LNC meeting, 1938–39, KNA, PC/NZA/4/7/7.

23. Uasin Gishu District Commissioner to Nyanza Provincial Commissioner, 18 January 1941, KNA, PC/NZA/3/18/21; White, *Comforts of Home*, 190–94.

24. North Kavirondo District Commissioner to Nyanza Provincial Commissioner, 7 January 1941, KNA, PC/NZA/3/18/21.

25. Minutes of North Kavirondo LNC meeting, 12 September 1941, KNA, PC/NZA/4/7/7.

26. Minutes of North Kavirondo LNC meeting, 3 December 1941, KNA, PC/NZA/4/7/7.

27. Majorie Mbilinyi, "Runaway Wives in Colonial Tanganyika: Forced Labour and Forced Marriage in Rungwe District 1919–1961," *International Journal of the Sociology of Law* 16, no. 1 (1988): 1–29; Hodgson and McCurdy, *"Wicked" Women*; White, *Comforts of Home*.

28. Richard Waller, "Rebellious Youth in Colonial Africa," *Journal of African History* 47, no. 1 (2006): 79.

29. Letters to the editor, *Baraza*, 2 August 1941, KNA, ARC(MAA) 2/5/43.

30. Matthew Carotenuto, "Repatriation in Colonial Kenya: African Institutions and Gendered Violence," *International Journal of African Historical Studies* 45, no. 1 (2012): 13.

31. In his tours of the district in the 1940s, Lord William Hailey observed the growth of "location consciousness" in North Nyanza. Hailey, *Native Administration in the British Territories, Part 1* (London: His Majesty's Stationery Office, 1950), 152.

32. Bunyore Welfare Society Constitution, amended 15 November 1953, KNA, DC/KMG/1/1/153; Bunyore Educated Peoples' Society Constitution, 1952, KNA, DC/KMG/2/1/114.

33. North Nyanza District Commissioner to Senior Educational Officer, 19 April 1948, KNA, DC/NN/3/6/1; C. H. Williams Safari Diary to Nyanza Provincial Commissioner, 20 September 1947, KNA, PC/NZA/3/1/425.

34. Maragoli Locational Council, "Kitabu kya Mulogooli na Vana Veve," 1946, KNA, PC/NZA/2/3/61.

35. C. H. Williams Safari Diary to Nyanza Provincial Commissioner, 30 September 1947, KNA, PC/NZA/3/1/425; Francis Chogo, interview by author, Mbale, 27 September 2007.

36. Minutes of Luyia Language Committee, 12 March 1954, KPA, DH/1/1.

37. Minutes of North Nyanza ADC, 1951, KNA, PC/NZA/3/1/106.

38. Mordecai Tamarkin, "Tribal Associations, Tribal Solidarity, and Tribal Chauvinism in a Kenya Town," *Journal of African History* 14, no. 2 (1973): 257–74.

39. Carotenuto, "Repatriation in Colonial Kenya," 10.

40. Peter Alegi, *African Soccerscapes: How a Continent Changed the World's Game* (Athens: Ohio University Press, 2010); Laura Fair, *Pastimes and Politics: Culture, Community and Identity in Post-abolition Zanzibar, 1890–1945* (Athens: Ohio University Press, 2001); Paul Darby, "Football, Colonial Doctrine and Indigenous Resistance: Mapping the Political Persona of FIFA's African Constituency," in *The Decolonization Reader*, ed. James D. Le Sueur (New York: Routledge, 2003), 358–73; Phyllis M. Martin, *Leisure and Society in Colonial Brazzaville* (Cambridge: Cambridge University Press, 1995).

41. John Iliffe, *Honour in African History* (Cambridge: Cambridge University Press, 2005), 299.

42. Günter Wagner, "Proposals for Completion of Research: Results of First Year," paper presented at the 11th Meeting of the IAI Bureau, London, 30 December 1935, IAI_2/13.

43. Laura Fair, "Kickin' It: Leisure, Politics and Football in Colonial Zanzibar, 1900s–1950s," *Africa: Journal of the International African Institute* 67, no. 2 (1997): 236.

44. Iliffe, *Honour in African History*, 300.

45. Jonathan Barasa to Nyanza Provincial Commissioner, 11 March 1946, KNA, PC/NZA/3/27/99A.

46. Ezekiel Alembi, *Elijah Masinde: Rebel with a Cause* (Nairobi: Sasa Sema Publications, 2000), 22.

47. Mordecai Tamarkin, "The Evolution of Urban Ethnic Associations among Abaluyia in Nakuru, Kenya," *Journal of Eastern African Research and Development* 10, no. 2 (1980): 141.

48. P. Martin, *Leisure and Society*, 99.

49. Wanga Educated Men's Association constitution, 1945, KNA, OP/1/1328.

50. For a similar argument among the Luo, see Carotenuto, "Cultivating an African Community," 178.

51. Minutes of North Kavirondo LNC meeting, 29–30 March 1938, KNA, PC/NZA/4/7/7.

52. Peterson, *Ethnic Patriotism*, 220–21.

53. "Report of the Joint Tribal Committee of Nairobi on the Subject of Preventing the entry of women into the large towns from the reserves and of returning them from those towns to their homes," 9 October 1946, KNA, DC/UG/1/5/1.

54. Marach Union, Eldoret to Uasin Gishu District Commissioner, 28 March 1950, KNA, DC/UG/1/5/1.

55. *Uasin Gishu and Trans Nzoia Annual Report*, 1948.

56. General Secretary, Bunyore Welfare Society, to Locational Council, [1953], KNA, DC/KMG/1/1/153.

57. Philippa Levine, *Prostitution, Race, and Politics: Policing Venereal Disease in the British Empire* (New York: Routledge, 2003); White, *Comforts of Home*.

58. Minutes of North Kavirondo LNC meetings, 15–16 March 1944, KNA, PC/NZA/4/7/7.

59. Maragoli Association to Central Nyanza District Commissioner, 23 December 1960, KNA, HT/1/6.

60. Minutes of the Meeting of Maragoli Association and Central Nyanza District Commissioner, 22 October 1960, KNA, HT/1/6.

61. Chief Jeremiah Ochieng' to North Nyanza District Commissioner, 4 October 1948, KNA, DC/KMG/2/1/133; "Report of the Joint Tribal Committee of Nairobi on the subject of preventing the entry of women," 9 October 1946, KNA, DC/UG/1/5/1; Abaluyia Peoples Association to Eldoret District Commissioner, 9 February 1956, KNA, DC/UG/1/5/1.

62. District Officer Majengo to North Nyanza District Commissioner, 15 October 1948, KNA, DC/KMG/2/1/133.

63. Secretary of Maragoli Locational Advisory Council to Maragoli Society, Kitale Branch, 7 August 1948, KNA, DC/KMG/2/1/133.

64. Mutongi, *Worries of the Heart*, 142–44.

65. Minutes of North Kavirondo LNC meetings, 15–16 March 1944, KNA, PC/NZA/3/7/7.

66. AWA to Secretary of State for the Colonies, 28 July 1946, KNA, PC/NZA/3/4/28; AWA Resolutions, 16 June 1950, KNA, OP/1/1341; David Parkin, *Neighbours and Nationals in an African City Ward* (London: Routledge, 1969), 167.

67. The Abaluyia Football Club is now the popular AFC Leopards team in contemporary Kenya.

68. Abaluyia Association, draft constitution, n.d., KNA, DC/KMG/2/1/111.

69. Abaluyia Friendly Society of Eldoret special meeting, 20 September 1945, KNA, DC/UG/1/5/1.

70. AFS Eldoret Secretary Arthur Kadima to Eldoret District Commissioner, 19 October 1945, KNA, DC/UG/1/5/1.

71. Uasin Gishu District Commissioner to AFS, Eldoret, 27 October 1945, KNA, DC/UG/1/5/1.

72. Uasin Gishu District Commissioner to Nyanza and Rift Valley Provincial Commissioners, with enclosed AWA petitions, 4 September 1950, KNA, DX/21/9/2.

73. AFS Eldoret Secretary to the Uasin Gishu District Commissioner, 5 December 1947, KNA, DC/UG/1/5/1.

74. *Uasin Gishu and Trans Nzoia Annual Report*, 1950.

75. Secretary APA to Eldoret District Commissioner, 28 February 1956, KNA, UG/1/5/1.

76. Joseph Munapi, Idakho, to North Nyanza District Commissioner, 15 April 1956, KNA, DC/KMG/2/1/133.

77. APA, Eldoret, to Uasin Gishu District Commissioner, 30 September 1955, KNA, DC/UG/1/5/1.

78. Hobley, *Eastern Uganda*.

79. Wagner, *Bantu of North Kavirondo*, 1:336.

80. Simani Sangale, *Tiriki Community Customs and Traditions* (Nairobi: Kul Graphics, 2004); C. H. Williams Safari Diary, 30 September 1947, KNA, PC/NZA/3/1/425.

81. North Nyanza Intelligence Report, August 1946, KNA, PC/NZA/3/1/432.

82. Patrick Wangamati, interview by author, Webuye, 17 October 2007.

83. Wagner, *Bantu of North Kavirondo*, 1:339–46.

84. Luo People's Association of North Nyanza to North Nyanza District Commissioner, 6 September 1962, KPA; Luo People's Association of North Nyanza to Nyanza Provincial Commissioner, 29 October 1962, both in KPA, DX/1/6.

85. Regional Government Agent to Chief Ali, 10 September 1963, KPA, DX/1/6.

86. Arthur Ochwada, interview by author, Funyala, 12 October 2007; William Okwemba, interview by author, Kima, 19 October 2007; Benedict Makhulo, interview by author, Port Victoria, 14 October 2007.

87. North Kavirondo LNC Resolution no. 2/25, 1925, KNA, PC/NZA/3/1/233.

88. Nyanza Provincial Commission to Chief Native Commissioner, 25 September 1948, KNA, PC/NZA/3/1/100. For more on the resolutions passed in other regions, see Kanogo, *African Womanhood*; L. Thomas, *Politics of the Womb*.

89. Lonsdale, "Moral Economy," 315–504; Peterson, *Creative Writing*, 103–13; Jocelyn Murray, "Church Missionary Society," 92–104; Kanogo, *African Womanhood*, 73–103; Jomo Kenyatta, *Facing Mount Kenya: The Tribal Life of the Gikuyu* (London: Secker & Warburg, 1938; repr., New York: Vintage Books, 1965), 125–48.

90. Kanogo, *African Womanhood*, 92.

91. Central Kavirondo Intelligence Report, June 1930, KNA, PC/NZA/3/45/12.

92. Kanogo, *African Womanhood*, 92.

93. North Kavirondo LNC, Resolution no. 2 of 1931, KNA, PC/NZA/2/1/53.

94. North Kavirondo Intelligence Report, May 1935, KNA, DC/KMG/2/1/80.

95. North Kavirondo District Commissioner to Eldoret District Commissioner, 12 January 1945, KPA, DX/1/6.

96. Trans Nzoia District Commissioner to North Kavirondo District Commissioner, 9 October 1937, KPA, DX/1/6.

97. Pius Wanyonyi Kakai, "Social Concepts in the Initiation Rituals of the Abatachoni: A Historical Study" (master's diss., Kenyatta University, 1992), 42.

98. North Kavirondo District Commissioner to Nyanza Provincial Commissioner, 13 November 1944, KPA, DX/1/6.

99. North Kavirondo District Commissioner to Trans Nzoia District Commissioner, 14 October 1937, KPA, DX/1/6; North Kavirondo District Commissioner to Eldoret District Commissioner, 12 January 1945, KPA, DX/1/6.

100. The female circumcision crisis in North Nyanza received very little mention, if at all, in the archives of the Church Missionary Society (Birmingham) or the Friends African Mission (Richmond, Indiana), the two dominant missions in the region. This silence was due in part to the cases of female circumcision emerging among non-Christian populations.

101. Wandibba, "Oral History of Abatachoni," 18–33; Were, *Western Kenya Historical Texts*, 91–95; Administrative Note, "The Tachoni," [1955], KNA, ARC(MAA) 2/5/2/274I.

102. Were, *Western Kenya Historical Texts*, 91.

103. Nyanza Provincial Commissioner to Chief Native Commissioner, 18 February 1949, KNA, PC/NZA/2/1/53.

104. L. L. Appleby, Sketch of Dialect Groups in North Nyanza, [1942], BFBS, Luyia Language file, BSA/E3/3/324.

105. North Nyanza District Commissioner to Nyanza Provincial Commissioner, 18 May 1951, KPA, DX/1/6.

106. Kakai, "Social Concepts," 36.

107. Tachoni Union to North Nyanza District Commissioner, 23 March 1951, KPA, DX/1/6.

108. Kakai, "Social Concepts," 42.

109. Kanogo, *African Womanhood*, 80.

110. African Assistant Administrative Officer to North Nyanza District Commissioner, 6 June 1951, KPA, DX/1/6.

111. Nyanza Provincial Commissioner to Chief Secretary, 10 February 1948, KNA, PC/NZA/2/1/53.

112. Bungoma District Officer to North Nyanza District Commissioner, 16 May 1951, KPA, DX/1/6; Tachoni Union to North Nyanza District Commissioner, 23 March 1951, KPA, DX/1/6.

113. African Assistant Administrative Officer to North Nyanza District Commissioner, 6 June 1951, KPA, DX/1/6.

114. Bungoma District Officer to North Nyanza District Commissioner, 13 March 1951, KPA, DX/1/6; L. Thomas, *Politics of the Womb*, 40.

115. L. Thomas, *Politics of the Womb*, 50.

116. Tachoni Union to North Nyanza District Commissioner, 5 November 1947, KPA, DX/1/6; Nyanza Provincial Commissioner to North Nyanza District Commissioner, 13 January 1948, KNA, PC/NZA/2/1/53.

117. A. Qadir Malik to Chief Secretary, 30 January 1948, KNA, PC/NZA/2/1/53.

118. Kenyatta, *Facing Mount Kenya*; Lonsdale, "Moral Economy of Mau Mau," 388–97; Peterson, *Creative Writing*, 90–91.

119. Bungoma District Officer to North Nyanza District Commissioner, 13 March 1952, KPA, DX/1/6.

120. North Nyanza District Commissioner to Nyanza Provincial Commissioner, 10 November 1951, KNA, PC/NZA/3/1/24.

121. North Nyanza District Commissioner to Nyanza Provincial Commissioner, 16 June 1951, KNA, PC/NZA/2/1/53.

122. Tachoni Union to Nyanza Provincial Commissioner, 6 February 1948, KPA, DX/1/6.

123. Derek Peterson notes a similar trend among the Kikuyu. Peterson, *Creative Writing*, 108–12.

124. A. T. Matson, "Mumia: The Man and the Myth: Parts One and Two," *Kenya Weekly News*, 20, 27 October 1961.

125. Lonsdale, "Comparative Patriotisms," 251–67.

126. Record of evidence given before North Kavirondo NLTC, 1 July 1930, KNA, DC/NN/8/1.

127. E. A. Andere, "Abaluyia Land Law and Custom," [1952], KPA, DX/21/2/17.

128. NCA to Chief Native Commissioner, 13 March 1944, KNA, DC/KMG/1/1/153; Bukusu Union to Nyanza Provincial Commissioner, 7 September 1946, KNA, PC/NZA/3/4/28; minutes of North Nyanza LNC meeting, 19–22 August 1947, TNA:PRO, CO1018/25.

129. *Nyanza Province Annual Report*, 1946; mintues of the meetings of the Nyanza Ex-soldiers Organisation, January–October 1950, KNA, PC/NZA/3/1/314.

130. Peter Wafula to Nyanza Provincial Commissioner, 19 November 1947, KNA, DC/KMG/1/1/153.

131. "Re: Owuluyali," letter to editor, *Habari*, [1944], KNA, DC/KMGA/1/16/12.

132. Lonsdale, "'Listen While I Read'"; Bravman, *Making Ethnic Ways*.

133. Michael Jennings, "'Very Real War': Popular Participation in Development in Tanzania during the 1950s and 1960s," *International Journal of African Historical Studies* 40, no. 1 (2007): 71–95; Joanna Lewis, *Empire State-Building: War and Welfare in Kenya, 1925–52* (Athens: Ohio University Press, 2000); Lonsdale, "KAU's Cultures."

134. Bruce Berman, *Control and Crisis in Colonial Kenya: The Dialectic of Domination* (Athens: Ohio University Press, 1990); Spencer, *Kenya African Union.*

135. John Lonsdale, "Some Origins of Nationalism in East Africa," *Journal of African History* 9, no. 1 (1968): 119–46; Iliffe, *History of Tanganyika.*

136. Lonsdale, "KAU's Cultures," 121.

137. J. D. Otiende, interview by author, Mbale, 9 October 2007.

138. J. D. Otiende, interview by author, Mbale, 20 June 2007.

139. Peter Wanyande, *Joseph Daniel Otiende* (Nairobi: East African Educational Publishers, 2002).

140. J. D. Otiende, interview by author, Mbale, 9 October 2007.

141. KAU Resolutions, 20 April 1947, KNA, PC/NZA/3/1/366.

142. Otiende, *Habari za Abaluyia.*

143. Ibid., publisher's note.

144. For similar projects across Africa, see Peterson and Macola, *Recasting the Past.*

145. Nyang'ori location petition to Governor of Kenya, 14 October 1957, KNA, PC/NCA/4/14/5.

146. Otiende, *Habari za Abaluyia,* 51.

147. North Nyanza District Commissioner to Nyanza Provincial Commissioner, 10 March 1947, KNA, DC/KMG/1/1/73.

148. North Nyanza District Commissioner to Nyanza Provincial Commissioner, 10 March 1947, KNA, DC/KMG/1/1/73; W. W. W. Awori, interview by John Spencer, Nairobi, 5 June 1972, Lonsdale Personal Archives; Fay Gadsden, "The African Press in Kenya, 1945–1952," *Journal of African History* 21, no. 4 (1980): 515–35.

149. Chief Agoi to Nyanza Provincial Commissioner, 15 February 1947, KNA, DC/KMG/1/1/73.

150. Joseph Otiende to Editor, *Baraza,* 10 February 1948, KNA, DC/KMG/1/1/73.

151. Kakamega District Commissioner to Nyanza Province Senior Commissioner, 27 March 1925, KNA, PC/NZA/3/17/2.

152. North Nyanza District Commissioner to Nyanza Provincial Commissioner, 18 January 1945, KNA, DC/KMG/1/1/107.

153. AWA, "Group Farming, Census, and Income Tax in Nyanza Province," 18 July 1950, KNA, PC/NZA/2/1/215; AWA and KAU Eldoret Branches Resolutions, 16 July 1950, KNA, OP/1/1341.

154. Nyanza Provincial Commissioner Williams to Tom Mbotela, 3 May 1951, KNA, PC/NZA/3/1/366.

155. People of North Nyanza to H. E., Acting Governor, memorandum, 31 July 1950, KNA, MAA/8/165.

156. AWA meeting agenda, 22 December 1947, KNA, PC/NZA/2/1/215.

157. AWA, Bunyore Branch, to Nyanza Provincial Commissioner, 19 November 1947, KNA, PC/NZA/2/1/215.

158. Central Nyanza District Commissioner to Nyanza Provincial Commissioner, 22 November 1947, KNA, PC/NZA/2/1/215.

159. Nyanza Provincial Commissioner to North Nyanza District Commissioner, 6 November 1947, KNA, PC/NZA/3/14/19.

160. C. J. Martin, "The East Africa Population Census, 1948: Planning and Enumeration," *Population Studies* 3, no. 3 (December 1949): 312.

161. Rights of African Women (1958–59), KNA, MAA/1/370.

162. H. F. Morris, "Native Courts: A Corner-Stone of Indirect Rule," in *Indirect Rule and the Search for Justice: Essays in East African Legal History*, ed. H. F. Morris and James S. Read (Oxford: Clarendon Press, 1972), 131–66; Mamdani, *Citizen and Subject*, 109–37; Martin Chanock, *Law, Custom and Social Order: The Colonial Experience in Malawi and Zambia* (Cambridge: Cambridge University Press, 1985).

163. A prime example, sociologist turned official Hans Cory created a compendium of Haya "customary" laws in the 1940s that he then exported throughout Tanganyika. Cory and M. M. Hartnoll, *Customary Law of the Haya Tribe* (London: P. Lund, Humphries and Co., 1945). For the ways such practices helped privilege African men over women and junior men, see Margaret Jean Hay and Marcia Wright, eds., *African Women and the Law: Historical Perspectives* (Boston: Boston University African Studies Center, 1982); Kristin Mann and Richard Roberts, eds., *Law in Colonial Africa* (Portsmouth, NH: Heinemann, 1991); Elizabeth Schmidt, *Peasants, Traders, and Wives: Shona Women in the History of Zimbabwe, 1870–1939* (Portsmouth, NH: Heinemann, 1992); Gregory H. Maddox, "Narrating Power in Colonial Ugogo: Mazengo of Mvumi," in *In Search of a Nation*, ed. James L. Giblin and Gregory H. Maddox (Athens: Ohio University Press, 2005), 99.

164. Sally Falk Moore, *Social Facts and Fabrications: "Customary" Law on Kilimanjaro, 1880–1980* (Cambridge: Cambridge University Press, 1986); Sara S. Berry, *No Condition Is Permanent: The Social Dynamics of Agrarian Change in Sub-Saharan Africa* (Madison: University of Wisconsin Press, 1993); Brett L. Shadle, *"Girl Cases": Marriage and Colonialism in Gusiiland, Kenya, 1890–1970* (Portsmouth, NH: Heinemann, 2006); Thomas Spear, "Indirect Rule, the Politics of Neo-traditionalism and the Limits of Invention in Tanzania," in *In Search of a Nation*, ed. James L. Giblin and Gregory H. Maddox (Athens: Ohio University Press, 2005), 79–81.

165. Spear, "Neo-traditionalism," 16.

166. J. S. S. Rowlands, "Notes on Native Law and Custom in Kenya: I," *Journal of African Law* 6, no. 3 (Autumn 1962): 192–209; Brett L. Shadle, "'Changing Traditions to Meet Current Altering Conditions': Customary Law, African Courts and the Rejection of Codification in Kenya, 1930–60," *Journal of African History* 40, no. 3 (1999): 411–31.

167. Lord Hailey's Preliminary Notes, North Nyanza, 17 October 1947, TNA:PRO, CO1018/25.

168. Shadle, "'Changing Traditions,'" 422–24; L. Thomas, *Politics of the Womb*, 108.

169. Luyia Civil Law Panel, [1954], KNA, RR/8/24; meeting of the Abaluyia Customary Law Panel, 16 May 1962, KPA, ATW/4/62.

170. Meeting of the Abaluyia Customary Law Panel, 3 October 1952, KPA, DX/1/5.

171. E. A. Andere, "The Abaluyia Customary Law Relating to Marriage and Inheritance," [1952], KNA, DC/NN/7/1/1; E. A. Andere, "Abaluyia Land Law and Custom," [1952], KPA, DX/21/2/17; meeting of the Abaluyia Customary Law Panel, 16 May 1962, KPA, ATW/4/62.

172. E. A. Andere, "The Abaluyia Customary Law Relating to Marriage and Inheritance," [1952], KNA, DC/NN/7/1/1.

173. Ibid.

174. North Nyanza District Commissioner to Nyanza Provincial Commissioner, 27 July 1949, KNA, PC/NZA/3/1/100.

175. North Nyanza District Commissioner to Nyanza Provincial Commissioner, 16 June 1951, KNA, PC/NZA/2/1/53; Felix Bryk, *Neger-Eros: Ethnologische Studien über das Sexualleben bei Negern* (Berlin: A. Marcus and E. Weber, 1928), 33; Jan J. de Wolf, "The Diffusion of Age-Group Organization in East Africa: A Reconsideration," *Africa: Journal of the International African Institute* 50, no. 3 (1980): 308; Chief Ali Wamukoya, interview by author, Mumias, 19 September 2007; Julius Kakai Opicho, William Khaemba Nandasuba, and Paulo Chemyati, interview by author, Bokoli, 13 March 2007; Günter Wagner, *Bantu of North Kavirondo*, 1:336.

176. North Nyanza District Commissioner to Nyanza Provincial Commissioner, 12 October 1951, KNA, PC/NZA/2/1/53; North Nyanza Intelligence Report, October 1951, KNA, PC/NZA/3/1/38.

177. Bukusu petitions to North Nyanza ADC, 12 November 1951, KNA, PC/NZA/3/1/38.

178. Inquiries into these cases often found the occurrences were localized within Bukusu and Kabras clans of Maasai origin, which Luyia historian John Osogo later linked to Tachoni clans. North Kavirondo District Commissioner to Nyanza Provincial Commissioner, 6 December 1944, KPA, DX/1/6; Osogo, *History of the Baluyia*, 82, 93.

179. Perus Angaya Abura, interview by author, Kakamega, 9 July 2008.

180. Phillip Masinde, interview by author, Bwamani, 17 September 2007; Samuel Aluda, interview by author, Mungavo, 21 October 2007.

181. North Nyanza District Commissioner to Nyanza Provincial Commissioner, 12 October 1951, KNA, PC/NZA/2/1/53.

182. Bukusu petitions to North Nyanza ADC, 12 November 1951, KNA, PC/NZA/3/1/38.

183. African Assistant Administrative Officer to North Nyanza District Commissioner, 6 June 1951, KPA, DX/1/6.

184. Nyanza Provincial Commission to Chief Native Commissioner, 25 September 1948, KNA, PC/NZA/3/1/100.

185. North Nyanza ADC (Circumcision of Females) By-Laws Resolution no. 7/51, 16 June 1951, KNA, PC/NZA/2/1/53.

186. Burudi Nabwera, interview by author, Kiminini, 23 October 2007; North Nyanza District Commissioner to Nyanza Provincial Commissioner, 12 October 1951, KNA, PC/NZA/2/1/53; B. T. Namasaka to District Officer, Lurambi Division, 6 November 1959, KNA, DC.KMG/2/1/115.

187. Tachoni Union Meeting Agenda, 29 May 1960, KNA, DC.KMG/2/1/115.

188. Lonsdale, "Moral Economy," 391.

189. Burudi Nabwera, interview by author, Kiminini, 23 October 2007.

190. Philip Ingutia to Nyanza Provincial Commissioner, "Ref: the Name Abaluyia," 23 July 1949, KNA, PC/NZA/2/1/158.

191. Deputy Chief Secretary to Nyanza Provincial Commissioner, 16 December 1949, KNA, PC/NZA/2/1/158; official gazette of Abaluyia, general notice no. 34, 10 January 1950, KNA, PC/NZA/2/1/158.

192. Peterson, *Ethnic Patriotism*, 140.

193. P. G. Fullerton, "Notes for the North Nyanza Annual Report, Southern Division," *North Nyanza Annual Report*, 1955.

194. *Report of the Commissioner Appointed to Enquire into the Methods for the Selection of African Representatives to the Legislative Council*, 12; Kimilili Locational Council Petition to Coutts Commission, 11 April 1955, KNA, DC/KMG/1/1/73.

195. Perus Angaya Abura, interview by author, Kakamega, 9 July 2008; Audrey Wipper, "The Maendeleo ya Wanawake Movement in the Colonial Period: The Canadian Connection, Mau Mau, Embroidery, and Agriculture," *Rural Africana* 29 (Winter 1975–76): 195–214; Audrey Wipper, "The Maendeleo ya Wanawake Organization: The Co-opting of Leadership," *African Studies Review* 18, no. 3 (December 1975): 99–120.

CHAPTER 6: ETHNIC GEOGRAPHIES IN THE
ERA OF MAU MAU

1. Gerald Masibayi, interview by author, Bumala, 4 October 2007.

2. David M. Anderson, *Histories of the Hanged: The Dirty War in Kenya and the End of Empire* (London: Weidenfeld and Nicolson, 2005), 188–95.

3. Flemming Commission, 1955, KNA, KA/1/61; Flemming Commission, 1961, TNA:PRO, T296/215.

4. For a detailed account of the functioning of the pipeline, see Caroline Elkins, *Britain's Gulag: The Brutal End of Empire in Kenya* (London: Pimlico, 2005), 149–53.

5. Elgon Nyanza District Commissioner to Nyanza Provincial Commissioner, "Jarat Masibai: Marach—Convict at Athi River Camp," 5 January 1956, KNA, PC/NZA/3/15/131.

6. Bethwell A. Ogot and Mordecai Tamarkin have both written on the ambiguous position of loyalists within the Central Province. Ogot, "Revolt of the Elders: An Anatomy of the Loyalist Crowd in the Mau Mau Uprising 1952–1956," in *Hadith 4: Politics and Nationalism in Colonial Kenya*, ed. Ogot

(Nairobi: East African Publishing House, 1972), 134–49; Mordecai Tamarkin, "The Loyalists in Nakuru during the Mau Mau Revolt and Its Aftermath, 1953–1963," *Asian and African Studies* 12, no. 2 (1978): 247–61.

7. Daniel Branch, *Defeating Mau Mau, Creating Kenya: Counterinsurgency, Civil War and Decolonization* (Cambridge: Cambridge University Press, 2009); Branch, "The Enemy Within: Loyalists and the War against Mau Mau in Kenya," *Journal of African History* 48, no. 2 (2007): 291–315.

8. Branch, *Defeating Mau Mau*, 22.

9. The cult of Mumbo was a millennial movement that spread across southwestern Kenya between 1914 and 1934. Brett L. Shadle, "Patronage, Millennialism and the Serpent God Mumbo in South-West Kenya, 1912–34," *Africa* 72, no. 1 (February 2002): 29–54.

10. Elijah Masinde's family and former Dini ya Msambwa members, group interviews by author, Kimilili, 10, 11 October 2007.

11. For detailed descriptions of the origins and activities of the Dini ya Msambwa movement, see Wipper, *Rural Rebels*; Jan J. de Wolf, "Dini ya Msambwa: Militant Protest or Millenarian Promise?," *Canadian Journal of African Studies* 17, no. 2 (1983): 265–76.

12. Arson was an increasingly common occurrence in the Bukusu region. Although Msambwa members were held responsible for this increase in arson, it is more likely that these attacks were uncoordinated and individual rather than a central strategy planned by the leadership of Dini ya Msambwa.

13. J. C. Carothers, Medical Officer-in-Charge, to North Nyanza District Commissioner, 25 April 1947, KNA, DC/NN/10/1/5; for more on Masinde's time at Mathari, see Sloan Mahone, "The Psychology of Rebellion: Colonial Medical Responses to Dissent in British East Africa," *Journal of African History* 47, no. 2 (2006): 241–58.

14. Nyanza Province Intelligence Report, November 1947, KNA, PC/NZA/3/1/432; Nyanza Provincial Commissioner to Chief Secretary, 10 February 1948, KNA, PC/NZA/2/1/53.

15. "Found in a Cave," *East African Standard*, 20 February 1948.

16. Elijah Masinde's family and former Dini ya Msambwa members, group interviews by author, Kimilili, 10, 11 October 2007.

17. Bukusu elders, group interview by author, Bokoli, 13 March 2007; Wagner, "Political Organization," 232; Schoenbrun, "Conjuring the Modern," 19–20; Wesonga, "Pre-colonial Military Organisation."

18. "Kimilili Situation Now Reported Quiet," *Standard*, February 1948.

19. I. Okwirry, African Assistant Administrative Officer's Report, 2 December 1949, KNA, DC/NN/10/1/5.

20. Nyanza Province Intelligence Report, December 1949, KNA, PC/NZA/3/1/432.

21. C. H. Williams Safari Diary, 27 October 1947, KNA, PC/NZA/3/1/425.

22. Nyanza Province Intelligence Report, July 1947, KNA, PC/NZA/3/1/432; *Nyanza Province Annual Report*, 1948.

23. Nyanza Province Intelligence Report, July 1947, KNA, PC/NZA/3/1/432; David M. Anderson, "Stock Theft and Moral Economy in Colonial Kenya," *Africa: Journal of the International African Institute* 56, no. 4 (1986): 416.

24. Kenya Colony and Protectorate, *Population Census 1948*.

25. Tabitha Kanogo, *Squatters and the Roots of Mau Mau, 1905–63* (Athens: Ohio University Press, 1987), 46–50.

26. Nyanza Province Intelligence Report, June 1950, KNA, PC/NZA/3/1/433.

27. Notice no. 368, Native Passes Rules, 1949, KPA, ATW/4/62.

28. Chief Secretary of Kenya, "Interpenetration and Infiltration in the Native Land Units," 3 May 1946, KNA, DC/KMG/1/1/5.

29. Ibid.; "Statement of Government Interim Policy with regard to Interpenetration and Infiltration in Native Land Units," circular, 13 August 1947, KNA, PC/NZA/4/14/5.

30. "Statement of Government Interim Policy with regard to Interpenetration and Infiltration in Native Land Units," circular no. 29, 5 July 1948, KNA, PC/NZA/4/14/5.

31. Parsons, "Being Kikuyu," 67.

32. Nyanza Provincial Commissioner, Memorandum for Discussion at Provincial Commissioners' Meeting, 25–27 July 1951, KNA, PC/NZA/3/1/493.

33. Parsons, "Being Kikuyu."

34. J. Pinney, "Report of the Boundaries of Trans Mara," [1949], KNA, PC/NZA/3/14/3.

35. South Nyanza District Commissioner to North Nyanza District Commissioner, 23 February 1950, KNA, DC/KMG/1/1/5.

36. For a similar argument for the Meru of Central Kenya, see Parsons, "Being Kikuyu."

37. Mahone, "Psychology of Rebellion," 241–58.

38. Benjamin E. Kipkorir, "The Kolloa Affray, Kenya 1950," *Transafrican Journal of History* 2, no. 2 (1972): 114–29; Kipkorir, "Colonial Response to Crisis: The Kolloa Affray and Colonial Kenya in 1950," *Kenya Past and Present* 2, no.1 (1973): 22–35; Nottingham and Rosberg, *Myth of "Mau Mau,"* 328; Wipper, *Rural Rebels*, 208.

39. *West Pokot Annual Report*, 1950–53.

40. Report of the Commission of Inquiry into the Affray at Kolloa, Baringo, 14 November 1950, KNA, MSS/66/195.

41. Barbara A. Bianco, "Songs of Mobility in West Pokot," *American Ethnologist* 23, no. 1 (February 1996): 25–42.

42. *Rift Valley Province Annual Report*, 1950.

43. Report of the Commission of Inquiry into the Affray at Kolloa, Baringo, 14 November 1950, KNA, MSS/66/195.

44. Kapenguria District Commissioner, "History in Suk," 24 January 1955, KNA, DC/TN/3/1.

45. *Rift Valley Province Annual Report*, 1951.

46. J. G. Peristiany, "The Age-Set System of the Pastoral Pokot: The 'Sapana' Initiation Ceremony," *Africa: Journal of the International African Institute* 21, no. 3 (July 1951): 188–206.

47. Ibid., 202; petitions from Bukusu of Kimilili Location to Nyanza Provincial Commissioner, 30 June 1952, KNA, DC/EN/4/2.

48. West Suk Handing Over Report, 31 December 1951, KNA, PC/RVP/3/1/2.

49. Members of ADC and Kimilili Locational Council, 14 April 1952, ACK, ACSO/CPN/2; petitions from the Bukusu of Kimilili Location, 30 June 1952, KNA, DC/EN/4/2.

50. Members of ADC and Kimilili Locational Council, 14 April 1952, ACK ACSO/CPN/2.

51. Nyanza Provincial Commissioner to North Nyanza District Commissioner, 30 June 1952, KNA, DC/EN/4/2.

52. Over 120 Bukusu families had already been forcibly repatriated from the Rift Valley in 1949. Bungoma District Officer to North Nyanza District Commissioner, 2 July 1949, KNA, DC/NN/10/1/5.

53. "People of North Nyanza" to Governor, 31 July 1950, KNA, MAA/8/165.

54. "Chiefs Ask More Power to Deal with Lawless," *East African Standard*, 29 April 1949.

55. Nyanza Province Intelligence Report, April 1952, KNA, PC/NZA/3/1/38.

56. Lonsdale, "Moral Economy of Mau Mau"; Peterson, *Creative Writing*, 191–214.

57. Branch, "Enemy Within," 291–315.

58. Elijah Masinde's family and former Dini ya Msambwa members, group interviews by author, Kimilili, 10, 11 October 2007.

59. "Mzee Mombasa" Batholomeo Munoko, interview by author, Kiminini, 16 March 2007.

60. Elijah Masinde's family and former Dini ya Msambwa members, group interviews by author, Kimilili, 10, 11 October 2007; Bukusu elders, group interview by author, Bokoli, 13 March 2007.

61. Michael Adas, *Prophets of Rebellion: Millenarian Protest Movements against the European Colonial Order* (Cambridge: Cambridge University Press, 1987), xx–xxi; David M. Anderson and Douglas H. Johnson, eds., *Revealing Prophets: Prophecy in Eastern African History* (Athens: Ohio University Press, 1995); Gail Presbey, "Is Elijah Masinde a Sage-Philosopher? The Dispute between H. Odera Oruka and Chaungo Barasa," in *Sagacious Reasoning: Henry Odera Oruka in Memoriam*, ed. Anke Graness and Kai Kresse (New York: P. Lang, 1997), 200.

62. Makila, *History of the Babukusu*, 150.

63. Bukusu elders, group interview by author, Bokoli, 13 March 2007.

64. Makila, *History of the Babukusu*, 221–25.

65. Deportation Trial, Elijah Masinde Testimony, His Majesty's Supreme Court of Kenya at Kakamega, 17 May 1948, KNA, ARC(MAA), 2/5/105.

66. "Dini Ya Msambwa: Memorandum by the Kenya Intelligence Committee," 17 November 1954, TNA:PRO, CO822/809.

67. Oginga Odinga, *Not Yet Uhuru: The Autobiography of Oginga Odinga* (London: East African Educational Publishers, 1967), 70.

68. W. R. B. Pugh, Superintendent of Police, Report on "Dini Msambwa," 15 March 1948, KNA, DC/NN/10/1/5; Wamyama Waseme, youngest brother of Elijah Masinde, interview by author, Kimilili, 10 October 2007.

69. Makila, *History of the Babukusu*, 220.

70. Elijah Masinde's family and former Dini ya Msambwa members, group interviews by author, Kimilili, 10, 11 October 2007.

71. Wanyama Waseme, youngest brother of Elijah Masinde, interview by author, Kimilili, 10 October 2007.

72. Deportation Trial, Elijah Masinde Cross Examination, His Majesty's Supreme Court of Kenya at Kakamega, 17 May 1948, KNA, (ARC)MAA 2/5/105.

73. Special Intelligence Report, North Nyanza, December 1949, KNA, DC/NN/10/1/5.

74. North Nyanza District Commissioner to Nyanza Provincial Commissioner, 9 December 1949, KNA, DC/NN/10/1/5; Special Branch Headquarters Report on Elijah Masinde, 31 March 1960, TNA:PRO, CO 822/809.

75. Peterson, *Ethnic Patriotism*.

76. *Trans Nzoia Annual Report*, 1951.

77. Trans Nzoia Handing Over Report, 1955.

78. Kenya Police, Bungoma, telegram to Nairobi, 16 October 1952, KNA, DC/KMG/1/6/52.

79. Horace M. Shelley, "An Investigation Concerning Mental Disorder in Nyasaland Natives," *Journal of Mental Science* 82, no. 341 (1936): 701–30; Thomas Christie, "Criminal Lunatics and the Crime of Arson," *British Medical Journal* 25, no. 1 (January 1930): 162–63.

80. For a full accounting of these rehabilitation programs during the Mau Mau rebellion, see Elkins, *Britain's Gulag*, 91–120.

81. North Nyanza Handing Over Report, 4 November 1950, KNA, PC/NZA/3/1/434b.

82. Bungoma Handing Over Report, August 1952, KNA, DC/NN/2/6.

83. Derek Peterson, "The Intellectual Lives of Mau Mau Detainees," *Journal of African History* 49, no. 1 (2008): 73–91; Bethwell A. Ogot, "Britain's Gulag," review of *Histories of the Hanged: Britain's Dirty War in Kenya and the End of Empire*, by David Anderson, and *Britain's Gulag: The Brutal End of Empire in Kenya*, by Caroline Elkins, *Journal of African History* 46, no. 3 (2005): 493–505; John Lonsdale, "Britain's Mau Mau" (draft paper, University of Cambridge, 2009); Joanna Lewis, "Nasty, Brutish and in Shorts? British Colonial Rule, Violence and the Historians of Mau Mau," *Round Table* 96, no. 389 (April 2007): 201–23

84. Louis Leakey, *Defeating Mau Mau* (London: Routledge, 1954), 85–86.

85. L. G. Miller, Community Development Officer, "Rehabilitation Report 'D.Y.M.' Prisoners and Detainees—Kapenguria Prison Works Camp," 1 September 1956, KNA, DC/TN/3/1.

86. Deportation Trial, Elijah Masinde cross-examination, His Majesty's Supreme Court of Kenya at Kakamega, 17 May 1948, KNA, (ARC)MAA 2/5/105.

87. Kavujai District Officer, memorandum on Dini ya Msambwa, 1949, KNA, DC/NN/10/1/5.

88. L. G. Miller, Community Development Officer, "Rehabilitation Report 'D.Y.M.' Prisoners and Detainees—Kapenguria Prison Works Camp," 1 September 1956, KNA, DC/TN/3/1.

89. Bishop L. C. Usher-Wilson, "Dini ya Msambwa," *East Africa and Rhodesia*, 29 November 1951, 345–46.

90. Minister for Internal Security and Defence, "Dini ya Msambwa Restricted Persons," 3 February 1961, TNA:PRO, CO822/2017.

91. North Nyanza Intelligence Report, December 1954, KNA, DC/KMG/1/16/2.

92. Minutes of Liaison Meeting on Kenya/Uganda security affairs, Kakamega, 19 March 1955–6 April 1955, KNA, DC/TN/3/1.

93. "Some Notes on East African Native Laws and Customs," *Journal of the Society of Comparative Legislation* 11, no. 1 (1910): 190.

94. Trans Nzoia Handing Over Report, 1955; "Dini Ya Msambwa: Memorandum by the Kenya Intelligence Committee," n.d., TNA:PRO, CO833/809; *Trans Nzoia Annual Report*, 1951.

95. *Trans Nzoia Annual Report*, 1953.

96. *Trans Nzoia Annual Report*, 1955.

97. Kapenguria District Commissioner to Nyanza Provincial Commissioner, 2 June 1956, KNA, PC/NZA/3/1/328.

98. North Nyanza Intelligence Report, May 1953, KNA, DC/KMG/1/16/2.

99. Nyanza Provincial Commissioner to Secretary for African Affairs, 1 June 1955, KNA, PC/NZA/3/1/29.

100. Senior Marketing Officer, Maseno, to Nyanza Provincial Commissioner, 1 February 1955, KNA, PC/NZA/3/1/29; Nyanza Provincial Commissioner to Minister of African Affairs, [1954], KNA, PC/NZA/3/1/29. For similar debates over market control across the border among the Bagisu, see Stephen G. Bunker, *Peasants against the State: The Politics of Market Control in Bugisu, Uganda, 1900–1983* (Urbana: University of Illinois Press, 1987).

101. North Nyanza District Commissioner to Nyanza Provincial Commissioner, 22 July 1954, KNA, PC/NZA/3/1/29.

102. P. G. Fullerton, "Notes for the North Nyanza Annual Report, Southern Division," *North Nyanza Annual Report*, 1955.

103. Kavujai District Assistant to District Officer, 16 June 1959, KPA, WD/4/3; Mumias District Officer to North Nyanza District Commissioner, 13 July 1959, KPA, WD/4/3.

104. Minutes of Nyanza Province Security Committee meeting, 29 November 1960, KNA, PC/NZA/4/20/3.

105. *Rift Valley Province Annual Report, 1959.*

106. Spencer, *Kenya African Union,* 225.

107. Ibid.

108. Arthur Moody Awori, interview by author, Nairobi, 21 July 2008.

109. J. D. Otiende, interview by author, Mbale, 7 July 2008.

110. E. S. Atieno Odhiambo, "The Formative Years," in *Decolonization and Independence in Kenya, 1940–93,* ed. Bethwell A. Ogot and William R. Ochieng' (Athens: Ohio University Press, 1995), 25. For Awori's position on these issues, see articles in *Radio Posta,* 10 October 1947–3 December 1947, KNA, MAA/8/105; W. W. W. Awori, "Danger of the Identity Cards: What Difference Has It [made] to 'KIPANDE'?," *Radio Posta,* 3 December 1947, KNA, MAA/8/105.

111. Security Liaison Officer, East Africa, to Director General, 14 November 1947, TNA:PRO, KV2/1788; record of meeting with Awori, 20 October 1947, KNA, MAA/8/109.

112. Timothy Oberst, "Transport Workers, Strikes and the 'Imperial Response': Africa and the Post–World War II Conjuncture," *African Studies Review* 31, no. 1 (April 1988): 125.

113. Sharon B. Stichter, "Workers, Trade Unions, and the Mau Mau Rebellion," *Canadian Journal of African Studies* 9, no. 2 (1975): 259–75; Frederick Cooper, *Decolonization and African Society: The Labor Question in French and British Africa* (Cambridge: Cambridge University Press, 1996).

114. Untitled article, *Radio Posta,* 3 January 1948, KNA, MAA/8/109; Paul Kelemen, "Modernising Colonialism: The British Labour Movement and Africa," *Journal of Imperial and Commonwealth History* 34, no. 2 (2006): 230.

115. David W. Throup, "The Origins of Mau Mau," *African Affairs* 84, no. 336 (July 1985): 420.

116. Arthur Moody Awori, interview by author, Nairobi, 21 July 2008.

117. Nyanza Province Intelligence Report, 31 December 1950, TNA:PRO, WO276/381.

118. Ibid.

119. Nyanza Province Intelligence Report, November 1951, KNA, PC/NZA/3/1/38; Harry Wamubeyi, interview by author, Butere, 5 October 2007; Shem Musee, interview by author, Kona Mbaya, 22 October 2007.

120. Shem Musee, interview by author, Kona Mbaya, 22 October 2007; Lonsdale, "KAU's Cultures," 116.

121. Mwaniki, H. Muoria, *Kenyatta ni Muigwithania Witu* (Nairobi: East African Educational Publishers, 1947), as quoted in Lonsdale, "KAU's Cultures," 116.

122. North Nyanza District Commissioner to Kakamega District Officer, 3 July 1952, KNA, DC/KMG/1/1/154.

123. W. W. W. Awori, advertisement for African member of the Legislative Council, 1952, KNA, PC/NZA/3/1/64.

124. W. W. W. Awori, interview by John Spencer, 7 June 1972, Lonsdale Personal Archives.

125. "New Acting President of KAU," *East African Standard*, 11 March 1953.

126. Resolutions of the Conference of Leading Nyanza Delegates Committee, 23 November 1952, KNA, DC/KMG/1/1/154.

127. Idakho Chief to W. W. W. Awori, 22 November 1952, KNA, DC/KMG/1/1/73.

128. Nyanza African Union, Nakuru, 18 January 1953, KNA, DC/KMG/1/1/73.

129. *Nyanza Province Annual Report*, 1952.

130. Ibid.; North Nyanza Intelligence Report, October 1952, KNA, DC/KMG/1/16/1.

131. W. W. W. Awori, interview by John Spencer, 7 June 1972, Lonsdale Personal Archives; Shiraz Durrani, *Never Be Silent: Publishing and Imperialism in Kenya, 1884–1963* (London: Vita Books, 2006).

132. North Nyanza Handing Over Report, 1953, KNA, DC/NN/2/6.

133. Operation Cowslip, "Papers Taken from the possession of J. D. Otiende," [June 1953], KNA, MAA/8/120.

134. J. D. Otiende, interview by author, Mbale, 20 June 2007.

135. J. D. Otiende, interview by author, Mbale, 7 July 2008; Superintendent of Police to Assistant Commissioner of Police, 23 March 1954, KNA, GH/3/13.

136. J. D. Otiende, interview by author, Mbale, 20 June 2007.

137. Ibid.; Wanyande, *Joseph Daniel Otiende*, 24.

138. APA meeting minutes, 19 July 1952, KNA, DC/KMG/2/1/147.

139. North Nyanza Intelligence Records, 1953, KNA, GH/3/13.

140. APA meeting minutes in 1952, 4 December 1955, KNA, DC/KMG/2/1/147.

141. APA meeting minutes, 4 December 1955, KNA, DC/KMG/2/1/147, emphasis added.

142. Tamarkin, "Urban Ethnic Associations," 146.

143. Carotenuto, "Cultivating an African Community"; White, *Comforts of Home*, 190–94; Peterson, *Creative Writing*.

144. APA meeting minutes, 19 July 1952, KNA, DC/KMG/2/1/147.

145. North Nyanza Handing Over Report, January 1953, KNA, DC/NN/2/6.

146. Ibid.

147. Emergency Measures in Nyanza Province, 1953, KNA, PC/NZA/3/15/128; Law and Order, 1953, KNA, PC/NZA/3/15/135; North Nyanza District Commissioner to all chiefs, 17 July 1953, KNA, DC/KMG/1/1/144.

148. Nyanza Province Intelligence Report, February 1953, KNA, PC/NZA/3/1/38.

149. South Maragoli Hills Association to Governor, 28 May 1957, KPA, DX/21/9/2.

150. "Security Situation in Nyanza Province: Appreciation by the Kenya Intelligence Committee," 1955, TNA:PRO, CO833/809.

151. Harry Wamubeyi, interview by author, Butere, 5 October 2007.

152. North Nyanza Handing Over Report, 1953, KNA, DC/NN/2/6; "Famine in North Nyanza," editorial, *Mulina*, 10 June 1953, KNA, ARC(MAA) 2/5/155I.

153. Nyanza Province Intelligence Report, October 1952, KNA, PC/NZA/3/1/38.

154. Paul H. A. Ogula, "Political Chief: A Biography of Ex-senior Chief Mukudi of Samia and Bunyala c. 1881–1969," *Kenya Historical Review* 2, no. 2 (1974): 175–87.

155. Bunyala Association to District Commissioners of Central Nyanza, North Nyanza and Nairobi, 4 January 1957, KPA, DA/1/18.

156. "Mau Mau Identified in Fresh Kenya Tribe," *Daily Telegraph*, 13 July 1953, TNA:PRO, CO833/809.

157. Director of Intelligence to Governor, "Aggrey Minga and W. W. W. Awori Political Activities in North Nyanza," 21 January 1954, KNA, GH/1/13.

158. AWA Bunyore Branch to Nyanza Provincial Commissioner, 24 November 1947, KNA, PC/NZA/2/1/215.

159. Nyanza Provincial Commissioner to Executive Officer, African Land Utilization and Settlement, 3 March 1951, KNA, PC/NZA/3/1/493; Kanogo, *Squatters*, 105–20.

160. Kigumba settlement in Masindi Uganda, 1957, KNA, DC/KMGA/1/1/6; William Okwemba, Pascal Nabwana, and J. D. Otiende to Governor of Kenya, 20 December 1960, KNA, OP/EST/1/112.

161. William Okwemba, interview by author, Kima, 19 October 2007; Ezekiel Alembi, "The Construction of the *Abanyole* Perceptions on Death Through Oral Funeral Poetry" (PhD diss., Helsinki, 2002).

162. Director of Intelligence to Governor, "Aggrey Minga and W. W. W. Awori Political Activities in North Nyanza," 21 January 1954, KNA, GH/1/13.

163. Stichter, "Workers, Trade Unions," 259–75; "APA—BWS—Babukha," [1954], KNA, GH/1/13.

164. Director of Intelligence to Governor, "Aggrey Minga and W. W. W. Awori Political Activities in North Nyanza," 21 January 1954, KNA, GH/1/13.

165. William Okwemba, interview by author, Kima, 19 October 2007; APA meetings throughout 1954, reported in letters from Director of Intelligence and Security to Governor, KNA, GH/1/13.

166. Director of Intelligence to Governor, "APA Meeting," 5 February 1954, KNA, GH/1/13.

167. *Nyanza Province Annual Report*, 1954.

168. Private Secretary Prichard, Director of Intelligence and Security, 5 April 1954, KNA, GH/1/13; Vihiga District Officer Yunis Mahat to North Nyanza District Commissioner, "Kakamega District Detainees 1952," 27 August 1975, KPA, DX/21/6.

169. Vihiga District Officer Yunis Mahat to North Nyanza District Commissioner, "Kakamega District Detainees 1952," 27 August 1975, KPA, DX/21/6; Thika District Commissioner to North Nyanza District Commissioner, "RE: Abaluhya Restrictee," 14 July 1959, KNA, DX/21/6/1.

170. North Nyanza ADC Resolution No. 5/54, 14 April 1954, KNA, PC/NZA/3/1/99.

171. For a full account of the loyalty qualifications in Central Province, see Branch, *Defeating Mau Mau.*

172. Daniel Branch, "Loyalists, Mau Mau, and Elections in Kenya," *Africa Today* 53, no. 2 (Winter 2006): 27–50.

173. *Trans Nzoia Annual Report*, 1954; Arthur Ochwada, interview by author, Funyala, 12 October 2007; Samuel Onyango, interview by author, Matayos, 21 September 2007.

174. D. Anderson, *Histories of the Hanged*, 205.

175. *Nairobi Extra-provincial District Annual Report*, 1954.

176. Peterson, "Intellectual Lives."

177. Caroline Elkins glossed over these inter-Kikuyu politics in the camps in her study *Britain's Gulag*, 154–232.

178. James Osogo, interview by author, Port Victoria, 28 September 2007.

179. S. D. Wayo, "What Happened on January 26th, 1953," *Muluhya*, March 1958.

180. Samuel Onyango, interview by author, Matayos, 21 September 2007; Arthur Ochwada, interview by author, Funyala, 12 October 2007; William Okwemba, interview by author, Kima, 19 October 2007; Dunston Makalu, interview by author, Kaptegi, 21 October 2007.

181. W. W. W. Awori, "Behind the Headlines," *Baraza*, 30 July 1955.

182. W. W. W. Awori, "Behind the Headlines," *Baraza*, 19 November 1955.

CHAPTER 7: MAPPING DECOLONIZATION

1. "West Nyanza District," debate in Legislative Council, 19 July 1962, KNA, EN/14.

2. Ernest Renan, *Qu'est-ce qu'une nation?* trans. Ida Mae Snyder (Paris: Lévy, 1883); Tom Mboya, *The Challenge of Nationhood* (Nairobi: Praeger, 1970); Jomo Kenyatta, *Harambee! The Prime Minister of Kenya's Speeches, 1963–1964* (Nairobi: Oxford University Press, 1964).

3. Prosser Gifford and William Roger Louis, *The Transfer of Power in Africa: Decolonization, 1940–1960* (New Haven: Yale University Press, 1982); John D. Hargreaves, *Decolonization in Africa* (London: Longman, 1996).

4. Terence Ranger, "Connexions between 'Primary Resistance Movements' and Modern Mass Nationalism in East and Central Africa," *Journal of African History* 9, no. 4 (1968): 437–53, 631–41; John Lonsdale, "The Emergence of African Nations: A Historiographical Analysis," *African Affairs* 67, no. 266 (1968): 11–28.

5. Iliffe, *Africans*, 234–35; see also Justin Willis, "'A Model of Its Kind':

Representation and Performance in the Sudan Self-Government Election of 1953," *Journal of Imperial and Commonwealth History* 35, no. 3 (September 2007): 485–502; Peter Pels, "Imagining Elections: Modernity, Mediation and the Secret Ballot in Late-colonial Tanganyika," in *Cultures of Voting: The Hidden History of the Secret Ballot*, ed. Romain Bertrand, Jean-Louis Briquet, and Peter Pels (Bloomington: Indiana University Press, 2007), 100–113.

6. Lonsdale, "KAU's Cultures," 113; Lonsdale, "Moral and Political Argument," 73–95; Bethwell A. Ogot and William R. Ochieng', eds., *Decolonization and Independence in Kenya, 1940–93* (Athens: Ohio University Press, 1995); Nottingham and Rosberg, *Myth of "Mau Mau."*

7. See, for example, Miles Larmer and Erik Kennes, "Rethinking the Katangese Secession," *Journal of Imperial and Commonwealth History* 42, no. 4 (2014): 1–21; Brennan, *Taifa*; Peterson and Macola, *Recasting the Past*; Giblin and Maddox, *In Search of a Nation*.

8. A. I. Salim, "The Movement for 'Mwambao' or Coast Autonomy in Kenya, 1956–1963," *Hadith* 2 (1970): 212–28.

9. James R. Brennan, "Lowering the Sultan's Flag: Sovereignty and Decolonization in Coastal Kenya," *Comparative Studies in Society and History* 50, no. 4 (2008): 831–61.

10. Julie MacArthur, "Mapping Dissent: Greater Somalia and the Decolonization of Kenya's Northern Frontier," *African Boundaries and Independence*, Palgrave, forthcoming; "A People in Isolation," statement by Somalis in the Northern Frontier District, March 1962, U.S. National Archives and Records Administration (hereafter, NARA), Maryland, RG 84, UD 2844, box 12; *Report of the Northern Frontier District Commission* (London, 1962); Mario I. Aguilar, "Writing Biographies of Boorana: Social Histories at the Time of Kenya's Independence," *History in Africa* 23 (1996): 351–67.

11. "Masai Discuss Problems and Their Future," *East African Standard*, 23 May 1960; Lotte Hughes, "Malice in Maasailand: The Historical Roots of Current Political Struggles," *African Affairs* 104, no. 415 (2005): 207–24.

12. Tito Winyi, *To the Queen's Most Excellent Majesty the humble petition of Rukirabasaija Agutamba Omukama Sir Tito Gafabusa Winyi IV of Bunyoro-Kitara for himself and on behalf of the people of Bunyoro-Kitara* (Kampala: Sidney Press, 1958); Shane Doyle, "From Kitara to the Lost Counties: Genealogy, Land and Legitimacy in the Kingdom of Bunyoro, Western Uganda," *Social Identities: Journal for the Study of Race, Nation and Culture* 12, no. 4 (2006): 457–70.

13. Derek Peterson, "States of Mind: Political History and the Rwenzururu Kingdom, Western Uganda," in *Recasting the Past: History Writing and Political Work in Modern Africa*, ed. Derek Peterson and Giacomo Macola (Athens: Ohio University Press, 2009), 172.

14. Statement by the Hon. Dr. Nyerere to Conference of Independent African States, "The Federation of East African States," Addis Ababa, 14–24 June 1960, NARA, US Consulate Nairobi, RG 84, UD 2843, box 131.

15. Frederick Cooper, "The Ambiguities of Sovereignty: the United States and the Global Human Rights Cases of the 1940s and 1950s," in *The State of Sovereignty: Territories, Laws, Populations,* ed. Douglas Howland and Luise White (Bloomington: Indiana University Press, 2009), 94–124.

16. Owen J. M. Kalinga, "The Master Farmers' Scheme in Nyasaland, 1950–62: A Study of a Failed Attempt to Create a 'Yeoman' Class," *African Affairs* 92, no. 368 (1993): 367–87; Sara S. Berry, "Hegemony on a Shoestring: Indirect Rule and Access to Agricultural Land," *Africa: Journal of the International African Institute* 62, no. 3 (1992): 327–55; Grace Carswell, "Multiple Historical Geographies: Responses and Resistance to Colonial Conservation Schemes in East Africa," *Journal of Historical Geography* 32, no. 2 (April 2006): 398–421.

17. Peter Pels, "Creolisation in Secret: the Birth of Nationalism in Late Colonial Uluguru, Tanzania," *Africa: Journal of the International African Institute* 72, no. 1 (2002): 14.

18. R. J. M Swynnerton, *A Plan to Intensify the Development of African Agriculture in Kenya* (Nairobi: Kenya, Department of Agriculture, 1954).

19. Berman, *Control and Crisis,* 369; Angelique Haugerud, "Land Tenure and Agrarian Change in Kenya," *Africa: Journal of the International African Institute* 59, no. 1 (1989): 61–90.

20. Scott, *Seeing Like a State,* 183; *Elgon Nyanza Annual Report,* 1957.

21. Land Consolidation files, Elgon Nyanza, KPA, HB/27/9/1.

22. Craib, *Cartographic Mexico,* 166–67.

23. D. M. Wannyumba to Regional Boundaries Commission, 21 August 1962, KNA, GO/3/1/13.

24. North Nyanza Land Court cases, 1956, KNA, PC/NZA/3/15/68; North Nyanza Land Court cases, 1957–58, KPA, ATW/4/50.

25. North Nyanza District Assistant of Land Consolidation to North Nyanza District Commissioner, 16 January 1961, KNA, DC/KMG/1/16/19.

26. Keith Sorrenson, *Land Reform in the Kikuyu Country: A Study in Government Policy* (Nairobi: Oxford University Press, 1967).

27. Fiona Mackenzie, "Gender and Land Rights in Murang'a District, Kenya," *Journal of Peasant Studies* 14, no. 4 (1990): 626.

28. Swynnerton, *Plan to Intensify,* 10.

29. Feierman, *Peasant Intellectuals,* 181–203.

30. P. G. Fullerton, "Notes for the North Nyanza Annual Report, Southern Division," *North Nyanza Annual Report,* 1955.

31. North Nyanza Intelligence Report, April 1958, KNA, PC/NZA/3/1/38.

32. North Nyanza Intelligence Report, June 1956, KNA, PC/NZA/3/1/38; House of Commons Debate, *Hansard,* 1 August 1956.

33. Land Consolidation in Marama Location Report, [1958].

34. Vihiga District Officer to North Nyanza District Commissioner, April 1957, KNA, PC/NZA/3/14/4.

35. District Assistant, Land Consolidation, to North Nyanza District Commissioner, 16 January 1961, KNA, DC/KMG/1/16/19.

36. Peterson, *Ethnic Patriotism*, 138.

37. Ibid., 247.

38. *Report of the Commissioner Appointed to Enquire into the Methods for the Selection of African Representatives to the Legislative Council* (Nairobi, 1955).

39. "The Vote for Africans," *Baraza*, 14 January 1956.

40. Nyanza Provincial Commissioner to Secretary of the Abaluyia Association, 8 September 1956, KNA, PC/NZA/3/1/65.

41. *African Election—Voters Roll 1957, North and Elgon Nyanza*, Nairobi, [1957], KPA, DB/14/123.

42. James Osogo, interview by author, Port Victoria, 3 October 2007.

43. People of Maragoli to Constituencies Delimitation Commission, [July 1962], TNA:PRO, CO895/3.

44. Festus L. Shilesera, ADC councillor, to North Nyanza District Commissioner, 5 August 1960, KNA, DC/KMG/2/1/11.

45. Senior Chief Jeremiah Sepers, Isukha, to North Nyanza District Commissioner, 18 July 1961, KNA, DC/KMG/2/1/11.

46. Tachoni Union to North and Elgon Nyanza District Commissioners, 31 January 1958, KNA, DC/KMG/2/1/115.

47. Tachoni Union to North Nyanza District Commissioner, 9 May 1958, KNA, DC/KMG/2/1/115; Tachoni Union Meeting Agenda, 15 June 1958, KNA, DC/KMG/2/1/115.

48. Tachoni Welfare Association Fund to Constituencies Delimitation Commission, 5 August 1962, KNA, GO/3/1/16; Tachoni Welfare Association Fund to Nyanza Provincial Commissioner, 28 January 1963, KNA, DC/KMG/2/1/115.

49. Tachoni Union to North Nyanza District Commissioner, 18 October 1959, KNA, DC/KMG/2/1/115.

50. Nyanza Provincial Commissioner to Tachoni Union, 22 December 1958, KNA, DC/KMG/2/1/115.

51. Bukusu Union petition, 11 October 1960, KNA, OP/EST/1/111.

52. Bukusu Welfare Association to Constituencies Delimitation Commission, 14 September 1962, KNA, GO/3/1/16.

53. Bukusu Delegation c/o Chief Joseph Khaoya to Constituencies Delimitation Commission, 12 September 1962, TNA:PRO, CO895/3.

54. For a fuller history of KADU's genesis, see David M. Anderson, "'Yours in Struggle for Majimbo': Nationalism and the Party Politics of Decolonization in Kenya, 1955–64," *Journal of Contemporary History* 40, no. 3 (2005): 547–64.

55. "Voting Results," *East African Standard*, 12 March 1957; Jackton Simbuku Nyakuri, driver to Muliro during the 1957 electoral campaign, interviews by author, Kitale, 9, 16 March 2007; Simiyu Wandibba, *Masinde Muliro: A Biography* (Nairobi: East African Educational Publishers, 1996).

56. *Nyanza Province Annual Report*, 1960

57. BPU meeting agendas, 6 July 1960–13 January 1962, KNA, DC/KMG/2/1/119.

58. George Bennett and Carl G. Rosberg, *The Kenyatta Election: Kenya 1960–1961* (London: Oxford University Press, 1961), 139.

59. Musa Amalemba to Chairman of BPU, [1960], KNA, PC/NZA/4/20/3.

60. D. Anderson, "'Yours in Struggle,'" 552.

61. MacArthur, "How the West was Won," 227–41; David M. Anderson, "Majimboism: The Troubled History of an Idea," in *Our Turn to Eat! Politics in Kenya since 1950*, ed. Daniel Branch and Nic Cheeseman (Berlin, Lit Verlag, 2010), 17–43; Gary Wasserman, *Politics of Decolonization: Kenya, Europeans and the Land Issue, 1960–1965* (Cambridge: Cambridge University Press, 1976); Donald Rothchild, *Racial Bargaining in Independent Kenya* (London: Oxford University Press, 1973); Keith Kyle, *The Politics of the Independence of Kenya* (Basingstoke: Palgrave Macmillan, 1999); Bethwell A. Ogot, "The Decisive Years 1956–63," in *Decolonization and Indepedence in Kenya, 1940–93*, ed. Bethwell A. Ogot and William R. Ochieng' (Athens: Ohio University Press, 1995), 48–79.

62. Clyde Sanger and John Nottingham, "The Kenya General Election of 1963," *Journal of Modern African Studies* 2, no. 1 (March 1964): 13.

63. D. Anderson, "'Yours in Struggle,'" 547.

64. *Daily Nation*, 24 September 1961.

65. P. J. H. Okondo, "Proposals for Regional Governments and a Federal Constitution for Kenya," October 1961, TNA:PRO, CO822/2242.

66. Sanger and Nottingham, "Kenya General Election," 12.

67. Okondo, "Proposals for Regional Governments."

68. Tom Mboya, "KANU's Alternative to Regionalism," *East African Standard*, 18 October 1961.

69. *Report of the Kenya Constitutional Conference*, 1962, TNA:PRO, CO118/238.

70. Maps sent to the Regional Boundaries Commission, 1962, KNA, GO/3/1/16.

71. Claire Médard, "Les conflits 'ethniques' au Kenya: Une question de votes ou de terres?," *Afrique Contemporaine*, no. 180 (October–December 1996): 62–74; Médard, "Dispositifs électoraux et violences ethniques: Réflexions sur quelques stratégies territoriales du régime kenyan," *Politique Africaine*, no. 70 (June 1998): 32–40.

72. BPU, Mombasa to Regional Boundaries Commission, [August 1962], KNA, GO/3/1/16; testimony of Abaluyia Association in Nakuru, 31 August 1962, KNA, GO/1/2/1.

73. North Ugenya Map to the Regional Boundaries Commission, [August 1962], TNA:PRO, CO/895/6.

74. Regional Boundaries Commission, Record of the Oral Evidence, pt. 1, August 1962, KNA, GO/1/2/4.

75. Sanger and Nottingham, "Kenya General Election," 22.

76. For the history of the Kalenjin ethnic identity, see Lynch, *I Say to You*.

77. Sanger and Nottingham, "Kenya General Election," 21.

78. Maragoli Association, Kisumu, to Regional Boundaries Commission, 5 August 1962, TNA:PRO, CO897/5.

79. Uholo and Wanga Joint Committee to Regional Boundaries Commission, 2 August 1962, KNA, GO/3/1/16.

80. KANU memorandum, Western Division of Elgon Nyanza, to Regional Boundaries Commission, 4 August 1962, TNA:PRO, CO897/4.

81. North Nyanza leaders to Governor, [December 1960], KNA, OP/EST/1/112.

82. BPU to Governor, 2 January 1963, KNA, DC/KMG/2/1/2.

83. Oral testimony at Kisumu, 12 September 1962, *Report of the Regional Boundaries Commission* (London, 1962).

84. Ibid.

85. Jared Akatsa to Regional Boundaries Commission, 8 September 1962, KNA, GO/3/1/16.

86. Gray, *Colonial Rule*, 113.

87. B. Anderson, *Imagined Communities*, 185.

88. Oral testimony of BPU leader Musa Amalemba to Regional Boundaries Commission, 27 August 1962, KNA, GO/1/2/1.

89. BPU to Regional Boundaries Commission, memorandum, 27 August 1962, KNA, GO/3/1/16.

90. Ibid.

91. Oral testimony at Bungoma, 5 September 1962, *Report of the Regional Boundaries Commission* (London, 1962).

92. Oral Testimony in Nairobi, 9 August 1962, *Report of the Regional Boundaries Commission* (London, 1962).

93. BPU to the Regional Boundaries Commission, 30 August 1962, KNA, GO/3/1/13.

94. The United Maragoli of East Africa to the Regional Boundaries Commission, August 1962, KNA, GO/3/1/16.

95. Jean Marie Allman, "The Youngmen and the Porcupine: Class, Nationalism and Asante's Struggle for Self-Determination, 1954–57," *Journal of African History* 31, no. 2 (1990): 263–79; Richard Rathbone, *Nkrumah and the Chiefs: The Politics of Chieftaincy in Ghana, 1951–60* (Athens: Ohio University Press, 2000).

96. D. Anderson, "'Yours in the Struggle,'" 558.

97. BPU to Governor, 5 September 1961, KNA, OP/1/243.

98. Abaluyia members, "Re-union of Abaluyia," Kenya Constitutional Conference, memorandum, 20 March 1962, KNA, GO/1/1/12.

99. BPU to Governor, 5 September 1961, KNA, OP/1/243.

100. Sitawa Mumia, *Daily Mail*, 26 November 1962.

101. Elijah Masinde to Governor, telegram, 8 September 1961, KNA, GH/1/13.

102. Oral testimony of BPU leader Musa Amalemba to Regional Boundaries Commission, 27 August 1962, KNA, GO/1/2/1.

103. BPU, Mombasa, to Regional Boundaries Commission, [August 1962], KNA, GO/3/1/16.

104. Samia Union petition to Governor, 31 August 1961, KNA, OP/EST/1/119.

105. Buluhya Political Union Constitution, [1960], KPA, DX/21/9/2.

106. APA meeting minutes, 19 July 1952, KNA, DC/KMG/2/1/147.

107. Abaluyia Association of East Africa constitution, n.d., KNA, DC/KMG/2/1/111.

108. Uholo and Wanga Joint Committee to Regional Boundaries Commission, 2 August 1962, KNA, GO/3/1/16.

109. Wako, "Principles and Procedures," 15.

110. Osogo, *History of the Baluyia*, 4.

111. Abaluyia Mumbo, Busia, Uganda, to Governors of Uganda and Kenya, 25 January 1961, KNA, OP/EST/1/110.

112. Abaluyia Mumbo to Governor of Uganda, 9 April 1962, UNA, S10488.

113. BPU leader Musa Amalemba to Regional Boundaries Commission, oral testimony, 27 August 1962, KNA, GO/1/2/1.

114. Joint Boundary Commission on borders with Kenya and Uganda, 1961, TNA:PRO, FO371/159116.

115. Ph. Pullicino to Chief Minister, 20 February 1962, UNA, S10488.

116. Teso National Political Union to Governor, 21 July 1961, KNA, OP/EST/1/117.

117. "Abaluyia" to Governor of Kenya, 25 September 1961, KNA, GH/3/13.

118. Oral testimony at Kakamega, 19 November 1962, *Report of the Regional Boundaries Commission* (London, 1962).

119. Oral testimony at Kisumu, 9 October 1962, *Report of the Regional Boundaries Commission* (London, 1962).

120. Elijah Masinde to Regional Boundaries Commission, 4 September 1962, TNA:PRO, CO897/5.

121. Gem-Seme-Kisumu Abaluhya Union to Regional Boundaries Commission, 2 August 1962, KNA, GO/3/1/16.

122. Abaluyia of Uasin Gishu, *Report of the Regional Boundaries Commission* (London, 1962), 71.

123. Gem-Seme-Kisumu Abaluhya Union Members Demand Ratification of the Present Boundary and Ultimate Secession to North Nyanza District to Regional Boundaries Commission, 2 August 1962, KNA, GO/3/1/16.

124. BPU memorandum to the Regional Boundaries Commission, 27 August 1962, KNA, GO/3/1/16.

125. KADU to Regional Boundaries Commission, [August 1962], KNA, GO/3/1/16.

126. Samia delegation to Governor of Kenya, 16 November 1961, KNA, OP/118.

127. KADU to Chairman of the Regional Boundaries Commission, [August 1962], KNA, GO/3/1/16.

128. *Report of the Regional Boundaries Commission* (London, 1962).

129. *Nyanza Province Annual Report*, 1962.

130. AWA press release, 1 March 1963, KNA, GH/3/13.

131. BPU to Governor, 2 January 1963, KNA, DC/KMG/2/1/2.

132. Secretary of State for the Colonies, inward telegram, 28 December 1962, TNA:PRO, CO822/2538.

133. Petition to Boundary Commission, [1962], TNA:PRO, CO822/2540; Secretary of State for the Colonies, inward telegram, 28 December 1962, TNA:PRO, CO822/2538.

134. Secretary of State for the Colonies, inward telegram, 28 December 1962, TNA:PRO, CO822/2538.

135. Donald Rothchild, "Majimbo Schemes in Kenya and Uganda," in *Transition in African Politics*, ed. Jeffrey Butler and A. A. Castagno (New York: Praeger, 1967), 302–3.

136. D. Anderson, "'Yours in the Struggle,'" 562.

137. For more on how the loss of Kitale prompted the collapse of KADU, see D. Anderson, "'Yours in the Struggle'"; Sanger and Nottingham, "Kenya General Election."

138. Branch, *Kenya*, 17.

139. "Resolution on Frontiers, Boundaries, and Federation, All African Peoples' Conferences," Accra, 5–13 December 1958, reprinted in *The Ethiopia-Somali-Kenya Dispute, 1960–67: Documents*, ed. Catherine Hoskyns (Dar es Salaam: Oxford University Press, 1969).

140. Resolution AGH/ Res. 16 (1) reprinted as "Resolution on the Intangibility of Frontiers," OAU meeting, July 1964, in *Documents of the Organization of African Unity*, ed. G. J. Naldi (New York: Mansell, 1992), 49.

141. "West Nyanza District," debate in Legislative Council, 19 July 1962, KNA, EN/14.

AFTERWORD: BEYOND THE ETHNOS AND THE NATION

1. Idi Amin, *The Making of Modern Uganda* (Kampala: Government Printer, 1976).

2. "Is Amin Bluffing?," *Weekly News*, 23 February 1976; "Official Warning for Uganda: Kenya Won't Give an Inch!," *Nation*, 18 February 1976.

3. Peter Wafula Wekesa, "Old Issues and New Challenges: The Migingo Island Controversy and the Kenya-Uganda Borderland," *Journal of Eastern African Studies* 4, no. 2 (2010): 331–40.

4. Justin Willis and George Gona, "*Pwani c Kenya?* Memory, Documents and Secessionist Politics in Coastal Kenya," *African Affairs* 112, no. 446 (December 2012): 1–24.

5. Archer, *Personal and Historical Memoirs*, 35–129.

6. Ibid., 46.

7. See MacArthur, "Mapping Dissent."

8. *Report of the Northern Frontier District Commission* (London, 1962).

9. "Bring Me a Somali Raider—Dead or Alive," *Daily Nation*, Nairobi, 29 November 1963.

10. Donald Crummey, "Banditry and Resistance: Noble and Peasant in Nineteenth-Century Ethiopia," in *Banditry, Rebellion and Social Protest in Africa*, ed. Crummey (London: James Currey, 1986), 133–49.

11. Kenya Delegation to African Summit Conference, memorandum, May 1963, NARA RG 59, Office of the Eastern and Southern Africa, 1951–65, box 1.

12. See Julie MacArthur, "States of Exception: Genealogies of Sovereignty, Violence, and Belonging along the Kenya-Somali Frontier," article currently under review.

13. Ann Laura Stoler, "On Degrees of Imperial Sovereignty," *Public Culture* 18, no. 1 (2006): 128.

14. David M. Anderson, "Encountering Islam in Eastern Africa: Transnational History and Imperialism, c. 1880–1930," Global and Imperial History Research Seminar Paper, University of Oxford, 9 February 2011.

15. Simon Turner, "Suspended Spaces—Contesting Sovereignties in a Refugee Camp," in *Sovereign Bodies: Citizens, Migrants and States in the Postcolonial World*, ed. T. B. Hansen and F. Stepputat (Princeton: Princeton University Press, 2005), 312.

16. Some recent studies are attempting to redress this absence; see, for example, the work of Myles Larmer on Katanga, Derek Peterson on the Rwenzururu, and Wolfgang Zeller and Jordi Tomas, eds., *Secessionism in Africa* (New York: Palgrave Macmillan, forthcoming).

17. There was a small flurry of publications around the subject of an East African Federation in the early 1960s, but this scholarship dried up by the late 1960s. See for example, Carl G. Rosberg, Jr., with Aaron Segal, *An East African Federation* (New York: Carnegie Endowment for International Peace, 1963).

18. Frederick Cooper, *Citizenship between Empire and Nation: Remaking France and French Africa, 1945–1960* (Princeton: Princeton University Press, 2014), 25.

19. Christopher Vaughan, Mareike Schomerus and Lotje de Vries, eds., *The Borderlands of South Sudan: Authority and Identity in Contemporary and Historical Perspectives* (New York: Palgrave Macmillian, 2013).

20. See, for example, the work of Pierre Englebert and his upcoming chapter with Heather Byrne, "Shifting Grounds for African Secessionism?," in Zeller and Tomas, *Secessionism in Africa*.

21. For more the history and culture of political pluralism in western Kenya, see MacArthur, "How the West Was Won," 227–41.

22. W. W. W. Awori, "Behind the Headlines," *Baraza*, 15 October 1955.

23. David W. Throup and Charles Hornsby, *Multi-party Politics in Kenya: The Kenyatta and Moi States and the Triumph of the System in the 1992 Election* (Athens: Ohio University Press, 1998), 518.

24. Kanyoro, "Post-research Experience," 103–4.

25. See Lonsdale, "Moral Ethnicity," 131–50; Berman, "Ethnicity, Patronage and the African State: The Politics of Uncivil Nationalism," *African Affairs* 97, no. 388 (1998): 305–41.

26. Lonsdale, "Moral and Political Argument," 94–95.

27. http://www.standardmedia.co.ke/ktn/video/watch/2000069230/n-a.

Bibliography

ARCHIVAL SOURCES

Anglican Church of Kenya (ACK), Nairobi, Kenya
British and Foreign Bible Society (BFBS), University of Cambridge, Cambridge, UK
Church Missionary Society (CMS), Birmingham, UK
Friends African Mission, East African Yearly Meetings Archives, Kaimosi, Kenya
Friends United Mission (FUM), Earlham College, Richmond, Indiana, USA
International African Institute Archives (IAI), London School of Economics, London, UK
Kakamega Provincial Archives (KPA), Kakamega, Kenya
Kenya National Archives (KNA), Nairobi, Kenya
John Lonsdale Personal Archives, Trinity College, University of Cambridge, Cambridge, UK
Library of Congress, Washington, DC, USA
The National Archives: Public Records Office (TNA:PRO), Kew Gardens, London, UK
Rhodes House Library, University of Oxford, Oxford, UK
Uganda National Archives (UNA), Entebbe, Uganda
US National Archives and Records Administration (NARA), Maryland, Virginia, USA

ORAL INTERVIEWS

Perus Angaya Abura. Kakamega, 9 July 2008, 6 October 2009.
Samuel Aluda. Mungavo, 21 October 2007.
Moses Shiroko Atsolo. Khwisero, 5 October 2007.
Arthur Moody Awori. Nairobi, 21 July 2008.
Paulo Chemyati. Bokoli, 13 March 2007.
Bukusu elders (group interview). Bokoli, 13 March 2007.
Francis Chogo. Mbale, 27 September 2007.
Johnstone Kadima. Butere, 5 October 2007.
Francis Malika Lubana. Butere, 5 October 2007.
Welis Lukalia Lumati. Kaptegi, 21 October 2007.
Dunston Makalu. Kaptegi, 21 October 2007.

Benedict Oguto Makhulo. Port Victoria, 14 October 2007.

Marama elders (group interview). Butere, 5 October 2007.

Gerald Masibayi. Bumala, 4 October 2007.

Chestimoa Masinde. Kimilili, 10 October 2007.

Elijah Masinde's family, former Dini ya Msambwa members (group interviews). Kimilili, 10, 11 October 2007.

Philip Masinde. Bwamani, 17 September 2007.

George Muliro. Kitale, 7 March 2007.

Batholemeo Munoko ("Mzee Mombasa"). Kiminini, 16 March 2007.

Shem Musee. Kona Mbaya, 22 October 2007.

Burudi Nabwera. Kiminini, 23 October 2007.

Elizabeth Nahomeja. Kimilili, 10 October 2007.

Gertrude Naliaka. Kimilili, 10 October 2007.

Samson Wasike Nandasuba. Bokoli, 13 March 2007.

William Khemba Nandasuba. Bokoli, 13 March 2007.

Haini Nanjala. Kimilili, 10 October 2007.

Sarah Nayaman. Kimilili, 11 October 2007.

Jackton Simbuku Nyakuri. Kitale, 9, 16 March 2007.

Arthur Ochwada. Funyala, 12 October 2007.

Joshua Odango. Khayega, 24 September 2007.

William Okwemba. Kima, 19 October 2007.

Samuel Onyango. Matayos, 21 September 2007.

Julius Kakai Opicho. Bokoli, 13 March 2007.

James Otala Opuka. Butere, 5 October 2007.

James Osogo. Port Victoria, 3 October 2007.

J. D. Otiende. Mbale, 20 June, 9 October 2007, 7 July 2008.

Zacharia Shimechero. Kakamega, 25 June 2007.

Julius Sikala. Bokoli, 13 March 2007.

Tiriki elders (group interview). Kaptegi, 21 October 2007.

Mark Nyongera Udoto. Ambundo, 23 September 2007.

Richard Wafula. Kimilili, 10 October 2007.

Paul Wamatuba. Bungoma, 20, 25 September 2007.

Harry Wamubeyi. Butere, 5 October 2007.

Chief Ali Wamukoya. Mumias, 19 September 2007.

Mama Wangamati. Webuye, 17 October 2007.

Patrick Wangamati. Webuye, 17 October 2007.

Wanyama Waseme. Kimilili, 10 October 2007.

PRINTED PRIMARY SOURCES

ANNUAL REPORTS

Elgon Nyanza Annual Reports
Kavirondo Province Annual Reports
Kenya Mines Department Annual Reports

Kisumu Province Annual Reports
Nairobi Extra-Provincial District Annual Reports
Nairobi Municipal Native Affairs Office Annual Reports
North Kavirondo Annual Reports
North Nyanza Annual Reports
Nyanza Province Annual Reports
Rift Valley Province Annual Reports
Trans Nzoia Annual Reports
Uasin Gishu Annual Reports
West Pokot Annual Reports

OFFICIAL PUBLICATIONS

African Election—Voters Roll 1957, North and Elgon Nyanza (Nairobi, [1957])
African Population of Kenya Colony and Protectorate, Population Census 1948,
    East Africa Statistical Department (Nairobi, 1950)
Hansard, House of Commons Parliamentary Debates
Hansard, House of Lords Parliamentary Debates
Kenya Land Commission Evidence, vol. 3 (Nairobi, 1934)
Kenya Legislative Council Debates
Kenya Political Map (Nairobi, 1958)
Report of the Commissioner Appointed to Enquire into the Methods for the
    Selection of African Representatives to the Legislative Council (Nairobi,
    1955)
Report of the Commission of Inquiry into the Affray at Kolloa, Baringo (Nairobi,
    1950)
Report of the Kenya Constitutional Conference (London, 1962)
Report of the Kenya Land Commission (London, 1934)
Report of the Northern Frontier District Commission (London, 1962)
Report of the Regional Boundaries Commission (London, 1962)

PERIODICALS

Baraza (Nairobi)
Daily Mail (London)
Daily Nation (Nairobi)
Daily Telegraph (London)
East African Standard (Nairobi)
Evening Standard (London)
Habari (Nairobi)
Habari za dunia (Nairobi)
Kenya Weekly News (Nairobi)
Labour Magazine (London)
Makerere College Magazine (Kampala)
Makerere Journal (Kampala)
Mulina (Nairobi)

Muluhya (Kampala)
Nation (Nairobi)
Ngao (Nairobi)
North Kavirondo News (Nairobi)
Omwoyo Kwomuluyia (Nairobi)
People (Nairobi)
Radio Posta (Nairobi)
Sauti ya Mwafrika (Nairobi)
Standard (Nairobi)
Star (Nairobi)
Weekly News (Nairobi)

BOOKS AND ARTICLES

Abwunza, Judith M. "Ethnonationalism and Nationalism Strategies: The Case of the Avalogoli in Western Kenya." In *Ethnicity and Aboriginality*, edited by Michael Levin, 127–54. Toronto: University of Toronto Press, 1993.

Adas, Michael. *Prophets of Rebellion: Millenarian Protest Movements against the European Colonial Order.* Cambridge: Cambridge University Press, 1987.

Aguilar, Mario I. "Writing Biographies of Boorana: Social Histories at the Time of Kenya's Independence." *History in Africa* 23 (1996): 351–67.

Alegi, Peter. *African Soccerscapes: How a Continent Changed the World's Game.* Athens: Ohio University Press, 2010.

Alembi, Ezekiel. "The Construction of the *Abanyole* Perceptions on Death through Oral Funeral Poetry." PhD diss., Helsinki, 2002.

———. *Elijah Masinde: Rebel with a Cause.* Nairobi: Sasa Sema Publications, 2000.

Allman, Jean Marie. "The Youngmen and the Porcupine: Class, Nationalism and Asante's Struggle for Self-Determination, 1954–57." *Journal of African History* 31, no. 2 (1990): 263–79.

Allman, Jean, Susan Geiger, and Nakanyike Musisi, eds. *Women in African Colonial Histories.* Bloomington: Indiana University Press, 2002.

Ambler, Charles H. *Kenyan Communities in the Age of Imperialism: The Central Region in the Late Nineteenth Century.* New Haven: Yale University Press, 1988.

Amin, Idi. *The Shaping of Modern Uganda.* Kampala: Government Printer, 1976.

Anderson, Benedict. *Imagined Communities.* London: Verso, 1983.

Anderson, David M. "Depression, Dust Bowl, Demography, and Drought: The Colonial State and Soil Conservation in East Africa during the 1930s." *African Affairs* 83, no. 332 (July 1984): 321–43.

———. "Encountering Islam in Eastern Africa: Transnational History and Imperialism, c. 1880–1930." Global and Imperial History Research Seminar Paper, University of Oxford, 9 February 2011.

———. *Histories of the Hanged: The Dirty War in Kenya and the End of Empire.* London: Weidenfeld and Nicolson, 2005.

———. "Majimboism: The Troubled History of an Idea." In *Our Turn to Eat! Politics in Kenya since 1950,* edited by Daniel Branch, Nic Cheeseman, and Leigh Gardner, 17–43. Berlin: Lit Verlag, 2010.

———. "Stock Theft and Moral Economy in Colonial Kenya." *Africa: Journal of the International African Institute* 56, no. 4 (1986): 399–416.

———. "'Yours in Struggle for Majimbo': Nationalism and the Party Politics of Decolonization in Kenya, 1955–64." *Journal of Contemporary History* 40, no. 3 (2005): 547–64.

Anderson, David M., and Douglas H. Johnson, eds. *Revealing Prophets: Prophecy in Eastern African History.* Athens: Ohio University Press, 1995.

Andreassen, Bård-Anders, and Arne Tostensen. "Of Oranges and Bananas: The 2005 Kenya Referendum on the Constitution." Chr. Michelsen Institute Working Paper 13, 2006, 1–20. http://aceproject.org/ero-en/regions/africa /KE/http___www-cmi-no_pdf__file-_publications_2006_wp_wp2006 -13.pdf.

Appiah, Kwame Anthony. *Cosmopolitanism: Ethics in a World of Strangers.* New York: Norton, 2006.

———. "Cosmopolitan Patriots." *Critical Inquiry* 23, no. 3 (Spring 1977): 617–39.

Appleby, L. L. *A First Luyia Grammar, with Exercises.* Nairobi: CMS, 1947.

———. *Luyia-English Vocabulary.* Nairobi: CMS, 1943.

———. "Luyia Old Testament Translation, Part I: Unifying the Written Form of the Language." *Bible Translator* 6, no. 4 (1955), 180–85.

———. "Luyia Old Testament Translation, Part II: The Work of the Translation Committee." *Bible Translator* 7, no. 1 (1956): 25–30.

———. "Luyia Old Testament Translation, Part III: Some Problems in Translation." *Bible Translator* 7, no. 2 (1956): 85–90.

———. "Luyia Old Testament Translation, Part IV: Translation and People." *Bible Translator* 7, no. 3 (1956): 101–4.

Archer, Geoffrey. *Personal and Historical Memoirs of an East African Administrator.* Edinburgh: Oliver and Boyd, 1963.

Atieno Odhiambo, E. S. "The Formative Years." In Ogot and Ochieng', *Decolonization and Independence,* 25–47.

Atieno Odhiambo, E. S., and John Lonsdale, eds. *Mau Mau and Nationhood: Arms, Authority, and Narration.* Athens: Ohio University Press, 2003.

Atkins, Keletso. *The Moon Is Dead! Give Us Our Money! The Cultural Origins of an African Work Ethic, Natal, South Africa, 1843–1900.* Portsmouth, NH: Heinemann, 1993.

Bak Rasmussen, Ane Marie. *A History of the Quaker Movement in Africa.* London: British Academic Press, 1994.

Barber, Karin, ed. *Africa's Hidden Histories: Everyday Literacy and Making the Self.* Bloomington: Indiana University Press, 2006.

Barth, Fredrik. *Ethnic Groups and Boundaries: The Social Organization of Culture Difference*. Long Grove, IL: Waveland Press, 1969.

Bastin, Yvonne. "The Interlacustrine Zone (Zone J)." In *The Bantu Languages*, edited by Derek Nurse and Gérard Philippson, 501–28. London: Routledge, 2003.

Bayart, Jean-François. *The State in Africa: The Politics of the Belly*. London: Longman, 1993.

Beachey, R. W. *A History of East Africa, 1592–1902*. London: I. B. Taurus, 1996.

Bennett, George, and Carl G. Rosberg. *The Kenyatta Election: Kenya 1960–1961*. London: Oxford University Press, 1961.

Berman, Bruce. *Control and Crisis in Colonial Kenya: The Dialectic of Domination*. Athens: Ohio University Press, 1990.

———. "Ethnicity, Patronage and the African State: The Politics of Uncivil Nationalism." *African Affairs* 97, no. 388 (1998): 305–41.

———. "Ethnography as Politics, Politics as Ethnography: Kenyatta, Malinowski and the Making of *Facing Mount Kenya*." *Canadian Journal of African Studies* 30, no. 3 (1996): 313–44.

———. "Nationalism, Ethnicity, and Modernity: The Paradox of Mau Mau." *Canadian Journal of African Studies* 25, no. 2 (1991): 181–206.

Berman, Bruce, Dickson Eyoh, and Will Kymlicka, eds. *Ethnicity and Democracy in Africa*. Athens: Ohio University Press, 2004.

Berman, Bruce, and John Lonsdale, eds. *Unhappy Valley: Conflict in Kenya and Africa, Book One: State and Class*. Athens: Ohio University Press, 1992.

Bersselaar, Dmitri van den. "Creating 'Union Ibo': Missionaries and the Igbo Language." *Africa: Journal of the International African Institute* 67, no. 2 (1997): 273–95.

Berry, Sara S. *Chiefs Know Their Boundaries: Essays on Property, Power, and the Past in Asante, 1896–1996*. Portsmouth, NH: Heinemann, 2001.

———. "Hegemony on a Shoestring: Indirect Rule and Access to Agricultural Land." *Africa: Journal of the International African Institute* 62, no. 3 (1992): 327–55.

———. *No Condition Is Permanent: The Social Dynamics of Agrarian Change in Sub-Saharan Africa*. Madison: University of Wisconsin Press, 1993.

Bianco, Barbara A. "Songs of Mobility in West Pokot." *American Ethnologist* 23, no. 1 (February 1996): 25–42.

Bode, Francis. "Anti-colonial Politics within a Tribe: The Case of the Abaluyia of Western Kenya." In *Politics and Leadership in Africa*, edited by Aloo Ojuka and William Ochieng', 85–135. Kampala: East African Literature Bureau, 1975.

———. "Leadership and Politics among the Abaluyia of Kenya, 1894–1963." PhD diss., Yale University, 1978.

Bogonko, Sorobea N. *Kenya 1945–63: A Study in African National Movements*. Nairobi: Kenya Literature Bureau, 1980.

Bohannan, Paul. "Homicide and Suicide in North Kavirondo." In *African Homicide and Suicide,* edited by Bohannan, 154–78. Princeton: Princeton University Press, 1960.

Branch, Daniel. *Defeating Mau Mau, Creating Kenya: Counterinsurgency, Civil War, and Decolonization.* Cambridge: Cambridge University Press, 2009.

———. "The Enemy Within: Loyalists and the War against Mau Mau in Kenya." *Journal of African History* 48, no. 2 (2007): 291–315.

———. *Kenya: Between Hope and Despair, 1963–2011.* New Haven: Yale University Press, 2011.

———. "Loyalists, Mau Mau, and Elections in Kenya." *Africa Today* 53, no. 2 (Winter 2006): 27–50.

Bravman, Bill. *Making Ethnic Ways: Communities and Their Transformations in Taita, Kenya, 1800–1950.* Portsmouth, NH: Heinemann, 1998.

Brennan, James R. "Lowering the Sultan's Flag: Sovereignty and Decolonization in Coastal Kenya." *Comparative Studies in Society and History* 50, no. 4 (2008): 831–61.

———. *Taifa: Making Nation and Race in Urban Tanzania.* Athens: Ohio University Press, 2012.

Brubaker, Rogers, and Frederick Cooper. "Beyond 'Identity.'" *Theory and Society* 29, no. 1 (2000): 1–47.

Brückner, Martin. *The Geographic Revolution in Early America: Maps, Literacy, and National Identity.* Chapel Hill: University of North Carolina Press, 2006.

Bryk, Felix. *Neger-Eros: Ethnologische Studien über das Sexualleben bei Negern.* Berlin: A. Marcus and E. Weber, 1928.

Bulimo, Shadrack Amakoye. *Luyia Nation: Origins, Clans and Taboos.* Bloomington, IN: Trafford Publishing, 2013.

———. *Luyia of Kenya: A Cultural Profile.* Bloomington, IN: Trafford Publishing, 2013.

Bunker, Stephen G. *Peasants against the State: The Politics of Market Control in Bugisu, Uganda, 1900–1983.* Urbana: University of Illinois Press, 1987.

Cannadine, David. *Ornamentalism: How the British Saw Their Empire.* Oxford: Oxford University Press, 2001.

Carotenuto, Matthew. "Cultivating an African Community: The Luo Union in 20th Century East Africa." PhD diss., Indiana University, 2006.

———. "Repatriation in Colonial Kenya: African Institutions and Gendered Violence." *International Journal of African Historical Studies* 45, no. 1 (2012): 9–28.

———. "Riwruok e teko: Cultivating Identity in Colonial and Postcolonial Kenya." *Africa Today* 53, no. 2 (Winter 2006): 53–73.

Carswell, Grace. "Multiple Historical Geographies: Responses and Resistance to Colonial Conservation Schemes in East Africa." *Journal of Historical Geography* 32, no. 2 (April 2006): 398–421.

Chanock, Martin. *Law, Custom and Social Order: The Colonial Experience in Malawi and Zambia.* Cambridge: Cambridge University Press, 1985.

Chatterjee, Partha. *Nationalist Thought and the Colonial World: A Derivative Discourse?* London: Zed Books, 1986.

Cheeseman, Nic. "Introduction: Political Linkage and Political Space in the Era of Decolonization." *Africa Today* 53, no. 2 (Winter 2006): 3–24.

Christie, Thomas. "Criminal Lunatics and the Crime of Arson." *British Medical Journal* 25, no. 1 (January 1930): 162–3.

Clough, Marshall S. *Fighting Two Sides: Kenyan Chiefs and Politicians, 1918–1940.* Niwot: University Press of Colorado, 1990.

Cohen, David William. "The Cultural Topography of a 'Bantu Borderland': Busoga, 1500–1850." *Journal of African History* 29, no. 1 (1988): 57–79.

Cohen, David William, and E. S. Atieno Odhiambo. "Ayany, Malo, and Ogot: Historians in Search of a Luo Nation." *Cahiers d'Études Africaines* 27, nos. 3–4 (1987): 269–86.

——. *Burying SM: The Politics of Knowledge and the Sociology of Power in Africa.* Portsmouth, NH: Heinemann, 1992.

——. *Siaya: The Historical Anthropology of an African Landscape.* Athens: Ohio University Press, 1989.

Comaroff, John L., and Jean Comaroff. *Ethnicity, Inc.* Chicago: University of Chicago Press, 2009.

Cooper, Barbara. "Oral Sources and the Challenge of African History." In *Writing African History*, edited by John Edward Philips, 191–215. Rochester: University of Rochester Press, 2005.

Cooper, Frederick. "The Ambiguities of Sovereignty: the United States and the Global Human Rights Cases of the 1940s and 1950s." In *The State of Sovereignty: Territories, Laws, Populations*, edited by Douglas Howland and Luise White, 94–124. Bloomington: Indiana University Press, 2009.

——. *Citizenship between Empire and Nation: Remaking France and French Africa, 1945–1960.* Princeton: Princeton University Press, 2014.

——. *Decolonization and African Society: The Labor Question in French and British Africa.* Cambridge: Cambridge University Press, 1996.

Cory, Hans, and M. M. Hartnoll. *Customary Law of the Haya Tribe, Tanganyika Territory.* London: P. Lund, Humphries and Co., 1945.

Craib, Raymond B. *Cartographic Mexico: A History of State Fixations and Fugitive Landscapes.* Durham: Duke University Press, 2004.

Crummey, Donald. "Banditry and Resistance: Noble and Peasant in Nineteenth-century Ethiopia." In *Banditry, Rebellion and Social Protest in Africa*, edited by Crummey, 133–49. London: James Currey, 1986.

Curzon, George, Lord of Kedleston. "Text of the 1907 Romanes Lecture on the Subject of Frontiers." https://www.dur.ac.uk/resources/ibru/resources/links/curzon.pdf.

Darby, Paul. "Football, Colonial Doctrine and Indigenous Resistance: Mapping the Political Persona of FIFA's African Constituency." In *The*

Decolonization Reader, edited by James D. Le Sueur, 358–73. New York: Routledge, 2003.

Dealing, James. "Politics in Wanga, Kenya, c. 1650–1914." PhD diss., Northwestern University, 1974.

Dorman, Sara, Daniel Hammett, and Paul Nugent, eds. *Making Nations, Creating Strangers: States and Citizenship in Africa*. Leiden: Brill, 2007.

Doyle, Shane. *Crisis and Decline in Bunyoro: Population and Environment in Western Uganda, 1860–1955*. Athens: Ohio University Press, 2006.

———. "From Kitara to the Lost Counties: Genealogy, Land and Legitimacy in the Kingdom of Bunyoro, Western Uganda." *Social Identities: Journal for the Study of Race, Nation and Culture* 12, no. 4 (2006): 457–70.

Draper, Jonathan, ed. *Orality, Literacy, and Colonialism in Southern Africa*. Atlanta: Society of Biblical Literature, 2003.

Durrani, Shiraz. *Never Be Silent: Publishing and Imperialism in Kenya, 1884–1963*. London: Vita Books, 2006.

Edney, Matthew H. *Mapping an Empire: The Geographical Construction of British India*. Chicago: University of Chicago Press, 1997.

Ehret, Christopher. *An African Classical Age: Eastern and Southern Africa in World History, 1000 B.C. to A.D. 400*. Charlottesville: University Press of Virginia, 1998.

Eliot, Charles. *The East African Protectorate*. London: E. Arnold, 1905.

Elkins, Caroline. *Britain's Gulag: The Brutal End of Empire in Kenya*. London: Pimlico, 2005.

Engel, Ulf, and Paul Nugent. *Respacing Africa*. Leiden: Brill, 2010.

Fair, Laura. "Kickin' It: Leisure, Politics and Football in Colonial Zanzibar, 1900s–1950s." *Africa: Journal of the International African Institute* 67, no. 2 (1997): 224–51.

———. *Pastimes and Politics: Culture, Community, and Identity in Post-abolition Zanzibar, 1890–1945*. Athens: Ohio University Press, 2001)

Fearn, Hugh. *An African Economy: A Study of the Economic Development of the Nyanza Province of Kenya, 1903–1953*. London: Oxford University Press, 1961.

Feierman, Steven. *Peasant Intellectuals: Anthropology and History in Tanzania*. Madison: University of Wisconsin Press, 1990.

Finnegan, Ruth. *The Oral and Beyond: Doing Things with Words in Africa*. Oxford: James Currey, 2007.

Flynn, Laurie. *Studded with Diamonds and Paved with Gold: Miners, Mining Companies and Human Rights in Southern Africa*. London: Bloomsbury, 1992.

Foley, W. A. *Anthropological Linguistics*. Oxford: Wiley, 1997.

Ford, John. *The Role of Trypanosomiases in African Ecology: A Study of the Tsetse Fly Problem*. London: Oxford University Press, 1971.

Foucault, Michel. "Questions on Geography." In *Power/Knowledge: Selected Interviews and Other Writings, 1972–1977*, edited by Colin Gordon, 63–77. New York: Pantheon, 1980.

Fulford, Ben. "An Igbo Esperanto: A History of the Union Ibo Bible 1900–1950." *Journal of Religion in Africa* 32, no. 4 (November 2002): 457–501.

Gadsden, Fay. "The African Press in Kenya, 1945–1952." *Journal of African History* 21, no. 4 (1980): 515–35.

Geiger, Susan. *TANU Women: Gender and Culture in the Making of Tanganyikan Nationalism, 1955–1965*. Portsmouth, NH: Heinemann, 1997.

Gengenbach, Heidi. *Binding Memories: Women as Makers and Tellers of History in Magunde, Mozambique*. New York: Columbia University Press, 2005. http://www.gutenberg-e.org/geh01/.

———. "'I'll Bury You in the Border!': Women's Land Struggles in Post-war Facazisse (Magude District), Mozambique." *Journal of Southern African Studies* 24, no. 1 (March 1998): 7–36.

Giblin, James L. *A History of the Excluded: Making Family a Refuge from the State in Twentieth-Century Tanzania*. With Blandian Kaduma Giblin. Athens: Ohio University Press, 2006.

———. *The Politics of Environmental Control in Northeastern Tanzania, 1840–1940*. Philadelphia: University of Pennsylvania Press, 1992.

Giblin, James L., and Gregory H. Maddox, eds. *In Search of a Nation: Histories of Authority and Dissidence in Tanzania*. Athens: Ohio University Press, 2005.

Gifford, Prosser, and William Roger Louis. *The Transfer of Power in Africa: Decolonization, 1940–1960*. New Haven: Yale University Press, 1982.

Gilbert, David, David Matless, and Brian Short, eds. *Geographies of British Modernity: Space and Society in the Twentieth Century*. RGS-IBG Book Series. Oxford: Blackwell, 2003.

Gilpin, Clifford. "The Church and the Community: Quakers in Western Kenya, 1902–1963." PhD diss., Columbia University, 1976.

Glassman, Jonathan. "Creole Nationalists and the Search for Nativist Authenticity in Twentieth-Century Zanzibar: The Limits of Cosmopolitanism?" *Journal of African History* 55, no. 2 (2014): 229–57.

———. *War of Words, War of Stones: Racial Thought and Violence in Colonial Zanzibar*. Bloomington: Indiana University Press, 2011.

Goldthorpe, J. E. *An African Elite: Makerere College Students 1922–1960*. Nairobi: Oxford University Press, 1965.

Goscha, Christopher. *Vietnam or Indochina? Contesting Concepts of Space in Vietnamese Nationalism, 1887–1954*. Copenhagen: NIAS Books, 1995.

Gray, Christopher. *Colonial Rule and Crisis in Equatorial Africa: Southern Gabon ca. 1850–1940*. Rochester: University of Rochester Press, 2002.

Gregory, Derek. *Geographical Imaginations*. Cambridge: Blackwell, 1993.

Hailey, Lord William. *Native Administration in the British Territories, Part I*. London: His Majesty's Stationery Office, 1950.

Hakansson, N. Thomas. "Grain, Cattle, and Power: Social Processes of Intensive Cultivation and Exchange in Precolonial Western Kenya." *Journal of Anthropological Research* 50, no. 3 (Autumn 1994): 249–76.

Hanson, Holly. *Landed Obligation: The Practice of Power in Buganda.* Portsmouth, NH: Heinemann, 2003.

——. "Mapping Conflict: Heterarchy and Accountability in the Ancient Capital of Buganda." *Journal of African History* 50, no. 2 (2009): 179–202.

Hargreaves, John D. *Decolonization in Africa.* London: Longman, 1996.

Harries, Patrick. *Butterflies and Barbarians: Swiss Missionaries and Systems of Knowledge in South-East Africa.* Athens: Ohio University Press, 2007.

——. "Exclusion, Classification and Internal Colonialism: The Emergence of Ethnicity among the Tsonga-Speakers of South Africa." In Vail, *Creation of Tribalism,* 82–117.

——. "The Roots of Ethnicity: Discourse and the Politics of Language Construction in South-East Africa." *African Affairs* 87, no. 346 (January 1988): 25–52.

Hartwig, Gerald W. "Demographic Considerations in East Africa during the Nineteenth Century." *International Journal of African Historical Studies* 12, no. 4 (1979): 653–72.

Harvey, P. D. A. *Maps in Tudor England.* Chicago: University of Chicago Press, 1993.

Hastings, Adrian. *The Construction of Nationhood: Ethnicity, Religion, and Nationalism.* Cambridge: Cambridge University Press, 1997.

Haugerud, Angelique. "Land Tenure and Agrarian Change in Kenya." *Africa: Journal of the International African Institute* 59, no. 1 (1989): 61–90.

Hawkins, Sean. *Writing and Colonialism in Northern Ghana: The Encounter between the LoDagaa and "the World on Paper,"* 1892–1991. Toronto: University of Toronto Press, 2002.

Hay, Margaret Jean. "Changes in Clothing and Struggles over Identity in Colonial Western Kenya." In *Fashioning Africa: Power and the Politics of Dress,* edited by Jean Marie Allman, 67–83. Bloomington: Indiana University Press, 2004.

——. "Local Trade and Ethnicity in Western Kenya." *African Economic History Review* 2, no. 1 (Spring 1975): 7–12.

Hay, Margaret Jean, and Marcia Wright, eds. *African Women and the Law: Historical Perspectives.* Boston: Boston University, African Studies Center, 1982.

Heald, Suzette. *Controlling Anger: The Sociology of Gisu Violence.* Manchester: Manchester University Press, 1989.

Hill, Jonathan D., ed. *History, Power, and Identity: Ethnogenesis in the Americas, 1492–1992.* Iowa City: University of Iowa Press, 1996.

Hippel, E. V. "Kavirondo." *Uganda Journal* 10, no. 2 (September 1946): 166–68.

Hobley, C. W. "British East Africa: Anthropological Studies in Kavirondo and Nandi." *Journal of the Anthropological Institute of Great Britain and Ireland* 33 (July–December 1903): 325–59.

——. *Eastern Uganda: An Ethnological Survey.* London: Anthropological Institute of Great Britain and Ireland, 1902.

———. "Kavirondo." *Geographical Journal* 12, no. 4 (1896): 361–72.

———. *Kenya: From Chartered Company to Crown Colony; Thirty Years of Exploration and Administration in British East Africa.* London: Frank Cass, 1970.

Hodgson, Dorothy L. *Being Maasai, Becoming Indigenous: Postcolonial Politics in a Neoliberal World.* Bloomington: Indiana University Press, 2011.

Hodgson, Dorothy L., and Sheryl A. McCurdy, eds. *"Wicked" Women and the Reconfiguration of Gender in Africa.* Portsmouth, NH: Heinemann, 2001.

Hodgson, Dorothy L., and Richard A. Schroeder. "Dilemmas of Counter-mapping Community Resources in Tanzania." *Development and Change* 33, no. 1 (2002): 79–100.

Hoehler-Fatton, Cynthia. *Women of Fire and Spirit: History, Faith, and Gender in Roho Religion in Western Kenya.* Oxford: Oxford University Press, 1996.

Hoskyns, Catherine, ed. *The Ethiopia-Somali-Kenya Dispute, 1960–67: Documents.* Dar es Salaam: Oxford University Press, 1969.

Howard, Allen M. "Nodes, Networks, Landscapes and Regions: Reading the Social History of Tropical Africa, 1700s–1920." In Howard and Shain, *Spatial Factor in African History,* 21–140.

Howard, Allen M., and Richard M. Shain, eds. *The Spatial Factor in African History: The Relationship of the Social, Material and Perceptual.* Leiden: Brill, 2005.

Hughes, Lotte. "Malice in Maasailand: The Historical Roots of Current Political Struggles." *African Affairs* 104, no. 415 (2005): 207–24.

Hunter, Emma. "In Pursuit of the 'Higher Medievalism': Local History and Politics in Kilimanjaro." In Peterson and Macola, *Recasting the Past,* 149–70.

———. "Languages of Politics in Twentieth Century Kilimanjaro." PhD diss., University of Cambridge, 2008.

Huntingford, G. W. B. *The Eastern Tribes of the Bantu Kavirondo.* Nairobi: CMS, 1944.

Hutchinson, Sharon E. *Nuer Dilemmas: Coping with Money, War, and the State.* Berkeley: University of California Press, 1996.

Iliffe, John. *Africans: The History of a Continent.* Cambridge: Cambridge University Press, 1995.

———. *Honour in African History.* Cambridge: Cambridge University Press, 2005.

———. *A Modern History of Tanganyika.* Cambridge: Cambridge University Press, 1979.

Ingham, Kenneth. "Uganda's Old Eastern Province: The Transfer to East Africa Protectorate in 1902." *Uganda Journal* 21, no. 1 (March 1957): 41–46.

International Institute of African Languages and Cultures. *Practical Orthography of African Languages.* London: The Institute, 1930.

Isaacman, Allen F., and Barbara S. Isaacman. *Slavery and Beyond: The Making of Men and Chikunda Ethnic Identities in the Unstable World of South-Central Africa, 1750–1920.* Portsmouth, NH: Heinemann, 2004.

Itebete, P. A. N. "Language Standardization in Western Kenya." In Whiteley, *Language in Kenya,* 87–114.

Jackson, Frederick. *Early Days in East Africa.* London: Edward Arnold, 1930.

Jameson, Fredric. "Cognitive Mapping." In *Marxism and the Interpretation of Culture,* edited by Cary Nelson and Lawrence Grossberg, 347–57. Urbana: University of Illinois Press, 1988.

Jeeves, Alan H. *Migrant Labour in South Africa's Mining Economy: The Struggle for the Gold Mines' Labour Supply 1890–1920.* Montreal: McGill-Queen's University Press, 1985.

Jeffers, Chike. "Appiah's Cosmopolitanism." *Southern Journal of Philosophy* 51, no. 4 (December 2013): 488–510.

Jennings, Michael. "'A Very Real War': Popular Participation in Development in Tanzania during the 1950s and 1960s." *International Journal of African Historical Studies* 40, no. 1 (2007): 71–95.

Johnston, Harry. *The Uganda Protectorate.* 2 vols. London: Hutchinson, 1902.

———. "The Uganda Protectorate, Ruwenzori, and the Semliki Forest." *Geographical Journal* 19, no. 1 (January 1902): 1–39.

Kakai, Pius Wanyonyi. "Social Concepts in the Initiation Rituals of the Abatachoni: A Historical Study." Master's diss., Kenyatta University, 1992.

Kalinga, Owen J. M. "The Master Farmers' Scheme in Nyasaland, 1950–62: A Study of a Failed Attempt to Create a 'Yeoman' Class." *African Affairs* 92, no. 368 (1993): 367–87.

Kanogo, Tabitha. *African Womanhood in Colonial Kenya, 1900–50.* Athens: Ohio University Press, 2005.

———. *Squatters and the Roots of Mau Mau, 1905–63.* Athens: Ohio University Press, 1987.

Kay, Stafford. "Local Pressures on Educational Plans in Colonial Kenya: Post–Second World War Activity among the Southern Abaluyia." *International Journal of African Historical Studies* 11, no. 4 (1978): 689–710.

Kanyoro, Rachel Angogo. "The Abaluyia of Kenya: One People, One Language: What Can Be Learned from the Luyia Project." *Proceedings of the Round Table on the Assuring the Feasibility of Standardization within Dialect Chains* (1988): 86–102.

———. "Post-research Experience: The Abaluyia of Western Kenya." *Proceedings of the Round Table on the Assuring the Feasibility of Standardization within Dialect Chains* (1988): 103–06.

———. *Unity in Diversity: A Linguistic Survey of the Abaluyia of Western Kenya.* Vienna: AFRO-PUB, 1983.

Kelemen, Paul. "Modernising Colonialism: The British Labour Movement and Africa." *Journal of Imperial and Commonwealth History* 34, no. 2 (2006): 223–44.

Kenyanchui, Simon. *Nabongo Mumia*. Nairobi: Heinemann Kenya, 1992.

Kenyatta, Jomo. *Facing Mount Kenya: The Tribal Life of the Gikuyu*. London: Secker & Warburg, 1938. Reprint, New York: Vintage Books, 1965.

———. *Harambee! The Prime Minister of Kenya's Speeches, 1963–1964*. Nairobi: Oxford University Press, 1964.

Kipkorir, Benjamin E. "Colonial Response to Crisis: The Kolloa Affray and Colonial Kenya in 1950." *Kenya Past and Present* 2, no.1 (1973): 22–35.

———. "The Kolloa Affray, Kenya 1950." *Transafrican Journal of History* 2, no. 2 (1972): 114–29.

Kisembe, Evelyne. "Dahl's Law and the Luyia Law in Luyia Dialects Spoken in Western Kenya." *Lwati: A Journal of Contemporary Research* 7, no. 4 (2010).

———. "Linguistic Effects of English on Luyia Languages." *Estudios de Lingüística Aplicada* 21, no. 37 (2003): 53–70.

Kodesh, Neil. *Beyond the Royal Gaze: Clanship and Public Healing in Buganda*. Charlottesville: University of Virginia Press, 2010.

———. "History from the Healer's Shrine: Genre, Historical Imagination, and Early Ganda History." *Comparative Studies in Society and History* 49, no. 3 (2007): 527–52.

———. "Networks of Knowledge: Clanship and Collective Well-Being in Buganda." *Journal of African History* 49, no. 2 (2008): 197–216.

Kopytoff, Igor. "The Internal African Frontier: The Making of African Political Culture." In *The African Frontier*, edited by Kopytoff, 3–86. Bloomington: Indiana University Press, 1989.

Kyle, Keith. *The Politics of the Independence of Kenya*. Basingstoke: Palgrave Macmillan, 1999.

Kyomuhendo, Grace Bantebya, and Marjorie Keniston McIntosh. *Women, Work and Domestic Virtue in Uganda, 1900–2003*. Athens: Ohio University Press, 2006.

Landau, Paul Stuart. *The Realm of the Word: Language, Gender, and Christianity in a Southern African Kingdom*. Portsmouth, NH: Heinemann 1995.

Larmer, Miles, and Erik Kennes. "Rethinking the Katangese Secession." *Journal of Imperial and Commonwealth History* 42, no. 4 (2014): 1–21.

Laszlo, Ervin, and Ignacio Masulli, eds. *The Evolution of Cognitive Maps: New Paradigms for the Twenty-First Century*. New York: CRC Press, 1993.

Leakey, Louis. *Defeating Mau Mau*. London: Routledge, 1954.

Lee, Christopher J. *Unreasonable Histories: Nativism, Multiracial Lives, and the Imagination in British Africa*. Durham: Duke University Press, 2014.

Levine, Philippa. *Prostitution, Race, and Politics: Policing Venereal Disease in the British Empire*. New York: Routledge, 2003.

Lewis, Joanna. *Empire State-Building: War and Welfare in Kenya, 1925–52*. Athens: Ohio University Press, 2000.

———. "Nasty, Brutish and in Shorts? British Colonial Rule, Violence and the Historians of Mau Mau." *Round Table* 96, no. 389 (April 2007): 201–23.

Lohrentz, Kenneth P. "The Campaign to Depose Chief Mulama in Marama Location: A Case Study in Politics of Kinship." *Kenya Historical Review* 4, no. 2 (1976): 249–57.

Lonsdale, John. "Britain's Mau Mau." Draft Paper, University of Cambridge, 2009.

———. "Comparative Patriotisms and Ethno-history in Eastern Africa." In Peterson and Macola, *Recasting the Past*, 251–67.

———. "The Emergence of African Nations: A Historiographical Analysis." *African Affairs* 67, no. 266 (1968): 11–28.

———. "KAU's Cultures: Imaginations of Community and Constructions of Leadership in Kenya after the Second World War." *Journal of African Cultural Studies* 13, no. 1 (2000): 107–24.

———. "Kikuyu Christianities." *Journal of Religion in Africa* 29, no. 2 (May 1999): 206–29.

———. "'Listen While I Read': The Orality of Christian Literacy in the Young Kenyatta's Making of the Kikuyu." In *Ethnicity in Africa: Roots, Meanings and Implications*, edited by Louise de la Gorgendière, Kenneth King, and Sarah Vaughan, 17–53. Edinburgh: Centre of African Studies, University of Edinburgh, 1996.

———. "Moral and Political Argument in Kenya." In Berman, Eyoh, and Kymlicka, *Ethnicity and Democracy*, 73–95.

———. "The Moral Economy of Mau Mau: Wealth, Poverty, and Civic Virtue in Kikuyu Political Thought." In Berman and Lonsdale, *Unhappy Valley*, 315–504.

———. "Moral Ethnicity, Ethnic Nationalism and Political Tribalism: The Case of the Kikuyu." In *Staat und Gesellschaft in Afrika*, edited by Peter Meyns, 93–106. Hamburg: Lit Verlag, 1995.

———. "Political Associations in Western Kenya." In *Protest and Power in Black Africa*, edited by Robert I. Rotberg and Ali Mazrui, 589–638. New York: Oxford University Press, 1970.

———. "A Political History of Nyanza, 1883–1945." PhD diss., University of Cambridge, 1964.

———. "The Politics of Conquest in Western Kenya." In Berman and Lonsdale, *Unhappy Valley*, 45–74.

———. "The Prayers of Waiyaki: Political Uses of the Kikuyu Past." In Anderson and Johnson, *Revealing Prophets*, 240–91.

———. "Some Origins of Nationalism in East Africa." *Journal of African History* 9, no. 1 (1968): 119–46.

———. "When Did the Gusii (or Any Other Group) Become a Tribe?" *Kenya Historical Review* 5, no. 1 (1977): 123–35.

Low, D. A. *Fabrication of Empire: The British and the Uganda Kingdoms, 1890–1902.* Cambridge: Cambridge University Press, 2009.

Lugard, F. D. "Travels from the East Coast to Uganda, Lake Albert Edward and Lake Albert." *Proceedings of the Royal Geographical Society and Monthly Record of Geography* 14, no. 12 (December 1892): 817–41.

Lynch, Gabrielle. *I Say To You: Ethnic Politics and the Kalenjin in Kenya.* Chicago: University of Chicago Press, 2011.

Mabogunje, Akin L. *Urbanization in Nigeria.* London: University of London Press, 1968.

MacArthur, Julie. "How the West Was Won: Regional Politics and Prophetic Promises in the 2007 Kenya Elections." *Journal of Eastern African Studies* 2, no. 2 (2008): 227–41.

———. "The Making and Unmaking of African Languages: Oral Communities and Competitive Linguistic Work in Western Kenya." *Journal of African History* 53, no. 2 (July 2012): 151–72.

———. "Mapping Dissent: Greater Somalia and the Decolonization of Kenya's Northern Frontier." In *African Boundaries and Independence.* Palgrave, forthcoming.

———. "The Perils of Ethnic History. Review of *I Say to You: Ethnic Politics and the Kalenjin in Kenya.* By Gabrielle Lynch." *Journal of African History* 53, no. 1 (March 2012): 122–23.

———. "States of Exception: Genealogies of Sovereignty, Violence, and Belonging along the Kenya-Somali Frontier." Draft Paper, University of Toronto, 2014.

———. "When Did the Luyia (or Any Other Group) Become a Tribe?" *Canadian Journal of African Studies* 47, no. 3 (2013): 351–63.

Mackenzie, Fiona. "Gender and Land Rights in Murang'a District, Kenya." *Journal of Peasant Studies* 14, no. 4 (1990): 609–43.

———. *Land, Ecology and Resistance in Kenya, 1880–1952.* Edinburgh: Edinburgh University Press, 1998.

Maddox, Gregory H. "Narrating Power in Colonial Ugogo: Mazengo of Mvumi." In Giblin and Maddox, *In Search of a Nation,* 86–102.

Maddox, Gregory H., and Ernest M. Kongola. *Practicing History in Central Tanzania: Writing, Memory, and Performance.* Portsmouth, NH: Heinemann, 2006.

Mahone, Sloan. "The Psychology of Rebellion: Colonial Medical Responses to Dissent in British East Africa." *Journal of African History* 47, no. 2 (2006): 241–58.

Makila, F. E. *An Outline History of the Babukusu of Western Kenya.* Nairobi: Kenya Literature Bureau, 1978.

Mamdani, Mahmood. *Citizen and Subject: Contemporary Africa and the Legacy of Late Colonialism.* Princeton: Princeton University Press, 1996.

———. *Define and Rule: Native as Political Identity.* Cambridge, MA: Harvard University Press, 2012.

———. "Political Violence and State Formation in Post-colonial Africa." International Development Centre Working Paper 1, 2007.

———. *When Victims Become Killers: Colonialism, Nativism, and the Genocide in Rwanda.* Princeton: Princeton University Press, 2002.

Mann, Kristin, and Richard Roberts, eds. *Law in Colonial Africa.* Portsmouth, NH: Heinemann, 1991.

Martin, C. J. "The East Africa Population Census, 1948: Planning and Enumeration." *Population Studies* 3, no. 3 (December 1949): 303–20.

Martin, Phyllis M. *Leisure and Society in Colonial Brazzaville*. Cambridge: Cambridge University Press, 1995.

Mason, A. T. "Uganda's Old Eastern Province and East Africa's Federal Capital." *Uganda Journal* 22, no. 1 (March 1958): 43–53.

Maxon, Robert M. "Colonial Conquest and Administration." In Ochieng', *Historical Studies and Social Change*, 93–109.

———. "'Fantastic Prices' in the Midst of 'an Acute Food Shortage': Market, Environment and the Colonial State in the 1943 Vihiga (Western Kenya) Famine." *African Economic History* 28 (2000): 27–52.

Mbembe, Achille. "At the Edge of the World: Boundaries, Territoriality, and Sovereignty in Africa." *Public Culture* 12, no. 1 (2000): 259–84.

Mbilinyi, Marjorie. "Runaway Wives in Colonial Tanganyika: Forced Labour and Forced Marriage in Rungwe District 1919–1961." *International Journal of the Sociology of Law* 16, no. 1 (1988): 1–29.

Mboya, Tom. *The Challenge of Nationhood*. Nairobi: Praeger, 1970.

McCann, James C. *Green Land, Brown Land, Black Land: An Environmental History of Africa, 1800–1990*. Portsmouth, NH: Heinemann, 1999.

McCaskie, Tom. *Asante Identities: History and Modernity in an African Village, 1850–1950*. Edinburgh: Edinburgh University Press, 2000.

McEwen, A. C. *International Boundaries of East Africa*. Oxford: Clarendon Press, 1971.

McIntosh, Roderick J. "Clustered Cities of the Middle Niger: Alternative Routes to Authority in Prehistory." In *Africa's Urban Past*, edited by David M. Anderson and Richard Rathbone, 19–35. Oxford: James Currey, 2000.

Médard, Claire. "Les conflits 'ethniques' au Kenya: Une question de votes ou de terres?" *Afrique Contemporaine*, no. 180 (October–December 1996): 62–74.

———. "Dispositifs électoraux et violences ethniques: Réflexions sur quelques stratégies territoriales du régime kenyan." *Politique Africaine*, no. 70 (June 1998): 32–40.

Mitchell, Timothy. *Rule of Experts: Egypt, Techno-politics, Modernity*. Berkeley: University of California Press, 2002,

Moodie, T. Dunbar. *Going for Gold: Men, Mines, and Migration*. Berkeley: University of California Press, 1994.

Moore, Donald S. *Suffering for Territory: Race, Place, and Power in Zimbabwe*. Durham: Duke University Press, 2005.

Moore, Henrietta L. *Space, Text, and Gender: An Anthropological Study of the Marakwet of Kenya*. Cambridge: Cambridge University Press, 1986.

Moore, Sally Falk. *Social Facts and Fabrications: "Customary" Law on Kilimanjaro, 1880–1980*. Cambridge: Cambridge University Press, 1986.

Morris, H. F. "Native Courts: A Corner-Stone of Indirect Rule." In *Indirect Rule and the Search for Justice: Essays in East African Legal History,* edited by Morris and James S. Read, 131–66. Oxford: Clarendon Press, 1972.

Muoria Mwaniki, H. *Kenyatta ni Muigwithania Witu.* Nairobi: East African Educational Publishers, 1947.

Murray, Jocelyn. "The Church Missionary Society and the 'Female Circumcision' Issue in Kenya." *Journal of Religion in Africa* 8, no. 2 (1976): 92–104.

Mutongi, Kenda. *Worries of the Heart: Widows, Family, and Community.* Chicago: University of Chicago Press, 2007.

Mwanzi, Helen Oronga A. "Reflections on Orality and Cultural Expression: Orality as a Peace Culture." *Journal des Africanistes* 80, nos. 1–2 (2010): 63–74.

Naldi, G. J., ed. *Documents of the Organization of African Unity.* New York: Mansell, 1992.

Nottingham, John, and Carl G. Rosberg, Jr. *The Myth of "Mau Mau": Nationalism in Kenya.* New York: Praeger, 1966.

Nugent, Paul. *Smugglers, Secessionists, and Loyal Citizens on the Ghana-Togo Frontier: The Lie of the Borderlands since 1914.* Athens: Ohio University Press, 2002.

Nugent, Paul, and A. I. Asiwaju, eds. *African Boundaries: Barriers, Conduits and Opportunities.* London: Frances Pinter, 1996.

Oberst, Timothy. "Transport Workers, Strikes and the 'Imperial Response': Africa and the Post–World War II Conjuncture." *African Studies Review* 31, no. 1 (April 1988): 117–33.

Ochieng', William R., ed. *Historical Studies and Social Change in Western Kenya.* Nairobi: East African Educational Publishers, 2002.

———. *An Outline History of Nyanza up to 1914.* Nairobi: East African Literature Bureau, 1974.

Ochwada, Hannington. "Negotiating Difference: The Church Missionary Society, Colonial Education, and Gender among Abetaaluyia and Joluo Communities of Kenya, 1900–60." PhD diss., Indiana University, 2008.

Odinga, Oginga. *Not Yet Uhuru: The Autobiography of Oginga Odinga.* London: East African Educational Publishers, 1967.

Ogot, Bethwell A. "The Construction of Luo Identity and History." In White, Miescher, and Cohen, *African Words,* 31–52.

———. "The Decisive Years 1956–63." In Ogot and Ochieng', *Decolonization and Independence,* 48–79.

———. "Historical Portrait of Western Kenya up to 1985." In Ochieng', *Historical Studies and Social Change,* 13–28.

———. *History of the Southern Luo.* Nairobi: East African Publishing House, 1967.

———. "Mau Mau and Nationhood: The Untold Story." In Atieno Odhiambo and Lonsdale, *Mau Mau and Nationhood,* 8–36.

———. "Britain's Gulag." Review of *Histories of the Hanged: Britain's Dirty War in Kenya and the End of Empire,* by David Anderson, and *Britain's*

Gulag: The Brutal End of Empire in Kenya, by Caroline Elkins. *Journal of African History* 46, no. 3 (2005): 493–505.

———. "Revolt of the Elders: An Anatomy of the Loyalist Crowd in the Mau Mau Uprising 1952–1956." In *Hadith 4: Politics and Nationalism in Colonial Kenya*, edited by Ogot, 134–49. Nairobi: East African Publishing House, 1972.

Ogot, Bethwell A., and W. R. Ochieng', eds. *Decolonization and Independence in Kenya, 1940–93*. Athens: Ohio University Press, 1995.

Ogula, Paul H. A. "Political Chief: A Biography of Ex-Senior Chief Mukudi of Samia and Bunyala c. 1881–1969." *Kenya Historical Review* 2, no. 2 (1974): 175–87.

Olumwullah, Osaak A. *Dis-ease in the Colonial State: Medicine, Society and Social Change among the AbaNyole of Western Kenya*. London: Praeger, 2002.

Omulokoli, Watson. "The Historical Development of the Anglican Church among Abaluyia, 1905–1955." PhD diss., University of Aberdeen, 1981.

Onyango, George M. "The Geographic Setting of Western Kenya." In Ochieng', *Historical Studies and Social Change*, 3–12.

Osborne, Myles. *Ethnicity and Empire in Kenya: Loyalty and Martial Race among the Kamba, c. 1800 to the Present*. Cambridge; Cambridge University Press, 2014.

———. "The Historiography in Mau Mau." In *The Life and Times of General China: Mau Mau and the End of Empire in Kenya*, edited by Osborne, 255–61. Princeton: Markus Wiener, 2015.

Osogo, John. *A History of the Baluyia*. Nairobi: Oxford University Press, 1966.

———. "The Significance of Clans in the History of East Africa." *Hadith* 2 (1970): 30–41.

Otiende, J. D. *Habari za Abaluyia*. Nairobi: Eagle Press, 1949.

Owen, W. E. "The Bantu of Kavirondo." *Journal of the East Africa and Uganda Natural History Society* 44–45 (1932): 57–77.

Parkin, David. *Neighbours and Nationals in an African City Ward*. London: Routledge, 1969.

Parsons, Tim. "Being Kikuyu in Meru: Challenging the Tribal Geography of Colonial Kenya." *Journal of African History* 53, no. 1 (March 2012): 65–86.

———. *Race, Resistance, and the Boy Scout Movement in British Colonial Africa*. Athens: Ohio University Press, 2004.

Peel, J. D. Y. "The Cultural Work of Yoruba Ethnogenesis." In *History and Ethnicity*, edited by Elizabeth Tonkin, Malcolm Chapman, and Maryon McDonald, 198–215. London: Routledge, 1989.

Pels, Peter. "Creolisation in Secret: The Birth of Nationalism in Late Colonial Uluguru, Tanzania." *Africa: Journal of the International African Institute* 72, no. 1 (2002): 1–28.

———. "Imagining Elections: Modernity, Mediation and the Secret Ballot in Late-colonial Tanganyika." In *Cultures of Voting: The Hidden History of the Secret Ballot*, edited by Romain Bertrand, Jean-Louis Briquet, and Pels, 100–13. Bloomington: Indiana University Press, 2007.

Peristiany, J. G. "The Age-Set System of the Pastoral Pokot: The 'Sapana' Initiation Ceremony." *Africa: Journal of the International African Institute* 21, no. 3 (July 1951): 188–206.

Peterson, Derek. "'Be Like Firm Soldiers to Develop the Country': Political Imagination and the Geography of Gikuyuland." *International Journal of African Historical Studies* 37, no. 1 (2004): 71–101.

———. "Colonizing Language? Missionaries and Gikuyu Dictionaries, 1904 and 1914." *History in Africa* 24 (1997): 257–72.

———. *Creative Writing: Translation, Bookkeeping, and the Work of Imagination in Colonial Kenya.* Portsmouth, NH: Heinemann, 2004.

———. *Ethnic Patriotism and the East African Revival: A History of Dissent, c. 1935–72.* Cambridge: Cambridge University Press, 2012.

———. "The Intellectual Lives of Mau Mau Detainees." *Journal of African History* 49, no. 1 (2008): 73–91.

———. "Language Work and Colonial Politics in Eastern Africa: The Making of Standard Swahili and 'School Kikuyu.'" In *The Study of Language and the Politics of Community in Global Context*, edited by David L. Hoyt and Karen Oslund, 185–214. Lanham, MD: Lexington Books, 2006.

———. "States of Mind: Political History and the Rwenzururu Kingdom, Western Uganda." In Peterson and Macola, *Recasting the Past*, 171–90.

———. "Writing in Revolution: Independent Schooling and Mau Mau in Nyeri." In Atieno Odhiambo and Lonsdale, *Mau Mau and Nationhood*, 76–96.

Peterson, Derek R., and Giacomo Macola, eds. *Recasting the Past: History Writing and Political Work in Modern Africa.* Athens: Ohio University Press, 2009.

Presbey, Gail. "Is Elijah Masinde a Sage-Philosopher? The Dispute between H. Odera Oruka and Chaungo Barasa." In *Sagacious Reasoning: Henry Odera Oruka in Memoriam*, edited by Anke Graness and Kai Kresse, 195–210. New York: P. Lang, 1997.

Ramaswamy, Sumathi. *The Goddess and the Nation: Mapping Mother India.* Durham: Duke University Press, 2010.

———. "Maps, Mother/Goddesses and Martyrdom in Modern India." *Journal of Asian Studies* 67, no. 3 (2008): 1–35.

Ranger, Terence. "Connexions between 'Primary Resistance' Movements and Modern Mass Nationalism in East and Central Africa, Parts One and Two." *Journal of African History* 9, no. 4 (1968): 437–53, 631–41.

———. "The Invention of Tradition in Colonial Africa." In *The Invention of Tradition*, edited by Eric Hobsbawm and Ranger, 211–62. Cambridge: Cambridge University Press, 1983.

———. "The *Invention of Tradition* Revisited: The Case of Colonial Africa." In *Legitimacy and the State in Twentieth-Century Africa*, edited by Ranger and Olufemi Vaughan, 62–111. London: Macmillan, 1993.

———. "Making Northern Rhodesia Imperial: Variations on a Royal Theme, 1924–38." *African Affairs* 79, no. 316 (1980): 349–73.

Rathbone, Richard. *Nkrumah and the Chiefs: The Politics of Chieftaincy in Ghana, 1951–60.* Athens: Ohio University Press, 2000.

Renan, Ernest. *Qu'est-ce qu'une nation?* Translated by Ida Mae Snyder. Paris: Lévy, 1883.

Richards, Paul. *Fighting for the Rain Forest: War, Youth and Resources in Sierra Leone.* Oxford: James Currey, 1996.

Roberts, A. D. "The Gold Boom of the 1930s in East Africa." *African Affairs* 85, no. 341 (October 1986): 545–62.

Rosberg, Carl G., Jr., with Aaron Segal. *An East African Federation.* New York: Carnegie Endowment for International Peace, 1963.

Rothchild, Donald. "Majimbo Schemes in Kenya and Uganda." In *Transition in African Politics,* edited by Jeffrey Butler and A. A. Castagno, 291–318. New York: Praeger, 1967.

——. *Racial Bargaining in Independent Kenya.* London: Oxford University Press. 1973.

Rowlands, J. S. S. "Notes on Native Law and Custom in Kenya: I." *Journal of African Law* 6, no. 3 (Autumn 1962): 192–209.

Sack, Robert David. *Human Territoriality: Its Theory and History.* Cambridge: Cambridge University Press, 1986.

Said, Edward W. *Orientalism.* New York: Vintage, 1979.

Salim, A. I. "The Movement for 'Mwambao' or Coast Autonomy in Kenya, 1956–1963." *Hadith* 2 (1970): 212–28.

Sangale, Simani. *Tiriki Community Customs and Traditions.* Nairobi: Kul Graphics, 2004.

Sanger, Clyde, and Nottingham, John. "The Kenya General Election of 1963." *Journal of Modern African Studies* 2, no. 1 (March 1964): 1–40.

Sangree, Walter H. *Age, Prayer and Politics in Tiriki, Kenya.* London: Oxford University Press, 1966.

——. "The Social Functions of Beer Drinking among the Bantu Tiriki." In *Society, Culture and Drinking Patterns,* edited by David J. Pittman and Charles R. Snyder, 6–21. London: Wiley, 1962.

Sapir, Edward. *Language: An Introduction to the Study of Speech.* New York: Harcourt, Brace, 1921.

Schmidt, Elizabeth. *Peasants, Traders, and Wives: Shona Women in the History of Zimbabwe, 1870–1939.* Portsmouth, NH: Heinemann, 1992.

Schoenbrun, David L. "Conjuring the Modern in Africa: Durability and Rupture in Histories of Public Healing between the Great Lakes of East Africa." *American Historical Review* 111, no. 5 (December 2006): 1403–39.

——. *A Green Place, A Good Place: Agrarian Change, Gender, and Social Identity in the Great Lakes Region to the Fifteenth Century.* Portsmouth, NH: Heinemann, 1998.

Scott, James C. *The Art of Not Being Governed: An Anarchist History of Upland Southeast Asia.* New Haven: Yale University Press, 2009.

——. *Seeing Like a State.* New Haven: Yale University Press, 1998.

Shadle, Brett L. "'Changing Traditions to Meet Current Altering Conditions': Customary Law, African Courts and the Rejection of Codification in Kenya, 1930–60." *Journal of African History* 40, no. 3 (1999): 411–31.

———. *"Girl Cases": Marriage and Colonialism in Gusiiland, Kenya, 1890–1970.* Portsmouth, NH: Heinemann, 2006.

———. "Patronage, Millennialism and the Serpent God Mumbo in South-West Kenya, 1912–34." *Africa* 72, no. 1 (February 2002): 29–54.

———. "Rape in the Courts of Gusiiland, Kenya, 1940s–1960s." *African Studies Review* 51, no. 2 (September 2008): 27–50.

Shanguhyia, Martin Shidende. "The State, Ecology, and Society in Western Kenya: Politics of Soil Conservation and Land Management in Vihiga, 1930–1950." PhD diss., West Virginia University, 2007.

Shell-Duncan, Bettina, and Ylva Hernlund. *Female "Circumcision" in Africa: Culture, Controversy and Change.* Boulder: Lynne Reiner, 2001.

Shelley, Horace M. "An Investigation Concerning Mental Disorder in Nyasaland Natives." *Journal of Mental Science* 82, no. 341 (1936): 701–30.

Shetler, Jan B., ed. *Gendering Ethnicity in African Women's Lives.* Madison: University of Wisconsin Press, 2015.

———. "'Regions' as Historical Production." In Howard and Shain, *Spatial Factor in African History,* 141–76.

Shilaro, Priscilla. *A Failed Eldorado: Colonial Capitalism, Rural Industrialization, African Land Rights in Kenya, and the Kakamega Gold Rush, 1930–52.* Lanham, MD: University Press of America, 2008.

Siegel, Brian. "Bomas, Missions and Mines: The Making of Centers on the Zambian Copperbelt." *African Studies Review* 31, no. 3 (December 1988): 61-84.

Simiyu, V. G. "The Emergence of a Sub-nation: A History of Babukusu to 1900." *Transafrican Journal of History* 20 (1991): 125–44.

Smith, G. E. "Road-Making and Surveying in British East Africa." *Geographical Journal* 14, no. 3 (September 1899): 269–89.

Smith, J. S. *A History of Alliance High School.* Nairobi: Heinemann Educational Books, 1976.

Snoxall, R. A. *Luganda-English Dictionary.* Oxford: Oxford University Press, 1967.

"Some Notes on East African Native Laws and Customs." *Journal of the Society of Comparative Legislation* 11, no. 1 (1910): 181–95.

Sorrenson, Keith. *Land Reform in the Kikuyu Country: A Study in Government Policy.* Nairobi: Oxford University Press, 1967.

Southall, Aidan W. "The Illusion of the Tribe." In *Perspectives on Africa: A Reader in Culture, History and Representation,* edited by Roy Richard Grinker and Christopher B. Steiner, 38–51. Oxford: Oxford University Press, 1997.

Spear, Thomas. "Indirect Rule, the Politics of Neo-traditionalism and the Limits of Invention in Tanzania." In Giblin and Maddox, *In Search of a Nation,* 70–85.

———. "Neo-traditionalism and the Limits of Invention in British Colonial Africa." *Journal of African History* 44, no. 1 (2003): 3–27.

———. "Toward the History of African Christianity." In *East African Expressions of Christianity*, edited by Spear and Isaria N. Kimambo, 3–24. Athens: Ohio University Press, 1999.

Spear, Thomas, and Richard Waller, eds. *Being Maasai: Ethnicity and Identity in East Africa*. Athens: Ohio University Press, 1993.

Spencer, John. *The Kenya African Union*. London: KPI, 1985.

Stanley, Henry Morton. "Letters of Mr. H. M. Stanley on his Journey to Victoria Nyanza, and His Circumnavigation of the Lake." *Royal Geographical Society Proceedings* 20 (1875–76): 134–61.

Stichter, Sharon B. *Migrant Labour in Kenya: Capitalism and African Response, 1895–1975*. London: Longman, 1982.

———. "Workers, Trade Unions, and the Mau Mau Rebellion." *Canadian Journal of African Studies* 9, no. 2 (1975): 259–75.

Stoler, Ann Laura. "On Degrees of Imperial Sovereignty." *Public Culture* 18, no. 1 (2006): 125–46.

Summers, Carol. "Grandfathers, Grandsons, Morality, and Radical Politics in Late Colonial Buganda." *International Journal of African Historical Studies* 38, no. 3 (2005): 427–47.

———. "Radical Rudeness: Ugandan Social Critiques in the 1940s." *Journal of Social History* 39, no. 3 (2006): 741–70.

———. "Young Buganda and Old Boys: Youth, Generational Transition, and Ideas of Leadership in Buganda, 1920–1949." *Africa Today* 51, no. 3 (2005): 109–28.

Swynnerton, R. J. M. *A Plan to Intensify the Development of African Agriculture in Kenya*. Nairobi: Kenya, Department of Agriculture, 1954.

Tamarkin, Mordecai. "The Evolution of Urban Ethnic Associations among Abaluyia in Nakuru, Kenya." *Journal of Eastern African Research and Development* 10, no. 2 (1980): 135–52.

———. "The Loyalists in Nakuru during the Mau Mau Revolt and Its Aftermath, 1953–1963." *Asian and African Studies* 12, no. 2 (1978): 247–61.

———. "Tribal Associations, Tribal Solidarity, and Tribal Chauvinism in a Kenya Town." *Journal of African History* 14, no. 2 (1973): 257–74.

Thomas, Lynn M. *Politics of the Womb: Women, Reproduction, and the State in Kenya*. Berkeley: University of California Press, 2003.

Thomas, Samuel S. "Transforming the Gospel of Domesticity: Luhya Girls and the Friends Africa Mission, 1917–1926." *African Studies Review* 43, no. 2 (September 2000): 1–27.

Thomson, Joseph. *Through Masai Land: A Journey of Exploration among the Snowclad Volcanic Mountains and Strange Tribes of Eastern Equatorial Africa*. Boston: Sampson Low, Marston, Searle, and Rivington, 1885.

———. "Through the Masai Country to Victoria Nyanza." *Proceedings of the Royal Geographical Society and Monthly Record of Geography*, n.s., 6, no. 12 (1884): 690–712.

Throup, David W. "The Origins of Mau Mau." *African Affairs* 84, no. 336 (July 1985): 399–434.

Throup, David W., and Charles Hornsby. *Multi-party Politics in Kenya: The Kenyatta and Moi States and the Triumph of the System in the 1992 Election.* Athens: Ohio University Press, 1998.

Tonkin, Elizabeth. *Narrating Our Pasts: The Social Construction of Oral History.* Cambridge: Cambridge University Press, 1992.

Turner, Simon. "Suspended Spaces—Contesting Sovereignties in a Refugee Camp." In *Sovereign Bodies: Citizens, Migrants, and States in the Postcolonial World*, ed. T. B. Hansen and F. Stepputat, 312–32. Princeton: Princeton University Press, 2005.

Vail, Leroy, ed. *The Creation of Tribalism in Southern Africa.* Berkeley: University of California Press, 1989.

——. "Ethnicity in Southern African History." Introduction to Vail, *Creation of Tribalism*, 1–19.

Vansina, Jan. *Habitat, Economy and Society in the Central African Rainforest.* Providence: Bloomsbury Academic, 1992.

——. *Oral Tradition: A Study in Historical Methodology.* Chicago: Aldine, 1965.

——. *Oral Tradition as History.* Madison: University of Wisconsin Press, 1985.

——. *Paths in the Rainforests: Toward a History of Political Tradition in Equatorial Africa.* Madison: University of Wisconsin Press, 1990.

Vaughan, Christopher. "Violence and Regulation in the Darfur-Chad Borderland c. 1909–56: Policing a Colonial Boundary." *Journal of African History* 54, no. 2 (2013): 177–98.

Vaughan, Christopher, Mareike Schomerus, and Lotje de Vries, eds. *The Borderlands of South Sudan: Authority and Identity in Contemporary and Historical Perspectives.* New York: Palgrave Macmillian, 2013.

Voss, Barbara L. *The Archaeology of Ethnogenesis: Race and Sexuality in Colonial San Francisco.* Berkeley: University of California, 2008.

Wagner, Günter. "The Abaluyia of Kavirondo." In *African Worlds: Studies in the Cosmological Ideas and Social Values of African Peoples*, edited by Daryll Forde, 27–54. Oxford: Oxford University Press, 1954.

——. *The Bantu of North Kavirondo.* 2 vols. London: Oxford University Press, 1949.

——. "The Political Organization of the Bantu of Kavirondo." In *African Political Systems*, edited by Meyer Fortes and E. E. Evans-Pritchard, 196–236. London: Oxford University Press, 1940.

Wainaina, Binyavanga. "Wangechi Mutu Wonders Why Butterfly Wings Leave Powder on the Fingers, There Was a Coup Today in Kenya." *Jalada*, 2014. http://jalada.org/tag/wangechi-mutu/.

Wainwright, Joel, and Joe Bryan. "Cartography, Territory, Property: Postcolonial Reflections on Indigenous Counter-mapping in Nicaragua and Belize." *Cultural Geographies* 16, no. 2 (2009): 153–78.

Wako, Daniel M. "Principles and Procedures of Conflict Resolution and Settlements of Disputes among the Luyia of Kenya." Master's diss., Makerere University, 1976.

———. *The Western Abaluyia and Their Proverbs*. Nairobi: Kenya Literature Bureau, 1954.

Waller, Richard. "Ecology, Migration and Expansion in East Africa." 84, no. 336 (July 1985): 347–70.

———. "Rebellious Youth in Colonial Africa." *Journal of African History* 47, no. 1 (2006): 77–92.

Wambunya, Tim. *Luyia Proverbs from Kisa, Marama, Tsotso and Wanga*. London: Luyia Publishing, 2005.

Wandibba, Simiyu, ed. *History and Culture in Western Kenya: The People of Bungoma through Time*. Nairobi: Gideon S. Were Press, 1985.

———. *Masinde Muliro: A Biography*. Nairobi: East African Educational Publishers, 1996.

———. "Notes on the Oral History of Abatachoni." In Wandibba, *History and Culture*, 18–33.

"Wanga-English Dictionary." http://www.academia.edu/9346974/Wanga-English _Dictionary, 2008.

Wanyande, Peter. *Joseph Daniel Otiende*. Nairobi: East African Educational Publishers, 2002.

Ward, Ida. *Ibo Dialects and the Development of a Common Language*. Cambridge: W. Heffer and Sons, 1941.

Wasserman, Gary. *Politics of Decolonization: Kenya, Europeans and the Land Issue, 1960–1965*. Cambridge: Cambridge University Press, 1976.

Wekesa, Peter Wafula. "Old Issues and New Challenges: The Migingo Island Controversy and the Kenya-Uganda Borderland." *Journal of Eastern African Studies* 4, no. 2 (2010): 331–40.

Werbner, Richard, and Terence Ranger, eds. *Postcolonial Identities in Africa*. Atlantic Highlands, NJ: Zed Books, 1997.

Were, Gideon. "Ethnic Interaction in Western Kenya: The Emergence of the Abaluyia up to 1850." *Kenya Historical Review* 2, no. 1 (1974): 39–44.

———. *A History of the Abaluyia of Western Kenya, 1500–1930*. Nairobi: East African Publishing House, 1967.

———. "The Masai and Kalenjin Factor in the Settlement of Western Kenya: A Study in Ethnic Interaction and Evolution." *Journal of Eastern African Research and Development* 2, no. 1 (1972): 1–11.

———. *Western Kenya Historical Texts: Abaluyia, Teso, and Elgon Kalenjin*. Nairobi: East African Publishing House, 1967.

Wesonga, R. "Pre-colonial Military Organisation of Babukusu." In Wandibba, *History and Culture*, 42–50.

White, Luise. *The Comforts of Home: Prostitution in Colonial Nairobi*. Chicago: University of Chicago Press, 1990.

———. *Speaking with Vampires: Rumor and History in Colonial Africa*. Berkeley: University of California Press, 2000.

White, Luise, Stephan Miescher, and David William Cohen, eds. *African Words, African Voices*. Bloomington: Indiana University Press, 2001.

Whiteley, W. H. "The Classification and Distribution of Kenya's African Languages." In Whiteley, *Language in Kenya*, 13–68.

———, ed. *Language in Kenya*. Nairobi: Oxford University Press, 1974.

Willis, Justin. "Clan and History in Western Uganda: A New Perspective on the Origins of Pastoral Dominance." *International Journal of African Historical Studies* 30, no. 3 (1997): 583–600.

———. "The Makings of a Tribe: Bondei Identities and Histories." *Journal of African History* 33, no. 2 (1992): 191–208.

———. "'A Model of Its Kind': Representation and Performance in the Sudan Self-Government Election of 1953." *Journal of Imperial and Commonwealth History* 35, no. 3 (September 2007): 485–502.

———. *Mombasa, the Swahili, and the Making of the Mijikenda*. Oxford: Clarendon Press, 1993.

———. "A Portrait for the Mukama: Monarchy and Empire in Colonial Bunyoro, Uganda." *Journal of Imperial and Commonwealth History* 34, no. 1 (March 2006): 105–22.

Willis, Justin, and George Gona. "*Pwani c Kenya?* Memory, Documents and Secessionist Politics in Coastal Kenya." *African Affairs* 112, no. 446 (December 2012): 1–24.

———. "Tradition, Tribe, and State in Kenya: The Mijikenda Union, 1945–1980." *Comparative Studies in Society and History* 55, no. 2 (2013): 448–73.

Wilson, E. G., ed. *Who's Who in East Africa, 1965–66*. Nairobi: Marco Publishers (Africa), 1966.

Winichakul, Thongchai. *Siam Mapped: A History of the Geo-body of a Nation*. Honolulu: University of Hawaii Press, 1994.

Winyi, Tito. *To the Queen's Most Excellent Majesty the humble petition of Rukirabasaija Agutamba Omukama Sir Tito Gafabusa Winyi IV of Bunyoro-Kitara for himself and on behalf of the people of Bunyoro-Kitara*. Kampala: Sidney Press, 1958.

Wipper, Audrey. "The Maendeleo ya Wanawake Movement in the Colonial Period: The Canadian Connection, Mau Mau, Embroidery, and Agriculture." *Rural Africana* 29 (Winter 1975–76): 195–214.

———. "The Maendeleo ya Wanawake Organization: The Co-opting of Leadership." *African Studies Review* 18, no. 3 (December 1975): 99–120.

———. *Rural Rebels: A Study of Two Protest Movements in Kenya*. London: Oxford University Press, 1977.

Wisner, Ben, Camilla Toulmin, and Rutendo Chitiga, eds. *Towards a New Map of Africa*. London: Earthscan, 2005.

Wolf, Jan J. de. *Differentiation and Integration in Western Kenya: A Study of Religious Innovation and Social Change among the Bukusu*. The Hague: Mouton, 1977.

———. "The Diffusion of Age-Group Organization in East Africa: A Reconsideration." *Africa: Journal of the International African Institute* 50, no. 3 (1980): 305–10.

———. "Dini ya Msambwa: Militant Protest or Millenarian Promise?" *Canadian Journal of African Studies* 17, no. 2 (1983): 265–76.

Wood, Denis. With John Fels and John Krygier. *Rethinking the Power of Maps.* New York: Guilford Press, 2010.

World Resources Institute. *Natural Benefits in Kenya: An Atlas of Ecosystems and Human Well-Being.* 2007. http://www.wri.org/publication/content /9506.

Zeitlyn, David, and Bruce Connell. "Ethnogenesis and Fractal History on an African Frontier: Mambila-Njerep-Mandulu." *Journal of African History* 44, no. 1 (2003): 117–38.

Zeller, Wolfgang, and Jordi Tomas, eds. *Secessionism in Africa.* New York: Palgrave Macmillan, forthcoming.

Index

Page references in *italics* denote illustrations on those pages.

postcolonial conflict, 224; and the
Regional Boundaries Commission,
31, 200, 203–10, 213, 215–17, 224;
relation to countermapping, 21, 168;
and social history, 6; and spatial
strategies, 16–17, 21–22, 27, 34, 59,
63; and subversion/sabotage, 15–16,
21–22, 27, 34, 60–62, 168, 204; and
territoriality, 16–17, 22, 59. *See also*
boundaries; cognitive mapping;
countermapping; mapping;
territoriality
census (2009), 1–4, 32, 232
census taking, 14, 30, 34, 60, 85, 122, 150,
154–56, 193, 197–98, 210
Central Province, 55, 89, 104–5, 163, 196
Chadwick, Reverend Walter, 118
Chetambe's Fort, 53, 175
Church Missionary Society (CMS), 54,
67, 69, 102, 117–19, 121, 124, 128, 241
Church of God, 54, 117–18, 121–22, 162
citizenship, 7–8, 17, 98, 108, 139, 198, 223,
227–28, 231
civic virtue, 7, 135, 178, 185, 217, 231; and
belonging, 7, 184; and identity, 5,
192, 217; and reputation, 30, 135, 165;
and responsibility, 8, 140
class, 7, 20, 125, 161, 193, 195–98
cognitive mapping, 16, 19, 20, 22, 34,
43–44, 53, 84, 86, 126, 199, 243n86
Cohen, David William, 43
Congo, 216, 222, 228
Constituencies Delimitation
Commission (1962), 199–200
constructivism (or the "invention of
tradition"), 7–9, 13, 25, 43, 111, 171,
157
Cooper, Frederick, 8, 194, 228, 232
cosmopolitanism, 5, 9; definition of,
12–13, 240n55; and gender, 13–14,
161; and language, 111, 132; and
mapping, 20; and Mau Mau
rebellion, 163, 165; and ethnic
patriotism, 12–15, 20, 30–32, 135,
153–54, 173, 217, 221, 231; and
pluralism, 6, 12, 20, 111, 135, 161,
221, 231; postcolonial debates over,
242n71
counterinsurgency, 31, 77, 165, 173, 176
countermapping (or ethnocartography),
15, 20–22, 34, 61–63, 65–66, 68,
77–78, 168, 193; and geographic
information systems, 21; and Global

Positioning Systems, 21. *See also*
cartography; mapping
Coutts Commission (1956), 11, 188, 215
Craib, Raymond, 62, 195
cult of Mumbo, 166, 282n9
Curzon, Lord F. D., 16
customary practices: and authority, 69,
72, 217, 232; and bridewealth, 159,
170; and circumcision, 144–50, 159–
61; conflicts over, 39, 133–39, 141,
179; and control, 29–30, 65, 141, 198;
diversity of, 11, 28, 60, 145, 153, 158,
217; and expertise, 43; and gender,
13–14, 25–26, 72, 133, 141, 144–50,
159–61; and identity, 7–8, 11, 14–15,
72, 144, 147, 149–50, 161, 170–72, 198,
217; and inheritance, 72, 157–58;
and interpenetration, 170–72, 216–
17; and land, 19, 72; and language,
125; legal codification of, 7, 10–11,
13, 14, 60, 68, 135–37, 145, 151, 153,
157–58, 162, 185, 196, 202, 279n163;
and marriage, 136–38, 145, 157, 159–
60, 185, 187; territorialization of, 5,
30, 83, 144, 146, 157–59, 161, 179

decentralized despotism, 65–68
demographic work, 10, 80, 135, 149–50,
154–55, 157–58, 161–64, 197. *See also*
census taking
destocking, 106, 108
Dini ya Msambwa, 30–31, 165; and
antiterritorial politics, 173; and
borders, 168, 171; and detention,
177, 180; as frontier rebels, 165,
167–68, 173, 179, 231; and gender, 25;
leadership of, 140, 167–68, 282n12; and
loyalism, 30–31, 165–67, 173, 176; and
Mau Mau, 165, 173, 176–79; meaning
of, 167; as moral reform movement,
167, 173–74, 176; and Mount Elgon,
168, 172, 174, 179; origins of, 167,
282n11; and postcolonial politics, 26,
201; among the Pokot, 171–72; and
prophecy, 174; and rehabilitation,
176–78; and repatriations, 172–73, 178;
and traditional religious practices,
175–76; use of arson, 167, 176, 282n12.
See also Bukusu; Kolloa Affray;
Malakisi riot; Masinde, Elijah; Mau
Mau rebellion; Pkech, Lucas
Dini ya Roho, 103
Dobbs, C. M., 61

65, 75, 83, 85–86, 88–89, 91, 97, 99, 105, 207; and prostitution, 80, 136; social impacts of, 79–81, 94

Gray, Christopher, 16–17, 48

Greater Luyia, 99, 193, 210, *214*, 215, 229

Habari za Abaluyia (Otiende, 1949), 112, 152–53

Hailey, Lord William, 158, 272n31

Hannington, Bishop James, 54

Harries, Patrick, 121–22

Hastings, Adrian, 127

Hawkins, Sean, 19, 53

Hay, Jean, 42, 113

Haya Union, 9, 13

Hayo (language Luhayo), 40, 45, 115, 118, 144, 190, 215

Heald, Suzette, 43

heterarchy, 21, 34, 43, 46–47, 63, 72, 98–99, 151

Hippel, E. V., 95

Hislop, F. D., 110

history writing, 14, 28, 38–40, 100–104, 121, 153

Hobley, C. W.: 1898 map of Kavirondo, 52; as ethnographer, 53–54, 71, 147; and the Hobley line, 57, 62–63, 101; as Kavirondo district commissioner, 52–54, 60

Hornsby, Charles, 230–31

household economies, 18; and discipline, 139, 141, 166, 174; as idioms, 48, 134–35, 162; and land consolidation, 196–97; and language 48, 125; and religion, 175; threats to, 77, 81, 86, 134, 136, 138–42, 145; and virtue, 145

Howard, Allen, 22

Howard, J. W., 220

Hunter, Emma, 102

Hunter, Kenneth L., 108, 149, 160, 167

Idakho, 45, 151, 186; and campaign against Chief Milimu, 66–67; and customary practices, 159; and language (Luidakho), 114–15, 129; and mapping, 198; and mining, 73, 78–79, 93; and naming, 53; and political organization, 89, 183

identification: and emotive power, 7; mobile processes of, 8, 173; multiple sites of, 8, 15, 32, 44, 46–47, 98, 171; and plurality, 231; precolonial forms

of, 27, 44, 46–47, 98; territorial forms of, 129, 179; and urban migration, 136

Iliffe, John, 7, 34, 139, 193

Ingutia, Philip, 10, 97, 153, 161

initiation, 14, 47, 97, 172–73

instrumentalism, 6–7, 16, 20, 123, 184, 231

intermarriage, 3, 13–14, 40, 46, 98, 144–45, 157, 160, 211

interpenetration, 14, 27, 112, 122, 145, 152, 161, 170–72, 179, 210–11, 217

Isukha, 1–2, 52, 66, 151, 154, 186; and customary practices, 159; and language (Luisukha), 114–15, 129; and mapping, 198; and mining, 73, 78–79, 93; and naming, 53, 66; and political organization, 89

Itebete, P. A. N., 115

Jackson, Sir Frederick, 49, 56, 102

Johnston, Sir Harry, 45, 55–56

Joint Boundary Commission (Kenya-Uganda), 215

Jubaland, 227

Jumba, Andrea, 89–92, 94, 97, 103, 108–9

Kabras (language Lukabrasi), 84, 105, 115, 118, 129, 146–47, 149, 160, 168–69, 198–99, 280n178

Kadenge, Rosa, 143

Kaimosi, 84, 105, 117, 128, 169, 183, 209

Kakai, Pius Wanyonyi, 147–48

Kakamega Forest, 91–92, 105

Kalenjin, 3, 9, 14, 36, 39–40, 42–43, 57, 83; and border conflicts, 153, 211; and circumcision, 95, 145–47, 160; and KADU, 200, 207, 209, 220–22; and language committee, 10; and naming, 28, 87, 99; and voting, 230. *See also* pastoralism

Kamakoiya River, 62, 84, 168

Kanogo, Tabitha, 95, 148

Kanyoro, Rachel, 110–11, 113, 115–17, 123, 230

Katanga, 216, 222, 228, 298n16

Kavirondo: campaigns against, 96–97, 99, 135; as a mapped space, 49–51, 55, 57, 81–86, 88, 131; origins of, 95–96, 246n8; as a people, 34, 52–53, 110, 112; and prostitution, 136–37, 144

Kavirondo Taxpayers' Welfare Association (KTWA), 76, 79, 99, 107

Kenya African Democratic Union
(KADU), 200–203, *206*, 207, 209–10,
217, 220–21, 293n54, 297n127
Kenya African National Union (KANU),
200–203, 208, 209–10, 216, 220–21
Kenya African Union (KAU), 30, 135,
152–54, 181–83, 185, 187
Kenya Land Commission (KLC) (1932),
11, 28, 65, 81–92, 102, 104, 109, 169–
70, 193, 207, 212
Kenya Mining Association, 79
Kenyanchui, Simon, 46
Kenya Regional Boundaries
Commission (1962), 24, 31, 192, 200,
203–10, 216–17, 219–20, 226, 292
Kenyatta, Jomo (Johnstone), 89–90, 149,
180–82, 192, 201, 216, 227
Khasakhala, Eric, 201, 216
Kibaki, Mwai, 1–2
kifagio campaign, 169
Kigumba settlement, 187
Kikuyu, 7–8, 70, 98, 103, 156, 212; and
circumcision, 95, 146–49, 151,
161; and gender, 141; and KANU,
200, 209; and KAU, 181–82, 184;
and the KLC, 82–84; and land
consolidation, 196; and language,
119–20, 122, 125, 129; and Mau Mau,
163–66, 169–70, 177–78, 186–87, 189;
and naming, 87, 258n87; political
influence of, 89–90, 107–8; and
postcolonial Kenyan history, 184;
and voting, 230. *See also* Kikuyu
Central Association; Mau Mau
rebellion
Kikuyu Central Association (KCA), 9,
89–90, 107–8, 135, 152, 181, 185,
259n19
Kimathi, Dedan, 183–84
kinship: cognitive mapping of, 16; and
friendship, 43; ideologies of, 67–68;
and language, 113; and lineage, 28,
40, 43–44, 48, 68, 70–71, 83, 85, 160,
169, 212, 216; as metaphor/strategy
for political organization, 28, 64,
66, 71, 83, 87, 96–99, 101, 139–40,
213; as primordial, 6; and relation to
clan, 44, 94; and territory, 9, 48, 86,
104–5, 197; and values, 153
kipande (also pass/identity card), 60, 147,
170, 198
Kisa (language Lukisa), 1, 40, 71, 115, 118,
132, 144, 153

Kisala, Lumadede, 12, 81–82, 84, 89–90,
92, 109
Kisii (also Gusii), 38, 87, 98, 170
Kisumu, 54–55, 80, 95, 136–37, 141, 207,
209, 216
Kiswahili, 79, 90, 95, 113, 118–21, 123, 125,
132, 151–52, 202
Kitale, 126, 207, 209, 220–21, 297n137
Kitosh Education Society, 138
Kodesh, Neil, 44
Kolloa Affray (1950), 171–73, 176, 178

labor: and gender, 80, 134; and migrancy,
59, 90, 134, 136, 155, 165, 172–73,
196–97; and mining, 75, 79, 80,
89–90, 93; and settler farms, 55, 75,
106, 168–69, 171; and strikes, 168, 181
Lamu, 50, 175, 178
Lancaster House conferences, 193–94,
202–3, 212
land consolidation, 107, 192, 195–98
Leakey, Louis, 177
Legislative Council, 10–11, 102, 104, 132,
153, 155, 161, 182–83, 192, 195, 201,
203, 209
life histories, 24–26, 245n123
Ligalaba, Erasto, 89–90
Limba (Sierra Leone), 111–12
Lisudza, Mudi, 92
Local Native Council (LNC): and
debates over naming, 98–99,
235n2; and decentralization, 202;
and football, 140; and gender
policing, 80, 136–37, 145–47, 149–50,
159–60; and land policies, 73, 75,
81–82, 105–6, 169, 172, 186; and
language, 120, 129–30; and political
organization, 67, 88
locational council, 12, 131, 137, 139
Logoli (also Maragoli): and
circumcision, 139, 144–45; and
customary practice, 11–12, 128,
138–39, 159, 170–71, 198; and FAM,
105; and foreign chiefs, 67; and
gold mining, 78–79, 89, 91; and
land, 47, 109, 136, 154, 169, 186; and
language (Luragoli), 105, 113, 115,
118, 122–24, 128–31; and mapping,
205, 207, 209–11, 217; and Mau
Mau, 186; and naming, 96, 153; and
political organization, 44–45, 83,
89, 109, 112, 128, 138–39, 151, 158;
and prostitution, 137, 141–42; and

relation to neighbors, 42, 230. *See also* Maragoli Association; Maragoli People's Association; Maragoli Society

Lonsdale, John, 7–8, 13, 53, 66, 70, 92, 161, 173–74, 193, 231

loyalism, 5, 30–31, 162–66, 173, 181, 184–85, 188–91, 197–98, 281n6

Lugard, Lord Frederick, 77

Luo (also Nilotic): and 2007 election, 2–3; and boundaries, 57, 83, 155–56, 170–71, 184, 186, 209–12, 216, 218–20; and circumcision, 95, 144–45; and ethnic patriotism, 9, 13, 98–99, 103, 135, 162, 185, 192, 217, 273n50; and the gold rush, 76; and the Kavirondo name, 50, 95–96; and land consolidation, 197; and language (Dholuo), 10, 42, 103, 112–14, 119–20, 132; and nationalism, 174, 182, 200, 222; and settlement in western Kenya, 38–40, 42–43, 53; and urban labor, 136, 189, 196. *See also* Luo Council of Elders; Luo Union

Luo Council of Elders, 26

Luo Union, 9, 13, 135, 185

Luyia Council of Elders, 24, 163

Luyia-English Vocabulary (1943), 124, 126

Luyia language: and amateur linguists, 110, 114; conflicts over inclusion in, 126–32, 199; and ethnic patriotism, 10, 29, 110–12, 120–21, 127, 132–33, 153, 161, 215; and gender, 125, 137, 272n21; and geography, 125–26; and land, 126; and missionary work, 117–19, 121, 123; and nation, 127; as nonexistent, 110; and orality, 4, 110–12, 123, 132–33, 184; and orthography, 123, 130; and pronunciation, 123, 128; and publications, 125, 127, 130; and questions of dialects/linguistic diversity, 10, 25, 50, 94, 111–19, 122–23, 147; and questions of translation, 113, 124–27, 272n21; standardization of, 29, 119–22, 127. *See also* Luyia Language Committee

Luyia Language Committee, 10, 29, 110, 119–20, 122, 126–30, 132, 147, 158

Lynch, Gabrielle, 14

Maasai, 36, 39–40, 43, 46, 53, 57, 112, 130, 145–47, 160–61, 170, 194, 200, 211–12

Mackenzie, Fiona, 82, 196

Macola, Giacomo, 100

Maendeleo ya Wanawake, 162

majimbo, 202, 216

Makerere College, 9–11, 29, 95, 112, 120–21, 127, 132, 138, 152–53, 189, 267n47; *Muluhya* (student quarterly), 11, 121, 132, 189–90

Malakisi riot (1948), 168, 171

male circumcision, 43, 95, 144–45, 148, 170

Malik, A. Qadir, 149

mapping: and alternative visions of postcolonial nations, 32, 194, 200, 202, 207, 209, 212–15, 217, 222, 224–29; amateur mapmakers, 17, 22, 34, 204; archives of, 20, 23–24; and census taking, 30, 34, 122, 135, 154–56, 193, 198–200, 207, 210–11; competing forms of, 34, 56, 62–63; competitive culture of, 18–19, 68–69, 78, 193, 195–98, 200, 202–3, 207, 209–12, 229; and colonial maps/surveys, 16–17, 27, 34, 49, 53–57, 59, 60–63, 65–66, 77, 81–82, 84, 106, 193, 199, 213, 224–31; and conquest, 4, 34, 53–54, 71; and customary practices, 30, 43, 65, 135, 141, 157, 162, 196, 198, 217; and decolonization, 192–94; and electoral politics, 135, 193, 197–200, 211; as fetish, 32, 228; and gender, 17, 30, 77, 134–35, 162, 193–97; and the gold rush, 28, 65, 76–78, 81–83, 85–86, 88–89, 97, 231; and KADU regional map, 202; and land claims, 18–21, 32, 66, 83–84, 88, 195–97, 204; and land consolidation, 195–97; and language, 114–17, 126, 129, 131; and local competition over resources, 17–20, 27–28, 32, 65, 67–68, 196, 198; and local geographic practices, 16–17, 20, 27, 34, 54, 62–63, 128, 195, 231–32; metaphors of, 15, 242n75; and migration, 39–41, 43, 112; and missionaries, 54, 122; and moral geographies, 5, 31, 34, 81, 86, 88, 164, 166–67, 230; and narrative maps, 39; and patriotic work, 5, 14, 20, 22–23, 30–32, 65, 81–89, 92, 97, 105, 135, 191, 194, 204, 221, 222–23, 228, 230–33; and power, 15–17, 20–22, 24, 27, 34, 62, 65–68, 81, 209;

mapping (*cont.*)
        and precolonial political
        organization, 44, 46; and the
        Regional Boundaries Commission,
        31, 198, 200, 203–10, 217; and soil
        conservation, 106, 195; and state
        formation, 16–17, 21–22, 34, 193,
        195, 202, 210, 229; as strategies of
        resistance/dissent, 16–17, 21–22,
        30–32, 61–63, 66, 68, 77–78, 168, 193,
        203–4, 207, 217, 221–22, 226, 228–29,
        233; and territoriality, 16–17, 22, 30,
        203; and topography, 16, 35, 52–53,
        56, 60; and urbanity, 26, 135, 139,
        155–56; uses of, 27; as way of "writing
        the world," 16, 63; of western Kenya,
        4–5, 17, 27, 50–53, 55–58, 60–63,
        95, 218–20. *See also* cartography;
        cognitive mapping; countermapping
Marach (language Lumarachi), 113, 115,
        118, 141, 163–64
Marach Union, 141
Maragoli Association, 141, 205, 209
Maragoli People's Association, 130
Maragoli Society, 128, 138, 141, 151, 158, 217
Marama (language Lumarama), 40, 48,
        52, 66–68, 102, 115, 118, 124, 132, 144,
        154, 230, 254n8
Maseno, 10, 118, 220–21
Masibayi, Gerald, 153–65, 177, 189
Masinde, Elijah: and capture, 168; as
        cultural nationalist, 174–75; and
        deportation trial, 175, 177; as leader of
        Dini ya Msambwa, 140, 165, 167–68,
        188; and Mathari Mental Hospital,
        167; and politics, 26, 180, 201, 209, 212,
        216; as prophet, 165, 174–75, 178
Mau Mau rebellion, 5, 7; and
        classifications, 177; and
        counterinsurgency, 31, 176–77, 180;
        and detention, 163–64, 166, 180; and
        Dini ya Msambwa, 31, 173–74, 176–
        78; and ethnic politics, 165, 189–90;
        and loyalism, 164–67; and national
        politics, 30, 181–84, 190; and oaths,
        164, 176–77; and rehabilitation,
        176–78, 285n80; and western Kenya,
        144, 178–79, 186–88
Mbembe, Achille, 15
Mboya, Paul, 10
Mboya, Tom, 187, 192, 202, 220–22
Médard, Claire, 203
Meru, 108, 148

Migingo Island, 226
migration, 3–4, 27, 33, 36, 38–41, 44,
        48–49, 53, 59, 66, 69–71, 83, 110, 112,
        115–16, 210, 212, 216–17, 247n16
Mijikenda, 3, 9, 28, 87, 98
Milimu (Chief), 66–67
Mill Hill Mission, 118, 121, 130–31
Minya, Aggrey, 187
Misri (Egypt), 39, 148
Mitchell, Timothy, 17
Mnubi (Chief), 109
mobility, 12, 29; and customary control,
        80, 138, 187; and gender, 135–36,
        147; and Msambwa rebels, 168, 179,
        231; and practices of territoriality,
        48, 207; and processes of
        identification, 8, 226
modernity, 12, 102, 161–62, 195, 198
Moi, Daniel arap, 10, 221
Mombasa, 11, 50, 80, 85, 136, 139, 142,
        181, 196, 226
Mombasa Republican Council, 226
monarchism (also royalism), 11, 39, 46,
        65, 100–104, 151, 153, 193, 210–13,
        216
Moore, Henrietta, 13
moral ethnicity, 7, 22, 230
msambwa, 45, 168
Mudavadi, Musalia, 4, 230
Muhanga, Moses, 89, 91, 107
Muhati, Reuben, 92
Mukholosi, J. L., 143
Mukudi (Chief), 186
mulembe, 12, 33, 48, 240n58
Muliro, Masinde, 200–201, 207, 209, 216,
        220–21
multilingualism, 12, 113, 132, 135, 154
Muluhya (student quarterly), 11, 121, 132,
        189–90
Mumia (Paramount Chief), 46, 51, 54,
        60–61, 95, 101–2, 122–23, 151, 212
Mumia, Sitawa, 212
murembe oaths, 33, 178
Murunga (Chief), 60, 62, 66, 68, 81, 84,
        148, 151
Mutesa (King), 101
Mutongi, Kenda, 78, 136–37, 142
Mutu, Wangechi, 23
mwambao, 194, 216, 226
Mwangale, Philip, 138
myths of origin (also founding figures), 5,
        7, 9, 14, 28, 38–39, 44, 67, 70–71, 87,
        96, 98, 101, 153

Peterson, Derek, 100, 125, 162, 173, 189, 197

Pkech, Lucas, 172, 175

pluralism, 3–5, 228–33; and cosmopolitanism, 6, 12, 20, 111, 135, 161, 221; and customary practices, 65, 68, 72, 83, 100, 145–46, 150; and ethnic patriotism, 13–15, 22, 30–32, 88, 97, 109, 121, 135, 157, 161, 166, 173, 191, 211, 217, 220; and language, 111–13, 132–33; and the making of "publics," 184–85; and political loyalties, 201–2, 230–33; rationalization of, 8, 10–11, 159, 193, 298n21

Pokot, 171–72, 206

political tribalism, 2, 3, 22, 150, 230, 232

precolonial markets, 42, 113

primordialism, 6–7, 114, 149, 171, 184

prophecy, 26, 70, 92, 140, 167, 174–76, 180

prostitution: and campaigns against, 29, 141–44; and ethnic patriotism, 134, 140–41, 160, 162, 197; and gold mining, 80–81, 94; and moral crisis, 136; and repatriations, 142–43; and urban migration, 136–37

race, 7, 81, 93, 163, 183, 226

railway, 54–55, 59, 67, 77, 141, 174

Ramaswamy, Sumathi, 22

Ramogi, 38–39

Ranger, Terence, 7

Ravenstein, E. G., 50–51

region: and alternative mappings of communities, 88, 184, 191–93, 202–4, 207, 209, 211, 215–17, 231–32; definition of, 15; and networks of exchange, 5, 8, 15, 27, 33–34, 42, 113; and settlement, 38–40, 112; and spatial analysis, 15

Renan, Ernest, 192

Renison, Patrick, 220

repatriation, 169, 172–73

Resolution on the Intangibility of Frontiers (OAU, 1964), 222, 225, 229

revivalists, 176

Richards, Paul, 8

Rift Valley, 57, 123, 141, 146–48, 155, 171, 174, 179, 187, 203, 210, 213, 218, 221

Rosberg, Carl, 99, 201

Rwenzururu (Kingdom), 194, 212

Sack, Robert, 16

Salvation Army, 175

Samia (language Lusamia), 42, 57, 68, 115, 118, 123–24, 144, 197, 209, 213, 216–18

Sauti ya Mwafrika, 152–53

Scott, James, 17, 21

secession, 3, 66, 194, 203, 212, 216, 222, 226–29

settlers (European): arrival of, 5, 55–56, 59; and Dini ya Msambwa, 174–76, 178; and the gold rush, 74–75, 82–84, 86, 88; in Kaimosi, 84; and *majimbo*, 202; and Mau Mau rebellion, 178, 190; and migrant labor, 134, 146–47; and sexual politics, 80; in the Trans Nzoia, 62, 106, 167, 169, 207. *See also* White Highlands

Shadle, Brett, 166

Shain, Richard, 22

Shams-ud-Deen, Mohamed, 102

Shifta War, 227

Shikuku, Martin, 230

Shilaro, Priscilla, 75

Siganga, C. N. W., 184–85, 188

Sio River, 57, 224

sleeping sickness (trypanosomiasis), 49, 60

soil conservation, 106–9, 137, 195, 263n119

soil erosion, 77, 106, 109, 136

Somali, 3, 119, 194, 200, 202, 216, 222, 226–27

Somaliland, 60, 229

Sore (Chief), 82–83, 151

South Sudan, 226, 229

sovereignty: alternative models of, 194, 200, 203, 221–22, 224–25, 227, 229; claims to, 81, 119, 193–94, 212–13, 215–16; colonial versions of, 53; histories of, 39, 46, 65–66, 100, 102, 212, 216, 221–22, 224; loss of, 2, 51, 102, 204, 210, 213; postcolonial debates over, 191, 222–23, 224–27; terms of, 31; threats to, 49, 127, 221–27, 229

Spear, Thomas, 8

speech community, 113

Spencer, John, 90

sphere of influence, 105, 118

Stanley, Henry Morton, 34, 49

statelessness, 16, 21, 101

Stoler, Ann, 227

Sudi (Chief), 60, 70, 103

Summers, Carol, 98

Sutton, J. E. G., 121
Swynnerton Plan, 195–96

Tachoni, 40, 105; and customary
    practices, 159–60; and female
    circumcision, 29, 135, 147–50,
    158–62, 231; and language, 114–15,
    118; and Luyia patriotism, 160–61;
    and mapping, 198–200, 211. *See also*
    Tachoni Union; Tachoni Welfare
    Association Fund
Tachoni Union, 149–50, 158, 161, 198–99,
    271n4
Tachoni Welfare Association Fund, 199
Taita, 10, 34, 68, 108, 151, 195
tenant farmers (also squatters), 67, 73, 84–
    85, 167, 169–71, 187, 196–97, 216, 231
Terrace War (Uluguru, Tanganyika), 195
territoriality: and customary law, 146, 161;
    definition of, 16–17; and identity, 16,
    22, 45, 169; instruments of, 59, 210,
    223; itinerant forms of, 33, 37, 207;
    and kinship, 47–48; and the "Luyia
    idea," 184; and patriotism, 30, 84,
    90; and power, 16, 34, 104; and the
    Regional Boundaries Commission,
    203, 217; and space, 16–17
territorial nationalism, 5, 11, 15, 19, 29–30,
    85, 152, 185, 190, 211
Teso (also Iteso/Wamia), 38, 59, 184, 186,
    209, 215, 230
Thomas, Lynn, 148
Throup, David, 230–31
tin-trunk literature, 23
Tiriki (language Lutiriki), 40, 42, 45, 73,
    89, 94, 115, 118, 129, 144–46, 159
Trans Mara, 170–71
Trans Nzoia, 53, 62, 66, 84, 106, 146, 155,
    167–73, 176, 178, 188, 199, 206–7,
    210–11, 218, 220
trenches, 57, 76–78, 90, 106, 109, 126
tribe: and census, 1–3, 155–56; claims
    to, 28, 65, 71, 75, 81–83, 85–86,
    90, 99, 109, 198–99; colonial
    preoccupations with, 6, 49–50, 114;
    and customary practices, 158–59,
    167; debates over usage of, 6–7;
    definition of, 4, 6, 43–44; and
    gender, 13–15; geographies of, 8,
    30, 57, 60, 160–61, 165, 169–71; and
    historiography, 6–8, 22, 236n22;
    language of, 9, 134; and loyalism,
    189; and nation, 127, 182, 192;

and social/moral reproduction,
    125, 138, 141, 144, 149; threat of
    "detribalization," 140; and violence,
    2. *See also* political tribalism

Uasin Gishu, 40, 141, 146–47, 155, 168,
    169, 199, 206, 209, 216, 218
Uganda, 10, 23, 29, 43, 51, 54–57, 59, 66,
    70, 100–102, 104, 118, 120, 131, 135,
    163, 168, 173, 187, 194, 203, 212–13,
    215–16, 224–26, 232
Ukamba Members Association, 108
Union Ibo, 111, 122
urban citizenship, 139
Usher-Wilson, Bishop L. C., 178

Vail, Leroy, 7, 13
van den Bersselaar, Dmitri, 111
Vansina, Jan, 16, 24, 43
Vaughan, Christopher, 53
Victoria, Lake, 4, 33, 35, 38, 40, 44, 46,
    49, 51, 57, 85, 95, 112, 114, 206, 213,
    216, 226, 252n121

Wabuge, Wafule, 216
Wafula, Peter, 151
Wafula, Samson, 167
Wagner, Günter, 37, 40, 42, 44–45, 47–
    48, 64, 78, 86, 97, 105, 112, 114–15,
    123, 127, 139
Wainaina, Binyavanga, 23
Wanga (kingdom): and anti-Wanga
    sentiment, 65–69, 72, 78, 96,
    102, 105, 148, 186, 198, 216; and
    circumcision, 144–45; and conquest,
    51, 53, 71; and customary practices,
    159; and language (Luwanga/
    Luhanga), 95, 112, 115, 118–19,
    121–25, 127–32, 209; and mapping,
    27, 60–61, 83; and paramount
    chief campaign, 101–4; and
    patriotic histories, 100–101, 103,
    212; and political organization,
    44–47, 72, 96; and rule, 62, 66; and
    urban associations, 140. *See also*
    anti-Wanga campaigns; Wanga
    Educated Men Association
Wanga Educated Men Association, 140
Ward, Ida, 122
Wayo, S. D., 190
ways of being, 8, 170, 231–32
Wekuke, Benjamin, 167
Werbner, Richard, 7

Were, Gideon, 9, 39–40, 41, 49, 71
West Suk, 170–73
White Highlands, 55, 59, 82, 106–7, 167, 169, 174. *See also* settlers (European)
Williams, C. H., 170–71
Willis, Justin, 3, 101
Winichakul, Thongchai, 16–17

Wipper, Audrey, 25
World War I, 59, 62, 84
World War II, 108–9, 120, 135–36, 151–52; and Defence Regulations, 108

Yala River, 66

Zanzibar, 140, 194